The Five Approaches to Acting Series

THE COLLECTED SERIES

WRITTEN BY DAVID KAPLAN

Hansen Publishing Group, LLC
East Brunswick, New Jersey
www.hansenpublishing.com

International Standard Book Number: 978-1-60182-180-5

Hansen Publishing Group, LLC
302 Ryders Lane
East Brunswick, New Jersey
732-220-1211
www.hansenpublishing.com

CREDITS

To Edwin W. Schloss,

Prince of friends, open-hearted, open-eyed.

CONTENTS

Part II. Playing Episodes

Part III. Building Images

Part V. Telling a Story

Part VI. Comparing, Choosing, and Combining Approaches

INTRODUCTION

Be warned: this book starts off slowly. Once you get past the mention of a three-year-old setting a fire on stage (the founder of twentieth-century acting: Stanislavsky), you will find yourself reading about Russian painting, the history of the English novel, Freud's theory of dreams, and the practice of Yoga. Before you get to how to perform a line of dialogue as simple as "One and one make two," you may very well be grumbling your own line: "What does this have to do with acting?" Be patient. What seem like digressions do have a connection. In this book, at least, acting is considered to be an art of human relationships, an art woven to other arts and sciences.

If we can agree that acting involves the theory and practice of human relationships—not just the relationships of actors with actors, but of actors with audiences—then the study of acting merits attention from anyone interested in behavior, character, and a relationship to the world from which ideas about such things evolve. The novel defined characters in ways that pre-date the theater by fifty years. Russian painters gave shape to psychology. Freud's obsessions are twined tightly around an actor's subconscious. It turns out that the founder of twentieth-century acting was a lifelong devotee of Yoga—although mention of it was edited out of his books in America and suppressed outright by censors in Russia.

Past the hurdle of history, the first chapter will respond to your question: "Once I'm onstage, what should I do?" The answer turns out to be more questions: What do you *need* to do? What actions might satisfy your needs? What obstacles might get in the way of your actions? What do you do about those obstacles?

By the second chapter, just when you think you're about to learn what do when you meet an obstacle, you'll meet some performers out of history. Among others, there will be a twelve-year-old pest named Master Betty, a dignified African-American actor named Ira Aldridge, and a lady dressed as a man who would exit the stage tied upside down on a horse. Yes, all this information is itself an obstacle to the subject of obstacles, but try thinking of it as an invitation to attend a family reunion. At first, you'll find yourself in the middle of a group of relatives (some rather strange) whom you've never met before. Once you do get to know them better, you will be able to see some family resemblance and claim kinship to your heritage.

How you deal with obstacles in life determines character. Just so with the characters you play onstage. When characters meet obstacles onstage, their behavior changes in order to meet their needs. Confronting obstacles on the stage and off, you can learn from the experience of actors who have come before you. You are not the first student to be told you weren't talented enough, you are not the first actor to fight with your parents over your choice of a profession, you are not the first girl in the world to be taunted as too thin or too fat or too plain ever to be an actress.

By the time you get to the third chapter, you will have been introduced to the Stanislavsky System, a performance approach that identifies acting as a series of tasks undertaken to satisfy a need, and that defines character by the way actions are adjusted when they encounter obstacles. Arguments over how to apply this idea have raged for a century, and the rest of the chapter will discuss who the arguers were and what they agreed and disagreed about. Just when you think you've understood the subject of the argument—and perhaps made up your mind what you yourself think—a new section will begin, undermining the basic principles you've spent so much time learning.

Not to worry. You'll land on your feet, this time among a group of men and women who lived through poison gas, the Russian Revolution, and the First World War. Shell-shocked for the rest of their lives—even as they watched a second and worse World War poison their lives—these idealists learned first-hand how good people can commit unapologetic evil. Their experience in life led them to think that character on and off the stage was a series of contradictory roles often performed in irreconcilable opposition, and behavior was determined by transactions—some fair, some unfair—that people entered into in order to survive. Perhaps in response to the selfishness of nationalism, they believed in common property. One cunning and lucky survivor, Bertolt Brecht, used that belief shamelessly to help himself to other people's property, including the ideas of his mentor, Erwin Piscator. Like many people in pursuit of a difficult ideal, these believers in dignity-for-all squabbled among themselves.

Their approach to acting was to cultivate oppositions in a performance and to demonstrate transactions to an audience. They believed that breaking a scene down into separate units—which we'll call episodes—helped an audience discover for themselves the contradictions of life. At roughly the same time, the Viennese psychologist Alfred Adler, prodded by his feminist wife Raissa Epstein, also came to view behavior as a series of transactions. Adler likewise defined character as a series of sometimes contradictory roles. Freud claimed Adler was crazy and forced him to resign from the Vienna Psychoanalytic Society. Adler claimed Freud was childishly sex-obsessed and that the basic human drive was toward mastery and power, not one's mother. You don't have to decide who was right.

The next approach presented will reintroduce the combatants of Chapter 3—and the slugfest between actors who like to dress up in masks and stare at themselves in the mirror and actors who avoid the mirror (and sometimes the audience) in order to stare deep inside themselves at repressed memories. Both sides will level charges at each other of sorcerer, witch, heretic, narcissist, and ham. Flamboyant entertainers like Sarah Bernhardt will be accused of deluding their audiences, and self-examining Method actors will be accused of deluding themselves. Frank Sinatra will make an appearance. You'll learn about Abstract Expressionist painters and *be-bop* jazz musicians; artists whose response to a regimented Cold War world was to find inspiration in sights and sounds of their own making. They were as mocked as any actor for abandoning the rules of traditional craft.

INTRODUCTION

In the midst of all these feuds you will learn that you are not the first performer to suffer devastating criticism. A British newspaper critic once noted that Laurence Olivier could move every muscle in his body, but "he could not move me." Directing a Method-obsessed Marilyn Monroe, Olivier himself was moved to shout at her impatiently: "Just be sexy!" As a way to reconcile outer appearance with inner conviction, you will read about the psychologist Carl Jung's claim that personality is a collection of inner and outer masks. Jung further claimed that behavior shaped itself to fulfill the pattern of images those masks referred to. (Freud called Jung insane, too.) Yet, gluing on a nose or soul-searching for emotional memories, when actors discover images that move them to play, those images—whatever their source—can be built up with an approach that ignites a performance with an inner flame.

By the time you've reached the fourth approach, the thread of the book should be clearer, if not clear: different approaches to acting are useful for different scripts for the same reason it is useful to pack differently for a safari and a sea voyage. Approaching a situation comedy or a Greek tragedy, it helps to be prepared—although not in exactly the same ways. You'll be reminded that as Gulliver traveled from island to island he was measured as a giant among the Lilliputians and a pipsqueak among the giants. Just so, within a play, character and actions are measured by comparison with the patterns of the text, and an analysis of the rules that govern the pattern of a play can help you decide how to perform it.

The cultural anthropologist Ruth Benedict offers a model for actors to identify the pattern that gives measure to the world of any play. The study of cultural anthropology may seem far afield from the study of acting, but it isn't really: actors adapt their behavior to the circumstances of a production the way voyagers adapt to a foreign land and learn the local customs in order to survive. Actors, though, go a few steps further than anthropologists: they inhabit the stage world as if born into it, learning an appropriate accent or learning how, circa 1965, to size up a divorced woman who is smoking a cigarette while waiting for a drink. This approach to acting, called a world of the play analysis, will reinforce the idea that there is no one correct way to act any more than there is one correct way to look at the world.

Next—in the company of a wise-cracking glamour girl and some French intellectuals—you will encounter the fifth approach, one that tackles the specialized problem of how to tell a story onstage. This is a chance to learn true witchcraft: the casting of a spell on audience members so that they see what isn't there. More, the telling of a tale can reveal the occult: what takes place in the mind of the speaker. Shakespeare's soliloquies offer an actor special opportunities to reveal the processes of thought, and there is a separate chapter on soliloquies from his plays. Like Mae West's sultry recitation of nursery rhymes, Romeo's bashful recitation of Juliet's charms works from the principle that it's not what you say, it's how you say it—and what happens to you while you say it.

So those are the *Five Approaches to Acting*: identifying tasks, playing episodes, building images, learning the world of the play, and telling a story. Each approach has its own definition of what it means to act, what it means to act well, what it means to be a character in a performance on stage, and, by extension, what it means to be a person in "real" life.

INTRODUCTION

The sixth part of the book compares these five approaches, shows you how and why to choose among them, and demonstrates a way to combine them so they support rather than trip each other up. You'll be reminded that the actors you've encountered throughout the text themselves borrowed, combined, and found their own approaches to work—just as you hope to find yours.

There's a lot of information here. It will take time to sort it out, much less put it to use. To help you find your way, following this Introduction is a chart you can consult that summarizes and compares the approaches. At the end of the book, there's a list of the people mentioned and their dates. If you'd like to know when Louis XIV reigned or when Elizabeth Taylor was born, you can look it up. Also at the book's end is a glossary that defines terms and phrases related to performance, the visual arts, pertinent history, and psychological theories. The definitions are taken from dictionaries, from history, and from customary and practical use. You can disagree with them, but at least you'll know what my bias is and what I mean (even if you're convinced I'm wrong) when I use a term.

I am an American, and my references throughout will be to America. Dates, for example, refer to George Washington or Orville Wright rather than to the Manchu emperors or a Soviet aviator. I've worked and gone to the theater in enough places to know that the American theater is by no means the last or even the latest word in acting. I'm not just talking about the obvious excellence of the British classical repertory or the latest cult-like theatrical commune in Poland. In 1995, when I first went to work in Mongolia, I jokingly fantasized that the repertory of the Mongolian Drama Theatre would include *Little Yurt on the Prairie* and *Sweet Yak of Youth*. The joke was on me. At the Mongolian National Theater in Ulaan Baator they were rehearsing Shakespeare's *Richard III* after a successful run of Lorca's *Blood Wedding*. Such a repertory is rarely staged in America.

In Mongolia and elsewhere, I've experienced firsthand that certain plays transcend their culture. I've chosen scene excerpts from among the Western canon—e.g., *Hedda Gabler*, *Richard III*—that any actor should know as a measure of excellence against which to compare other scripts. I wish I could have included more comedies as examples, but they aren't so easy to make sense of out of context. Throughout the book, women are represented as performers and directors, though rarely as playwrights, which reflects women's historic lack of such opportunities in the theater. (Some of Bertolt Brecht's most important texts, by the way, were collaborations with women who remain uncredited.) Despite a similar lack of opportunity for people of color within the Western theater, actors such as the Chinese Mei Lanfang—who shared his art with the world through his extensive touring—and the African-American Ira Aldridge—who taught the techniques of classical acting in Sarajevo—are included for their uniquely significant contributions to the practice of acting in the West.

The text includes film examples that serve to demonstrate how different actors using different approaches achieve differing forms of excellence. The films chosen—all of them American—are distant enough in time so that performances can be evaluated without the bias of a contemporary definition of "realism" or the distraction of a response to pertinent and immediate subject matter. The most recent film acting discussed is Robert De Niro's forceful performance in Martin Scorsese's *Raging Bull* (1980), the old-

INTRODUCTION

est is Lillian Gish's silent but equally forceful performance in D.W. Griffith's *Orphans of the Storm* (1921). Although film performances are assembled by editors and directors—artists in their own right—in all the scenes used as examples it is the craft of the actor that is on display. If you do nothing more than view the rest of the films featured in this book—*A Place in the Sun, Dinner at Eight, Touch of Evil, Night of the Hunter,* and *Long Day's Journey into Night*—you will have experienced a visceral way to remember, and argue about, the differences in good acting.

By now you've probably figured out for yourself that the tone of this book will be at times informal, reflecting its origins as classroom lectures and explanations given during rehearsals. I was taught, as were many others, by teachers and colleagues who themselves had been students of Lee Strasberg, Stella Adler, Bertolt Brecht, Mei Lanfang, and Erwin Piscator. I am lucky enough to have learned Russian and luckier still to have met—and worked with—the custodians of the legacies of Stanislavsky and Meyerhold. Whether in Russia or America, I learned, yes, by reading, but also by watching and listening in class and rehearsals—and hearing a good deal of backstage gossip and anecdote. When I have been able to trace a good story back to a source in print, I have cited that as the reference, although in most cases that's not where I first learned it.

I come by my enjoyment for a contrast in techniques from experience as a student in an acting class taught by two instructors, one trained by Erwin Piscator, the other by Stella Adler. While each spoke, one would make faces behind the other's back. Since they did it to each other, they knew it was being done to them. This helped me to understand that different opinions could disagree playfully. You will not agree with all points of view—you're not supposed to. What these approaches do have in common is the rigor of learning and interpreting lines (rather than improvisation) and the pleasure of representing a character other than yourself. Each of the five approaches traces a route for you to take on a journey from text to performance. There are other ways to work, of course; these are the ones I've found most useful on my own journeys.

Five Approaches to Acting limits itself to comparing the ways an actor might work from a script. Even so, the readership for the book is not necessarily limited to actors. Given its emphasis on the interconnection of action, personality, and social environment, the art of human relationships has something to reveal to other disciplines as well. It is easy to make fun of an actor's instinctive vanity and cultivated self-awareness, but an actor's awareness of other people needs to be just as cultivated—if not instinctive. As an art, rather than an instinct for showing off, acting requires a sensitivity to others and the technical skill to develop and apply that sensitivity.

The models acting proposes for understanding other people's behavior might well be emulated and studied by anyone interested in human relationships because, in human relationships, even those as spontaneous as love or revenge, there is a need to reflect, to reconsider, and to refine. I hope *Five Approaches to Acting* will help its readers to do just that.

ACKNOWLEDGMENTS

My students, of course, should be thanked first. Their faith, talent, support, imagination, and questions have been the necessary partner to my thinking about acting. Jef Hall-Flavin taped my lectures, typed four transcripts, and forced me to read them, which jolted me enough into writing a full-length manuscript after years of preliminary drafts. Among contributions large and small from twenty-five years of students: Michael Winther, Jessica Weglein, Lowell Smith, Phllip Walker, Charles Arnesto, Jim Kohn, Kristina Purcell, Robin Romeo, Matt Ashford, Nancy Casarro, Richard Stegman, Rick Corley, Joey Hoeber, Adam Adams, Debby Van Nostrand, Judy Sheehan, Chris Frachiolla, Jack Fris, Liz Dennehy, Diane DiMemo, Tom McGowan, Sterling Swan, Nancy Sigworth, Paul Boocock, Debbie Leeds, Suki John, Roy Clyde Baldo, Bonnie Max, Rose Kalajian, Steve Massa, Susan Selig, Heather Robinson, and the ladies who put themselves at risk of public attack by announcing the episodes to the audience: Jane Ross and Roberta Platt.

Other people's contributions along the way have been long range. In 1981, Laurence Senelick patiently listened to my ideas for an acting text, made several valuable suggestions, and encouraged me to pursue the connection between Stanislavsky's theories and the psychology of Russian novelists. Almost twenty years later, he pointed me toward Sharon Marie Carnicke's Stanislavsky research. Professor Carnicke took the time to quickly and enthusiastically answer my questions about her work. In 1984, Tony Holland insisted that the story of how Stanislavsky's teachings diverged in America was essential to their understanding. Lou Criss, my directing teacher at Yale, who had been a student of Piscator and an assistant to Charles Laughton and Harold Clurman, generously shared his experience and his understanding of Piscator's importance. Also at Yale, Norma Brustein explained the mystery of Stanislavsky in clear, concise language, and with good humor. Ditto Jan Kott and Lee Breuer for Brecht. At Clark, Michael Spingler brought me up on Molière, Beckett, and Ionesco, and arranged for me to teach my first college classes.

Other people have contributed in unique ways, in particular, my colleagues: Patricia Norcia, who, since 1979, maintains the Ruth Draper monologues with inspiring craftsmanship and dedication. Leslie Ayvazian—writer, actress, and good friend—took my class in 1980, read the first draft of this book and insisted I could do a better job of it, and told me when I did. Patti and Leslie rounded up my first private students and organized my first classes in New York. Lyuba Filimonovna and the company of the Samara Drama Theater took me down the Russian rabbit hole to join the company of international theater artists. Special thanks to Professor Naudikova and the faculty of the Siberian Academy of Fine Arts in Ulan Ude for their invitation to teach among

ACKNOWLEDGMENTS

them. Friends who read or listened to early drafts and offered substantial help and suggestions include Alan Havis, Chris Markle, and Kate Clarke.

Special thanks, and apologies, to my family for their sometimes uncomplaining patience during this often anti-social process, in particular my parents (who contributed my computers) and my brothers (and now sister-in-law), as well as my long-term extended family: the laughing Scott Baron, the leggy Kristina Kinet, the lovely Olga Kogan, and the loving Jerry Stacy. Special pleadings for unreturned phone calls to my friends in New York, among them: Jennie Moreau, Debra Roth, Marty and Camilla Kenner, Bob Abrams and Ann Gillen, Kathryn Freed, Kai and Hiro Ito, Carol Friedman, and the inspirational Dorothy Warren. In California: Juliet Green, Marilyn B. Atlas, Glenn Shaddix, and Tom Sullivan. In Berlin: Manja Barth and Volker Ratzmann. In Italy, Pia Mortari, now gone, gave me a house overlooking her olive trees in Puglia in which to write. Mark Addy gave me a place to write in Los Angeles during the summer of 1984.

Thanks also to: Cathy Spingler, Maria DeLaCruz, and my beach neighbors: Melody and Christian, Lydia, Stanley, the entire Verdeschi Office, Lucy and Bob Brunelli, John Marsala, and Tom Cipolla. Also: Lennon Shannon, Penguin's Carol Slattery, Warner Brothers' Rosemarie Gawelko, and the New York Public Library's Anne Lauder.

Brenda Currin has also collaborated with me for more than twenty years, in particular on the stage adaptation of Eudora Welty's work called *Sister and Miss Lexie*. Working with Brenda, I learned the techniques of storytelling on stage and much else besides, personal and professional. Her enthusiasm and expectations for this book, her constructive criticism, and honest appreciation have improved the manuscript at every step of the way, especially the fine-tuning of the references to Ruth Benedict.

On behalf of the publisher, thanks to Barbara Mars, Dr. Donald Mars, Nathaniel Mars, Dr. Benjamin Kent, Jim Weikart and everyone at Weikart Tax Associates, and Leon Friedman. Thanks also to Aldon James, President of The National Arts Club, which has served as a cultural and intellectual haven for my publisher and myself. We appreciate Aldon's friendship and his moral support for this project. Thanks also from author and publisher to Joseph Frappaolo and the Club's Dining Room staff for keeping us well fed.

With quiet determination, my editor, Ron Kaehler, extended his wit, courtesy, professionalism, patience, and passion to this project, and has woven a design that reflects his own balance and calm. Dave Strauss, the art director, braided in his own strand with admirable calm. Faye Zucker, who produced the book, had the wisdom to invite Ron and Dave to join this project.

Many happy accidents of fate attended the creation of this book, none happier than the miracle of finding the ideal publisher: Jill Seiden. Jill's performance of her role is what they call the eleven o'clock number. The manuscript caught fire under her appreciative eye. Her bone-deep knowledge of art history and psychology made her an ideal partner for the oddly punctuated pages that multiplied, thanks to her unstinting generosity of spirit, resources, and good humor. Her decision to publish was and is an act of faith. Her belief in the merit of getting it right (rather than written) allowed (and financed) an extensive and expensive rewrite in the middle of the editing process. Many people encouraged and contributed to this book. Sections have been passed around for years in blurry photocopies. Jill is the person who committed her resources so that it may reach a wider audience as the eye-candy you now hold in your hands.

And yes, thanks to R.D, once domestic, once pickled, and now aged (and exported) ham.

ABOUT THE AUTHOR

David Kaplan has held classes for actors since 1975. He has taught and lectured at Bard, Clark, Hofstra, New York University, Columbia, Rutgers, the University of New Mexico, the Siberian Academy of Fine Arts (in Russian), and the Hong Kong Academy of Performing Arts. His professional students in New York and Los Angeles have won numerous stage awards, including the Tony. Three theater companies have formed out of Mr. Kaplan's classes, including Artificial Intelligence, the creators of the long-running *Tony 'n Tina's Wedding*.

During the same time, he has staged plays around the world with professional companies in indigenous languages and settings: *King Lear* in a Sufi interpretation in Tashkent, Uzbekistan, performed in the Uzbek language; Genet's *The Maids* in Ulaan Baator, Mongolia, performed in Mongolian; *A Midsummer Night's Dream* in Buddhist Buryatia, performed in the Buryat language with traditional shamanic imagery. In Russia, and in the Russian language, Mr. Kaplan staged the first production of the American comic classic *Auntie Mame* at the 200-year-old Penza Theater, and the first production of Tennessee Williams's *Suddenly Last Summer* (the subject of a TASS documentary), as well as Shakespeare's *Macbeth*, both in Samara, Russia.

Plays directed by Mr. Kaplan have appeared in 40 of the 50 United States. These include his own adaptations of Charles Finney's *The Circus of Dr. Lao*, Stephen Foster's *Beautiful Dreamer*, and Gertrude Stein's *Dr. Faustus Lights the Lights*. More traditional repertory staged by Mr. Kaplan include Genet's *The Maids* in New York, Chekhov's *Cherry Orchard* in Los Angeles, and Tina Howe's *Painting Churches* for the Provincetown Players. He has had the pleasure of staging spectacles at the Atlantic City Convention Center, in Las Vegas, at the Coney Island Wax Museum, and a multi-ethnic celebration (with animals) in the Central Park Zoo.

Since 1979, Mr. Kaplan has worked on two one-woman shows that he adapted and continues to direct. Among them is the long-running revival of Ruth Draper's monologues performed by Patricia Norcia. Over twenty years of rehearsals, Mr. Kaplan and Miss Norcia have built up a repertory of 14 Draper pieces in 12 languages (some of them invented), which play for a total of nine hours. A portion of the Draper repertory performs annually to sold-out audiences at Carnegie Recital Hall in New York and has been presented in Tokyo, Munich, Rome, and London's West End. Mr. Kaplan's tribute to Mississippi writer Eudora Welty, *Sister and Miss Lexie*, has been performed by Brenda Currin since 1980 in critically acclaimed appearances throughout the United States.

Mr. Kaplan holds degrees from Clark University and the Yale School of Drama. His teachers include Jan Kott, Richard Gilman, Robert Brustein, Lee Breuer, Stanley Kaufman, Lou Criss, and, in Russia, Peter Monastersky.

SCRIPT ANALYSIS COMPARATIVE REFERENCE CHART

	TASK/ACTION ANALYSIS	EPISODIC ANALYSIS	BUILDING IMAGES ANALYSIS	WORLD OF THE PLAY ANALYSIS	NARRATIVE ANALYSIS
BASIC UNIT	Task	Episode	Image	Social context; behavior and form	Event Point of view
ILLUSION OF CHARACTER	Web of relationships	Playing the opposition	String of masks	Distinctions within the context of the world	Intersection of point of view and events
DRAMATIC ACTION	Action meeting an obstacle	Transaction or *gest*	Moment when mask changes	Breach in the rules of the world	Shifting the point of view
KEY QUESTION	What do I need to do?	What do I do? What is my role?	What is this like? What does this make me think of?	What are the values of the world?	What am I describing? What is my point of view?
UNIFYING IMAGE	Oil painting	Poster	Collage	Frame	Film camera angles
RELATIVE THEORY	Freud Psychoanalysis	Alfred Adler Transactional analysis Marxism	Carl Jung Personae	Ruth Benedict Cultural anthropology	Derrida Literary deconstructionism
SUITABLE PLAYWRIGHTS	Chekhov Ibsen Strindberg	Shakespeare Brecht Ionesco	Strindberg Lorca Genet Williams	Molière Wilde O'Neill Beckett	Shakespeare the Greeks Williams Shepard
AUDIENCE	Compassionate	Judgmental	Passionate	Transported	Participatory

PART I

GETTING TO THE TASK

Reading List

The Lesson by Eugene Ionesco

Hedda Gabler by Henrik Ibsen

An Actor Prepares (chapters 3, 5, 7, and 15) by Konstantin Stanislavsky

Stanislavsky in Focus (chapters 3 and 4) by Sharon Marie Carnicke

Viewing List

Orphans of the Storm directed by D.W. Griffith

A Place in the Sun directed by George Stevens

Ilya Repin, detail from *Ivan the Terrible and His Son Ivan: 16 November 1581*

CHAPTER 1

WHAT SHOULD I DO?

Why Is Stanislavsky Important?

Russia is cold and theaters are warm. For this reason, among other reasons, attending the theater in Russia is and was extraordinarily popular. One hundred years before the American Revolution, demand for theater was so strong in Russia that foreign companies and stars braved the distance, the cold, and the lack of dependably hot water to perform there. Inspired by their visitors to form acting companies of their own, Russian actors learned to imitate the popular European styles of exaggerated poses and sing-song declamation. By the end of the nineteenth century—twenty years before the start of the Russian Revolution—Russian actors too were tearing their hair to show despair, placing their hands over their hearts to indicate love, and—reliable report has it—staring open-mouthed with wonder at the mention of death.

A prematurely gray young man from a wealthy family in Moscow (they manufactured gold thread) (1) changed all that, not only in Russia, but in theaters throughout the world. He was stagestruck at the age of three, when he set the tree branch in his hands on fire while playing the role of "Winter" (2). On a business trip to Paris he enrolled in the famous Conservatory and began to study the craft of performing. To save his family embarrassment, he exchanged his last name (Alexeyev) for that of a Polish actor who was retiring from the stage. From then on he was known as Konstantin Stanislavsky. He is the Orville Wright of actors: he taught us to fly. Stanislavsky's soaring approach to acting had no use for hand-over-the-heart sincerity or the pregnant pause. His concern was the spiritual life of an actor, as a creative as well as interpretive artist.

Find the bag of nails

Stanislavsky always claimed he gained his practical insights by watching the performances of two Italian actors, Eleonora Duse and Tommaso Salvini. Although they never acted together, Duse and Salvini both shaped their art with passion and precision; it was this mix that prompted Stanislavsky to develop the craft of creative acting.

Many people had seen Duse and Salvini perform without understanding how these artists accomplished their effects. Most critics discussed what Salvini and Duse did by describing what they did not do. Salvini, though he acted in the grand manner of vivid gestures and thrilling speech, seemed to live on the stage—as if nothing offstage entered his mind. Duse acted in a subtler way; it seemed as if she came from no school at all. She made no displays of any kind, no effort to impress; she didn't make her voice sound interesting, she didn't even wear make-up. Yet out of this seeming nothingness, these two actors took the stages of the world by storm.

It was Stanislavsky who understood the technique of the great Italians. The best example of Stanislavsky's insight is from *An Actor Prepares*, the title given by his American translator to the first of three influential books on training actors. By his fifth page, Stanislavsky is describing a student, whose invented surname, Nazvanov, means "The Chosen One" in Russian (3). Nazvanov, though doing nothing more than sitting on the stage, is unable to rehearse—much less act. He feels oppressed by the size of the stage floor and pulled into the black hole of the audience. Then a workman drops a bag of nails that scatter along the floor. The Chosen One gets on his hands and knees to find the nails, and—for the first time—he feels at home on the stage. Stanislavsky expands on this later when a group of students hunt for a lost pin and a lost purse. Why did searching look and feel real, while simply sitting onstage looked and felt fake? Because individually or as a group, when actors are looking for something, they have *a task*.

That's the first step toward all else that follows: A TASK.

The essence of Stanislavsky's thinking is that behavior and emotions are functions of *wanting to do something for a purpose* on the stage. Behavior and emotion derive from desire. In the illustrations above, the students want to pick up nails or find a pin. That's their purpose for being onstage, rather than to make a display of themselves to the audience. In this way, their simple hunt parallels the sophisticated acting of Duse and Salvini; their emotions are convincing because they derive from *purpose*. When they find a nail, they're happy. When a nail rolls away from them, they're frustrated, but continue in their pursuit.

This was Stanislavsky's radical idea—radical in the real meaning of the word, because it uprooted the rules of acting. Instead of defining behavior, it defined *motivation* as the technical basis of good acting. This was not an original idea of Stanislavsky's, but his genius was to include the art of acting in a trend that was developing in Western culture at the same time.

Inner drama in fiction

A comparable transition had begun at least fifty years before, in another art form with conventions for characters and plot: the novel. In nineteenth-century Europe and America, novels occupied the place in mass culture that film occupies today. For those who could read and the many more who liked to be read to, novels provided—at a comfortably safe distance—visits to exotic places and the vicarious experience of other people's lives. We get an idea of the novel's popular appeal when we read that anxious crowds lined the docks of New York in 1841 to secure the latest serial installment of Charles Dickens's novel *The Old Curiosity Shop*—just to learn what had happened to its pathetic heroine, Little Nell. They weren't asking about the snappy dialogue or secret motives. They wanted to know what happened.

Since the days of Robinson Crusoe racing from the cannibals, what authors offered their audiences were narratives composed of curious events succeeded by events curiouser and curiouser. This happened, that happened, and any and all of what happened next was external and describable. As its title suggests, *The Old Curiosity Shop* has much to offer in the "what happened" department, and a cast of colorful characters to whom these things happen. There is an ugly yet strangely attractive dwarf, with the memorable name of Quilp, who steals the life savings from a good but gullible man. There is the gullible good man's noble granddaughter, frail Little Nell, who lies languishing near death for a few suspenseful chapters. "Is Little Nell dead?" the crowds shouted as the boat with the latest installment docked into New York harbor. *What had happened?*

Other writers, though, many of them women, were interested in *why* events and behavior happened.* In England, thirty years before Little Nell, Jane Austen wrote novels in which the unspoken machinations of matchmaking were laid bare. Even her titles—*Sense and Sensibility, Pride and Prejudice*—demonstrate a clash of ideas, not arms. Austen knew herself enough to politely decline an invitation from the Court of Queen Victoria to write a historical adventure in the style of the sword-and-maiden specialist Walter Scott. Scott himself understood the difference between his and Austen's styles, and referred to his own work, books like *Ivanhoe*, as written in the "bow-wow style."

By the middle of the century, George Eliot, an Englishwoman with the mask of a masculine name, used her powerful intelligence to create novels that portrayed the *inner drama* of characters. Her first novel was called *Adam Bede* (1859), and there was adventure enough in it: Adam Bede is a modest carpenter in love with a poor woman who appears to have killed her own child. Significantly, the novel continues for an eighth of its length after the woman's execution and describes what could never be seen in an adventure, or written in a letter, or even thought about consciously: how Adam is restored to life by wrestling with his anguish, "which he must think of as renewed with the light of every new morning" (4). George Eliot made the processes of wrestling with feelings seem as dramatic and interesting as adventures. Her books included the evolution of characters—not only what happened to them, but also the adventure of what happened *inside them*.

Other novelists in other places unveiled the drama of inner action, sometimes enhancing it by contrasting it with outer action. In France, Gustave Flaubert's novel *Madame Bovary* (1857) presented the romantic drama of a bored middle-class woman who imagines that she has found true love outside her marriage with an adventurer. Flaubert ironically stirred his heroine's sentimental dreams into the muck of her real-life entanglement. Emma Bovary eventually kills herself when her adventurer leaves her. About the same time as Flaubert, over in America, Herman Melville was writing

---

*Since the Renaissance, there were novels—in Spain, in France, in England—made up of collections of imaginary letters that gave insight into the diverse thoughts and points of view of different characters, even as they described adventures.

Moby Dick—a meditation on a whale hunt, rather than the series of sea adventures that his previous two novels had been. In 1881, the American émigré Henry James wrote *Washington Square*, in which very little of what we would call adventure takes place. The novel's principle action is that a young heiress does *not* get married.

James admired Eliot's quiet insight and Flaubert's irony, and though indifferent to the example of his countryman Melville, he was especially impressed by the person and the writings of a Russian novelist who lived in Paris, Ivan Turgenev. Turgenev's novels delicately and subtly depicted characters whose drama was their lack of drama (James particularly liked that nothing happened). Turgenev's heroes were incapable of heroism; his heroines *didn't* consummate their love affairs. Another Russian master of internal action was Leo Tolstoy, who began his writing career with the intention of becoming an adventure writer—the Russian Walter Scott—but ended up punctuating his battle scenes in novels like *War and Peace* with his characters' equally momentous internal battles.

It might be said that the Russian emphasis on internal drama in fiction culminated in the work of Fyodor Dostoyevsky, whose writing traces the beautiful ambiguity of motivation. In his *Crime and Punishment* (1866), the main character takes nine pages to kill an old lady—and over four hundred pages to agonize about it before he confesses (in two pages). The condemned killer's train ride to exile in Siberia—which must have been a long and agonizing experience—is mentioned in an aside. Dostoyevsky demonstrates that what goes on in a person's mind can be forty-five times more dramatic than what that person does or says, even if—and maybe *especially* if—that person is an ax murderer.

Dostoyevsky's reputation grew in the 1880s, about the same time Stanislavsky began his search for substance in the art of acting. It was Stanislavsky's ambition to put onstage, and make dramatic, the inner process of the actor—to reach to the substance that Dostoyevsky was mining when he detailed the inner processes of the characters in his novels. Stanislavsky's interest in revealing the inner process of acting was not just technical, or even aesthetic. His commitment was based on compassion, and he rode the wave of a social movement—at that point unnamed—that sympathized with all people of all classes. George Eliot was part of that movement too, as she wrote in *Adam Bede*:

These fellow mortals, every one, must be accepted as they are: you can neither straighten their noses, nor brighten their wit, nor rectify their dispositions; and it is these people—amongst whom your life is passed—that it is needful you should tolerate, pity, love: it is these more or less ugly, stupid, inconsistent people whose movements of goodness you should be able to admire—for whom you should cherish all possible hopes, all possible patience. And I would not, even if I had the choice, be the clever novelist who could create a world so much better than this, in which we get up in the morning to do our daily work, that you would be likely to turn a harder, colder eye on the dusty streets and the common green fields—on the real breathing men and women, who can be chilled by your indifference or injured by your prejudice; who can be cheered and helped onward by your fellow-feeling, your forbearance, your outspoken brave justice.

So I am content to tell my simple story without trying to make things seem better than they were; dreading nothing, indeed, but falsity, which in spite of one's best efforts, there is reason to dread. Falsehood is so easy, truth so difficult. The pencil is conscious of a delightful facility in drawing a griffin—the longer the claws, and the larger the wings, the better; but that marvelous facility which we mistook for genius is apt to forsake us when we want to draw a real unexaggerated lion. Examine your words well, and you will find that even when you have no motive to be false, it is a very hard thing to say the exact truth, even about your own immediate feelings—much harder than to say something fine about them which is *not* the exact truth (5).

Inner drama in art

Stanislavsky was a cultured man—his first important job was to chair a *Society of Art and Literature*, which was, in part, an amateur theater where he directed. His search for ways to depict the truth, while stimulated by the achievement of Russian writers, was also shaped by the assumptions of Russian painters. In the visual arts, as in theater, Russia had copied Western Europe by setting up a state Academy that taught artists to draw from plaster casts of Greek statues and to paint with a technique that blended oil paints to a porcelain finish. Art students were assigned subjects from classical mythology or the Bible.

In France, artists rebelled against Academy training by painting subjects from life, not plaster casts. They applied paint so that it blended in the eye of the viewer, not on the canvas. The *Impressionists* painted subject matter significant for its physical beauty, whatever its cultural associations, negative or positive, traditional or contemporary. If there happened to be social implications to French subject matter, and there could be (squalid drunks or stolid bourgeoisie), those social concerns were secondary to the new ways of seeing form and new methods of applying paint.

Russian painters rebelled against their Academy in a different way. Their technique of applying paint stayed roughly the same, but their subject matter changed dramatically. *Genre painting* depicting scenes of recognizable middle-class life (which, by the way, George Eliot claimed to be her inspiration) was already a convention throughout Europe, but Russian painters, moved by the miserable circumstances of their country, made genre painting pointedly political and topical. The *Itinerants*—so called by themselves because they had no fixed place to show their work or, at times, to live—painted contemporary and often dramatic events: fathers unexpectedly coming home from prison, a woman bravely handing out pamphlets to poor people, a bank failure, smug policemen guarding a religious procession. French Impressionist artists most often painted a model's vague cheerfulness or detached and moody pensiveness, a sort of rainy-day patience that was probably an honest representation of the model's mood while posing. Russian Itinerant painters *staged scenes*, like theater directors.

Look, for example, at Nikolai Yaroshenko's *Life Is Everywhere*, painted in 1888. It requires an explanation today, but its meaning was clear to the public when it was first painted. It is a picture of a scuffed boxcar, and resembles a still frame from a filmstrip.

The initials on the side of the boxcar indicate that it is transporting prisoners to Siberia. Inside the car, a woman holds a grinning baby up to the bars of a window. The child reaches out through the bars. He's throwing crumbs to pigeons that have gathered below the window. A smiling man inside the boxcar holds a chunk of brown bread in his weathered hand, which just touches the child's pink fingers. Behind them is an older man with a beard, and another middle-aged man's face topped by a cap. They crowd behind the mother so that they may share the baby's pleasure. Another figure in the boxcar, seen from the back, stares out at the blank sky through the bars of the opposite window. With its blended color and even lighting, the style of the painting is not that different from academic technique. Yet Yaroshenko utilized that technique to evoke the child's pleasure—and doing so he portrayed the ironic *relationship* between the caged prisoners forcibly carted to Siberia and the birds free to fly away south.

The Russians were certainly not the first to paint relationships or contemporary political events, but the Itinerants were seized with a mission to make psychological subject matter worthy of investigation and refinement in its own right. Even episodes taken from the Bible or Russian history were illustrated for psychological and social significance. A wonderful example is a small canvas painted by Ilya Repin entitled *Ivan the Terrible and His Son Ivan: 16 November 1581*. Actually, the Russian word is not "Terrible," it is *Grozny*, and this painting helps to explain the meaning of the word. *Grozny* means more than terrible; it is related to the Russian word for thunderstorm, *groza*. *Grozny* implies fear and wonder and the breath-catching response to an overwhelming storm. There is something of this in the root meaning of the English word *awful*—"full of awe."

On November 16, 1581, Tsar Ivan *Grozny* quarreled with his son and killed him with a fire poker. Repin depicts this event in the painting as if it were on stage. The evidence of the murder is literally in front of the viewer: the bloody fire poker lies in the foreground three inches from the edge of the frame. The bottom half of the painting is a red Oriental rug, rumpled as it would be after a struggle. Repin painted this work in 1885, and its subject matter—the Tsar killing the younger generation—resonated with its viewers. This was a period in Russian history analogous to 1960s America for its liberalism and the reaction liberalism provoked. Parricide was the subject of Dostoyevsky's *The Brothers Karamazov* of 1880 and Turgenev's *Fathers and Sons* a few years before that. The meaning of the painting was not lost on the then-reigning Tsar. On his personal order, the canvas was removed from its gallery.

But this painting is significant even beyond its politics. At the same time in France, Seurat was dabbing on points of color to portray *Sunday Afternoon on the Island of La Grand Jatte*, and Monet was whisking feathery brushstrokes onto canvas to depict the changes of light on the façade of the Rouen Cathedral. Yet nothing in the well-known French Impressionist art of the 1880s prepares a viewer for the psychological depth Russian Itinerant painters achieved. What artists in the West dismiss to this day as sentimental genre painting, nineteenth-century Russian artists developed into a high art.

The greatness of Repin's painting is not in its technical innovations. This is a great painting because the artist—using crushed rocks mixed with oil pressed from seeds, applied with an animal's hair tied to a stick, and spread onto dried grass—has given form to an unspeakable but universal feeling: the horror of a sin that cannot be atoned for. *Grozny*. Awe-ful. In Repin's scene the Tsar cradles his dying son's head. The open eye of the son indicates that he is still alive. He knows that he is dying and he stares at his own blood with wonder and surprise. The father looks out, his eyes focused on what seems to be a vast depth. The surroundings, the furniture, the lighting, the gestures, the facial expressions—all are meant to involve the viewer in a psychological relationship with the subject matter, to evoke compassion for the murdered and for the murderer.

Just as Repin used the physical materials of paint to express the immaterial, it was Stanislavsky's ambition to create a craft for actors that could rouse the spiritual power of their art. His search for a way to tap into the power of the mind drew from various sources in art and literature—as well as Indian Yogic teachings that the mind and body were indivisible. The mechanism Stanislavsky eventually conceived was his own, yet it closely paralleled groundbreaking psychological theories that were being developed at the same time by Sigmund Freud in Vienna.

The science of inner process

Freud's central idea, which marks the beginning of twentieth-century psychology, is that emotions and behavior are functions of desire. People don't do things because a genie slips into their ear during the night. People don't have bad dreams because they eat spoiled fruit before bed. People do things, including dream, because they have desires. These may not be conscious desires, but conscious or not, desires structure behavior.

One of Freud's essential contributions to an understanding of desire and human relationships is this: what you want but never get means more in life than what you want and *do* get. Beginning with desire for a parent, which Freud called the *Electra* and *Oedipus complexes*, some desires inevitably meet immovable obstacles. In the case of lust for a parent, social convention and incest taboos are such obstacles.

The names Electra and Oedipus are taken from Greek plays where characters with these names meet tragic ends when their desires are revealed or perversely fulfilled. But in life, thwarted desires don't usually meet tragic ends. Once desires meet an obstacle, they don't die; they retreat into the mind, below the surface of awareness, in the region called the *subconscious*. According to Freud, because gratified desires have been relieved and their energy spent, character is determined more by thwarted desires that remain in the subconscious to linger or fester unsatisfied—and unseen.

Thwarted desires determine character more than gratified desires. We'll soon see how this theory parallels Stanislavsky's work. According to Freud (and Stanislavsky), in order to understand and *choose* appropriate behavior with which to encounter obstacles in the world, one needs to move beyond conscious explanations and reach down to the subconscious. There one can view and identify unseen desire.

Neither Freud nor Stanislavsky ever heard of the other, although the foundations of Freud's research began in 1888, almost simultaneously with Stanislavsky's research into a performer's use of the subconscious.*

Stanislavsky's investigation below the conscious mind for the source of behavior was sustained not by psychology, but by his life-long interest in Yoga. The Indian religious approach called Yoga has many paths. Stanislavsky was interested in two of them: *Hatha Yoga* and *Raja Yoga*. Hatha Yoga, the more familiar, teaches the mind to observe the processes of the body in order to relax and ultimately eradicate stress. Raja Yoga, more pertinent here, teaches the mind to observe its inner desires in order to choose which desires to pursue, but only to refine and ultimately *eradicate* desire. Stanislavsky, however, differs from Raja Yoga when he asks that the actor's mind observe its inner desires in order to creatively *pursue* desire.

Terms to Work with: Tasks and Actions

This chapter limits itself to the ways Stanislavsky suggested that an actor organize a text with a structure of motivation. Even that is complex. Drawing ideas from several sources, Stanislavsky developed his insights during forty years of rehearsals, performances, and classes, eventually organizing them into a system for working in the theater. Today, around the world, the study of the *Stanislavsky System* is a field of its own. In theory or in practice, it takes more than a lifetime to master it. Stanislavsky wrote about this system expansively. The vast majority of his writing was taken down as notes and notebooks for himself, and never intended for publication. Some writings were published during his lifetime; most were not. When Stanislavsky died, a state commission was formed to sort through and organize the thousands of pages in manuscript he left behind. Nine volumes of the *Collected Stanislavsky* have been published in Russia, several of them multiple books—and some very different from their English "translations."

Stanislavsky's theories on acting have not only been translated into the many languages of the world, they've been translated into the many fancies of various acting teachers. Each teacher seems to have his own vocabulary of words that express the same basic ideas. The written word is just as suspect: at the turn of the twenty-first century, the field has cracked open once again with evidence—brought forward by American scholar Sharon Marie Carnicke—that the American translation of the most influential of Stanislavsky's books is abridged and inaccurate, and that the Soviet version of the same book is censored. More than a hundred years after the start of the Russian Revolution in acting, the full breadth of Stanislavsky's contribution has yet to be published, much less read, understood, or applied.

Many ideas about Stanislavsky in America were passed down orally from teacher to

---

*The psychologist whom Stanislavsky did read was the Frenchman Théodule Ribot, who claimed that a very small number of the sixty people he surveyed on the subject were so affected by emotional experience that the memory of past sensations was ingrained in their bodies. When so-called "affective memories" were recalled, they supposedly revived both sensation and emotion. Stanislavsky used Ribot's theory as support for his own investigations into memory and emotion, deciding on his own that affective memory wasn't rare, but inherent in all people and capable of development in all actors. Even so, Ribot's theory offered no support for an investigation of motivations for action.

student and repeated. One of the reasons for the variations in American interpretations is the American mishearing of Russian accents in English. During the very first speech about Stanislavsky's system in America, listeners took notes as the speaker mentioned the importance of *"beets"*—segments of a scene determined by a single task. Did the speaker mean "beats" as in musical "beats" (as some thought)? Was it "bits" as in show-biz "bits" (as someone claimed to have heard from Stanislavsky himself)? Was it "beads" on a string? Or was it Borscht?*

What's called the "Stanislavsky System" and how close it is to what Stanislavsky actually said, wrote, or meant, you can spend your life arguing. Don't. For the purposes of this text, these are the terms that an actor faced with a script can use. Learn them and you can put them to use in your work.

Task

The basic premise of Stanislavsky's approach to acting is that the text sets a **task,** which in turn challenges an actor to answer the question *What do I need to do?* The word we're calling a *task* can also be translated as a *problem,* for which the actor must find a solution. The task provides the need that drives an actor's activities, speeches, relationships, and behavior on stage. Four examples:

- I need to pass this class.
- I need to teach this student a lesson.
- I need to escape this prison of a marriage.
- I need to get back with my old boyfriend.

Within the rules of this approach, the place where a performer tries to satisfy any needs is onstage, and only onstage. You don't try to satisfy your needs out in the audience; an invisible wall stands in your way. Because of the three-sided box-like sets of Stanislavsky's time, this invisible wall became known as *the fourth wall,* closing off the actors from the audience. Because of the fourth wall, although you might need to escape, you don't run off the stage, down the aisles, and out the doors of the theater.

Action

An **action** is what you perform onstage to accomplish the task. The action answers the question *What do I do to get what I need?* An action is written in the form of an *infinitive verb,* in the *active* voice, in the *transitive* case. An action is a verb because it's something that you *do:*

- teach (*not* a teacher)
- study (*not* a student)
- escape (*not* an escapee)

---

*At Le Siècle Stanislavsky Conference in Paris, translators did translate the word as *beets.* Is this the root of organic acting?

11

The *infinitive* is the simplest form of the verb, always preceded by the word *to*:

- to teach
- to study
- to escape

Actions use verbs in the *active* voice—not the passive voice—because they are something that you do, not something done to you:

- to study (*not* to be taught)
- to escape (*not* to be untied)
- to arouse or to entice (*not* to be desired or to be chased after)

The action is never a state of being. You don't want "to be" anything; you want to do something. You don't want to be passive onstage. Even when you are listening, you want to be listening *actively*:

- I want to enjoy (*not* I want to be happy)
- I want to remove myself (*not* I want to be left alone)
- I want to graduate (*not* I want to be a graduate)

Now for the essential part: The action is expressed as a *transitive* verb because a transitive verb requires an *object* to complete its action. You want to put yourself in an *active relationship* with *somebody else*. For example, if the task is *I need to escape this prison of an acting class*, the actions can be:

- to charm my teacher
- to evade my teacher
- to confuse my teacher
- to beg for mercy from my teacher

The task is not simply *to run* from acting class, but *to escape it*. You want to run? Go ahead. Run! You don't need anyone else to run. But *I want to escape* . . . puts you in a *relationship* with something or someone else. When you are looking for ways to meet your task, you look to the other actors onstage. You may not want to, but that's what's there to look at. In this approach, acting is not the art of emotional display or contented being. Acting is the art of human relationships.

Script analysis

Armed with this information, let's poke at a script. By doing so we are reversing the usual order for working in rehearsal. *Script analysis* is not meant to be something you do at home and then display in the rehearsal hall to the wonder of your colleagues. It's meant to organize your work in rehearsal, and, ideally, it should follow the rehearsal as a way of recording what happened so that you can repeat the circumstances that achieved results.

When he first tried to apply his ideas to rehearsals, Stanislavsky spent a lot of time sitting at a table with his actors analyzing the text for tasks and actions. Later, following the example of Hatha Yoga and its physical exercises meant to unite body and mind (the word *yoga* means *union*), Stanislavsky led his actors to work on their feet at once, so, as he put it, there would be no divide between the spiritual and physical aspects of work. Either way of working is useful for discovering tasks; the way you choose will depend on the play, of course. Some texts are so dense or have so many characters that nothing more than a traffic jam will happen if the early rehearsals begin with the actors standing.

Let's pretend that you've had a rehearsal where you sat at a table and read lines with another actor. The text you read was simple and—seemingly—simple-minded:

> YOUR PART One and one make two, one and two make three, one and three make four, one and four make five.

These are hardly deathless words. You can probably even memorize them without too much trouble. There isn't much leeway in the interpretation of their meaning. They mean what they say. So how would you make them active?

A Web of Relationships: Rehearsing a Scene from *The Lesson*

The lines quoted above are from a scene in Eugene Ionesco's 1954 play, *The Lesson* (6). A Professor who gives lessons at home begins working with a new Pupil. When the Pupil arrives, she is self-assured and intimidates the Professor. The Professor begins the lesson by asking the Pupil a series of comically easy questions. Her quick responses fluster him. Then the Professor's questions get harder. Slowly the balance of power changes. The Professor deliberately confuses the Pupil. He sadistically insists that she answer his trick questions, even when she cries out that she suffers from a painful toothache. Eventually he teaches her how to escape the pain he causes her. He stabs her while teaching her to say the words, "The knife kills."

> PROFESSOR How much are one and one?
>> [The Professor's task is *to trap the Pupil*]
> PUPIL One and one make two.
>> [The Pupil's task is *to satisfy the Professor*]
> PROFESSOR (*marveling at the* PUPIL'S *knowledge*) Oh, but that's very good. You appear to me to be well along in your studies. You should easily achieve the total doctorate, miss.
>> [The Professor's action is *to flatter the Pupil*]
> PUPIL I'm so glad. Especially to have someone like you tell me this.
>> [The Pupil's action is *to soften up the Professor*]

These choices for tasks and actions are by no means the only choices. The lines could be interpreted differently:

> PROFESSOR How much are one and one?
>   [task: *to encourage the Pupil*]
> PUPIL One and one make two.
>   [task: *to earn her degree quickly*]
> PROFESSOR (*marveling at the* PUPIL'S *knowledge*) Oh, but that's very good. You appear to me to be well along in your studies. You should easily achieve the total doctorate, miss.
>   [action: *to coax the Pupil*]
> PUPIL I'm so glad. Especially to have someone like you tell me this.
>   [action: *to prod the Professor*]

Either way, the structure of the lines remains the same. The Professor speaks because he wants to fulfil his task. So does the Pupil. The Professor wants to trap the Pupil, so he flatters her. Or he wants to encourage the Pupil, so he coaxes her. The Pupil wants to satisfy the Professor, so she tries to soften him up. Or she wants to get out in a hurry, so she prods him.

Let's accept one set of choices and organize the scene. Although we're exaggerating the change in actions by introducing a new one with practically every sentence, an action can be played for much longer than a line. On the other hand, there can be more than one action to a line. While you're preparing a role, you'll usually use smaller units at first. Later, in rehearsal and performance, the actions will be absorbed into larger ones meant to meet the needs of a task. This resembles learning a dance or gymnastics routine. First you learn the individual steps and repeat them until they flow into each other. Then you can waltz or roll into a somersault without being aware of separate movements (7). What follows is one of many possible interpretations.

> PROFESSOR Let's push on: how much are two and one?
>   [task: *to push the Pupil*]
> PUPIL Three.
>   [task: *to stand up to the Professor*]
> PROFESSOR Three and one?
>   [action: *to press*]
> PUPIL Four.
>   [action: *to volley*]
> PROFESSOR Four and one?
>   [action: *to corner*]
> PUPIL Five.
>   [action: *to escape*]

PROFESSOR Five and one?
   [action: *to attack*]

PUPIL Six.
   [action: *to protect herself*]

PROFESSOR Six and one?
   [action: *to decoy*]

PUPIL Seven.
   [action: *to snap at*]

PROFESSOR Seven and one?
   [action: *to pounce*]

PUPIL Eight.
   [action: *to satisfy*]

PROFESSOR Seven and one?
   [action: *to trick*]

PUPIL Eight again.
   [action: *to show off*]

PROFESSOR Very well answered. Seven and one?
   [action: *to trick*]

PUPIL Eight once more.
   [action: *to show off*]

PROFESSOR Perfect. Excellent. Seven and one?
   [action: *to set her up, to confuse*]

PUPIL Eight again . . .
   [action: *to bite*]

PUPIL And sometimes nine.
   [action: *to shut him up*]

Activity

The stage direction reads: *marveling at the* PUPIL'S *knowledge*. But *marveling* is not an action, it's an *activity*. Marveling, teaching, questioning, studying, testing, or answering are all activities. The **activity** is the behavior taking place on stage. Bowling, fishing, reading, or looking at a picture album are all activities. The specific activity is determined by the *given circumstances* of the scene, in this case a classroom where studying, testing, and answering are typical activities.

The activity can change and the actions will still be what organize the performance. You may be bowling when you meet your old boyfriend, or you may be showing him a picture album from your honeymoon, but ten-pins or snapshots of tourist traps notwithstanding, your task will still be *to see if your old boyfriend still loves you*. The actions are what you'll do onstage in order to find out if he does.

In the scene from *The Lesson*, the activity, *marveling*, is given by the playwright, but why is the Professor marveling at the Pupil's ability to add one and two? There are many possible choices of actions that would motivate his *marveling*:

- to set the Pupil up
- to get the Pupil to let her guard down
- to seduce the Pupil
- to mock the Pupil

Paradoxically, the activity can be motionless, as when you work on a task with inner actions—*I need to resolve my doubt about my old boyfriend*. At an early period of developing his system, Stanislavsky, mindful of Yoga and concentrating on his own search for inner dramatic action, considered these inner activities far more important artistically than gestures or outer behavior.

Obstacles

The things that stand in your character's way are called **obstacles**. In order to create dramatic action you want to make an obstacle of the other actors. Often they will make obstacles of themselves. You can also make an obstacle out of the physical environment, your costume, or any other aspect of the production or the role. The Professor wants to trip up the Pupil—to dominate her—but she knows the answer to his question. That is the Professor's obstacle.

> PROFESSOR Now, let's look at subtraction. Tell me, if you're not exhausted,
>   how many are four minus three?
>   [His action: *to push her*
>   The obstacle in his way: *she bluffs him*]
> PUPIL Four minus three? . . . Four minus three?
>   [Her action: *to evade him*
>   The obstacle in her way: *he pursues her*]

Opportunities

Although Stanislavsky doesn't mention it directly, you can also identify **opportunities**, those things that will help you to accomplish the task.

> PROFESSOR Yes. I mean to say: subtract three from four.
>   [His task: *to demoralize her*
>   His action: *to corner her*
>   The opportunity: *she is confused and disoriented*]
> PUPIL That makes . . . seven?
>   [Her task: *to save face*

Her action: *to guess the answer*

The opportunity: *the possibility that she might guess correctly*]

PROFESSOR I am sorry but I'm obliged to contradict you. Four minus three does not make seven. You are confused: four plus three makes seven, four minus three does not make seven . . . This is not addition anymore, we must subtract now.

[His task now is *to sabotage the Pupil*

His actions are *to pounce and to punish*

The opportunity is *she gave a wrong answer*]

What Stanislavsky tried to create onstage was an active *web of relationships* among people. To create that active web, the actions you take on stage to accomplish your tasks must be transitive actions that relate to the other actors on the stage. The other actors present obstacles to getting the tasks done, or provide you with opportunities to succeed at your tasks. If you take advantage of the opportunities, or succeed in overcoming the obstacles, your desire is satisfied. If you don't overcome the obstacles, your desire is thwarted. In either case, the outcome is truthful emotion.

- *Completed desire*: I want something from my new professor. I got it. My task is accomplished and I'm happy.
- *Thwarted desire*: I want something from my new professor. I didn't get it. As a result, I am frustrated and angry. I might cry or I might do something desperate.

Don't go onstage and *be* angry, or *be* frustrated. Frustration or anger will come about when you try to meet the demands of your task.

Through-line

Dramatic action, as well as emotion, occur when a task meets up with an obstacle and the actor changes course in the same way that a riverboat pilot on the Mississippi might change course when he finds his craft heading toward an unexpected sandbar. The Russian word for *through-line* is the same word as *channel*, and Stanislavsky makes a point that a pilot navigates his boat down the river by *sticking to the channel*. The diagram Stanislavsky gives for a through-line:

Action ⟶ Obstacle   New Action ⟶ Task
⟍   ⟋
New Action ⟶ Obstacle

The riverboat pilot wants to get from St. Louis to Natchez. But the course of the journey will be altered by any number of circumstances: where the rocks are, where the rapids are, where the banks of the river have shifted. That's the metaphor for organizing the elements of this approach. As you attempt to accomplish your tasks in rehearsal, you will establish a **through-line** by the intersection of action and obstacles. In rehearsal, you want first to identify your tasks and then to establish what helps and what hinders any actions you take to achieve those tasks.

Transitions and adjustments

When the Professor redirects himself to his task by trying another action, that tacking movement from *flattering the Pupil* to *coaxing the Pupil* is called **making an adjustment.** The actor makes an adjustment so that he can try a different action in order to meet the demands of the same task. Making adjustments to onstage obstacles is a constant process in rehearsal and in performance. It is what keeps a performance fresh and alive.

When the Professor *accomplishes* his task and moves on to try another task, that switch from *encouraging the Pupil* to *demoralizing the Pupil* is called **making a transition.** The Pupil has been encouraged enough for the Professor to move on and sabotage her. If the Pupil fails at her task and attempts another, that switch also is called making a transition. When she realizes there is no pleasing the Professor, the Pupil might switch to pleading with him. In making the transition, she abandons one task in the face of an immovable obstacle and moves on to a new task that might have more success.

Transitions happen when you switch tasks. That doesn't happen as often as switching actions, but when it does happen, it is more significant. The part of a scene dominated by a single task is experienced by the audience—usually without their being aware of it—as a single unit called a *beat*. Or a bead. Or a bit. You choose.

Super-task

Sometimes a task will challenge a character for the entire play. *I want to teach this girl a lesson*, thinks the Professor. *I want to satisfy my teacher*, thinks the Pupil. This is given the awkward term of **super-task** (it doesn't sound any better in Russian). Harold Clurman, one of the first American stage directors to apply the Stanislavsky System in rehearsals, called the super-task the *spine* of the character. The image is a good one: the spine holds upright and supports.

The advantage of identifying the super-task, or the spine, is that it organizes all the other tasks. You're not just sailing down the river; oh no, you're sailing to Natchez. Practically speaking, when you don't know what to do in performance and rehearsal—or when an unforeseen circumstance happens—you can always fall back on the spine of the character, or hope that the super-task will swoop down from your thoughts and save you from disaster. In Ionesco's *The Lesson*, the Professor's super-task is *to murder the Pupil* or *to teach her a real lesson about life* or *to excite her to rapture* or—any interpretation you choose.

Let's Review Terms

task	what you need to do onstage
action	what you do to accomplish your task
activity	your behavior while you're acting on your task
obstacle	whatever interrupts the progress of your actions
opportunity	what helps you get the task done
super-task	what you need to do throughout the play
making a transition	moving from task to task
making an adjustment	moving from action to action when you encounter an obstacle
through-line	a repeatable progression of actions encountering obstacles and opportunities

The Chart

At the beginning of the book is a chart that compares five different ways of organizing and analyzing a text. There are categories for each form, including *basic unit*, *dramatic action*, *key question*, and *relative theory*.

- **Basic unit.** The basic unit is the building block of each system; the way the actor will organize the text. For Stanislavsky, a dramatic text is analyzed and organized into basic units of *tasks*.
- **Dramatic action.** For the actor, dramatic action is what is meant to happen onstage when the words of the play are spoken aloud and performed. In this technique, an *action meant to accomplish a task should meet an obstacle*.
- **Key question.** Like a key unlocking a door to understanding, the basic unit often answers a question. For Stanislavsky the key question is *What do I need to do?*
- **Relative theory.** Acting is the art of human relationships. Besides acting teachers and playwrights, other thinkers have defined human relationships: psychologists, anthropologists, historians, and economists. These theories often parallel theories about acting. The relative theory for Stanislavsky is *Freud's psychoanalysis*. Both place an emphasis on motivated and thwarted desire.

In Chapter 2 we'll fill in the rest of the chart: *the illusion of character, unifying image, suitable playwrights*, and *the intended reaction of the audience*.

Notebook: Getting to the Task

What follows is an example of how your notebook would look after several weeks of rehearsal if you were organizing the material into tasks and obstacles. The example is from *The Lesson*.

PROFESSOR Good. Let us arithmetize a little now.

PUPIL Yes, gladly, Professor.

PROFESSOR It wouldn't be too tiresome for you to tell me . . .

PUPIL Not at all, Professor, go on.

PROFESSOR How much are one and one?

PUPIL One and one make two.

PROFESSOR (*marveling at the* PUPIL'S *knowledge*) Oh, but that's very good. You appear to me to be well along in your studies. You should easily achieve the total doctorate, miss.

PUPIL I'm so glad. Especially to have someone like you tell me this.

PROFESSOR Let's push on: how much are two and one?

PUPIL Three.

PROFESSOR Three and one?

PUPIL Four.

PROFESSOR Four and one?

PUPIL Five

The actions are not
to question or *to answer*.
Those are paraphrases
of the activity.

The Professor's task? For this
you have to read the play. The
Professor kills the Pupil at the end.
That might be the Professor's
super-task, to teach the Pupil by
killing the Pupil.

The Pupil's super-task?
To be taught is passive, *to learn* is
better, but still not good. How about
to satisfy the Professor?

If the Professor's task is
to kill the Pupil, the Professor's actions
will include tripping the Pupil up:
to flatter, to confuse.
(Notice that these all involve the Pupil)

The Professor's actions are not
to praise (this is the activity): but
*to trap the Pupil, to inflate the Pupil's
ego, to stroke*

The Professor's actions can all change:
to strike, to whip, to flick, to dab

The Pupil's actions: *to slake,
to fend off, to avoid*, (not the
passive and intransitive *to respond*)

WHAT SHOULD I DO?

PROFESSOR Five and one?

PUPIL Six.

PROFESSOR Six and one?

PUPIL Seven.

PROFESSOR Seven and one?

PUPIL Eight.

PROFESSOR Seven and one?

PUPIL Eight again.

PROFESSOR Very well answered. Seven and one?

PUPIL Eight once more.

PROFESSOR Perfect. Excellent. Seven and one?

PUPIL Eight again. And sometimes nine.

PROFESSOR Magnificent. You are magnificent. You are exquisite. I congratulate you warmly, miss. There's scarcely any point in going on. At addition you are a past master. Now, let's look at subtraction. Tell me, if you're not exhausted, how many are four minus three?

PUPIL Four minus three? . . . Four minus three?

PROFESSOR Yes. I mean to say: subtract three from four.

PUPIL That makes . . . seven?

PROFESSOR I am sorry but I'm obliged to contradict you. Four minus three does not make seven. You are confused: four plus three makes seven, four minus three does not make seven . . . This is not addition anymore, we must subtract now.

PUPIL (*trying to understand*) Yes . . . yes . . .

PROFESSOR Four minus three makes . . . How many? . . . How many?

PUPIL Four?

PROFESSOR No, miss, that's not it.

PUPIL Three, then.

PROFESSOR Not that either, miss . . . Pardon, I'm sorry . . . I ought to say, that's not it . . . excuse me.

The Professor's obstacle:
The Pupil knows the answers
The Pupil's opportunity:
These questions are easy

The Professor's action:
to mask (own anger)
(Note: The Professor's action is not
to praise. That's the activity.)

The Professor's action: *to fool, to trick*

The Pupil's action:
to stall the Professor, to keep the Professor at a distance

The Professor's action:
to push the Pupil
The Pupil's action:
to evade the Professor
The Professor's action:
to chase after the Pupil

The Pupil's action: *to grasp*
(not only the Professor's meaning, but for help)
The Professor's action:
to close in on the Pupil
The Pupil's action:
to hide from the Professor

The Professor's action: *to pounce*
(Perhaps *not that either* is shouted, which is why the Professor apologizes later)

PUPIL Four minus three . . . Four minus three. Four minus three? . . . But now doesn't that make ten?

The Pupil's action: *to distract the Professor,* not *to bluff* (that's the activity)

The Professor's action: *to unhinge the Pupil*

PROFESSOR Oh, certainly not, miss. It's not a matter of guessing. You've got to think it out. Let's try to deduce it together. Would you like to count?

PUPIL Yes, Professor. One . . . two . . . uh . . .

PROFESSOR You know how to count? How far can you count up to?

The Professor's action: *to mock* or

The Professor's action: *to torture*

PUPIL I can count to . . . to infinity.

The Pupil's action: *to rescue (self)*

PROFESSOR That's not possible, miss.

PUPIL Well then, let's say to sixteen.

PROFESSOR That is enough. One must know one's limits.

The Professor's action: *to slam down on*

CHAPTER 2

THE IMPORTANCE OF OBSTACLES

In Stanislavsky's approach to performance, dramatic action happens when a performer tries to meet the demands of a task and an obstacle gets in the way. The through-line of a performance is a series of intersections between task and obstacle. It is this intersection that characterizes your role to the audience: they see you *choose* something else to do when your action runs into an obstacle. If you can't do one thing, then you choose to do another.

When you define character by obstacles, you don't define what you need, you define what you do when you don't get what you need. Cleverly trying another tack? Backing up, giving up, or smiling and deceiving other people? As in Freud's interpretation of behavior, emotion comes from the same intersection:

- I need this. I get it and I'm pleased.
- I need that. I don't get it and I'm annoyed.
- If I figure out a way to get past the obstacle, I'm pleased and satisfied.

In choosing tasks and actions, it is important to understand that they are most effective if they create a relationship with someone else—and they become especially interesting if they overcome an obstacle. Thinking about or striving for your needs is not the same as communicating or accomplishing your needs. The art of fulfilling your tasks will lead you to listen, to watch, and to respond sensitively to the environment, including the other people around you who have their *own* needs.

When onstage actions seem weak or passionless, the problem is usually that the obstacle onstage is too weak to challenge the actions to greater strength. It doesn't help to squeeze the task (or repeat the desperate acting teacher's command: *need it more!*), it helps to raise the obstacles. This is what spurs pole-vaulters to go higher. Coaches don't shout, "Jump higher, fool!" The bar to be jumped over is raised as an incentive for the pole-vaulter to go another tenth of an inch. Same thing here. To heighten the behavior onstage, challenge the action by making the obstacle *more difficult to overcome*.

But don't start with yourself; start with an active relationship. Every aspect of the rehearsal process, including investigating the meaning of the text, should involve creating a relationship with other actors. The fourteenth-century Japanese acting teacher Zeami wrote that every acting school has its secret. What is the secret song of an actor trained to accomplish tasks?

Sometimes I'm happy.
Sometimes I'm blue.
My disposition depends on you . . . (8)

Enlarging the Circle of Concentration

What you'll do in rehearsal is what Stanislavsky called **enlarging the circle of concentration**. The exercise is taken directly from a Raja Yoga practice. As you've read in Chapter 1, Stanislavsky was influenced by two schools of the Indian religious path called Yoga. He derived his relaxation and breathing exercises for actors from Hatha Yoga, which teaches meditation and relaxation through physical techniques. More applicable to our discussion of script analysis is Raja Yoga, which teaches that the mind observing itself can discriminate among its actions and, before it acts, can notice, respond, and achieve communion with increasing aspects of the world.

In practice, at every rehearsal you will consider new aspects of the production or your partner's ability to help or hinder your accomplishment of your task. Less noble than Yoga, we'll call it the Paranoid Theory of Acting. Everyone—and everything—onstage is either for you or against you. There's nothing neutral. Every aspect of the production should be included in the widening circle.

Now, of course you can't do that at once. Slowly, over time, you become increasingly sensitive to what's around you—not just noticing other people's and other things' presence, but letting their presence affect you. Today you're going to extend your concentration to the light, tomorrow to the other actor's hands, the next day to his neck, or his costume. This is a way to keep a performance fresh by discovering new ways to connect to the environment. Make a game of it if you like. At every rehearsal add one more thing to assign value as obstacle or opportunity.

Avoid extending concentration into the audience, though, or bang and bounce you'll go against the invisible fourth wall. Working strictly in this way, the task never, never, *never* involves the people in the audience. There are exceptions—even Stanislavsky had the actors enter through the audience for a production of Shakespeare's *Twelfth Night*—but these exceptions are rare. The illusion of a self-contained world is created by placing the actions and the obstacles on the stage.

The whole point is to create a real—not simulated—sequence of behavior onstage that is motivated by the given circumstances happening in front of the audience. Good acting is like good lying: tell 95 percent of the truth and you can slip in 5 percent that isn't the truth. Creating a relationship with someone else is so rare and so powerful that if you can do that for real, it's a lot easier to convince the audience, among other fibs, that you're sitting in Norway even though the audience is sitting in northern Illinois, ten feet away. The key to recreating a living truth on the stage: don't copy the form of truth; repeat the structure of relationships that got you to the truth. This is how twentieth-century acting theory and practice differ from what came before. In order to further understand Stanislavsky's contribution to the art of acting, it helps to know what came immediately before.

A Little History

Great acting—in the eyes of the beholder

Before we compare Stanislavsky's approach to acting to any approach that preceded it, it's important to recognize that long-gone acting is just that: long gone. Before the invention of the camera, audiences realized that the great theatrical performances they were witness to were precious, fleeting moments in time. They also recognized that great performances, like any great art work, somehow needed to be recorded and passed down to posterity as evidence of what the human spirit might achieve.

Yet, to try to fix a reliable portrait of "great" acting into words is as difficult as trying to capture the shifting appearance of the ocean's surface: what is being described keeps moving and changing. The descriptive words in the chronicles of acting throughout history likewise shift, their meanings relative to their time and place. When we read accounts of "great" performances—be they Eleonora Duse's or Bugs Bunny's—the same words appear, yet they are describing obviously different stories. The meaning of phrases such as "truthful emotions," "believably lifelike," and "natural" changes as rapidly and regularly as the ocean's waves; they have as fixed a meaning from century to century as the words "up-to-date." What is "believable" or "lifelike" depends on the beliefs and lives of the audience. An old saying goes that an actor's fame is written in water—or, as one actor said about himself, in hot water. Hot, cold, or tepid, that water keeps changing.

Nevertheless, behind the imprecise words that try to capture what is gone forever lies an undeniable passion. The writers trying to describe what they had witnessed on stage knew these performances were *already* gone forever. There is poignancy in that, and although we may not agree with or understand their assessments, we can't deny that they were moved by what they saw.*

We can also be curious about performances we would consider good that audiences of the past might have overlooked, or, having been blinded by their circumstances, not appreciated. In 1850, one of the first international stage stars in history, a dark-skinned African-American named Ira Aldridge, toured to Russia at the height of his fame to play Othello, Shylock, and Macbeth. The Russian actor Michael Schepkin, always credited as an earlier version of Stanislavsky because of Schepkin's eighteenth-century "realism," criticized Aldridge's calm and majesty in the role of Othello. Schepkin reminded Aldridge (who had won prizes for Latin composition in his youth) that Othello was a *Moor*: "hot southern blood seethes in his veins . . . he ought to rush at Desdemona and grab at her, and only then remember that he is a general and people are staring at him" (9). Schepkin's version might be realistic or not; it is certainly affected by his eighteenth-century vision of black people.

---

*Throughout this book, scenes from films are often used as examples of a performance. Film performances, of course, are the result of a team effort: the words can be dubbed, the mood manipulated by lighting or the musical soundtrack, the meaning of the performance rearranged by editing or computer graphics. Even so: when we watch a film performance, at least we can agree on what we're talking about.

In 1775, just before the American Revolution was about to start, a well-connected twenty-one-year-old girl made her London stage debut. Her married name was Mrs. Sarah Siddons, but she was better known in theater circles as the daughter of the celebrated Kemble acting family. Despite her connections, critics and audiences of 1775 didn't think much of Sarah Siddons, and she retreated to the provinces. Seven years later she returned to London and the same stage to be acclaimed as the greatest English actress who ever lived. Did Mrs. Siddons get better? Or did tastes change so that audiences appreciated what the actress had been doing all along?

When it comes to performances that date back to the time of George Washington, let's agree that we can't really know just what was "believable." Still, thanks to the distance of time, we can deduce a period's general trends. Again, as with the sea: there are calms, there are storms, there are tides. Before the rising tide of Stanislavsky's system, there were other systems of acting—classical and romantic—that, conveniently enough, can be remembered as a calm and a storm.

Classical acting

Classical acting was deliberately calm, though hardly calming. From letters, newspaper reviews, and engraved illustrations (which were as popular as baseball cards in their day), we can deduce that by the time the American Revolution was over and George Washington was President, Mrs. Siddons was London's reigning actress. Her younger brother, John Phillip Kemble, was the reigning actor-manager of Drury Lane, the same theater where Mrs. Siddons had her lackluster London debut and subsequent triumph. John was two years younger than his sister Sarah, and at the time of her debut he was off in a seminary studying to be a priest. Soon after, conveniently armed with a good working knowledge of Greek and Latin, he returned to the family acting trade.

Classical actors like Mrs. Siddons and John Phillip Kemble were concerned with posing and propriety. They stood on stage with dignity. They studied classical statues for ways to drape their clothes and to build their scenery. It was rumored they also copied their *gestures* from statues—why not imitate poses that would express emotion? In her spare time Mrs. Siddons sometimes sculpted, and her attitude toward her onstage gestures was that of someone scrupulously concerned with graceful expression, carefully shaping the human form.

Classical acting was an approach of artful deliberation. It was lifelike—within its forms.* According to the tastes of the time, this meant balanced, stately movements and harmonious tones that were equally poised, balanced, and orderly—especially when expressing disorder. Once Sarah Siddons fainted onstage, something she did very believably in certain roles, but her audience knew it was for real and not an act because *they could see her legs*—which would never have been admitted to plain view if the lady was conscious. Of course, contemporary descriptions didn't say that. True to the discretion of the day, they referred to the sight of Mrs. Siddons's *uncovered limbs*.

---

*Stanislavsky called this kind of acting *representation*, because the performers *re-presented* their characters rather than embodied them.

THE IMPORTANCE OF OBSTACLES

We mustn't think that because legs couldn't be seen or spoken about directly that classical acting was cold—although it certainly was calculated. Mrs. Siddons was so emotional and convincing that other actors could choke up onstage when playing a scene with her. She herself was put out during her first tour to Edinburgh when, after one of her better speeches and effects, her Scottish audience failed to interrupt the scene with thunderous applause. Mrs. Siddons wrote in her *Reminiscences* that, while she was grateful for the silent appreciation, she needed time to breathe in order to work herself up for the next effect (10).

She wasn't being self-indulgent to expect a breather between bravos. The claptrap Mrs. Siddons was reciting was mostly rhetoric, and it required great gusts of wind. It was her practiced technique to draw energy and renewed concentration from a crowd's approval—unlike other actors, who would simply become distracted.*

This was one reason Sarah Siddons succeeded; her talent met the demands of the time. It also demonstrates that talent is a relative term. The ability to make love to the camera, for example, was not a recognized talent until film acting called for it. Turning pages of turgid rhetoric into thrilling stage events is no longer the necessary skill it was in Sarah's day, when actors were asked to say lines like:

Oh! give me daggers, fire, or water:

You can still view Mrs. Siddons's scripts, marked by her own hand in blue pencil, and the underlined words and phrases with which she wanted to "bring out" her "points" to the audience. This is what her book looked like. The scene is from *Venice Preserved*, by Thomas Otway (10).

Oh! give me daggers, fire, or water:
How I could bleed, how burn, how drown, the waves
<u>Huzzing and foaming round my sinking head</u>
Till I descended to the peaceful bottom
Oh! there's all quiet, <u>here</u> all rage and fury:
The air's too thin and pierces my weak brain;
I long for thick substantial sleep: <u>Hell! Hell!</u>
<u>Burst from the centre, rage and roar aloud</u>
If thou art half so hot, so mad as I am.

Notice, by the way, that two of the lines to be "brought out" describe actions so clearly that they could be confused with stage directions. Huzzing? Sarah Siddons and other trained actors of her time could do so much huzzing with lines like the above that playwrights wrote similar speeches to show off actors' talents—something we'll notice happening in other times and places as well.

In addition to acting, audiences, critics, and theater professionals of the period

---

*This was training, not instinct. Before Sarah was ten, she had turned tail to the wings after an audience laughed at her. Her mother took her by the hand to the edge of the stage, calmed the crowd, and Sarah started again (10).

wanted the old plays to be harmoniously balanced, too. Shakespeare's *The Tragedy of King Lear* became a little less tragic with the addition of a happy ending. To balance the horrors of *Macbeth*, new scenes incorporated singing fairies and dancing elves.

At its worst, classical acting became a collection of poses and vocal tricks. One hand on the breast, the other extended in gesture, classical acting was called by detractors "the teapot school," and its practitioners were said to spout. In 1804, the rage of the London season was a little spouter, a twelve-year-old boy named Master Betty. Yes, that really was his name.* Master Betty could act up a storm of classical gestures. He played Hamlet, Macbeth, and Richard III. While he was popular, Mrs. Siddons withdrew from the London season and went as far as Ireland for another tour. Her brother, on the other hand, had the good sense to book Master Betty while he was hot: Master Betty's Romeo took in more than double the Drury Lane's box office average (11). Master's Betty's star did wane, however, and Mrs. Siddons returned in force—sternly and nobly—to the London stage the next season.

Master Betty brushed aside, classical acting continued its calm reign in England, albeit briefly. It did go on to flourish in France, however, and in 1837 culminated in the person of a sixteen-year-old Jewish girl named Rachel. Actually, her name was Eliza Felix, but *Rachel* had more showbiz appeal than *Miss Felix* did. Rachel had been taught to stand like a statue and intone her lines with fever and passion. Far from being a monster like Master Betty, the teenage Rachel was acclaimed within months as a genius who excelled in high-minded, strong-willed princesses—Greek and Roman roles for which she could have had little life experience while strumming her guitar on the streets of Lyons where she had been discovered. Rachel's most successful role was Phaedra, a stepmother who lusts after her younger stepson. Rachel was twenty-two when she first played Phaedra; how old could the stepson have been? Fifteen? Where was Master Betty when they needed him? But Rachel's life experience didn't matter. She personified perfect forms, like a well-cut diamond. Don't think they didn't call her believable and lifelike. By the standards of the day, she *was*—and by any standards, brilliant.

Germany had its own classical acting, with rules laid down by the philosopher Goethe that decreed an actor must not only imitate nature, but present "her" ideally. That was Rule 35 (11). Other European countries had similar rules. It was considered very tasteful. People who didn't act "classically" were criticized for tastelessness.

Romantic acting

Romantic acting can be thought of as the storm after the calm. For all the success of classical acting, by the mid-nineteenth century there were people who wanted a little more life in their poses. The romantic literature, which had been tempered by the classical approach of what was sarcastically called the Kemble Religion, was now dispensed full strength (and then some) by actors of the romantic school. Romantic actors knew few rules of restraint. They believed poses should be less balanced, less poised, and less de-

---

*Master William Henry West Betty, to be precise. He made his debut at eleven, a year after seeing Mrs. Siddons in Belfast and declaring to his father: I shall certainly die if I do not become an actor!

liberate. An actor's poses should be, in theory, free to rise spontaneously from the performer's genius. Romantic acting, as with all romantic art, trusted that the soul of the artist would create its own evocative forms.

Edmund Kean was the British exemplar of this more dynamic style. When Mrs. Siddons was on tour in Ireland during Master Betty's flash in the pan, she played opposite an eighteen-year-old Kean. Did she recognize him from when he was eight? When Kean had been thrown out for misbehavior from a Kemble production of *Macbeth*—in which he played an elf? Within a short time—and for a short time—Edmund Kean was to become recognized around the world as a phenomenon of romantic acting, a style that maintained poses were formed by the personality of the performer, not by a rule of grace or the model of a statue. Kean executed some of the same roles that John Phillip Kemble had portrayed. The contrast was striking: the critic Leigh Hunt called it Kean's tears versus Kemble's cheeks of stone (12). Hamlet—a role Kemble had made moody and thoughtful—was played by Kean violently, his hands shattering the air in rapid and compulsive movement, his body trembling in fits and jerks, his voice ringing out in growls and roars. His listeners were awestruck; he was literally unnerving, his force of life so unbridled that audiences fainted at the sight and sound.

Don't think his gestures and poses were spontaneous. They were just as calculated as the ones derived from rules of taste. Kean counted the steps he took onstage, and complained that people thought he was making up what he took great pains to make appear spontaneous. When asked about the earnestness of a scene in which he choked another actor onstage, Kean replied, "In earnest! I should think so. Hang the fellow! He was trying to keep me out of the focus!" (13).

Athletic acting was the American contribution to all these poses. It's usually called by a fig leaf of a name—"heroic" acting—but perhaps "athletic" more captures what it was about. It was democratic as well: Adah Isaacs Menken, an African-American woman light-skinned enough to hide her racial background, was very famous for playing the male role of *Mazeppa*, galloping onto the stage on a "wild California mustang" and refusing to have a straw dummy double for her when it was time to be carried off upside down on the same horse. Wow.

Edwin Forrest was the greatest of the athletic actors. At eighteen, Forrest had played opposite Edmund Kean during Kean's American tour and was motivated to invent his own brand of over-the-top theatrics. Forrest's booming voice, fine physique, and horsemanship—he was bow-legged (which shows that "fine physique" is relative too)—made him wildly popular in America. He was less appreciated in England: when he played Macbeth in London, the audience hissed. Forrest always thought the British actor William Macready led the hissing. When Macready had the nerve to play his Macbeth in New York City, Forrest fans rioted in Astor Place. It may be inconceivable, but yes, they once cared about acting styles in America as much as they care about sports teams today.

The line between classical and romantic actors was hardly a fixed one. For example, Macready, who seems to have annoyed people in both camps, was criticized in classical quarters for performing with his necktie undone—as if he was in his own living room, complained the critic William Hazlitt (12). Whether their approach to acting was romantic or classical or some mix of the two, what actors using these approaches did was read a script and look for opportunities to illustrate the emotional state of their characters. The big question was which poses were better.

Melodrama

What happened to change all this posturing? The plays changed. As the theater became increasingly popular with audiences of different social backgrounds and education, *melodrama* became a dominant form. Today we think of melodrama as unrealistic because of its sensational situations (*the poor girl's house is on fire!*) and flat characters (*the bad man set the fire! the good man stopped it!*). To the audience of its day, melodrama seemed lifelike, realistic, and truthful, not least because the characters in melodramas began to include shop girls, sailors, and factory workers. It would be ludicrous for such down-to-earth types to roll on the floor, let alone copy a Greek statue. Posing seemed at odds with what these characters were saying, which required that they *did* look like they were spouting in their living room.

Did the subject matter of these plays invite the lower-class audience to attend the theater? Did the lower-class audience create a demand for plays that depicted lower-class people? A little of both. The excitements of melodrama compensated factory workers and clerks for their uneventful working hours. After a hard day at the factory, watching a play was easier than reading a book.

The hoi polloi had already been coming to the theater in Sarah Siddons's day. All too often on tour the cheaper seats would shout out: "Sally, me jewel, that's no bad!" Once when Mrs. Siddons was drinking the poison as Juliet, someone from the galleries yelled out: "Sip it up, lass!"* In order to satisfy the kind of spectator who didn't quite appreciate the nuances of a queen's hauteur or classical restraint—yet knew when a sailor or his girl was talking phony—melodrama required, before Stanislavsky's revelation of the importance of internal structures, a vocabulary of realistic poses to rival the gestures of classical or romantic acting. Called *naturalism*—the name is similar to that of a literary movement (more about that later)—this new style urged artists, including actors, to study nature.

Naturalism and naturalistic acting

The study of nature is an instinctive place to learn about acting. Making use of those observations, however, is a result of training. One of the first books of acting instruc-

---

*This happened in Leeds. The wit called out, in dialect: "Soop it oop, lass." At her curtain call, Mrs. Siddons said: "Goodbye, you brutes." Once again on a tour, this time to Scotland, the theater Mrs. Siddons was appearing at was so hot that the actress knew in advance she would be thirsty when she finished her Lady Macbeth. She asked that a beer be delivered to her at a certain time. The woman from her dressing room placed an order with the nearest tavern. The boy from the tavern arrived, hot on his task with a frothy mug, calling at the stage door for "Mrs. Siddons!" He asked a stagehand where the lady might be and the stagehand jerked his finger in the direction of the stage. Seizing the opportunity for a tip, the delivery boy walked onstage, mug in his outstretched hand, right in the middle of the sleep-walking scene. Mrs. Siddons proved an obstacle, and waved him away grandly, but he made an adjustment to ignore the meaning of her gestures and kept on coming until a stage manager ran out to grab both mug and boy. The lad was whisked off, with no chance to make a transition, his action thwarted, the task over, and the beer spilled. No tip, either (14).

tion in the English language, written in 1746, declares that observation of nature will produce a total of ten emotions in all (15). It recommends buying a three-quarter-length mirror, so that when the actor finds himself feeling one of the ten he can run to the mirror (three-quarter, not half) in order to make sure his forehead is smooth for joy or ruffled for anguish. Another acting treatise, written slightly later, points out that rolling eyes are the sign of quick wit in a man and loose morals in a woman (15). Observation, just as much as talent and truthfulness, depends on expectations.

A slightly more scientific approach to observation was taken in the 1840s by a Frenchman by the name of François Delsarte. Delsarte used to go to the park in Paris to observe people and take detailed notes about the ways happy people sat and sad people slumped. He had an eye for detail. He noticed that mothers who loved their children reached toward their child with the thumb lifted, and that hired nurses who were simply doing a job reached toward the child with the thumb turned inward. Delsarte made charts, too, which demonstrated the poses used for declarations of love and the grimaces of abject misery—along with notes, drawings, and schemes for the physical representation of other emotions. The original idea was to replace formulae by recording scientifically what could be found in nature. Delsarte's ideas, charts, and drawings became a formula of their own, of course—"naturalism."

Even with naturalism, one still analyzed a script to discover opportunities for effective poses and appropriate tones. The big question was the *source* of the gestures: copied from life, copied from statues, or free-form? This was not as zany as it sounds. Actors performing in a classical or romantic or naturalistic style were playing inside very large theaters. Any effective pose was welcome when one was entertaining houses that held over fifteen-hundred people—sometimes more than twice as much.* On those vast stages, in front of thousands of listeners, an actor's task involved speaking louder and clearer than in everyday life. Gestures had to be projected across the distance as well. Whether in broad daylight, lit by candles, or in the flicker of the gaslight that eventually illuminated the stage, performers needed to use big, bold shapes that could be seen and understood from afar—the visual equivalent of louder and clearer.

We can see the end of this style—the very tail end of it—in silent movies. The first professional silent movie actors were, for the most part, performers who had grown up with a vocabulary of familiar illustrative stage gestures. To avoid such mannerisms, the American director D.W. Griffith often used young actors with little if any stage experience; among them were the Gish sisters, Lillian and Dorothy. Lillian Gish said in an interview that she received her first and only acting lesson as a little girl: go out there and speak loudly and clearly so that everyone in the theater can hear you—*or they'll get another little girl who can* (16). Despite or because of their lack of more formal training, the Gish sisters' silent film performances are as nuanced, astute, and psychologically subtle as any ever since.

Watch their films and see for yourself. In *Orphans of the Storm* (1921), the sisters

---

*The size of stages expanded so much during Sarah Siddons's lifetime that she needed to enlarge her moves—make longer strides and slower turns, lead her movements from her hip, and move her arms more than she would have on a small stage. Siddons confessed to a friend that had she been starting out on such a large stage, her talent would have been lost.

play two orphans, one blind (Dorothy), one seeing (Lillian), separated by the French Revolution, the storm of the title. Throughout the film, the manner of acting is so understated and natural that whatever old-fashioned gestures remain stick out—you should pardon the expression—like sore thumbs. Sometimes the actors display overly-theatrical outstretched arms—silent film's equivalent to melodrama's cries for longing, mercy, or justice—but the scenario for *Orphans of the Storm* was adapted from an 1874 stage melodrama that included situations where outstretched arms would have been very effective onstage: for example, the cruelly separated sisters—one in a high balcony, the other on the street below—vainly reaching for each other.

More subtle and telling differences in approaches to acting in *Orphans of the Storm* can be noticed by paying attention to the close-ups in which different performers express the process of thinking. An experienced character actress, Lucille LaVerne, indicates her character's wicked thoughts with a malevolent side-long glance and a clenching fist to indicate "Gotcha!" The Gish sisters and most of the other actors do nothing of the kind and Griffith's camera records the genuine process of thought, as when Lillian's naturally wide eyes radiate delight, shock, understanding, or whatever else is on her mind.*

The Pioneers of Realism: Ibsen, Chekhov, Strindberg

Think of all the time that you've saved not having to study poses, copy Greek sculptures, or watch your forehead creasing in the mirror. Working to fulfil tasks, you'll try to create an inner dynamic structure that is active and changing, not fixed and static. Because of the nature of our medium—human relationships—we don't fix a formula of evocative forms. We believe inner emotion will lead to an evocative form, and we try to identify and reproduce the formula of the *inner emotion*.

Melodrama paved the way for realistic situations onstage and realistic plays, which, like the novels of George Eliot and Ivan Turgenev, dramatized interior action as much as outer action. The three pioneering authors who wrote plays that emphasized inner action and the drama of shifting relationships were from cold climates. Their names were infamous in their time but are celebrated in ours: Norway's Henrik Ibsen, Russia's Anton Chekhov, and Sweden's August Strindberg.

Could it be that these Scandinavian and Russian writers understood from birth the difference between a frozen outside and a burning inside? Maybe. Whatever the reasons, they created plays that required realistic and understated acting. Yes, they knew about each other. No, they didn't like each other, or each other's work. But they accomplished similar goals: they freed realistic plays from naturalistic formulae and presented the drama of the subconscious onstage. Within a short time of their writing, their plays revolutionized theater practices throughout the world.

The theater is notoriously the most conservative of art forms to digest new content. Because innovations in the theater cannot wait a hundred years in an attic before they are appreciated—because they must take place in front of a crowd—most innova-

---

*A transcript of Stanislavsky working with actors who are preparing a 1927 stage version of *Orphans of the Storm* appears in *Stanislavsky's Legacy*, translated by Elizabeth Reynolds Hapgood (Theatre Arts Books, 1958).

tions first suffer a baptism of uncomprehending fire. When Ibsen, Chekhov, and Strindberg started to create plays without clichés—texts that created the same internal drama that nineteenth-century novels did—critics and audiences were at first unready and unwilling to accept the change.

When Ibsen or Chekhov were performed in the typically large theaters in the accustomed style, it was often to disastrous reviews and dissatisfied audiences. Fortunately, understanding contemporary theater artists rose to these playwrights' challenges. Stanislavsky's inspiration, Eleonora Duse, excelled in roles written by Ibsen; they allowed her to demonstrate the best and subtlest aspects of her technique. Stanislavsky excelled in staging and performing Chekhov's work. Strindberg specifically called for a more intimate "chamber" theater where the behavior of the actors could be noticed in detail; he too had his champions and interpreters.

One of the first psychological dramas to achieve notoriety throughout Europe and America was *Hedda Gabler*, written by the self-exiled Norwegian, Henrik Ibsen. Nowadays one of the most admired plays in the repertory, *Hedda Gabler* was hissed and whistled down at its premiere performance on January 31, 1891, in Munich. Despite this initial reception, the play was quickly staged in other cities around Europe. Uncomprehending (and powerful) critics called Ibsen a "funereal clown." As to the play, Robert Buchanan of the *Illustrated London News* wrote: "For sheer unadulterated stupidity, for inherent meanness and vulgarity, for pretentious triviality . . . no Bostonian novel or London penny novelette has surpassed *Hedda Gabler*." "A bad escape of moral sewage-gas . . ." reported the *Pictorial World*. And *The People* concurred with "tedious turmoil of knaves and fools" (17).

The most indirectly perceptive of the negative critics was in Norway. Gerhard Gran, in *Samtiden* (1891) wrote:

> It is a law, or anyway has until now been a law, that drama, in its present state of technical development, can only present comparatively simple characters. . . . Everything that should make this curious being intelligible to us, her development, her secret thoughts, her half-sensed misgivings and all that vast region of the human mind which lies between the conscious and the unconscious—all this the dramatist can do no more than indicate. For that reason, I think a novel about Hedda Gabler would be extremely interesting, while the play leaves us with a sense of emptiness and betrayal (18).

Stanislavsky's technique, of course, was to release onstage just that "vast region of the mind between the conscious and the unconscious."

Organizing a Text for Its Obstacles: Rehearsing a Scene from *Hedda Gabler*

It seems appropriate, then, to use a scene from *Hedda Gabler* (19) as our example of how to organize a text for its *obstacles*. The play is named for its central character, the independent daughter of a General Gabler. After her father dies, Hedda marries the dull but well-meaning George Tesman. On her honeymoon Hedda realizes that her marriage is a mistake; by staying with her husband she is condemning herself to a living death as a trophy in a middle-class home. At the end of the four-act play she kills herself.

The scene we will look at is from the second act. Back from her honeymoon with Tesman, Hedda is meeting her old beau Mr. Løvborg for the first time since her marriage—and in her new home. Tesman is entertaining a guest of his own, Judge Brack.

HEDDA I'll keep Mr. Løvborg company a while.
TESMAN All right, Hedda dear, you do that.

> *He and* BRACK *go into the inner room, sit down, drink punch, smoke cigarettes, and talk animatedly during the following.* LØVBORG *remains standing by the stove.* HEDDA *goes to the writing table.*

HEDDA (*slightly raising her voice*) I can show you some photographs, if you like. Tesman and I traveled through the Tyrol on our way home.

> *She brings over an album and lays it on the table by the sofa, seating herself in the farthest corner.* LØVBORG *comes closer, stops, and looks at her. Then he takes a chair and sits down on her left, his back toward the inner room.*

HEDDA (*opening the album*) You see this view of the mountains, Mr. Løvborg. That's the Ortler group. Tesman's labeled them underneath. Here it is: "The Ortler group, near Meran."
LØVBORG (*whose eyes have never left her, speaking in a low, soft voice*) Hedda— Gabler!
HEDDA (*with a quick glance at him*) Ah! Shh!
LØVBORG (*repeating softly*) Hedda Gabler!

Examples of obstacles and opportunities

Let us agree that Hedda, like most people, would like to lead a fulfilled life. Her *supertask* will be *to escape from this marriage* and free herself from the strictures of social convention. One opportunity Hedda has to accomplish her task is this scene's visit from Mr. Løvborg. In the days before her marriage, when Hedda and Løvborg were close friends, Løvborg had been a hell-raiser. Hedda has heard that Løvborg is reformed, but she wishes it wasn't so. Could Løvborg rescue her from her prison? Why has he come to see her now that she's married?

Hedda's first *task* in this scene will be *to probe Løvborg's expectations*. Her first *action* will be *to overcome the obstacle of her husband* by putting Tesman at ease. Her manner in doing so will be shaped by another *obstacle*: she can be seen from the inner room as she sits with her old beau. The photo album gives Hedda and Løvborg some innocent-seeming *activity*; leafing through its pages is an *opportunity* to cover their actions.

THE IMPORTANCE OF OBSTACLES

In rehearsal, Løvborg's task, *to test whether Hedda still loves him*, meets the obstacle of Hedda's aloof cool as she seats herself in the farthest corner of the sofa and opens the photo album—without looking at him. The closeness of Tesman and Judge Brack are obvious obstacles to Løvborg, so his manner must be discreet if he is to speak with Hedda at all. Using the photo album, Hedda teases Løvborg, and perhaps baits him with the appearance of a happy marriage.

Løvborg's next action will be *to pierce Hedda's reserve*, to slice open her mask of contentment. His next actions will be determined by the obstacles that he encounters as he pursues her. He goes as far as he can before Hedda stops him. When he calls her by her maiden name, Hedda has gotten what she wanted: Løvborg has come to remind her of who she was before she married—Hedda *Gabler*, not Hedda *Tesman*. The sensuality of the scene is heightened by being *channeled* past obstacles.

Let's review the structure of the scene, which follows from Hedda's super-task of trying to *escape from this marriage*:

- task: *to probe Mr. Løvborg's expectations*
- obstacle: *her husband's kind attention*
- action: *to divert her husband*
- obstacle: *being seen*
- actions: *to mask* (herself), and then *to bait*, *to tease*, *to provoke Løvborg* until she gets what she wants and she makes a *transition* to the next task.

Note that Ibsen included stage directions that describe the activities:

HEDDA (*opening the album*)

LØVBORG (*whose eyes have never left her, speaking in a low, soft voice*)

HEDDA (*with a quick glance at him*)

LØVBORG (*repeating softly*)

HEDDA (*looks at the album*)

HEDDA (*turning the pages*)

LØVBORG (*resentment in his voice*)

HEDDA (*looks at him sharply*)

Ibsen had been a stage director in the relatively large city of Bergen and he understood that without such specific stage directions the actors and producers reading his script wouldn't understand what was happening in the scene. Even so, it was difficult for contemporary actors to interpret their roles in Ibsen's plays because the characters didn't declare their emotions as they did in melodramas. The stage directions in Ibsen are indications of inner actions and should be read as clues for motivation. *Why* does Hedda turn the pages? To tease Mr. Løvborg? Within the boundary of obstacles, Hedda has no other way to flirt with him. If you establish *to flirt* as the action, you might point at a specific mountain peak, rather than turn the page. Ibsen won't mind. In a letter to a young actress playing the heroine of *Rosmersholm*, the play he wrote before *Hedda Gabler*, Ibsen advised:

No declamation! No theatricalities! No grand mannerisms! Express every mood in a manner that will seem credible and natural. Never think of this or that actress whom you may have seen. Observe the life that is going on around you, and present a real and living human being (20).

Expanding the circle of concentration in rehearsal

The scene continues in this way:

> LØVBORG (*repeating softly*) Hedda Gabler!
>
> HEDDA (*looks at the album*) Yes, I used to be called that. In those days—when we two knew each other.
>
> LØVBORG And from now on—for the rest of my life—I have to teach myself not to say Hedda Gabler.
>
> HEDDA (*turning the pages*) Yes, you have to. And I think you ought to start practicing it. The sooner the better, I'd say.
>
> LØVBORG (*resentment in his voice*) Hedda Gabler married? And to George Tesman!
>
> HEDDA Yes—that's how it goes.
>
> LØVBORG Oh, Hedda, Hedda—how could you throw yourself away like that!
>
> HEDDA (*looks at him sharply*) All right—no more of that!
>
> LØVBORG What do you mean?
>
> TESMAN *comes in and over to the sofa.*

A quick list of Hedda's actions would include:

- to bait Løvborg
- to egg him on
- to tease him, yet to keep him at a distance
- to disguise her hurt

Every aspect of the production can be brought into the circle of concentration to help or hinder these and other actions. Begin with the setting. Tesman's Aunt Juju has decorated the room with overstuffed vases and Victorian furniture. The conventional décor is an obstacle to Hedda's need to escape; wherever she looks she is reminded of her new identity as an ornament. To Hedda, her home is a cage. Yet, if the light in the room is not bright, that is an opportunity for the two old lovers to sit close to each other using the photo album as a cover. There is also the opportunity to mask their feelings by leaning back into the shadows.

The sound of voices as the men smoke and drink in the inner room will be a constant obstacle, one Hedda and Løvborg will listen to actively. The smell of the men's cigarette smoke can also be included in the circle of concentration as one more aspect of the home's claustrophobic atmosphere. The clink of the punch glasses has the possibility to distract the teetotaler Mr. Løvborg, or to remind Hedda of her husband's unwanted presence.

If the production is accurate to the period (it doesn't have to be), Hedda will probably be corseted. Her tight dress will be an obstacle to any action. If she looks attractive in her costume, that will be an opportunity to arouse Løvborg and to charm her husband. The album, of course, is a world of possibilities. It is an opportunity for Hedda to sit next to Løvborg, and to bring her hand closer to his. She can bore her eyes into the album when her action is *to disguise her hurt*. She can point to its charmless photographs when her action is *to bait Løvborg* and mock her husband. The album is an obstacle for Løvborg, who would probably like to be talking about something other than Hedda's honeymoon with another man.

The specifics of the scene and its interpretation will naturally arise out of the relationship the two actors develop in rehearsal. If the actress playing Hedda is easily swayed by Løvborg, then Løvborg will be a different lover from one that Hedda can brush off. When Løvborg says, "Hedda Gabler married? And to George Tesman!" will Løvborg attack? Mock? Plead? The tone of the actress's response, "Yes—that's how it goes," will determine Løvborg's "Oh, Hedda, Hedda—how could you throw yourself away like that!"

The illusion of character is a web of relationships

If Hedda's behavior is molded by her dependence on other people and the environment, just what kind of person is she?

LØVBORG Oh, Hedda, Hedda—how could you throw yourself away like that!

HEDDA (*looks at him sharply*) All right—no more of that!

LØVBORG What do you mean?

TESMAN *comes in and over to the sofa.*

HEDDA (*hears him coming and says casually*) And this one, Mr. Løvborg, was taken from the Val d'Ampezzo. Just look at the peaks of those mountains. (*looks warmly up at* TESMAN) Now what were those marvelous mountains called, dear?

TESMAN Let me see. Oh, those are the Dolomites.

HEDDA Why, of course! Those are the Dolomites, Mr. Løvborg.

TESMAN Hedda dear—I only wanted to ask if we shouldn't bring in some punch anyway. At least for you, hm?

HEDDA Yes, thank you. And a couple of *petits fours*, please.

In any acting technique, character is an illusion. You're not Hedda Gabler. You're just not. If you think you are, you should be in a mental institution, not on the stage. There is no such person, okay? It's a name on a page. You're an actor creating an illusion. The way you create the illusion of character for Stanislavsky—and the illusion of reality—is by *the web of active and dynamic relationships.*

Hedda is opposed in her tasks by all the characters in the play. That's what characterizes her. Tesman's Aunt Juju is suspicious of Hedda's fidelity and has installed a loyal maid to spy on the new wife. The neighbor, Judge Brack, is aware that Hedda chafes under the restrictions of convention and offers himself as a sexual diversion. But to Hedda, an affair with Brack would be only one more banality. The challenge for the actress is to make the dullness of the bourgeoisie such an obstacle to a fulfilled life that Hedda kills herself to escape it. When all the other characters act as obstacles to Hedda's task, they strengthen her character and the dramatic action of the play.

As the play develops, relationships shift. Hedda is pregnant as a consequence of her honeymoon (her corset will grow even tighter). The responsibilities of caring for a child will end any chance Hedda might have had to be an independent woman. Løvborg cannot save her; at a crucial time he fails her. Hedda's behavior in response to Løvborg grows so ambivalent that by the end of the third act she burns the manuscript for the book Løvborg has written, a book into which he has poured his life's thoughts. Løvborg's precious manuscript can be understood by the actress playing Hedda as competition for Løvborg's affections. Destroying the book destroys the obstacle of such a fascinating rival.

Tesman's concern for his wife is an obstacle of a different sort. It is a mistake when actors play Tesman as a joke because if Hedda cannot take Tesman seriously, the audience finds him dull, not funny. There is humor in his misplaced attentions only if they are heartfelt. To create the illusion of a realistic character, the actor playing Tesman must have an effect on Hedda. If he is deeply in love with his wife, that is an obstacle that will drag on her resolve to leave him.

Hedda is sly when she flirtatiously orders her husband out of the room for petit fours. She is also naïve enough to be cornered in Brack's trap, and romantic enough to try to rouse Løvborg to heroics. These relationships will be created in rehearsals and form a composition that changes in time. Again, the actress playing Hedda will not BE romantic or BE naïve. Her actions will create those changing qualities; the intersection of actions with obstacles will create her evolving emotions.

The analogy of oil painting

There is a parallel between Stanislavsky's technique of building a character and the illusion of depth in oil painting. In an oil painting, the artist puts down layer upon layer of paint. Beneath one layer the under-painting can be subtly seen. The effect of different layers viewed simultaneously is a sense of depth on the flat surface of the canvas. Similarly, in Stanislavsky's rehearsal technique, the dense layers of relationships between and among characters create the illusion of depth in an onstage role. Like the layers of oil paint, the layers of relationships take time to establish. A painter working in oil usually waits for one layer to dry before he puts down another. Likewise, in rehearsal the actor needs time to establish (and develop) each of the overlapping relationships.

THE IMPORTANCE OF OBSTACLES

For example, Tesman's task *to put his guest at ease* is an obstacle to Løvborg's task *to regain intimacy with Hedda*, yet it serves Hedda's action in deflecting Løvborg's attack on her façade. Ibsen was a master at writing scenes where different characters fulfil their chosen tasks even when they seem to be at odds. This is one of the ways in which Ibsen's work differs from melodrama; there is no agreed-on interpretation of the meaning of actions. There are only struggling ideas of what is right. It is exactly this moral relativism that made the Victorian critics identify *Hedda Gabler* as "moral sewage gas."

The sympathetic relationship with the audience

Although the character is an illusion, the emotions of the character are not. You experience real emotions onstage when you play your actions and attempt to accomplish your tasks. It is this, as much as anything, that Stanislavsky learned when observing Eleonora Duse. Inner conviction is so truthful it creates the illusion that what it speaks about is true. Genuine emotions onstage persuade the audience to sympathize with you.

Stanislavsky wanted his public to sympathize with characters. The actor's art, like the novelist's of the period, was meant to make the inner life of the characters available and emotionally resonant to the audience. As in the fiction written by Turgenev, Tolstoy, and Dostoyevsky, there are no villains or even heroes. There are only people who perform different actions for understandable—if not always shared—reasons. In his novel *Resurrection*, Tolstoy writes:

> One of the most widespread superstitions is that every man has his own special, definite qualities; that a man is kind, cruel, wise, stupid, energetic, apathetic, etc. Men are not like that. We may say of a man that he is more often kind than cruel, oftener wise than stupid, oftener energetic than apathetic, or the reverse; but it would be false to say of one man that he is kind and wise, of another that he is wicked and foolish. And yet we always classify mankind in this way. And this is untrue. Men are like rivers: the water is the same in each, and alike in all; but every river is narrow here, is more rapid there, here slower, there broader, now clear, now cold, now dull, now warm. It is the same with men. Every man carries in himself the germs of every quality, and sometimes one manifests itself, sometimes another, and the man often becomes unlike himself, while still remaining the same man (21).

With this in mind, it is important that the audience be sympathetic to Hedda's motivations as well as the motivations of her unwitting oppressors: her husband, his aunt, and the maid. Following Stanislavsky's dictum, even the amoral Judge Brack should be played for the basic humanity of his task. In his own mind Brack is trying to help Hedda as best as he can. Done well, the role of Brack can become a figure of pity to the audience because, in his ignorance, Brack knows no better than to frighten the person he would comfort. No matter what the role, the performance of action and obstacles is meant to elicit *compassion*.

Notebook:
Obstacles and Opportunities

HEDDA I'll keep Mr. Løvborg company a while.

TESMAN All right, Hedda dear, you do that.

> *He and* BRACK *go into the inner room, sit down, drink punch, smoke cigarettes, and talk animatedly during the following.* LØVBORG *remains standing by the stove.* HEDDA *goes to the writing table.*

HEDDA *(slightly raising her voice)* I can show you some photographs, if you like. Tesman and I traveled through the Tyrol on our way home.

> *She brings over an album and lays it on the table by the sofa, seating herself in the farthest corner.* LØVBORG *comes closer, stops, and looks at her. Then he takes a chair and sits down on her left, his back toward the inner room.*

HEDDA *(opening the album)* You see this view of the mountains, Mr. Løvborg. That's the Ortler group. Tesman's labeled them underneath. Here it is: "The Ortler group, near Meran."

LØVBORG *(whose eyes have never left her, speaking in a low, soft voice)* Hedda—Gabler!

HEDDA *(with a quick glance at him)* Ah! Shh!

LØVBORG *(repeating softly)* Hedda Gabler!

HEDDA *(looks at the album)* Yes, I used to be called that. In those days—when we two knew each other.

LØVBORG And from now on—for the rest of my life—I have to teach myself not to say Hedda Gabler.

Hedda's super-task:
to escape her marriage
Løvborg's super-task: *to rise again*

Hedda's task:
to see if Løvborg can rescue her
Løvborg's task:
to see if Hedda still loves him

Hedda's action:
to put Tesman at ease

Obstacle:
Hedda can be seen by Brack

Opportunity:
She can't be heard
if she speaks softly

Hedda's action:
to tease/to cover/to test
(Does he still love her?)

Opportunity (Hedda):
The album is an excuse
to sit close to Løvborg

Opportunity (Løvborg):
Hedda leaves room for
Løvborg on the sofa

Løvborg's action: *to test her*
(Is she still the same person?)

Hedda's action: *to bait*

Løvborg's action:
to pierce, to slice open

HEDDA (*turning the pages*) Yes, you have to. And I think you ought to start practicing it. The sooner the better, I'd say.

Hedda's action: *to egg him on*
Løvborg's action:
to lure her out of her cover
Hedda's action: *to tease him,
yet keep him at a distance*

LØVBORG (*resentment in his voice*) Hedda Gabler married? And to George Tesman!

HEDDA Yes—that's how it goes.

Løvborg's action: *to jab her*

LØVBORG Oh, Hedda, Hedda—how could you throw yourself away like that!

Hedda's action: *to tickle him*

Løvborg's action: *to pierce her reserve
(to mock)*

HEDDA (*looks at him sharply*) All right—no more of that!

Hedda's action: *to disguise her hurt*

LØVBORG What do you mean?

Løvborg's action: *to wake her up*
Hedda's action: *to slap him*

TESMAN *comes in and over to the sofa.*

Obstacle (Løvborg):
the husband arrives

Opportunity (Hedda):
the husband arrives

HEDDA (*hears him coming and says casually*) And this one, Mr. Løvborg, was taken from the Val d'Ampezzo. Just look at the peaks of those mountains. (*looks warmly up at* TESMAN) Now what were those marvelous mountains called, dear?

Løvborg's action: *to pounce*
Obstacle: Tesman's solicitude
Opportunity: Tesman's solicitude

TESMAN Let me see. Oh, those are the Dolomites

HEDDA Why, of course! Those are the Dolomites, Mr. Løvborg.

Hedda's action: *to divert Tesman,
to show off to Løvborg*

Hedda's action: *to mock Tesman,* but
to tease Løvborg

TESMAN Hedda, dear—I only wanted to ask if we shouldn't bring in some punch anyway. At least for you, hm?

HEDDA Yes, thank you. And a couple of *petits fours*.

Tesman's action:
to make them comfortable
(Ironically, he is the obstacle
to their comfort)

Practical Tips for Working

Why rehearse?

You rehearse in order to identify which actions work to meet the demands of your task and which actions do not. At the end of the rehearsal, take time to write notes for yourself. You might identify tasks. At the next rehearsal, if you play actions to accomplish those tasks, you'll learn what obstacles you encounter from the other actors. If that doesn't work, you're going to find obstacles and opportunities by using a prop, or a costume, or the scenery, or something else physically present in the room—including the heat or lack of it. But you're always going to start with what the other people onstage are doing. The rehearsal process is meant to be interactive between you and the other actors.

Many people think a rehearsal process is a series of less bad performances. Their process is to criticize each rehearsal in order to eliminate more and more bad choices until, after painstaking attacks, the choices become stage-worthy. A rehearsal process need not be a savage removal of bad choices, but a steady build-up of good and better choices. During productive rehearsals you plant the seeds of what works, watch what flourishes, and encourage what is successful so that it can overtake what isn't. If you find something that succeeds, the chances are good you will abandon what doesn't. What does not help will often drop away naturally.

Use what's there first

At the first reading, always focus on the other people as much as you focus on the text. Always use the immediate circumstances: having the book in your lap, not knowing the lines, meeting the other people in the cast. That's all you may have, so make the most of it. Don't pretend you're doing anything but reading the play to each other. The presence of the book can be a tool in creating a relationship.

Listen actively—nothing is lost

Listen actively so that the words being spoken provoke a response within you. Don't be so concerned with picking up the cue or losing your place. This isn't a performance; it's an investigation. In some languages the word for *rehearsal* is the same word as *probe*. Your earliest responses in rehearsal are like pencil sketches. The historical process of rehearsal and of art (and of life, by the way) is such that all sketches build depth to your eventual choices, even if they are replaced later by more effective ones.

There is a wonderful book written by the psychologist of art Rudolf Arnheim on the subject of Picasso's mural *Guernica*. It contains all the sketches for the mural, from Picasso's first doodle—which is a composition study on a little scrap of paper—to photographs of the wall-sized painting in progress. During the time of *Guernica*'s creation Picasso explored its themes by finishing several other paintings with similar subject matter. The figure of a bull, for instance, received a lot of the artist's repeated attention.

Picasso sketched it as a cave drawing, as a wise Greek face, and as a realistic animal. Doing so, he learned for himself what the varying nature of the bull could be to him in his work. You will do similar sketches of your relationships in rehearsal.

Get your nose out of the book

End and begin sentences with your eyes on the other person, not on the book. This is because (presumably) the other person will have been listening and will have some reaction to what you say. The book will not have a reaction. It will lie there flat. From the beginning, you want to be in the habit of speaking with the purpose of creating and observing a response in the person to whom you are speaking. Don't take it for granted that the other person has had a reaction; take the time to notice it. Look up from the book not only to listen, but also to see the effect of what you've just said. *This is especially important if you get what you want.* See it. Don't assume it.

Use what you have around you, because that is truthful. Use that you're nervous or that the words are confusing. Again, as with good lying, acting is slipping in a few untruths among many truths.

Learn from Mae West (take notes for yourself)

Take notes for yourself; don't just record what the director tells you. As that lowdown 1920s vaudevillian turned glamorous 1930s movie star Mae West always said: *Keep a diary, girls, and one day it'll keep you.* It's true. All too often in rehearsal you see actors writing down the notes given to them by the director, as if they had no ideas of their own. Yes, performers are called actors, not writers, and their work should be done playing actions, not writing about them. Yes, it is true that to write actions down is to distort them by translating them into another medium. If you have the luxury of a long rehearsal period and not much else to think about during the long rehearsal period, you will not need to keep your own notes. If you're one of those people who remembers everything, you won't need to keep notes. Most people can risk the distortion of writing something down, and should use notes to organize themselves.

Should a director give you notes, you can write them down and translate them into your own structure of actions and obstacles. Suppose the director has something typically vague to relay like: "It's not interesting enough. Make it more interesting." What should that mean to you? That the director is bored? Don't panic and react by playing the action harder. No. Raise the difficulty of the obstacle. To increase the heat of the action and the size of your behavior, make the obstacle more difficult to overcome. Yes, look more deeply into yourself, in order to react to the other people onstage.

Learn from Bugs Bunny (go backward to go forward)

Before Bugs Bunny—the cartoon character who's as fast on his feet as he is with a quip—springs forward, he does a little preparation move backward. Think of yourself doing the same before playing an action. Take a moment to take in the situation. Your action will take place in order to solve a problem, or to enter an environment. Take the time to assess or be affected by the problem you are about to solve.

Work with an image

If you find that the task organizes itself around an image—an animal in a cage or a fox-hunt, for example—let that image provide a vocabulary for the actions: *to claw, to chase to the ground*. In another section of the book we will talk about organizing a text primarily with images, but here, let's recognize their power to refine the actions. Choosing the right word for a task is not meant to be a task in itself, as if an actor's work was to find the solution to a crossword puzzle, but the power of a word used to specify action will help you to specify your performance. You may find that once you've established the image you will go back and relabel the task.

For Michael Chekhov, the playwright's nephew and a member of Stanislavsky's first studio, the image for a task was always a "psychological gesture," a physical movement that summed up the super-task. For example, the Professor in *The Lesson* might compulsively ball his hands into fists. This could be very effective—and it wouldn't necessarily have to happen in performance or rehearsal. The gesture could remain most useful as a wordless way of specifying his super-task.

A sign of a good action is when you start to gesture as you try to find an apt word. That usually means the action is something you already do. Giving it a name clarifies it so that it is repeatable. When choosing a word or wordless images to organize your thinking, always remember to pick tasks that move you and excite you to act out the scene.

Work with the other actors

Should you tell the other actors your tasks? Should you ask them to play obstacles to increase the dramatic action of the scene? Unless you're paying the other actors' salaries, that isn't advisable. Even if you are paying their salaries, don't tell the other actors what to do. Let's put it this way: it's like making love. It works better (for most people) if you *do* it rather than talk about it. If your partner is doing something that arouses you, it's better for him to notice your response himself and increase or continue or cease what he is doing. It's probably better if there isn't much discussion about it, so that it remains physical, ambiguous, and changeable. As a lover, so as an actor. You could say a discreet *I like when you do that*, perhaps. There are exceptions: some people like to be told what to do. That doesn't mean they're going to do it. Acting is like any other partnership; you establish your own communication, in this case onstage.

The most celebrated partnership in cinematic ballroom dance, Fred Astaire and Ginger Rogers, didn't socialize together. They didn't even particularly like each other, which probably made their communication in performance and rehearsal all the more critical. Going into rehearsal, you hope that all your acting partners will have instincts and be sensitive to what the two or three or five of you are creating together. Once in a blue moon the director will help you define or refine what's going on between you, although more likely the director will be worried about the lighting.

THE IMPORTANCE OF OBSTACLES

What if the other actors aren't doing anything? The obstacle is that they are *no* obstacle. Well, that's not as bad as it sounds. It's worse when the other actors are doing too much. When they're not doing anything, you can endow them in your imagination with the ability to affect your behavior. Better yet, you can over-sensitize yourself to what they do. If you interpret every pause your partner takes as hostile, then the audience will project onto your partner the ability to affect you in that way. As in all perception, we understand the significance of something by the way it affects or relates to something else. If the other actors don't move you, pretend that they do. Channel your frustration with their wooden behavior into an active relationship with them.

What if the other actor does too much? There are so many obstacles that getting to an action that might further the task seems impossible. Learn from the masters: sit back. There is nothing so powerful as actively listening onstage and reacting. Look at Audrey Meadows as Alice in the classic television series *The Honeymooners*, how wonderful her performance is. It's Jackie Gleason's show, but Meadows is doing a remarkable job of holding her own with him. She doesn't do it by trying to top him; she goes underneath by having what he does affect her selectively. She doesn't respond to his large theatrics, she bides her time for something to be significant to her. This is also a good lesson for dealing with overly dramatic people in life. Let them have their little or gigantic fit. When they're out of breath, you can pounce.

The B choice (as in grade-B) is to attack and provoke the partner or group into some desired behavior. Let's call this the Sweaty Approach. It can be wonderful in rehearsal. It is rarely wonderful in performance. Usually it comes across as loud and intense. But mostly loud. The last resort of a sterile imagination and a dull way to avoid dealing with the other people onstage is to break the furniture or the props. It's like screaming: a little of it goes a very long way. It's better to hold back and let the possibility for violence act as a menace.

In a film, shouting, screaming, and throwing things can be made effective when such behavior is focused, selected, and edited. Onstage, more often than not, it's simply a wash of emotion. Even in a film—and with the best of actors—the results can still be lackluster. An example: one of the few dull sequences in the film *Citizen Kane* (1941) is when Kane tears apart the room after his wife leaves him. Off the set, Orson Welles, who was directing and playing Kane himself, scandalously tore apart a room at a restaurant. He decided to quote his shameful behavior in the film. The crew preparing to shoot the scene were shocked that Welles would use his own private life so openly. A room to be destroyed (with mirrors!) was set up, cameras were safely placed, and self-referential Orson went in there and tossed the chairs around. As exciting as this may have been on the set, in the film the sequence is uninvolving. After the first two seconds we don't need or want to see or hear the rest of the scene. Orson Welles acting with the furniture is simply not as engaging as Orson Welles acting with people.

Don't toss people around onstage, either.

Of course, not everything in the environment is going to be an obstacle. There will be opportunities to further the tasks. Opportunities are less dramatic than obstacles onstage, unless they come after a long series of obstacles. Turning an obstacle into an opportunity is always an appealing choice, but the script will not always allow this to happen.

The Chart

Near the end of Chapter 1 we reviewed the chart that compares five different ways of organizing and analyzing a text. There are four more categories: the *illusion of character*, the *unifying image*, *suitable playwrights*, and the *intended reaction of the audience*.

- **The illusion of character.** The illusion of depth in a drawing is most simply created by placing one figure over another. The illusion of depth in a character is created by different means. For Stanislavsky, a *web of relationships* between people creates the illusion of character on stage.
- **Unifying image.** Building a role in rehearsal by overlaying relationships among characters is similar to the process of an *oil painting*, where depth is built up with layers of paint.
- **Suitable playwrights.** Different approaches to organizing a text are appropriate, though by no means limited to the work of certain authors. Although Stanislavsky would never have limited his Stanislavsky System to specialize in or exclude any one form or style, the approach, with its emphasis on the illusion of reality, is particularly appropriate for those realistic playwrights like *Chekhov, Strindberg*, and *Ibsen*. Paradoxically, it also works well for absurdist playwrights like *Ionesco, Beckett*, and *Pinter*, where an inner logic organizes the behavior of the roles.
- **The intended reaction of the audience.** It was intended by Stanislavsky that his audience have *compassion* for the actions of the actors. No character should be seen as a villain or a hero, but only as a human being with recognizable hopes, dreams, and ambitions with which the audience can identify.

CHAPTER 3

STANISLAVSKY'S LEGACY

Konstantin Stanislavsky stressed that his system was a basic vocabulary. He applied it to melodrama, opera, realistic plays, and stylized verse plays written by Shakespeare and Molière. He insisted that, although it came from Russia, his system was applicable to all the stages of the world. Time has shown he was right. Russian émigrés would teach the Stanislavsky System in New York and Hollywood, in London, in Paris, and in Beijing.

Stanislavsky in Russia

When Stanislavsky died in 1938, he was seventy-five. He had been born in Russia under an all-powerful Tsar, two years before the freeing of Russia's serfs. During his lifetime his country passed through a revolution whose leader, Vladimir Ilyich Lenin, held out the hope, justified or not, that there would be freedom for all in the new Soviet Union. In the last fifteen years of Stanislavsky's life, Russia regressed under the rule of a latter-day Tsar, Josef Stalin, who studied Ivan Grozny for ways to subdue his own countrymen (remember Repin's painting?).

In Stanislavsky's youth, his father was rich enough to build and equip an amateur theater on their family estate; after the Revolution, the family property was confiscated by the government. Despite his later success onstage, Stanislavsky was desperately poor and hadn't money enough for decent clothes or his own son's tuberculosis treatments. The minister of culture appealed to Lenin that Stanislavsky was down to his last pair of pants. Fortunately, Lenin had seen and enjoyed Stanislavsky's performances, and authorized the government to give Stanislavsky a small house with two rooms to rehearse in.

Adaptation

The humanism of Stanislavsky's work and its accessibility fit in well with the Soviets' task of bringing art called *Socialist Realism* to the masses. Socialist Realism is an approach to art dedicated to the display of positive role models. It takes as its mission the inclusion of groups that have not previously been represented or active in art, especially the lower classes. It is also meant to invite those previously excluded groups to participate in art as creators and enthusiasts. It emphasizes realism because it assumes realistic art is most accessible to all groups.* The Itinerant painters, depicting criminals on the way to Siberia, or revolutionaries passing out pamphlets, fit the bill and were marched into Soviet art history as prophetic predecessors.

Stanislavsky's Soviet "protectors" made sure Socialist Realism became the *only* approach to art—including the art of acting—permitted by the all-powerful government. Stanislavsky somehow came to terms with the new regime. Sometimes he merely misunderstood what was going on, or lived blissfully ignorant. He did use his position to do good. When radical artists were attacked for not making their work accessible enough, Stanislavsky did what he could to shield them with his prestige. True, in many cases it made no difference, but he made public efforts when it was dangerous for him to do so. In *An Actor Prepares*, Stanislavsky illustrates an actor's technique of adapting to circumstances with an example so revealing in its specifics that it would lose its meaning if it were simplified or paraphrased. Here is the quote:

> "Suppose that you, Kostya, hold some high position and I have to ask a favor of you. I must enlist your aid. But you do not know me at all. How can I make myself stand out from the others who are trying to get help from you?
>
> "I must rivet your attention on me and control it. How can I strengthen and make the most of the slight contact between us? How can I influence you to take a favorable attitude toward me? How can I reach your mind, your feelings, your attention, your imagination? How can I touch the very soul of such an influential person?
>
> "If only I can make him conjure up a picture in his mind's eye that in any way approximates the dreadful reality of my circumstances, I know his interest will be aroused. He will look into me more attentively, his heart will be touched. But to reach this point I must penetrate into the being of the other person, I must sense his life, I must adapt myself to it." (22)

Towards the end of his life Stanislavsky was a respected figure of culture who had known other respected Russian figures of culture to be arrested, jailed, or executed. As with other prestigious artists who were elderly, Stanislavsky was surrounded by nurses and attendants who screened him from the world. In the last few years of his life, it seems Stanislavsky was under virtual house arrest.

The Story of the Book

In line with Stalin

There was sustained pressure on Stanislavsky to align his system with Communism, but his system had always been playfully contradictory, choosing to emphasize one aspect

---

*It isn't always.

and then another of union between body and mind, guided by the practices of Yoga and reinforced by the psychological theories of Théodule Ribot that motion could produce emotion and vice versa. The Soviet government wanted acting theory, and any other theory in the land, to be a clear, rigid, and unified set of rules—and not ever vice versa. Soviet thinking held that all behavior was determined by physical circumstances, not by thoughts. Knowledge of Freud was derided or suppressed and any aspect of Stanislavsky's system that unknowingly paralleled that theory was held suspect as subversive. Talk of Yoga, or any mystic religious practice, was probably even worse in aggressively atheist Soviet Russia.*

Revisions

One of the prices Stanislavsky paid for survival in this environment was extracted when his first book was adopted as a textbook for model Soviet theater schools. This meant the book had to be approved by Communist censors and, when it deviated from the prescribed path, brought back in line. In 1928, Lyubov Gurevich, a woman who had been Stanislavsky's literary advisor for over thirty years, warned Stanislavsky to avoid references in his book to Ribot's affective memory and to become more aware of the claptrap that passed for psychology in Stalin's Russia.† She had a point. Among other terms the censors objected to: the spirit, the soul, intuition, and the subconscious. Out, of course, went the references to Yoga that ran throughout the text, including key Hindu words like *prana* (the Yogic concept of vital energy) and *chakras* (the bundles of concentrated energy within the spine). Stanislavsky responded with supple adaptation; words may have changed, but he held to his key concepts. The government urged teachers who worked from the book to emphasize its physical exercises and ignore the half concerned with psychology. If, at the end of his life, Stanislavsky also stressed the physical side of his theory, perhaps it was his way to make peace with his captors.

Stanislavsky's death provided the Soviet commissars with an opportunity to bronze his quicksilver thought into an unyielding doctrine, something it had never been in his lifetime. Until the end his mind was flexible. In his last work with actors, held in his home, he abandoned table talk for active rehearsals. He was preparing a production of Molière's *Tartuffe*—not a realistic play, but one in verse. Three months before he died, he told his directing students: "One must give actors various paths. One of these is the path of action. There is also another path: you can move from feeling to action, arousing feeling first" (23).

---

*Eastern religions were particularly threatening to the Soviet Union because they had the potential to encourage the Eastern countries under Russian control to establish separate national and ethnic identities. Beginning in the 1920s, and continuing into the 1930s, the Communist government went out of its way to suppress and humiliate Eastern thought, going so far as to make sure it was publicized that a hippopotamus was dissected inside a famous Buddhist temple in Saint Petersburg—a gross sacrilege for that sect.

†Stanislavsky had never graduated from school and felt the need for more book learning. Lyubov Gurevich advised him. Throughout Stanislavsky's life, she urged to him write books of his own and looked out for him in other ways as well.

The Story of the Theater Claimed for Him After His Death

In 1897 Stanislavsky formed a theater company with Vladimir Nemerovitch-Danchenko, a Russian writer, educator, and producer. The troupe was called the Moscow Art Theater. In Russia, the company is known by its initials as MXAT and called in Russian *Moohat* (accent on the second syllable, the *h* slightly breathy). MXAT's aim was to improve the standards of Russian theater and bring it in line with what has since been called the Silver Age of Russian arts: a rebirth of the spirit in literature, dance, and painting.

Stanislavsky's MXAT performances as an actor were riveting to his audiences, especially his portrayals of Dr. Stockman in Ibsen's *An Enemy of the People* and the difficult title role of *Othello*—the latter being Stanislavsky's homage to his idol Tommaso Salvini. Stanislavsky had no system of working as an actor when the Moscow Art Theater was founded, and he only began to search for a system after his successful performances of Dr. Stockman began to lose their power.

Neither the actors of MXAT nor Stanislavsky's partner were eager to use the techniques Stanislavsky discovered. But by 1911 Stanislavsky had become so certain of his techniques that he threatened to quit if they weren't adopted by the company. The actors agreed, for a year, then chafed under the discipline of having to learn what they termed "eccentric." Eventually, Stanislavsky went outside MXAT to create a studio where he taught and worked on his system more systematically.

Still, it was while working at the MXAT that the Russian pioneer of psychological realism in acting found the ideal vehicles for his explorations—the psychologically realistic plays of Anton Chekhov. Stanislavsky learned from staging and acting in long-running, critically acclaimed productions of Chekhov's *Seagull* and *Uncle Vanya* even before his system was in place. These popular productions, after disastrous earlier versions at more established theaters, made MXAT's—and Chekhov's—reputations. Chekhov wrote two other plays specifically for MXAT, *The Cherry Orchard* and *The Three Sisters*. MXAT was also where he met the company actress who would later become his wife.*

Although these productions had been created without Stanislavsky's system, Stanislavsky toured the world with them as examples of his work. The tours, beginning in 1906, brought awareness of the achievement of Stanislavsky's approach to acting to France, to Germany, and, on an especially fateful tour in 1923, to America. There were other plays in the repertory by that time that had been created using his system, but as Stanislavsky put it: "America wants to see what Europe already knows" (23). Stanislavsky toured America for two years, during which his company gave three-hundred and eighty performances, with special matinees on Fridays so theatre professionals could attend.

Stanislavsky in America

Stanislavsky's American tour was performed in Russian, of course. In the history of acting, the observation of foreign performers has often had powerful consequences. Re-

---

*It was also where his nephew Michael Chekhov would later work.

member how Stanislavsky was inspired by watching Duse and Salvini perform in Italian? It is no accident that he learned by watching foreign actors acting in a language he didn't speak. Without the distractions of such technical considerations as diction, accent, volume (up to a point), and, most importantly, the information value of the words, an audience watching a foreign language performance must concentrate on the relationships and reactions of the performers. To understand a foreign language, we very often gain meaning by seeing what effect the speaker has on other people. Duse and Salvini performed in Italian while the actors they were performing with spoke English. Ira Aldridge performed Othello in English while the actors around him spoke German or Russian or Polish, depending on the country they were in. The experience of watching operas performed in foreign languages had taught European audiences to enjoy onstage action without regard to the unknown (or unclear) words issuing from a singer's throat. American audiences in 1923 had experience watching silent films and had learned the habit of paying attention to behavior separately from any spoken language. The American audience's inability to understand Russian freed them to focus on and appreciate the nuances of psychological realism.

The Teachers

Eight days after MXAT opened in New York,* the first lecture on the subject of the Stanislavsky System in America was given by Richard Boleslavsky, an original member of the MXAT company who had left for America four years earlier but had been pressed into service for the MXAT tour. His was the accent that began the *beets/beads/bits* disagreement—and much else besides, depending on the expectations of the listeners.

Sitting in the audience at that lecture were Lee Strasberg and Harold Clurman, who were to become two of Stanislavsky's foremost disciples in America. Strasberg and Clurman took classes at the American Laboratory Theatre, where Boleslavsky taught in New York with another MXAT alumna, Maria Ouspenskaya. (She too had an unforgettable accent that, during the 1940s, would land her lucrative jobs in Hollywood B-pictures.)†

Clurman studied with Boleslavsky, Strasberg more often with Ouspenskaya. Boleslavsky's group, which also tried to produce plays, lasted until 1930, when it collapsed financially—despite the producer mortgaging her house and the actors providing weekly sums of money. A year later Clurman and Strasberg formed their own company, the Group Theatre, which also staged shows commercially. The Group Theatre began informally with Harold Clurman's Messianic post-performance lectures inside Broadway theaters on Friday nights. In the summer the company left the city and lived communally in the country. After rehearsals, the eager Americans would gather to listen as their cook (!), who knew Russian, would read out loud to them from Russian actors' diaries and theater history related to Stanislavsky.

The Group Theatre modeled itself on MXAT, cultivating socially aware play-

---

*January 18, 1923, at the Princess Theater.

†*The Wolf Man* (1941), *Frankenstein Meets the Wolf Man* (1943), *Tarzan and the Amazons* (1945).

wrights like Clifford Odets, whose first great success, *Waiting For Lefty* (1935), dramatized a labor strike. Sympathetic to the many people whose lives were ruined by the Depression—but ignorant of what was really going on in Russia—Group members flirted with Communism. Innocent that they were echoing Soviet censors, they insisted the plays they staged have upbeat endings. Before they demanded a change, Odets's play *Awake and Sing!* was originally titled *I Got the Blues*. Harold Clurman's book about this era sums it up in its title: *The Fervent Years*. Fervently, the members of the Group Theatre believed that by discovering Stanislavsky they had discovered a new way to live. More significantly, they had discovered a link between theater craft and the technique of Freudian psychoanalysis.

The Link with Freud

Freud's ideas were gaining legitimacy in America at this time, and the Group Theatre tried to combine the two similar interpretations of behavior. Freud's theories of repression seemed especially applicable to an actor's craft, and removing repression from an actor's subconscious seemed an obvious way to expand the emotional range of performing artists. The Group Theatre developed exercises to improve access to emotional memories hidden by repression. These became a specialty, and in time playwrights would include a speech or so in their plays to tap into the ability of actors to recall their past. Some talented and intuitive actors felt they were unsuited for their trade because, no matter how hard they tried, they were unable to mine their psyches for repressed emotional memories.

American arguments

In 1934 a key member of the Group Theatre, the actress Stella Adler, tracked Stanislavsky down in France. She first said to him, referring to the burden of emotional memory, "I loved the theater until you came along. And now I hate it!" (23). Stanislavsky wrote to a friend that Adler had been pestering him (she reports herself as being shy), but he felt sorry for her, and so, in his words, he wasted a month working with her. In all, Adler and Harold Clurman, to whom she was married at the time, spent six weeks with Stanislavsky discussing the American developments of his system. At the time, Stanislavsky was involved with the later, more physical developments of his approach that would be emphasized in Russia. He was to die four years later.

Adler returned to New York and announced that the Group Theatre had gotten it wrong—there was too much emphasis placed on emotional memory and uncovering repression. And it was *bits*, not *beats*.* But Strasberg said that he preferred his interpretation—it was a method that got results, and he called it just that: "the Method."

Strasberg insisted the emphasis on emotional memory developed Stanislavsky's ideas. Adler thought otherwise; she had learned from Stanislavsky himself that fantasy

---

*She asked the wrong person. It was Boleslavsky who had said the word *bead*.

was just as potent as memory, and emotional memory was a dead end, not a route to a performance. Of course, she didn't consider why Stanislavsky might have told her that. When she had her conversations with him, the concept of emotional memory was suspect in Russia and dangerous to talk about.

It wasn't that Strasberg had gotten it wrong, or Stanislavsky had changed his mind—as Strasberg accused—but that Stanislavsky's thinking had shifted to emphasize another aspect of the same basic idea that emotion and motion were linked. The discussion of emotional memory was a non-issue in Russia, where teachers were working through their notes from the last of Stanislavsky's developments in physical acting.

Stanislavsky training in America split into two camps. Strasberg continued to emphasize the earlier part of the training, Adler kept Stanislavsky's later emphasis on a method of physical action, which included actors improvising the story of the play before any line analysis or investigation of psychological tasks—much less memories.

The Books—Lost in the Translation?

The field of Stanislavsky studies has cracked open with Sharon Marie Carnicke's startling discoveries that were set off in 1978 when she was serving as interpreter for a MXAT director working with Strasberg-trained actors in New York and she personally encountered the obstacles of American and Russian mutual misunderstanding.* One of the reasons such misunderstanding exists is the history of Stanislavsky's books. The story that follows is from Carnicke's *Stanislavsky in Focus*, as important a book in Stanislavsky studies as the original edition of *An Actor Prepares*.

The reason for the rights

In the late 1920s, Stanislavsky had a heart attack. He was in his sixties by then, and like many teachers facing death, before and since, he decided to put his notes in order. Because Communist Russia held property in common—including an author's royalties—Stanislavsky would have made no money if his book was published in Russia. So he decided to have the first version published in English and in the United States, where he had made money on his autobiography.

He invited Elizabeth Reynolds Hapgood to become his translator. Her husband, Norman Hapgood, was a theater critic, but Reynolds Hapgood herself initially knew little about the theater.† She had been Stanislavsky's interpreter at the White House—an odd job, considering protocol at the time held that foreigners could speak to the President only through an ambassador. In 1923, Soviet Russia was unrecognized by America and so had no ambassador. Therefore, Stanislavsky was not allowed to speak with Calvin Coolidge—although he did pose for photos.

---

*Strasberg himself would whisper critiques.

†One of the few non-émigré Americans at the time who could read and write Russian, Reynolds Hapgood founded the Russian Department at Columbia University.

Elizabeth Reynolds Hapgood must have made a good impression during her photo opportunity, because not only did Stanislavsky ask her to translate his books, he awarded her the rights in all languages in all countries for all time. Because Stanislavsky was irritated by the task of combing through many years' accumulation of contradictory notes—he'd been scribbling to himself about acting since he was fourteen years old—he urged Reynolds Hapgood not only to translate but to cut, edit, and rearrange; in essence to do anything to get the manuscript into shape. She took him up on the offer. Even so, it took her so long that after five years there was still no finished book. The original publisher withdrew.

Another American publisher offered to publish the first half of the unfinished manuscript, and in 1936 the book came out in America under the title *An Actor Prepares*. Reynolds Hapgood was under intense pressure from the new publisher to cut even this first half of the repetitive manuscript. She held out as best she could, but, perhaps less experienced than Stanislavsky facing his Russian censors, she did make cuts, some of substance.

The differences

As in Russia, gone were most direct references to Yoga—the publisher felt that Yoga didn't appeal to "Anglo-Saxons." Other changes were made, some big, some small, some as the result of requested cuts, but some also due to Reynolds Hapgood's free hand at interpretation. The key concept of *tasks*—which Reynolds translated as the word *objectives*—became, in America, the most commonly used term for speaking about Stanislavsky's system. Yet the word obscures the essence of Stanislavsky's approach: that acting is something you *do*. You can't do an objective. You can't attempt an objective. An objective is the goal. The Russian word for "objective" is very different from the Russian word more commonly translated as "tasks" or "problems."

Where did this word *objective* come from? At the time of this writing the link is unproved, but even a quick glance at the vocabulary used in the 1930s—and still used—to explain Raja Yoga in English reveals word clusters like "the object of desire" and statements that the conscious mind "acts in order to grasp the objects" (24). Other familiar word clusters occur in Raja Yoga literature: "hindered by obstacles," "analyze your thoughts," "scrutinize your motives." Perhaps the word *objective* is transmuted from this source, and the Yogic principles of Stanislavsky are woven deeper into the American translation than previously known or admitted.

There are other changes in *An Actor Prepares*, large and small. The published American book is 295 pages, while the published Russian that it purports to be translating is 575 pages! The manuscript in Russian, by the way, is 700 pages. Yet, legally, the English is the only authorized and easily accessible version. Legally, the extra 175 pages in Russian exist like hovering ghosts, prevented from translation by a vigorously enforced protection of the American copyright. Attempts to translate from the Russian original have been thwarted not only in America, but in Italy, Japan, and France. In 1954, when someone pointed out the differences in the texts, Reynolds Hapgood had a friend who had been a MXAT actress write an article defending the translation, and the American publisher went so far as to have a comparison made and a notarized statement issued that nothing important had been eliminated! The copyright is still held in America, although soon enough the Russian manuscript will be in the public domain and new translations might be published.

The gap between Russia and America

The Reynolds Hapgood version, whatever its connection to Stanislavsky, has nevertheless shaped understanding of Stanislavsky in America. In addition to the differences in the text, there is also the matter of the title, *An Actor Prepares*. Stanislavsky's original manuscript grew so large it split into two parts. He reluctantly agreed to have the first half published separately. The book's Russian title could be translated as *An Actor's Work on Himself, Part One*. At the insistence of the publisher, the American title was made to seem complete—the result being that the teachings of Stanislavsky in this county derive only from the first half, without anyone being told there was more.

In 1948, ten years after Stanislavsky's death, a second book came out in Russia. The next year a book was issued under Stanislavsky's name in English, called by Reynolds Hapgood *Building a Character* (1949). Although it gives the appearance of a unified whole, *Building a Character* is made up of different articles from a span of twenty years. A third book published in America called *Creating a Role* (1961) is even more divergent from any Russian source. Joshua Logan, who wrote the introduction to *Creating a Role*, reports in his biography that Stanislavsky said to him, "Oh, I see you've read my books. Well . . . . We have extended past that. Now that's for the bathroom" (25). There is no Russian word for "bathroom," not in the English sense, and Logan's translator was being polite. What Stanislavsky said was more properly translated: "Now that's for the toilet."*

The American identity of Stanislavsky was further sealed off from Russia by the Cold War isolation between the two countries. Although Stanislavsky's system changed over time, the instructors who were in America to teach it were early Russian émigrés who had no further contact with their native country—at least regarding acting theory—and so taught the early version they had learned with its emphasis on sitting around the table. Later developments in Russia went unnoticed and untranslated.

"The System" or "The Method"?

American understanding of Stanislavsky has thus been shaped by willfulness and political reality, linked to a psychology Stanislavsky would have been arrested for had he ever discussed it. The interpretive abridged American translation of Stanislavsky's writings, the opportunity to create an independent way of thinking during the publication gap between the first and second volumes, the reluctance of professionals to revisit their

---

*"Banya" is the Russian word for "bath." The Russian word for "toilet" is—"toilet."

basic training—all these helped to create a new identity for Stanislavsky's system until it became, in America, indistinguishable from Lee Strasberg's "Method."

In addition, an entire set of jargon has evolved, added by various teachers: not just "objectives" but also "intentions," "indicating," and "beats." Strasberg's knowledge of Stanislavsky was genuine; working from an unauthorized German translation,* he taught the basic principles of desire and obstacles at the Actors Studio—the school he was initially excluded from but eventually took over. The students who emerged from the Studio, many of them popular and influential, assumed they were receiving Stanislavsky training, and, in the essentials, they were.

Among certain performers, however, the Method, which was initially meant to root out acting styles, became an acting style itself, and the popularity of that style—like Delsarte's attempts at "naturalism"—created its own bouquet of poses: the grunt, the yawn, the yearning pause. Stanislavsky himself had talked about "stencils" of such behavior. When old-fashioned Russian actors played peasants, they spat on the floor for "realism." In the place of classical or romantic poses, the Method substituted psychological poses and prompted endless discussion in rehearsal about motivation.

The Method was so popular that it invited attack. There are many anecdotes told about the old-style hams meeting the new-style narcissists. The emphasis on motionless action seemed like the emperor's new clothes, and the chapter of *An Actor Prepares* in which an actor is asked to be a tree became a surefire joke. The period excesses of Method acting claiming to be derived from the Stanislavsky System can be seen in 1950s television and film performances, where scratching, grunting, and other details of *verismo* are the studied clichés of "acting naturally." When it works, however, Method acting can be glorious, especially in film, where the technical skill of Method actors allows for great sophistication.

Application in Film

The link between Stanislavsky and America is not only personal. The demands of American film (and later television) for realistic acting gave the Stanislavsky System great opportunities for application. Look at the performances in the 1951 film *A Place in the Sun*, directed by George Stevens, who was an early member of the Actors Studio. The story is told primarily through reactions and the web of relationships between people rather than dialogue, description, declarations, or even action. Many of the camera set-ups include the full figures of more than one actor instead of individual close-ups.

The novel on which the film is based, Theodore Dreiser's *An American Tragedy*, tells a complex psychological story. The film adaptation relies on the technical ability of American actors to execute Russian techniques. Two of its stars became Strasberg-trained performers. Shelley Winters plays a trusting factory girl in love with a socially connected cad, played by Montgomery Clift. Winters, who would later become a serious devotee of Strasberg, has said that working with George Stevens on this film taught

---

*Unavailable to Strasberg's students.

56

her the principles of the Method even before she took her first class at the Actors Studio (26).

Winters's shy fragility is powerful and moving, especially the way she listens—still and silently wary throughout her increasing intimacy. Clift's obsessive attraction to another girl (Elizabeth Taylor) is established without his uttering a word, created entirely through his reactions to her wealth and beauty. His own lower social class is expressed by his wordless awkwardness in society. The scene where he wrestles with his task of drowning the factory girl (now pregnant) is dramatically heightened by the obstacle of her nervous chatter—motivated by her attempt to overcome the obstacle of his silent unease (her futile task being to make him love her again).

The Range and Limitations

Stanislavsky's techniques have also been influential in China and other parts of Asia. It was introduced in Communist China by the Russians as part of the Communist-approved art forms of Socialist Realism. A theater created by motivated actions was easier for mass audiences to appreciate than the traditional forms of Chinese theater, which played to the expensive, cultivated tastes of its elite public. A school of realistic plays was encouraged in China and Chinese actors learned Stanislavsky's techniques. Chinese playwrights studied Ibsen and Chekhov.

They continue to do so today, even though Russia and China stopped being comrades after a few decades. The authoritarian control of the arts in China means that certain topics are encouraged, certain others forbidden. Chekhov's ironic prophecies about a new wind coming are interpreted as meaning the eventual triumph of Socialism. But in 1996 a production of Ibsen's *Enemy of the People* took China by storm, demonstrating that Ibsen, after all these years, was still venerated as a great realist playwright and Stanislavsky-inspired actors were his dedicated interpreters.

Stanislavsky's revolution in the theater is permanent. No matter the country or culture, theater is an art of human relationships, and Stanislavsky's emphasis on compassion propels his system's survival past changing theatrical styles and national borders. Like Freud's interpretation of psychology, Stanislavsky's system offers genuine insight into the mechanism of behavior and feeling.

In America, Stanislavsky is the core of a serious actor's training, and most actors in this country are now trained to use an Americanized version of Stanislavsky's system of motivated actions. American universities and high school classes proudly teach aspects of the Method. Professional actors review Stanislavsky's technical vocabulary in studio classes. American students—and teachers—accept their duty to chase away hokey acting with zeal.

There is another mission, too, that actors inspired by Stanislavsky take on seriously: his appeal for artists who work onstage to love the theater in themselves, not themselves in the theater. Faith in the value of Stanislavsky's system, however, sometimes leads to disbelief in any other way to work.

Stanislavsky himself recognized no limitations to his system, although some limits were intended: no caricature, no talking to the audience, no exaggeration, no stylized speech or gestures. Stylization, though, is not necessarily a bad thing onstage. Some very good scripts are written in verse, involve caricature, or can only be performed while acknowledging the audience.

No art form, including acting, has any one way of working, any one true method. Scripts, audiences, interpretations, and the physical setup of performance vary and require different techniques. The painter working in watercolor applies the paint differently than when painting in oil. The technique of carving stone is very different from those of casting bronze or molding clay, yet any of these skills can create a sculpture.

There isn't any one way to interpret behavior, either. The unexamined prejudices of his society clouded even Freud's vision (his assumption that women were inevitably envious of men is particularly ludicrous). Stanislavsky experimented with stylization,* but accepted without too much questioning the assumption of his day that imitating reality was the highest calling of art. The commissars of Socialist Realism helped to shape this aesthetic by shooting dead those who disagreed.

Even without a gun to their heads, Russians are fond of realism. Gertrude Stein reported that in 1908 when Sergei Shchukin, a collector of Picasso's early romantic paintings, saw Picasso's newest work, *Les Demoiselles d'Avignon*, with its mutilated forms and unnatural perspectives, Shchukin wept at the loss for art. We recognize now that a stretched canvas covered with paint doesn't need to pretend to be a mirror to be art. The stage doesn't need to pretend to be a mirror, either. The theater can show us more than what we are; it can show us what we might be, or what we might avoid becoming.

This book teaches five approaches an actor can take while reading a script and developing ideas in rehearsal and performance. We've begun with Stanislavsky's system for organizing a text through analysis of its characters' tasks and obstacles. Why would we abandon such a good idea for anything else? Because, even though Stanislavsky tried to make his system universal, *it doesn't work with every script*. In its Russian developments or in its American variants, this approach is not always appropriate or the most useful way to work on texts by authors as diverse as Shakespeare, Sam Shepard, or Gertrude Stein.

The next part of the book examines Bertolt Brecht's idea of *episodes*; an approach, Brecht took pains to point out, that was bent on the *task* of sweeping Stanislavsky's compassion off the stage.

---

*Often disastrously, but persistently nonetheless.

PART II

PLAYING EPISODES

Reading List
In the Jungle of Cities by Bertolt Brecht
King Richard III by William Shakespeare
Brecht on Theater (section 24) by Bertolt Brecht

Viewing List
The Night of the Hunter directed by Charles Laughton
Raging Bull directed by Martin Scorsese

George Grosz, *Getting the Axe*

Chapter 4

Episodes

The Trouble with Stanislavsky

In 1908, Stanislavsky himself stumbled onto a definition of *episodic acting* after the actress Olga Knipper (who was Chekhov's widow) fled a Moscow Art Theater rehearsal in tears. Knipper was preparing the central role in a revival of Ivan Turgenev's *A Month in the Country*; Stanislavsky was directing her. Turgenev had written the play sixty years before, never expecting his words to be spoken in a theater. More novelist than playwright, Turgenev doubted it was possible to depict the intricacies of behavior outside of fiction and believed his text would be most effective read silently at home. Stanislavsky, however, was eager for the challenge of dramatizing the interior lives of onstage characters and looked forward to the play's inaction, the better to display "a lacework" of psychology (27).

In rehearsal, however, it quickly became apparent that the central role of Natalya Petrovna was as exasperating to her interpreter as she was to the other characters in the play. Natalya Petrovna is a married woman pursued by a devoted admirer. When Natalya Petrovna falls in love with her son's boyish tutor (played by a nineteen-year-old Richard Boleslavsky), she finds herself vying with an inexperienced eighteen-year-old girl (Natalya Petrovna's ward) for the tutor's affections. Natalya Petrovna's behavior is capricious, perverse, contradictory—and very true to life. A hunt for the motives of her caprice was tormenting the actress Olga Knipper as she built the role. Stanislavsky was similarly frustrated directing the play. It was a critical moment for the director and his actress. After two months spent discussing the script without getting out of their chairs, they discovered that their approach had run them into a dead end. Isaiah Berlin writes in the Introduction to his translation of *A Month in the Country*:

> Stanislavsky wrote [Olga Knipper] a famous letter in which he tried to express his understanding of her condition and his profound sympathy with it. She was grateful and comforted. When she finally returned, he explained to her that in his view the play was best acted in sections, that is, without necessary continuity either of mood or tone . . . The part could only be successfully acted by dividing it into segments: in one segment Natalya Petrovna is amusing, charming, enthusiastic, untroubled; in the next segment she is at the beginning of a new mood—jealousy, suspicion, uneasiness, and the like. Other

constant changes of tone, feeling and mood follow, carefully separated from each other . . ." (28)

That's as good a way to begin to define *episodic acting* as any other you'd read: the play is best acted in segments, carefully separated from each other, without continuity.

Why does Natalya Petrovna flirt with the tutor? Bully her ward? Antagonize her lover? Remain with her husband? She doesn't know. Her creator didn't know. Why should a performer pretend to know? In order to release the actress from the crushing responsibility of explaining away the role's inexplicable motivation, Stanislavsky was cornered into organizing the performance into episodes. It worked. Olga Knipper's Natalya Petrovna was deliciously unpredictable.

The rehearsals of *A Month in the Country* provided Stanislavsky with his first opportunity to put his system into practical use while directing and acting in a play. Understandably, he concentrated on the techniques of task, action, and obstacle at the expense of investigating playing separate segments. Soon, though, other theater artists elaborated the techniques of episodic acting, for it had sturdy roots in the most ancient traditions of performing and, paradoxically, satisfied the demands of the twentieth century's avant-garde.

The Basics of an Episode

The skills of episodic acting are crude:

- Figure out what you're supposed to do.
- Do it.
- Make sure the people watching you understand that it happened.

Like telling a story, which it resembles, organizing a performance episodically is a technique so old it's prehistoric, and so basic that it gets reinvented whenever there's a parade or a fourth-grade health pageant. Using definitions given by the British novelist E.M. Forster in his book of lectures, *Aspects of the Novel*:

"The King died and then the Queen died" is a story.
"The King died and then the Queen died of grief" is a plot (29).

What an episodically structured performance does is act out a *story*, or sequence of *events*, rather than attempt to perform a *plot* linked together by cause and effect. In theory, each event in a story can be understood separately from the sequence. *The Queen died*, for example, is an event—no matter if it's due to grief or unlucky coincidence. *The Professor kills his Pupil* is another event, no matter why. Performed onstage—no matter why—an event becomes an *episode*.

Onstage, as in a parade, when episode succeeds episode, unexpected juxtapositions and the mystery of what will happen next create an engaging sequence for an audience.

Often there is a deliberate ambiguity to the connections between episodes in a play—a dramatic ambiguity that the playwright intends. As a literary device, episodic structure organizes anonymous medieval texts, plays by Shakespeare, and texts by twentieth-century playwrights like Bertolt Brecht or Samuel Beckett. Some examples:

- *The Stations of the Cross*
- *The Crimes and Punishment of Richard III*
- *The Business Deals of Mother Courage*
- *What Happens While Waiting for Godot*

While clearly different in tone and intention, these sequences are similar in that they require an actor to *identify and perform a series of events for an audience.*

The Spokesman for Episodes: Bertolt Brecht

Although episodic acting renews itself vigorously whenever it can—even at the sources of motivated acting—it wasn't codified as a system until the middle of the 1930s, when an approach to acting to rival Stanislavsky's was set forth by the brash, opportunistic, and foul-smelling German writer Bertolt Brecht.

Brecht cultivated his odor. He smoked cheap cigars and he seldom bathed. He willfully groomed himself like a truck driver and wore cheap steel-rimmed glasses and a loose leather jacket. Early photographs show him scrawny and bookish, strumming a guitar. Brecht was born in 1898 to a middle-class family. Once he moved from the south of Germany to Berlin, he worked up a coarse, direct way with language, art, and women. Just as Stanislavsky's personal elegance* tells us something about his aesthetic, Brecht's vulgar poses tell us something about his. If Stanislavsky's ambition was to coax the spirit of an actor to soar, Brecht meant to plant an actor's feet firmly into the earth.

These two founders of twentieth-century acting differed in other radical ways. Although he did strum the guitar once or twice for pay, Brecht, unlike Stanislavsky, was never an actor. He began his career in the theater as a writer, part of a generation of German artists who referred to themselves as the primitives of a new era. Their intention was to create art that was coarse, crude, and direct. The title of Brecht's early plays, set in Chicago and Berlin, convey his attitude toward urban life: *In the Jungle of Cities* and *Drums in the Night*. Brecht constructed these texts out of scenes unconnected by cause and effect, and they needed to be staged—like Turgenev's *A Month in the Country*—with an approach to acting very different from Stanislavsky's "psychological lace."

When the Moscow Art Theater played Berlin in the early 1920s, Brecht was in attendance with his musical collaborator Kurt Weill. They were accompanied by, of all people, Isadora Duncan and her boyfriend, the Russian poet Yesenin. During a performance of Chekhov's *Three Sisters*, the four of them dissolved into giggles at the actors'

---

*Stanislavsky's appearance as an elegant gentleman was hard-won. While on tour in Berlin, the financially strapped actor was ashamed to leave his hotel room because his clothes were so shabby.

concentrated effort to maintain the fourth wall. The believable and rounded characters, the illusion of reality—even the audience's compassion—all seemed laughably outdated to Bertolt Brecht (30).

Theater more to Brecht's liking were the plays staged by the daring Berlin director Erwin Piscator* at the Volksbühne ("the People's Stage"), where seats were cheap and the audience smoked. During Volksbühne performances, projectors showed documentary footage and narrators or choruses described the onstage action, even as it was happening. Film, choruses, and actors at the Volksbühne combined forces to tell the story of the play, the modern-day equivalent of a bard reciting an epic around a fire. The actors themselves addressed the public directly so that the experiences of the characters in the play could be understood by the audience *objectively*, not shared in, as Stanislavsky would have wanted. Piscator called these innovations in staging *epic theater*.

In 1927, Brecht was invited to assist Piscator, who was then forming a new theater in Berlin. Brecht worked on texts for Piscator and collaborated in directing the work. But by the next year Brecht and Kurt Weill had written an unexpectedly popular musical play that has since become a standard of the international repertory—*The Threepenny Opera*. Soon after, Brecht began to direct on his own, developing Piscator's experiments in his own way.

In the course of the next thirty years, as a director and writer, Brecht redefined Piscator's epic theater, and under that name developed a system of acting to rival Stanislavsky's. Unfortunately, *epic acting* already means something in English—Elizabeth Taylor as Cleopatra.† We need to use another term. Piscator reclaimed his own identity by renaming his work *objective theater* (*objective* in the sense of *matter-of-fact*, rather than Stanislavsky's translator's fruitful misinterpretation of the Russian word for "tasks" as "objectives"). Other artists used other words to describe similar techniques, among them *constructivist* theater. Whatever the term, all were approaches to organizing a performance into separated events onstage. Let's agree to call them *playing an episode*.

Like Stanislavsky, Brecht wrote essays defining a grammar of terms for performers, gave practical advice to professionals, and suggested exercises for developing the expertise of students. Also like Stanislavsky, he founded a theater—the Berliner Ensemble—where actors were trained in these techniques and directed by Brecht. At home or on tour, the actors of the Berliner Ensemble dazzled audiences with the assured, quiet mastery of their craft.

When he died in 1956 (the cigars?), Brecht left behind five volumes of collected essays and over forty plays. Throughout his life he wrote poetry as well; Brecht the poet is considered to be among the greatest of twentieth-century Germans. Moreover, there is an industry of writing *about* Brecht. His influence as a director and writer is studied, debated, exalted, and reviled. We will concentrate on what can be put into use by actors. But first, in order to appreciate the scope and limits of Brecht's contribution, it's important to understand the circumstances of his time and place.

---

*Pronounced pis-KAH-tor. It's telling that the name of this pivotal yet neglected figure in the American theater is all too often mispronounced.

†D.W. Griffith's *Orphans of the Storm* calls itself an epic, too.

Sources for Brecht

Brecht's work rose on foundations—sometimes credited, sometimes not—laid by others. By force of his personality and persuasive writing, he became the spokesman for episodic acting.

Zola's social novel and roles

To begin with, an actor who organizes a text into episodes defines "character" as a *role* within an onstage action. The question *who are you?* is answered by *what you do*:

- Natalya Petrovna: The Woman Who Flirts with Her Child's Tutor
- Ionesco's Professor: The Teacher Who Kills His Students
- Hedda Gabler: The Unhappy Wife Who Shoots Herself

Fiction, like acting, also proposes models for understanding human relationships. The definition of personality as a role in an episode was anticipated by a particular kind of fiction, the *social novel* of the nineteenth century. Even as it told its story, the social novel also investigated the role of its characters in society. No fiction writer did this more systematically or seriously than the French author Emile Zola. In 1868, around the time when most other novelists were intent on teasing out the nuances of personal motivation, Emile Zola declared that his own writing was meant to establish the "natural laws of society"—that fate and character were functions of environment and heredity. Before he wrote a word, Zola rigorously structured his writing to display how individuals survived or perished due to heredity and social milieu.

Zola lived in poverty for twelve years as he worked on a series of novels depicting the rise and fall of a single family. Not until 1877 did the seventh of the series, a portrait of alcoholics called *L'Assommoir* (the title derived from the French verb *to beat down*—"assommer"), bring him fame and sufficient money.* Despite his lack of popular success, Zola was well thought of by other authors. Turgenev, who lived most of the year in Paris (he wrote *A Month in the Country* there) arranged for a five-year contract for Zola to write short stories for a Russian magazine. The third of the series, "Comment on meurt" ("How One Dies"), was published in August 1876, while Zola was working at his fortune-changing *L'Assommoir*.

There is no plot to "Comment on meurt." There are five separate stories, each a self-contained vignette in which someone dies. Each richly detailed vignette demonstrates how death inevitably takes shape according to class and social position: A Count lies dying with decorum and decency, fastidious and ready to receive visitors. An upper middle-class woman, overhearing her sons planning to divide her estate, goes into her death rattle as she frantically lifts herself up from her sickbed to protest. A shopkeeper's wife dwindles slowly, ruining her health and working all hours to save for the future. A

---

*Three film versions of the story of *L'Assommoir* were made before the First World War; Hollywood borrowed the basic plot for *The Lost Weekend* in 1945.

desperately sick child lies in a fever on a thin mattress; his parents pull tufts of the wool padding out from under him in order to raise enough money for his medicine. A seventy-year-old peasant falls like a tree, ending his life when he has no more strength to work the earth—the same earth into which he is laid as if into a lover's arms. Zola had used this scheme of parallel events among different social classes before in a story called "How One Weds," written for the same Russian magazine.

Zola wanted to lay bare the mechanism of society with the amoral vision of a scientist. No mechanisms of cause and effect are given in the vignettes. The reader is left to conclude for himself how each death is explained by its circumstances. Zola himself found explanations for the mechanism of social evolution in the observations of naturalists. In the forests of the newly industrialized Europe, the fate of an individual white moth trying to hide from birds in a smoke-blackened wood had more to do with the moth's changing environment than with the moth's personal feelings or inclinations. Similarly, according to Zola, the fate of a sick child whose parents couldn't afford medicine, or the life of a woman too overworked to take care of herself, had little to do with their individual actions and a lot more to do with the evolving structure of industrial society.

One of Brecht's earliest published letters (November 10, 1914) "proposes Zola as a model because 'the soul of the people has not yet been explored'" (31). Although Brecht and other twentieth-century advocates of episodic theater disagreed with Zola's explanations of how roles form in society, they did agree that character was not a function of motivations, but could be understood better as a role within a social situation. Three months before Brecht wrote his letter about Zola, the First World War began*—a war that would teach Brecht, and many other people, the insignificance of any individual's actions.

The First World War and after

For many Germans who lived through the First World War, the consequences of personal motivations were shot down in combat and buried for good during the post-war collapse of their society. From 1914 until 1918, in battle after battle, no matter who won, the role of any individual—foot soldier or general—was dwarfed by the destructive power of modern weapons. The weapons' increased capacity to kill so outpaced the capabilities of leaders to command or troops to resist that the number and rapidity of casualties in the First World War still shock today—even with our knowledge of Hiroshima and the Holocaust. Let one battle serve as an example for them all.

It was the summer of the second year of combat, July 1, 1916. As an early light rain gave way to brilliant sunshine along the sluggish Somme River in northern France, twenty thousand men died in battle—ten thousand of them within the first hour of combat, and most of those *in the first few minutes* of the fighting (32). When a soldier faced machine guns firing six hundred bullets a minute, personal traits like bravery, heroism, commitment, and passion, while admirable in some abstract sense, had no real signifi-

---

*The first week of August 1914.

cance. Cowardice, fear, and selfishness had no real significance either, except perhaps as low-level survival skills.

A poem called "Lament" by the British writer F.S. Flint (33) captures a generation's sense of being coerced to play a role in this episode of history. Any personal feelings the actors playing this role might have had really didn't matter:

> The young men of the world
> Are condemned to death.
> They have been called up to die
> For the crime of their fathers . . .
> They have been cast for a cruel purpose
> Into the mashing-press and furnace.
>
> The young men of the world
> No longer possess the road:
> The road possesses them.
> They no longer inherit the earth:
> The earth inherits them.
> They are no longer the masters of fire:
> Fire is their master . . . .

Bombs flew overhead from far-off cannons, poison gas seeped quietly and invisibly into lungs. That the source of death was unseen added to one's sense of powerlessness. A son, a farm, a life's work—all could be destroyed, impersonally, in seconds. Individual action seemed as consequential as the efforts of a white moth trying to hide on a smoke-blackened tree.

Piscator always claimed that his experiences in the war forever sparked his work in the theater. He was drafted as a soldier when he was seventeen. At the first order to fire, he froze in fear and blurted out, as if it were an excuse, that he was an actor. He spent the rest of his life—he says—trying to live down his shame by making his trade socially responsible. Brecht, who was younger, was drafted into the German army in 1918 and ended up as an orderly in a military hospital ward for venereal diseases. A famous poem of his describes (in bouncy verse) how the doctors, in order to put more bodies on the frontlines, would certify even the dead as fit for battle.

When the war ended in November of 1918, Germany lost territory, self-respect, and military strength. Under pressure from the winning side to pay war damages, the German economy collapsed. Brecht first came to Berlin in 1923, but he nearly starved to death and left in three weeks. He was lucky he had a home in the south to escape to. In the city, crowds begged on the streets and scavenged the carcasses of dead horses (34). They were further demoralized by their inability to save their children from a similar fate. Like the soldiers in the First World War—or characters in a social novel by Zola—they were compelled to play roles assigned to them by society.

Artists' response to the social crisis

As soon as the war ended, German painters, architects, composers, industrial designers, playwrights, and stage directors (including Brecht and Piscator) banded together and proclaimed they would dedicate their work to the necessity—and opportunity—of building a new and better world. In the context of the social crisis, making art was recognized as a trade among other trades, not unlike manufacturing. An artist assembled raw materials, produced a finished product, and—just like any other worker—was poorly compensated for his hard work and skill. A quote from Bernard Meyers's *The German Expressionists: A Generation in Revolt* (35) sums it up:

> We painters and poets are bound to the poor in a sacred solidarity. Have not many among us learned to know misery and shame of hunger?

In Weimar, in the south of Germany, a new school of industrial design rose to meet the challenge of rebuilding after the war. It was called the Bauhaus and it took as its spiritual mission the reshaping of this new world. The Bauhaus took full advantage of the technical abilities of mass production to redesign common articles, including soup spoons, and looked to machines for aesthetic inspiration. The designer/craftsman/artist's task was to retool machines to produce new products and, ultimately, new people. Brecht would repeat this idea in his poetry and plays for the rest of his life.

Mass production of art, which had always lessened the value of an art object in the past, now enhanced value because it made it possible for art to reach a mass audience. In order to reach a wide group of people, the forms of art were made simpler to comprehend. No longer was there a need for cultural references that required an expensive education in order to be understood. No longer were shabby clothes and hollow eyes just picturesque details in novels or paintings. Now these images provoked a response among readers and viewers who themselves were poor and hungry.

Sculptors were no longer content to carve marble and cast bronze; they began to assemble the overlooked detritus of everyday life into their work. The sculptor Kurt Schwitters assembled cardboard box tops, newspapers, the soles of shoes, and tin cans—even the valueless German currency (which was probably the cheapest paper one could get).

In Russia, Moscow was undergoing a similar reorganization politically and artistically after the Russian Revolution, which ended at roughly the same time as the First World War. Cultural exchange between Berlin and Moscow was direct and strong at this time, and mass production and the virtues of industry were the trade secrets Moscow had to offer. The Russian sculptor El (for Eliezor) Lessitsky brought the aesthetic of gear shafts and pistons to Berlin. The Hungarian artist László Moholy-Nagy (pronounced NADJ) designed the curriculum at the Bauhaus, educating the next generation of German artists in the Russian approach. Russian experiments in theatrical form, begun by a renegade disciple of Stanislavsky's named Vsevolod Meyerhold, set off a response in the German theater world as well. At first the experiments were in stagecraft and scenery: Moholy-Nagy designed sets for Piscator with turntables, treadmills, slide projections, and machine parts. There were more innovations to come.

EPISODES

The example of Georg Grosz

Close ties between visual and theater artists helped to transform avant-garde German theater. Among the most influential visual artists was the painter Georg Grosz. Although he worked in watercolor and oil, Grosz was best known for his lithographs and black-ink drawings. He also designed scenery for Piscator, and almost went to jail over one of his backdrops. Grosz knew Brecht from the start; he'd illustrated Brecht's poem of the doctor sending a rotting corpse to the war front.

That particular sketch was one of a series that Grosz drew between 1918 and 1926, and published in Berlin in 1930, under the title *The Marked Men (Die Gezeichneten)*. The collection begins with a quote from the Bible (Genesis 1:28): *And God said to them be fruitful and multiply and subdue the earth*. With a ruthless, unblinking eye and superb technique, Grosz illustrated the multiple ways Berliners had subdued the earth—and each other. In the drawings, women of all ages sell themselves, unkempt unemployed men loiter on street corners, and a rich man hauls bread out of the reach of poor children.

Grosz's work usually depicts a relationship between people—just like good acting. Background scenery is rudimentary: a wall, a potted plant, a window (in which, often enough, a murder is being committed). Yet the essential details of class that define people's social roles are etched with precision: the expensive silk underwear of the whores, the crisp striped cravat tied around Hitler's neck, the stubble on the faces of the poor.

No single plot connects the pictures. Like the scenes of an episodic play, each of the sixty plates is a little scene complete in itself: a poor family contemplates the goods it cannot buy, an ax murderer washes his bloody hands at the kitchen sink, a bloated old man eyes a bare-breasted young girl. Often the scenes have a central *gesture*. In one sketch, for example, a well-fed dandy lifts his well-shod foot to avoid the artificial leg of a war veteran who is begging in the street. This is captioned, by the way: *Don't Trip!*

The devices of Grosz's lithographs—social roles, episodic tableaux, essential gestures, captions, cartoonish distortions mixed with precise realistic details—paralleled Piscator's and Brecht's techniques in creating the devices of modern episodic acting. Many of Grosz's drawings are captioned because they first appeared in newspapers and needed to be quickly and easily understood by a wide mass of readers (who were no less connoisseurs of everyday life than wealthy collectors of oil paintings). The captions summed up the action of each little scene in the same way that banners or actors announced the title of an episode directly to the audience in episodic theater productions.

Even the degree of finish of Grosz's drawings was influential. Grosz spattered, scratched, dropped, and dragged the ink across the nubby surface of the paper. His lines were spare and spiky. His images had a job to communicate directly, simply, and immediately; they didn't need the careful modeling and creamy finish of oil painting. The deliberate distortions and use of simplified and cartoonish effects were sufficient to animate the scene and clarify the episode on the paper. Episodic acting was similarly bold. Brecht and Piscator had their actors mix distortions with the precise details of observed behavior to achieve a style of acting more real than realism.

69

Rival episodic theater: politics

During this period in Germany, distraction was as necessary as bread. Episodic entertainments such as circuses, pageants, and musical reviews were very popular—and easier to sit through than classical theater or a composed symphony. But even some twentieth-century operas were episodic in structure: both Richard Strauss's *Elektra* (1909) and Alban Berg's *Wozzeck* (1925)* had librettos comprised of scenes that depicted unrelated incidents rather than aspects of one continuous plot.

Other, more sinister episodes were being staged in Brecht and Piscator's Berlin as well—and not on the stage. As drama became more political, politics became more dramatic. In stadiums and open squares, Nazi rallies and parades were essentially staged performances that used techniques similar to those used by Piscator's People's Stage. They even copied the look of his posters. Rallies featured speeches clarified by banners and slogans. Arms outstretched in salute were effective essential gestures. Historical and current events were presented as simply as possible, with roles assigned to individuals and ethnic groups.

In 1932, Nazi thugs staged a real-life episode by burning Berlin's parliament building—then acting out the role of Innocent Victim. In the next episode, the Nazis, playing the role of Protector, seized control of the central government and cast their opponents in the role of Criminals. Piscator, Brecht, Grosz, and Weill fled the country—as did other intellectuals and artists, including Albert Einstein, Sigmund Freud, and Marlene Dietrich.

Inspiration: Mei Lanfang

Brecht and Piscator—in exile from Germany—separately made their wandering ways to Russia. Piscator had visited the Soviet Union first in 1931, directing a film and helping to organize a German-speaking theater in a part of Central Asia then called the Volga German Republic, now Kazakhstan; although he was too busy at the time to go there. In the spring of 1935, Brecht and Piscator were both in Moscow at the time the great Chinese actor Mei Lanfang was performing there on tour.

Mei Lanfang played only women's roles. He performed only in Mandarin Chinese. Usually, his make-up was an elaborate pink and white mask that took two hours to apply. His touring repertory was comprised almost exclusively of scenes from the traditional Peking opera.† In Peking opera roles, Mei Lanfang's costumes were intricately stylized, so much so that the costume could be used to set the scene. Aside from the costume, Mei Lanfang appeared onstage without scenery, except for two chairs and a table. In order to be understood by audiences who didn't share the language of his texts, his performance was organized to present one complete event that could be understood from the beginning of the scene to the end: *The Concubine Forsakes the Losing General*,

---

*Based on *Woyzeck*, a series of fragmentary scenes written by Georg Büchner in 1837, unpublished until 1879.

†He also played shop girls—but never abroad.

for example. The Chinese film *Farewell My Concubine* (1993, directed by Chen Kaige) shows just such a scene, by the way, performed by students of students of Mei Lanfang.

Mei Lanfang's technical skill was such that he became his own cooperative ensemble. He could play two roles at once: his legs and feet could play the horse he was riding, while the upper part of his body could perform the rider's emotions and expressions. Like Grosz's drawings, details of precise realism were simultaneously juxtaposed with stylization. Like the Bauhaus aesthetic, Mei Lanfang's craft was openly on display; he could be seen watching his own gestures. The audience was invited to notice the artificiality of the acting and appreciate the craft necessary to act the onstage event.

At his first Moscow appearance Mei Lanfang had the assurance to perform out of make-up, in a dinner jacket. Brecht went to watch—and he didn't giggle. He was entranced. So were Meyerhold and, by the way, Stanislavsky. Meyerhold was captivated by the vocabulary of gestures and the elegant, streamlined stagecraft. What appealed to Stanislavsky was that the performer's inner commitment, like Duse's, was manifest in beauty and grace. Piscator, on the other hand, dismissed it as oriental exotica. As for Brecht, just as Stanislavsky was inspired by Salvini and Duse to form his ideas on motivated acting, so too was Brecht now inspired by Mei Lanfang to form concrete ideas about epic acting (distinct from epic *staging*). When he saw the Chinese actor perform, Brecht recognized the possibility of a systematic acting style that could fulfil his episodic plays—and revolutionize acting in the West.

Terms to Work with: Episodes and Captions

Brecht's definitions are buried amid charts and essays. Often they have to be deduced. Late in life, after rereading his own writing, Brecht realized he'd left out the most obvious principles. As we did with Stanislavsky's terms, let's agree on some basic terms for *episodic acting* in order to put them into practical use. In 1936, after his first trip to New York, Brecht wrote to Piscator: ". . . it's quite wrong that we should be making no propaganda for our view of theater and film. We ought to write articles, possibly an illustrated booklet, all this mass of material must at last be got into shape and made usable. I read Stanislavsky's *My Life in Art* with unease mixed with envy. The man got his system straight, with the result that in Paris and New York everyone's becoming a Stanislavsky disciple. Is that unavoidable?" (36).

Episode

An **episode** is an event performed onstage that is understood by its audience complete and by itself, separate from the whole of the play. Some examples:

- Natalya Petrovna flirts with the tutor.
- The Professor stumps the Pupil.
- The Professor stomps the Pupil.
- The Chinese Princess leaves her King.

The relationships between actors in an episode always imply the relationship between the actors and the audience. The essence of an episode is that something changes in the course of its playing, and the audience notices that it has changed.

As in good industrial design, all aspects of the performance—scenery, costumes, lighting, even the acting—are parts of a machine designed to perform the episode. It is not necessary to convince the audience that they are watching anything other than performers on stage. Any means of getting the episode across to the public is legitimate.

Caption

For purposes of analysis for actors, episodes are captioned. Like newspaper headlines, or the titles of Grosz's lithographs, an actor's **caption** for an episode should paraphrase or sum up the onstage event. A good caption is in the form of a complete sentence: it includes a subject, a verb, and object. A caption should answer the questions:

- What happens?
- Who makes it happen?
- To whom does it happen?

For example: HEDDA REVOLTS is insufficient as a caption because it is vague. HER SPIRIT IS FREED is not much better. What that will produce onstage is a tableau vivant. Better is: HEDDA REVOLTS AGAINST HER HUSBAND'S WORLD. Or: HEDDA DECLINES TO JOIN HER HUSBAND'S WORLD. HEDDA SHOOTS HERSELF is good, too, especially if you can avoid the temptation to explain why. Headlines out of sensationalist newspapers are a good model for the style of a caption (but not necessarily the style of your performance): MANIAC PROF OFFS STAR PUPIL. WIFE'S EX VISITS HONEYMOON COUPLE.

A caption can also answer *when* and *where*, but it does not include *how* and *why*. The *how* will be demonstrated onstage. *Why* is immaterial, or will be deduced by the audience. At first, the episodes in a rehearsal will usually be identified as brief units. After repetition in rehearsal—and performance—these smaller episodes will coalesce into larger ones.

Applying Episodic Techniques: Rehearsing a Scene from *In the Jungle of Cities*

Let's continue illustrating episodic techniques as if we were rehearsing the first scene of Bertolt Brecht's *In the Jungle of Cities* (1922) (37). This is from the playwright's prologue:

> *You are in Chicago in 1912. You will witness an inexplicable wrestling match between two men and observe the downfall of a family that has moved from the prairies to the jungle of the big city. Don't worry your head about the motives for the fight, keep your minds on the stakes. Judge impartially the technique of the contenders, and be prepared to concentrate on the finish.*

This scene begins with the central character, Garga, alone onstage, quietly working in the library wrapping books.

> SKINNY If we read the sign right, this is a lending library. We'd like to borrow a book.
>
> GARGA What kind of a book?
>
> SKINNY A fat one.
>
> GARGA For yourself?
>
> SKINNY (*who looks at* SHLINK *before each answer*) No, not for me, for this gentleman.
>
> GARGA Your name?
>
> SKINNY Shlink, lumber dealer, 6 Mulberry Street.
>
> GARGA (*taking down name*) Five cents a week per book. Take your pick.
>
> SKINNY No, you choose one.
>
> GARGA This is a detective story, it's not good. Here's something better—a travel book.
>
> SKINNY Just like that you say the book is no good?
>
> SHLINK (*stepping up to him*) Is that your personal opinion? I'll buy your opinion. Is ten dollars enough?
>
> GARGA Take it as a gift.

Why does Shlink, a bully of a lumber dealer, want to buy the clerk's opinion? The reason is not important, the playwright says, just pay attention to what happens. Garga refuses to sell.

Identifying roles

Why does Skinny look at Shlink before each answer? In an episodic structure an actor does not so much play a character as take a **role** in the episode (Bully or Bookworm). The question is not so much *Who am I?* as it is *What do I do?* or *How does it fit in with what other people do?* In order for the episode to work, its roles must interconnect. There is a theater game where actors pretend to be parts of a machine—making noises and swinging their arms, or twisting their bodies like a clockwork made of human beings. This exercise is a metaphor for what must happen onstage: that all the actors play roles that fit together like the parts of a machine in order to produce the effect of the episode.

In *In the Jungle of Cities*, Shlink is the Man Who Wants to Buy an Opinion. Garga is the Man Who Refuses Him. Skinny is the Man Who Speaks for Shlink. If you play Skinny, it is a noble waste of time to figure out *why* you speak for Shlink. Looking at Shlink before he speaks makes Skinny's role clear to the audience. Skinny is the role of the Man Who Speaks for Shlink.

> SHLINK You mean you've changed your opinion and now it's a good book?
>
> GARGA No.

SKINNY Ten dollars will buy you some fresh clothes.

GARGA My job here is wrapping books, that's all.

SKINNY It drives the customers away.

GARGA What do you want of me? I don't know you. I've never seen you before.

As rehearsals progress, roles will be defined fully from the beginning to end of the play:

- I'm the Pupil Who Gets Killed.
- I'm the Maniacal Teacher Who Kills His Pupil to Teach Her a Lesson.
- I'm the Woman Trapped in a Bourgeois Marriage.
- I'm the Husband Who Wishes His Wife Were More Like Other Men's Wives.

At first in rehearsal, the roles will be simpler:

- I'm the Bully.
- I'm the Bully's Henchman.
- I'm the Innocent Man Wrapping Books.

Similarly, you will begin with a rough draft of a caption. For example:

BULLY TRIES TO BRIBE THE BOOKWORM

GARGA I never heard of this book and it doesn't mean a thing to me.

SHLINK I'm offering you forty dollars for your opinions of it.

GARGA I'll sell you the opinions of Mr. J.V. Jensen and Mr. Arthur Rimbaud but I won't sell you my own opinion.*

SHLINK Your opinion is just as worthless as theirs, but right now I want to buy it.

GARGA I indulge in opinions.

SHLINK Are your family millionaires?

GARGA My family lives on rotten fish.

SHLINK (*obviously pleased*) A fighter! I'd have expected you to come across with the words that would give me pleasure and get your family something better than fish.

By the end of this scene, the thoughtful Garga has been provoked into a reckless fight. That's the outcome of the entire scene, but it will take us time to get there.

---

*The references are to books Brecht was reading at the time he wrote the play: the French writer Arthur Rimbaud's *A Season in Hell* (part template for Brecht's idea of Chicago) and the Danish novelist J. V. Jensen's *The Wheel*, a homosexual murder story set in Chicago. One of Brecht's early notes indicates that Garga should resemble Rimbaud in appearance and Garga's love/hate relationship with Shlink should parallel Rimbaud's stormy relationship with the poet Verlaine.

SKINNY Forty bucks! That's a lot of fresh shirts for you and your family.

GARGA I'm not a prostitute.

SHLINK (*with humor*) I hardly think my fifty dollars interferes with your inner life.

GARGA Raising your offer is one more insult and you know it.

SHLINK (*naïvely*) A man's got to know which is better, a pound of fish or an opinion. Or two pounds of fish or the opinion.

SKINNY Dear sir, your stubbornness will get you into trouble.

GARGA I'm going to have you thrown out.

SKINNY Having opinions shows you don't know anything about life.

Report to the audience

In order to make the episode clearer, this last line of Skinny's could be said directly to the audience. In fact, without the barrier of a fourth wall, much of the scene could be directed to the audience in order to clarify the episode. Skinny can show the audience the money offered to Garga, bill by bill, before he sticks the cash under Garga's nose. Many of Garga's lines can be delivered directly to the audience:

- *My job here is wrapping books, that's all.*
- *I never heard of this book and it doesn't mean a thing to me.*
- *I indulge in opinions.*
- *My family lives on rotten fish.*
- *I'm not a prostitute.*

As can both of the following:

SHLINK A man's got to know which is better, a pound of fish or an opinion.

SKINNY Having opinions shows you don't know anything about life.

This direct contact with the audience breaks one of Stanislavsky's rules that contribute to the illusion of the stage: that the actors behave with each other and ignore the audience. In one of his essays, Piscator dismisses Stanislavsky's example of actors ignoring the audience in a hunt for a dropped nail or a lost shoe, and adds that he himself is always embarrassed when actors looking out to the audience pretend not to notice the hundreds of staring eyes.

Demonstration

Brecht once gave his definition of good epic acting by saying it would be like watching the actor who plays Hamlet teaching his understudy what to do, late at night in the theater, while both are a little drunk. Imagine what that "Hamlet" says: "Okay, in this scene you get down on your knees, and you pick up the skull real slow. You say the first word,

'Alas,' then you make the audience wait while you think of something really sad, then you turn the skull toward them and continue the line (*mournful sigh, followed by a hiccup*) 'Poor Yorick.'"

The actor playing Hamlet is giving his understudy a **demonstration**.

Demonstration is different from enactment and its rules of good taste are different, too. Asides, indicating, direct address, playing to the house are—when playing an episode—no longer cheap theatrics and in bad taste. Properly done, they call attention not to the actor, but to the events of the play. Cartoons, exaggerations, and dismantling the illusion that the actor is a different person are anathema to Stanislavsky's aesthetic. In episodic theater, however, whatever makes the episode clear is appropriate. Just as the drunken actor demonstrates Hamlet's believable confusion, episodic theater has a place for realistic behavior and motivation. It also drops those things when it is effective to do so.

Demonstration is not meant to move the audience in the same way as enactment. Brecht and Piscator said the actor should prod the audience to judge the action, not seduce them into sharing the character's emotions. Empathy would confuse the audience about what was going on.

This desire not to be caught up in the emotion of a crowd was not a personal quirk of Brecht's or Piscator's; keeping one's head in the middle of pandemonium was a strategy for survival. The best-attended theatrical events in Berlin were Nazi rallies, parades, and public meetings that fully exploited the techniques of swaying the emotions of a crowd. If the theater trained people to be receptive to emotions without thinking, if the theater got people in the habit of being moved by captivating speakers, then tyrants like Hitler would be in power forever. Theatergoing would be one of those perverse ceremonies of a culture—like witch-burning and public hangings—that enjoys a long and rich performance history throughout the world.

Brecht and Piscator wanted a theater where what happened onstage and offstage would be questioned rather than wept at or laughed over. That doesn't mean the theater's emotions are taken away; it means emotions are not an end in themselves. "Are you enjoying this?" Garga asks the audience. The audience is meant to ask itself the same question.

In fact, in the best of all possible worlds, you play an episode to the little old matinee ladies in the balcony who have joined your grandmother for a theater weekend in the city. (They're staying at a hotel in midtown and they've just had Salad Niçoise for lunch.) You want those happy ladies sitting in the balcony to shout out in piercing voices: "Oh, look, he's minding his own business when that strange man comes in and picks a fight." It's a confirmation of good episodic acting when the ladies in the balcony comment on what's happening onstage and say the episode's caption aloud. "Will that librarian take the money?" "Turn him down!" "That Skinny is a pest." "Oh! *I* get it! Shlink wants to buy his soul."*

As the scene progresses, another caption may suggest itself:

---

*Brecht himself wrote dialogue critiquing his play *Man = Man*. Fake matinee ladies saying these lines in the audience can turn a performance of *Man = Man* into an impromptu debate over the play's merits.

EPISODES

GARGA I'm going to have you thrown out.

SKINNY Having opinions shows you don't know anything about life.

SHLINK Miss Larry says you wanted to go to Tahiti!

GARGA How do you know Jane Larry?

SHLINK She's starving. She's not getting paid for the shirts she sews. You haven't been to see her in three weeks.

GARGA *drops a pile of books.*

Why does Garga drop the books? Is he nervous? Angry? Just drop the books. The sound they make hitting the floor will alert the balcony to pay attention. Let *them* argue why you dropped the books.

SKINNY Watch your steps! You're only an employee.

GARGA You're molesting me. But there's nothing I can do about it.

SHLINK You're poor.

GARGA I live on fish and rice. You know that as well as I do.

SHLINK Sell!

SKINNY Are you an oil king?

SHLINK The people in your neighborhood feel sorry for you.

GARGA I can't shoot down the whole neighborhood.

SHLINK Your family that came from the prairies . . .

GARGA Sleep three in a bed by a broken drain pipe. I smoke at night, it's the only way I can get to sleep. The windows are closed because Chicago is cold. Are you enjoying this?

That last line can be spoken directly to the audience, who, freed from the responsibility of suspending disbelief at what they are watching, are allowed to think about what they enjoy.

Transactions

Zola's model for the mechanism of roles in society was natural science; Brecht's model for roles derived from economic science. Brecht shared a worldview that all forms of human behavior—onstage and off—were functions of power and commerce, and essentially political. "Political" aspects of power and commerce are inherent in all human relationships. The founders of twentieth-century episodic acting would all have agreed that an actor's performance should bring such political aspects into focus for an audience. Working with this approach, an episode includes an additional set of questions related to **transactions:**

PLAYING EPISODES

- What is being bought or sold?
- Who is the buyer?
- Who is the seller?
- What is the price?
- Is the deal concluded?

Sell! says Shlink. Just what is Shlink buying when he offers forty dollars for Garga's "opinion"? Is the price fair? The answers to these questions organize the first scene of *In the Jungle of Cities* much better than any investigation of the character's inscrutable motives.

The *gest*

In order to fully reveal the episode, the moment that the deal is concluded or fails has to be made clear onstage. Let's agree to call this playing the **gest,** from the same root word as for *gesture.** Think of it as the *gist* of the scene. Better yet, think of the moment of the *gest* as the photograph in the tabloid that would accompany the episode's headline. Yet the *gest* is not frozen in time, like a tableau; a *gest* implies the movement of an offer, an exchange, or a rejection.

A *gest* always involves a human gesture, an interaction between at least two people—or in some cases, two aspects of one person's character. It's different from the *psychological gesture* of Michael Chekhov, mentioned in Chapter 3, which is personal, symbolic, and without political content. For Brecht and Piscator, all *gests* had social significance, which for them implied politics, and, according to their notion of politics, *commerce.* The smallest social unit, Brecht claimed, was *two.*

caption	*gest*
SHLINK OFFERS GARGA MONEY FOR HIS OPINION	Skinny sticks the money under Garga's nose. Garga turns his head away.
HEDDA BURNS LOVE OUT OF HER HEART	She flings the manuscript into the fireplace.
THE PROFESSOR STUMPS THE PUPIL	His finger in her face, her eyes crossed.
THE PROFESSOR STUMPS THE PUPIL	His body coming within inches of her face, but never touching her.

---

*The contradictory and convoluted definitions of *gest* or *gestus* are, in part, what prevent Brecht's ideas from being applied by working actors. It does not further the cause of propaganda to repeat, as Peter Thomson does in "Brecht and Actor Training" from *Twentieth Century Acting Training* (38), "Gestus is 'the aesthetic gestural presentation of the economic and socio-ideological construction of human identity and interaction,' something which 'finds ultimate expression in the corporeal and intellectual work of the performer.'" Try saying that in a rehearsal.

EPISODES

At the beginning of *In the Jungle of Cities*, Garga is quietly wrapping books as Shlink and Skinny lurk in the door of the lending library. This could be the first tableau for *In the Jungle of Cities*. At the end of the first scene the library is a shambles. Shlink and Skinny stand amidst the wreckage, Garga is gone. In case the ladies in the balcony missed the point of the scene, Skinny will tell them: *We finally drove him out of his skin.* The *gest* might be the moment Garga threw his coat and shoes to the ground and ran out barefoot.

Would-be directors, take note: the episode can be given its essential structure by staging in rehearsal a tableau of the scene's beginning, a tableau of the scene's end, and the *gest* in between. Draw little sketches with stick figures, if you like. Just as you can rehearse a scene in order to uncover and elaborate its motivations, you can rehearse a scene with the intention of discovering the *gest*, or, once it's discovered, polishing the *gest*.

Very good examples of *gests* are in Grosz's cartoons, of course.

A *gest* can include a prop. In fact, the use of props in episodic technique is called, by Brecht, the **object lesson.** The object, onstage, represents an essential part of the episode, and is understood by the audience in this way. Hedda *burning Løvborg's manuscript* or the civilized Garga *tearing off his shoes* are good examples. The resemblance of the *gest* to the poses of melodrama are what make *gests* so potent in an object lesson. *Gests* and object lessons are sometimes given by the playwright, but very often you will rehearse the scene hoping to discover an effective *gest* with which to play the scene.

With the use of effective episodes and *gests*, the performance should be understandable apart from the language in which the play is being performed. This is not to rob the words of their theatrical power. Just the opposite, it gives the words the dramatic structure necessary to achieve theatrical power. The lack of such a structure is the problem with an approach based exclusively on tasks. If all you are doing is pursuing your task, you can become selfish, not as a character, but as a ham whose self-centeredness diverts the scene from its point, or gist, or—as you now know to call it—episode.

Let's Review Terms

episode	an event played out onstage that is understood by the audience independently of the play
role	your job in performing the episode
transaction	the underlying structure of behavior; trade: something is bought or sold
caption	the summary of the event in the episode
demonstration	making the episode clear to the audience
gest	the moment between people when the trade is made or denied
the object lesson	use of a physical object to demonstrate the gest

The Chart

The chart compares five different ways of organizing and analyzing a text. Let's begin to fill in the categories for *Episodic Analysis*: basic unit, key question, and dramatic action.

- **Basic unit.** The basic unit for the actor is the *episode*, an event that happens onstage, understood by the audience.
- **Key question.** The key question for an actor to answer in an episode is *What do I do?*
- **Dramatic action.** The dramatic action is defined as a *transaction* between characters, clarified by a *gest* at the moment when the transaction is successfully completed or falls apart.

CHAPTER 5

COMBINING EPISODES

Playing an Opposition

When a character performs a role in an episode reluctantly—his reactions at odds with his actions even as he performs them—that is called *playing an opposition*. Some examples:

- Hedda Gabler weeps as she destroys Løvborg's manuscript.
- Shlink apologizes sincerely for the pain he causes Garga.
- Skinny politely dumps the library books on the floor.

When a role played in one episode contradicts another of the same character's roles in other episodes, that too, is playing an opposition. Some examples:

- Hamlet plots to avenge his father; Hamlet hesitates when he might kill.
- Hamlet is in love with Ophelia; Hamlet pushes Ophelia off his lap.
- Natalya Petrovna defends her marriage; Natalya Petrovna competes with her ward for the love of her ward's tutor.

As Olga Knipper and Stanislavsky discovered in their rehearsals for *A Month in the Country*, playing **oppositions** frees actors from thinking that inconsistent behavior is a puzzle to be solved by the revelation of consistent need. Playing oppositions makes incongruity fun, not a problem; the tension of contradiction makes such theater theatrical.

The contradictions among a series of roles in an episodic performance create depth in the illusion of a character.

- Ionesco's Professor would like to please his Pupil. The Professor kills the Pupil.
- Hedda Gabler loves Løvborg, burns his manuscript, lies to him, and kills herself.
- Natalya Petrovna, a kind mother, fickle wife, and cruel mistress, flirts with a boy.

When actors demonstrate the kindness of a cruel action, or the harshness of doing good, they are playing oppositions. Performers have done it for centuries, acting on an artist's instinct to give shading to what otherwise would be flat. For a performance that is organized episodically, opposition does more than create interest; it provokes the audience to respond to the text and participate in the performance.

With oppositions left raw and unblended, the reconciliation of opposites (or lack of reconciliation) is left to be done by the audience—not the characters or the actors or the playwright or the director. The dramatic tension between the opposing forces invites such a synthesis. For those who like to use the stage as a tool for expanding social consciousness, the synthesis of oppositions is completed by the actions of the audience after it leaves the theater.

Even without social commitment, the technique of playing an opposition works with episodic structure to build depth for characters and suspense during performances. The use of opposition is meant to provoke the audience to stand apart from any one side of the opposition—including the feelings of any one character—in order to respond to the dynamic of the opposed forces.

Oppositions may sound like Stanislavsky's obstacles, but they aren't. An obstacle interrupts the pursuit of a task, altering actions. Oppositions coincide with each other. They do not blend or interrupt each other; they run parallel. An actor's job is to play each aspect of an opposition so that it holds its own in creating dynamic tension. You hope the combinations that create oppositions add up to something unexpectedly different from the sum of the parts, the way fire and water, carefully brought together, make steam.

Alienation

Alienation is the term Brecht used to describe the process by which actors playing episodes establish *gests*, transactions, and oppositions. What Brecht meant by alienation is to take something familiar, especially familiar human behavior, and *alienate* it from its surroundings so that it seems strange, or alien.* This, in part, was the reason for the captions and labels of epic productions: to get the audience to alienate events and concentrate on the circumstances that produced them. The crash of the books on the floor during the scene from *In the Jungle of Cities* would do the same thing.

For Brecht, alienation does NOT mean shining bright lights in the audience's eyes. It does NOT mean playing ear-splitting music. In fact, it doesn't have anything, anything, *anything* to do with alienating *the audience*. Anyone who tells you that is wrong. Not slightly incorrect. Wrong. Because of the confusion from the word *alienate*, some translators use another term, *estrangement*. But in the English-speaking theater, *estrangement*—like the phrase *epic acting*—already means something related to Elizabeth Taylor: what happened between the actress and most of her husbands. Some translators substitute the coded terms *A-affect* or *E-affect* for *A*-lienation or *E*-strangement. This is

---

*The German word is a translation of the term "alienation," coined by the Russian literary critic Viktor Shklovsky, who used the term to define Tolstoy's technique of describing the familiar as a collection of oddities. Brecht probably learned the word, an uncommon one in German, from his translator during Brecht's second trip to Moscow.

like calling Mrs. Siddons's legs her *limbs*. Let's agree here to call the process alienation—and promise not to shine lights in the audience's eyes.*

When an actor takes what is commonplace, everyday behavior and makes it worthy of aesthetic consideration, that fits the definition of alienation—*making the familiar strange*. Onstage, we alienate casual gestures like shaking hands, signing a deed, tipping the head, or bowing, so that they become significant to the audience. This way they may contribute to the episode. Some alienated gestures even move up the ladder to *gest*.

American Pop Art includes memorably witty examples of alienation. By framing an enlarged Campbell's soup can label or copying the graphics of a Brillo box, Andy Warhol called attention to the aesthetic of commercialized America. Roy Lichtenstein's use of cartoon style and cartoon imagery, including Donald Duck, is another illustration of alienation of the familiar. Then there is Claes Oldenburg, whose sculpture of a lipstick was so huge that its resemblance to a missile was unmistakable enough to draw protests during the Vietnam War. Oldenburg made giant toilet seats, too, and colossal hamburgers and teabags; the more mundane, the more worth looking at again.

The alienation of commonplace objects in Pop Art is a model for behavior alienated onstage: made strange, significant, and worthy of scrutiny. In this way, shoving a pile of books on the floor politely can be understood—by the audience—as an opposition. The Pupil's reflex parroting of nonsense phrases can be understood—by the audience—as a transaction. The nod of Shlink's chin toward the servile Skinny can be understood—by the audience—as a *gest*.

Even a structure of actions and obstacles can be alienated—in order to include realistic behavior within an episode. Because it is alienated, like the words of a quotation inside a larger paragraph—"Say what?"†—the action in pursuit of a task may come to an abrupt end once the episode is over. Brecht urged actors to understand and exploit this sophisticated combination of tasks within episodes.

The combination of objectives within episodes is also what Stanislavsky used for the 1909 rehearsals of *A Month in the Country*. Twenty-five years later, Stanislavsky again played in rehearsal with the technique of organizing a play into segments of action, this time perhaps adapting his system to include the innovations of Meyerhold. Stanislavsky wrote to his son in 1935: "We break the whole play, episode by episode, into physical actions . . ." (39)

The resemblance of Stanislavsky's 1934–1938 rehearsal techniques to episodic acting is striking in other ways, but the essential difference—the unconnected playing of events—was *not* part of Stanislavsky's technique. Stanislavsky's letter to his son goes on to stress that the episodes are rehearsed through improvisations until they look believable and establish a line. That line included cause and effect, rising and falling action, and other devices of *plot*, not story. Oppositions are understood to be *counter-actions* to be overcome, not played simultaneously. Complex characters are built by hidden connections between seeming contradictions (40).

---

*Or yell at them. There is a play by Peter Handke in which the actors verbally attack the audience. This is not alienation, either, although it is offensive. Handke's play is called, aptly, *Offending the Audience*.

†You see?

Analyzing Episodes: Rehearsing a Scene from *Richard III*

Shakespeare's use of episodes makes it possible for actors to build such complex characters by playing *roles* that revel in the contradictions of personality. The performer playing Lady Macbeth, for example, has the opportunity to juxtapose episodes of demonic possession with contradictory and intimate episodes of tenderness and fear. These oppositions build depth to the character of the murderous Lady Macbeth in the way contradictory episodes make Turgenev's mercurial Natalya Petrovna so charming. In more than one of Shakespeare's plays contradictions define the character: Hamlet, of course, but also Cleopatra, Iago, King Lear, Falstaff, Romeo, Juliet, and the crowd in *Julius Caesar*. Shakespeare's texts also provide good opportunities to examine *gests*, transactions, and episodes. Brecht studied them for structure and their implication for actors. So can you.

Let's organize the episodes of Shakespeare's *Richard III*, Act I, scene ii. In the course of the play, Richard of Gloster becomes sovereign the old-fashioned way: by killing anyone who stands in his way. On his way to the throne he stops to marry a politically well-connected widow, and tells the audience his plan before his scene with her begins. In many of his plays, Shakespeare wrote lines to explain action—before, during, and after the actor's performances of it. That's the case here:

> GLOSTER [RICHARD] . . . I'll marry Warwick's youngest daughter:
> What though I kill'd her husband and her father?
> The readiest way to make the wench amends
> Is to become her husband and her father . . .

Caption the episodes

As the next scene begins, Warwick's youngest daughter, better known as Lady Anne, enters, probably during the speech describing her. She accompanies her father-in-law's body on its way to burial. Her husband is also dead, murdered by Richard, Duke of Gloster, who intrudes on and interrupts the burial procession. Let's skip over Anne's monologue; the technique to be used for Shakespeare's monologues will be described—at length—in Chapter 13, "Shakespeare's Soliloquies." Even so, we can *caption* the first episode:

WIDOW ON WAY TO CEMETERY

The scene continues after the monologue. Lady Anne speaks to her gentlemen followers:

> ANNE . . . And still, as you are weary of the weight,
> Rest you, whiles I lament King Henry's corpse.
>
> *Enter* GLOSTER

GLOSTER Stay, you that bear the corpse, and set it down.
ANNE What black magician conjures up this fiend,
    To stop devoted charitable deeds?

Anne just announced the episode: *Fiend interrupts charitable deeds*. Richard himself told the audience he killed Anne's husband and father-in-law; from his own words and Anne's we know that Richard is unnaturally shaped. For the fun of it, let's caption the episode onstage in the style of tabloid newspapers:

DEFORMED KILLER CRASHES FUNERAL PROCESSION

GLOSTER Villains, set down the corpse; or, by Saint Paul,
    I'll make a corpse of him that disobeys.
GENTLEMAN My lord, stand back, and let the coffin pass.
GLOSTER Unmanner'd dog! stand thou, when I command:
    Advance thy halberd higher than my breast,
    Or, by Saint Paul, I'll strike thee to my foot,
    And spurn upon thee, beggar, for thy boldness.

This is the first transaction: *Put down the body / and I won't kill you.*

ANNE What, do you tremble? Are you all afraid?
    Alas, I blame you not; for you are mortal,
    And mortal eyes cannot endure the devil.

Based on what Anne describes, the Gentlemen, trembling and afraid (and so playing an opposition), accept the deal. The *gest* is the moment they lower their spears (halberds) from Richard's heart or put down the coffin as he has commanded. Clever directors and cleverer actors can polish the *gest* so it gleams:

Richard standing on top of the coffin, the spears of the guards pointed at him like a hunted boar. He swings his ax over the heads of Anne's guards, who lower the coffin submissively.

Or, if you don't trust the guards to lower the coffin smoothly:

Richard suddenly points his sword at the throat of the Gentleman. The guards, in fear, first lower their spears, then their eyes, then their heads. The loud clatter of the spears hitting the ground makes for a pause that alienates what follows.

The actress playing Anne will look at the *gest* while it happens, or turn her head away in fear and disgust, or in some other way *alienate* the moment for the audience—so that the public knows the moment is significant. What grief Anne might feel or exhibit should be focused on the event onstage. If she weeps so feelingly that we sympathize with her and lose the point of the scene, that's the same as if she sobbed so loudly we couldn't hear the other people's lines. Even if that is what the character would have done if she were a real person, *which she isn't*, every actor on stage should cooperate as part of an ensemble to perform the *gest*.

As the guards submit, we learn something about the social relations in the world of this play: even at a funeral, might makes right.

Choose opportunities for opposition

Richard can be gentle and soft while he threatens the guards: "It hurts me more than it hurts you to hold this sword to your trembling larynx." This would be one way to play the opposition, and it would be appropriately charming and witty. Snarling and hissing like a boar at bay might be better, though, since the next lines reveal that the playwright has another opposition in mind.

> ANNE Avaunt, thou dreadful minister of hell!
>   Thou hadst but power over his mortal body,
>   His soul thou canst not have; therefore, be gone.
> GLOSTER Sweet saint, for charity, be not so curst.

This is an opposition of Richard's roles from episode to episode—"unmannerly dog" with the lady's guards, "sweet saint" when speaking to the lady herself.

> ANNE Foul devil, for God's sake, hence, and trouble us not;
>   For thou hast made the happy earth thy hell,
>   Fill'd it with cursing cries and deep exclaims.
>   If thou delight to view thy heinous deeds,
>   Behold this pattern of thy butcheries.
>   O, gentlemen, see, see! dead Henry's wounds
>   Open their congeal'd mouths and bleed afresh!

It was a popular superstition in Shakespeare's day that a corpse would bleed in the presence of its killer. Richard killed Anne's husband, and also her father-in-law, whose corpse lies in front of her. The body bleeds in Richard's presence.

> ANNE Blush, Blush, thou lump of foul deformity;
>   For 'tis thy presence that exhales this blood
>   From cold and empty veins, where no blood dwells;
>   Thy deed, inhuman and unnatural,
>   Provokes this deluge most unnatural.
>   O God, which this blood mad'st, revenge his death!

There's a transaction here. She offers up the blood to God in exchange for righteous punishment. No deal. God doesn't respond. That's the next episode. Here's a caption:

COMBINING EPISODES

> ANNE O earth, which this blood drink'st revenge his death!
>   Either heaven with lightning strike the murderer dead;
>   Or, earth, gape open wide and eat him quick,
>   As thou dost swallow up this good king's blood
>   Which his hell-govern'd arm hath butchered!

There needs to be a *gest* here, too. *Now* Anne can sob loudly, satisfied that everyone is watching her do so. Richard can smile, Anne can weep, the guards can pray. The audience can even sympathize, since they understand that, within the episode, Anne's tears are one side of an opposition that won't help her any more than the guards' prayers.

Identify the transactions

The next episode begins. We'll label it a little later, when we know a little more about its conclusion. It begins with an announcement:

> GLOSTER Lady, you know no rules of charity,
>   Which renders good for bad, blessings for curses.

Richard has just announced the transactions that will follow: "Good for bad, blessings for curses"—*If you call me Saint / I'll call you Devil.*

The line itself can be split. The first part, "Lady, you know no rules of charity" can be said to Lady Anne. But, if you like, "Which renders good for bad, blessings for curses" can be spoken directly to the audience. This report to the audience is not a melodramatic whispered aside. The information is declared at full volume so that the audience watching Gloster and Anne can savor the exchanges that will follow. The actress playing Anne doesn't have to stand there and pretend she doesn't hear this report to the audience. She can respond from Anne's point of view about Richard's rending "blessings for curses."

> ANNE Villain, thou know'st no law of God nor man:
>   No beast so fierce but knows some touch of pity.
> GLOSTER But I know none, and therefore am no beast.

And if the actress playing Anne wishes to, she can make her *own* report to the audience:

> ANNE O wonderful, when devils tell the truth!

The two can vie for the audience's understanding:

> GLOSTER More wonderful, when angels are so angry.

And Richard can return to speaking to Anne:

> GLOSTER Vouchsafe, divine perfection of a woman,
>   Of these supposed evils to give me leave,
>   By circumstance, but to acquit myself.
> ANNE Vouchsafe, defus'd infection of a man,
>   For these known evils but to give me leave,
>   By circumstance, to curse thy cursed self.

The pattern of the transaction is for every curse he'll give her a blessing—perfection for infection, fair for foul, angel for devil. There are more:

> GLOSTER Fairer than tongue can name thee, let me have
>   Some patient leisure to excuse myself.
> ANNE Fouler than heart can think thee, thou canst make
>   No excuse current, but to hang thyself.
> GLOSTER By such despair, I should accuse myself.
> ANNE And, by despairing, shouldst thou stand excused;
>   For doing worthy vengeance on thyself,
>   Which didst unworthy slaughter upon others.
> GLOSTER Say that I slew them not?
> ANNE Then say they were not slain:
>   But dead they are, and devilish slave, by thee.
> GLOSTER I did not kill your husband.
> ANNE Why, then he is alive.
> GLOSTER Nay, he is dead; and slain by Edward's hand.

Another transaction is happening here, as Richard offers Anne his version of her husband's death.

> ANNE In thy foul throat thou liest:

She doesn't seem to be buying this history.

> ANNE Queen Margaret saw
>   Thy murderous falchion smoking in his blood;
>   The which thou once didst bend against her breast,
>   But that thy brothers beat aside the point.
> GLOSTER I was provoked by her slanderous tongue,
>   That laid their guilt upon my guiltless shoulders.
> ANNE Thou wast provoked by thy bloody mind.
>   Which never dreamt on aught but butcheries:
>   Didst thou not kill this king?
> GLOSTER I grant ye.

COMBINING EPISODES

Okay, he'll buy her version. What will Richard want her to grant him in exchange?

> ANNE Dost grant me, hedgehog? then, God grant me too
>   Thou mayst be damned for that wicked deed!
>   O, he was gentle, mild, and virtuous!
> GLOSTER The fitter for the King of heaven, that hath him.
> ANNE He is in heaven, where thou shalt never come.
> GLOSTER Let him thank me, that holp to send him thither;
>   For he was fitter for that place than earth.
> ANNE And thou unfit for any place but hell.
> GLOSTER Yes, one place else, if you will hear me name it.
> ANNE Some dungeon.
> GLOSTER Your bed-chamber.

Here is the essential transaction of the scene. Notice how the playwright helps to alienate the moment by changing the rhythm of the verse. Several overlong lines with twelve or eleven beats—not just the familiar ten—precede two short lines of three and four beats: *some' dun'geon / your bed'—cham'ber.* If you'd like to further admire Shakespeare's technique, notice how the vowels of *some, dun, geon,* and *your* precede the very different sound of *bed.*

The episode is obvious now. If tabloids had been around in the 1480s, they might have read:

KILLER HUNCHBACK PITCHES WOO TO VICTIM'S WIDOW

> ANNE I'll rest betide the chamber where thou liest!
> GLOSTER So will it, madam till I lie with you.
> ANNE I hope so.
> GLOSTER I know so. But, gentle Lady Anne,
>   To leave this keen encounter of our wits,
>   And fall somewhat into a slower method,

The announced change to a slower tempo alienates the lines that follow. But first, there comes another report to the audience, or rather, a question.

> GLOSTER Is not the causer of the timeless deaths
>   Of these Plantagenets, Henry and Edward,
>   As blameful as the executioner?

Anne supplies her own answer.

> ANNE Thou wast the cause, and most accurs'd effect.
> GLOSTER Your beauty was the cause of that effect;
>   Your beauty, that did haunt me in my sleep

89

> To undertake the death of all the world,
> So I might live one hour in your sweet bosom.

The beauty of these lines, alienated by the change in tempo, is meant to be understood as part of an opposition in which the cold-blooded killer speaks rapturous verse.

Notice that Richard is creating a *role* for Anne as his sweetheart. A woman cast as darling to the man whom she hates is, yes, another opposition. The weirdness of the scene is that, say what she will, do what she wants, Anne finds herself playing a love scene. There are at least two personae so far for each of the roles. Richard: Lying Killer and Poetic Lover. Anne: Good Faithful Widow and Poet's Beloved.

> ANNE If I thought that, I tell thee, homicide,
>   These nails should rend that beauty from my cheeks.
> GLOSTER These eyes could not endure sweet beauty's wreck;
>   You should not blemish it, if I stood by:
>   As all the world is cheer'd by the sun,
>   So I by that; it is my day, my life.
> ANNE Black night o'ershade thy day, and death thy life!
> GLOSTER Curse not thyself, fair creature thou art both.
> ANNE I would I were, to be reveng'd on thee.
> GLOSTER It is a quarrel most unnatural,
>   To be reveng'd on him that loveth thee.

That loveth thee! That's the full offer. He offers her his love. Perhaps in exchange for her life?

> ANNE It is a quarrel just and reasonable,
>   To be reveng'd on him that killed my husband.
> GLOSTER He that bereft thee, lady, of thy husband,
>   Did it to help thee to a better husband.
> ANNE His better doth not breathe upon the earth.
> GLOSTER He lives that loves thee better than he could.
> ANNE Name him.
> GLOSTER Plantagenet.

Richard and the men he killed come from the same family, Plantagenet. Offering himself to Anne as a Plantagenet is Richard's deceptive advertising for a contract with a lot of other hidden clauses.

> ANNE Why, that was he.
> GLOSTER The self-same name, but one of better nature.
> ANNE Where is he?
> GLOSTER Here.

He offers himself. A stage direction is included: *she spits at him*. This certainly could be a *gest*. Does Anne hesitate before spitting? Does she do it impulsively? Does Richard wipe it off, let it hang on his face? Lick it as if it were delicious?

> GLOSTER Why dost thou spit at me?
> ANNE Would it were mortal poison, for thy sake!
> GLOSTER: Never came poison from so sweet a place.
> ANNE Never hung poison on a fouler toad.
>   Out of my sight! thou dost infect mine eyes.
> GLOSTER Thine eyes, sweet lady, have infected mine.
> ANNE Would they were basilisks, to strike thee dead!

Basilisks were mythological animals that killed their prey by staring at them. Notice that another transaction is taking place: *If you'll behave like a toad / I'll behave like a basilisk.*

> GLOSTER I would they were, that I might die at once;
>   For now they kill me with a living death.
>   Those eyes of thine from mine have drawn salt tears,
>   Shamed their aspect with store of childish drops;

She gives him spit, he will give her tears; valuable tears at that, as he points out to her:

> GLOSTER These eyes, which never shed remorseful tear,

His tears are rare. Richard never cries—not even at the story of his father's death.

> GLOSTER No, when my father York and Edward wept,
>   To hear the piteous moan that Rutland made
>   When black-faced Clifford shook his sword at him;
>   Nor when thy warlike father, like a child,
>   Told the sad story of my father's death,
>   And twenty times made pause, to sob and weep,
>   That all the standers-by had wet their cheeks,
>   Like trees bedash'd with rain: in that sad time
>   My manly eyes did scorn an humble tear;
>   And what these sorrows could not thence exhale,
>   Thy beauty hath, and made them blind with weeping.

How shall the actor playing Richard do this? By isolating the episode, playing it by itself. Don't manipulate Anne. Don't try to persuade her. Act out the caption:

THE HARDENED KILLER WEEPS

The sight of an actor working up his tears—and calling the audience's attention to his craft in doing so—is quite useful for this episode. In this way and others, Richard's tears are alienated.

GLOSTER I never sued to friend nor enemy;
   My tongue could never learn sweet smoothing word;
   But, now thy beauty is propos'd my fee,
   My proud heart sues, and prompts my tongue to speak.

Another episode is happening here, but it's not one you could necessarily derive from the lines. Once again, for the purposes of analysis we are reversing the usual process of taking notes after the rehearsal. But imagine what is happening onstage. In rehearsal, the episode would be obvious:

WIDOW HEARS THE MURDERER OUT

That Anne stops and does not leave while her husband's murderer speaks at length is a significant onstage event. Why does she do it? It doesn't matter. She does it, and that's enough for you to establish. Let the ladies in the balcony argue why. The opposition Anne can play during this episode is that while Richard is weeping, Anne can be listening critically and yet—against her will—be moved.

   The transaction proposed here is that Anne buy Richard's tears in exchange for her sympathy. Her response to the offer is announced by a stage direction:

She looks scornfully at him.

GLOSTER Teach not thy lips such scorn, for they were made
   For kissing, lady, not for such contempt.
   If thy revengeful heart cannot forgive,
   Lo, here I lend thee this sharp-pointed sword;
   Which if thou please to hide in this true breast
   And let the soul forth that adoreth thee,
   I lay it naked to the deadly stroke,
   And humbly beg the death upon my knee.

He lays his breast open: she offers at it with his sword.

A new caption—HE OFFERS HER HIS LIFE—and with it a new transaction: *You may kill me / but you must accept that you are guilty too.*

GLOSTER Nay, do not pause; for I did kill King Henry,
   But 'twas thy beauty that provoked me.

Anne is unable to pay the price.

GLOSTER Nay, now dispatch; 'twas I that stabb'd young Edward,
   But 'twas thy heavenly face that set me on.

COMBINING EPISODES

Here Anne lets fall the sword. This, too, is a *gest*. The transaction is stated openly now:

GLOSTER Take up the sword again, or take up me.
ANNE Arise, dissembler: though I wish thy death,
   I will not be thy executioner.

Gloster rising is another alienated moment. Anne tries to wriggle out of the deal, but we in the audience know that by dropping the sword she is taking up her husband's killer. Reluctant to pay the price of killing Richard (the mess, the sin, the scandal!), she's accepted his other offer. The proud warrior, rising in front of his lady love, is the meaning of the *gest*—whether Anne likes it or not.

If you consider the scene separately from the *emotions* of the individual roles, and concentrate on what the roles *do* despite their "feelings" (or lack of feelings), another episode can be understood and made clear to the audience. Anne is the Good Faithful Widow, Richard is the Lying Killer. Playing her role of Good Faithful Widow, Anne will not commit the sin of murder, and she will behave according to this role during what follows, even offering her goodness and faith toward a miserable liar—in exchange for more misery and lies. A possible line of interpretation, then, is to label the next episode ANNE EXTENDS HER FAITH TO THE FAITHLESS. Playing this episode, Anne will maintain not just her role as Good Faithful Widow, but also the role Richard has cast her in: his Beloved.

Anne may act on the premise *it is a sin to kill, it is a sin not to forgive*, but the audience does not have to limit their understanding to Anne's understanding. Although the actors will not establish cause and effect as a way to connect this episode with episodes that follow (episodes in which Richard orders the death of children and happily slaughters innocent men), the audience will be able to witness the progression and make up their own minds about the sequence that leads from the personal (her grief, his ambition), to the "larger" and more "political" aspect of the entire scene, which might have as its caption THINKING TO DO GOOD, THE GOOD PROMOTE EVIL.

At this point in the progression, the smaller episode can be labeled ANNE EXTENDS HER FAITH TO THE FAITHLESS. The finer points of their contract follow over the stated offer: *take up the sword / or take up me*.

GLOSTER Then bid me kill myself, and I will do it.
ANNE I have already.
GLOSTER Tush, that was in thy rage:
   Speak it again, and, even with the word,
   This hand, which for thy love did kill thy love,
   Shall, for thy love, kill a far truer love;
   To both their deaths shalt thou be accessory.

In order to better get the sense of this as sales pitch, say it out loud and see where the natural emphasis of the rhythm of the verse hits.

Speak it again, and, even with the word,
This hand, which for thy LOVE did kill thy LOVE,

> Shall, for thy LOVE, kill a far truer LOVE;
> To both their deaths shalt thou be accessory.

Anne now begins to haggle over details of the offer she accepted when she allowed Richard to rise. Within the episode of ANNE EXTENDS HER FAITH TO THE FAITHLESS, Anne weighs Gloster's offer of love:

> ANNE I would I knew thy heart.
> GLOSTER 'Tis figured in my tongue.
> ANNE I fear me both are false.
> GLOSTER Then never man was true.
> ANNE Well, well, put up your sword.
> GLOSTER Say, then, my peace is made.
> ANNE That shall you know hereafter.
> GLOSTER But shall I live in hope?
> ANNE All men, I hope, live so.

The back-and-forth haggling here includes his tongue for her heart, her truth for his truth, his pursuit in exchange for her evasion, and a bargain proposing that Richard's act of putting away his sword be done in exchange for Anne's words of acceptance—or, better yet, her *public* act of acceptance.

> GLOSTER Vouchsafe to wear this ring.
> ANNE To take is not to give.

Anne saying "to take is not to give" could be an episode in itself: ANNE AGREES WITHOUT UNDERSTANDING THE PRICE.

> *She puts on the ring.*

> GLOSTER Look, how this ring encompasseth finger.
> Even so thy breast encloseth my poor heart;
> Wear both of them, for both of them are thine.

The entire scene now seems to be organized around one episode. There is not one interpretation, but several: HUNCHBACK ADVANCES FROM DESPISED KILLER TO LOVER or ANNE AGREES WITHOUT UNDERSTANDING THE PRICE or THINKING TO DO GOOD, THE WIDOW PROMOTES EVIL.

Polish the *gest*

How does Anne receive the ring? Is there a smile on her face? A gleam in her eye? A catch in her throat? Is her head bent away from Richard, even as her hand reaches out to him—an opposition? Does he take her hand in his? Does she slip the ring on herself? Does she shiver as she does it?

From where does Richard get the ring? His own finger? How carefully, quickly, readily does he slip it off? Are his hands clean? Does he treat the ring as if it were valuable? Does he hold it up in the air for the audience to see it sparkle? Does he hold it up in the air so that *Anne* may see it sparkle? Does he drop it? Does he thoughtfully hand it to her in a cloth so her hand doesn't need to touch his? As Anne's hand reaches out for the ring, does Richard playfully snatch it back, alienating her gesture of reaching out to him? Perhaps the guards smile as Anne reaches out for the ring. This, too, would alienate her outstretched hand—and Richard could then play an opposition, deadly serious and disapproving in what should be for him a moment of pleasure.

The rehearsal process of testing, trying, and perfecting these nuances can be thought of as *polishing the gest*. As with forks, so with rehearsals: once polished, the *gest* should gleam, burnished with use and care. *Gests* are not shaped by the internal desire of the characters who perform them; they are physical activities that require an actor's skill, forethought, and practice. They clarify the episode, so that even though Anne says, "to take is not to give," an audience watching the *gest* knows better.

This *gest* of Anne receiving Richard's ring has the potential to alienate a familiar transaction: how once-powerful women accept the favors of unpleasant-but-powerful men. Could the wedding of Jacqueline Kennedy to Aristotle Onassis give you some ideas? He handed her the ring on a pillow. Why? Let the ladies in the balcony argue over the *why*; it's more than enough to present the *how*.

Review the tableaux

You should be able to confirm the episode by comparing the beginning tableau with the ultimate tableau. In this scene, the *gests* resemble photographs in a tabloid: *Richard interrupting the funeral procession. Richard slipping the ring on Anne's finger.* Shakespeare was so concerned that the audience understand what happened in this scene that Richard announces the caption of the episode before the action begins—"I'll marry Warwick's youngest daughter"—and repeats the caption after the episode is complete:

> GLOSTER Was ever woman in this humor wooed?
>   Was ever woman in this humor won?

Let's Review Terms

opposition	contradictions, simultaneous or sequential, deliberately included in a performance in order to create a dynamic fusion of opposing forces
alienation	making the familiar seem strange—or alien—by taking what is familiar out of context

Notebook: Combining Episodes

Richard's role: The Poetic Lover
Anne's role: The Beloved
Transaction offered: *his body*

GLOSTER Why dost thou spit at me?
ANNE Would it were mortal poison, for thy sake!
GLOSTER Never came poison from so sweet a place.
ANNE Never hung poison on a fouler toad.
　　Out of my sight! thou dost infect mine eyes.
GLOSTER Thine eyes, sweet lady, have infected
　　mine.
ANNE Would they were basilisks, to strike thee
　　dead!
GLOSTER I would they were, that I might die at
　　once;
　　For now they kill me with a living death.
　　Those eyes of thine from mine have drawn
　　salt tears,
　　Shamed their aspects with store of childish
　　drops;
　　These eyes, which never shed remorseful
　　tear,
　　No, when my father York and Edward wept,
　　To hear the piteous moan that Rutland made
　　When black-faced Clifford shook his sword
　　at him;
　　Nor when thy warlike father, like a child,
　　Told the sad story of my father's death,
　　And twenty times made pause, to sob and
　　weep,
　　That all the standers-by had wet their cheeks,
　　Like trees bedash'd with rain: in that sad time
　　My manly eyes did scorn an humble tear;
　　And what these sorrows could not thence
　　exhale,
　　Thy beauty hath, and made them blind
　　with weeping.
　　I never sued to friend nor enemy;
　　My tongue could never learn sweet
　　smoothing word;
　　But, now thy beauty is propos'd my fee,
　　My proud heart sues, and prompts my
　　tongue to speak.

gest: She spits at him
(his offer rejected)

Transactions:
toad / sweet
infection / affection
love / spit
spit / tears

Transaction offered:
his tears / for her sympathy

Alienation: the tears are rare

Opposition:
Despite herself, Anne is moved

gest: She turns her head away
so he can't see her reaction

Transaction offered:
his word / for her acceptance

Opposition: The beauty of his speech,
the ugliness of his body and mind

Opposition: Her wanting to be kind to
the cruel

She looks scornfully at him.

GLOSTER Teach not thy lips such scorn, for they
            were made
    For kissing, lady, not for such contempt.
    If thy revengeful heart cannot forgive,
    Lo, here I lend thee this sharp-pointed
            sword;
    Which if thou please to hide in this true
            breast.
    And let the soul forth that adoreth thee,
    I lay it naked to the deadly stroke,
    And humbly beg the death upon my knee.

He lays his breast open:
she offers at (it} with his sword.

GLOSTER Nay, do not pause; for I did kill King
            Henry,
    But 'twas thy beauty that provoked me.
    Nay, now dispatch; 'twas I that stabb'd
            young Edward,
    But 'twas thy heavenly face that set me on.
                She lets fall the sword.
GLOSTER <u>Take up the sword again, or take up me.</u>

ANNE Arise, dissembler: though I wish thy death,
    I will not be thy executioner.
GLOSTER Then bid me kill myself, and I will do it.
ANNE I have already.
GLOSTER Tush, that was in thy rage:
    Speak it again, and, even with the word,
    This hand, which for thy love did kill thy
            love,
    Shall, for thy love, kill a far truer love;
    To both their deaths shalt thou be accessory.

Offer rejected:
She looks scornfully at him

EPISODE: HE OFFER HER HIS LIFE
Transaction offered:
You may kill me / the cost is hidden

gest?: He gets down on
his knees and bares his breast

EPISODE: ANNE CAN'T BRING
HERSELF TO KILL HIM
Transaction offered:
*You may kill me / but you must accept
that you are guilty too*

Offer rejected:
gest. Her hand shaking, but not
reaching the sword or *gest:* He rises

EPISODE: ANNE EXTENDS HER
FAITH TO THE FAITHLESS
Transaction offered:
<u>Take up the sword again /
or take up me.</u>

Transaction offered:
*to replace her old husband /
with a new husband (himself!)*

ANNE I would I knew thy heart.

GLOSTER 'Tis figured in my tongue.

ANNE I fear me both are false.

GLOSTER Then never man was true.

ANNE Well, well, put up your sword.

GLOSTER Say, then, my peace is made.

ANNE That shall you know hereafter.

GLOSTER But shall I live in hope?

ANNE All men, I hope, live so.

GLOSTER Vouchsafe to wear this ring.

ANNE <u>To take is not to give.</u>

She puts on the ring.

GLOSTER Look, how this ring encompasseth thy
        finger.
    Even so thy breast encloseth my poor heart;
    Wear both of them, for both of them are
        thine.

Transactions:
heart / tongue
true / false
her evasion / his pursuit
his act / her words:
he'll put away his sword /
she'll say for all to hear that they're at
peace

EPISODE: ANNE AGREES
WITHOUT UNDERSTANDING THE PRICE
<u>To take is not to give</u>

Offer accepted:
<u>She puts on the ring</u>
gest: Richard slipping the ring on
Anne's finger

Alienation?: He drops the ring, she
reaches for it with a reflex action, the
watching guards smile

Opposition?: Richard is annoyed that
the ring fell and that the guards smile

EPISODE:
HUNCHBACK ADVANCES FROM
DESPISED KILLER TO LOVER
or
ANNE SIGNS A CONTRACT
UNAWARE OF THE PRICE
or
THINKING TO DO GOOD,
THE WIDOW DOES EVIL

Practical Tips for Working

Watch each other

Gests and episodes are aimed at the audience; it's helpful to sit in the audience yourself. If the director will allow you, ask another actor to imitate what you do in a scene. Watch someone else perform your *gest* and learn how effectively it communicates to an audience. You might ask other actors to perform your *gest* their own way and then, like Brecht, help yourself to their ideas.* If you have an understudy, or are doubling a role, watch while the other person rehearses. If you can't get off the stage to get some distance, still try to be aware of the stage picture and what other people are doing around you. These things help to define your role.

Share ideas

Episodic work is collaborative. The people performing an episode need to work together for the same reason machine parts should fit together. This happens more often than you think; learn to pay attention when it does. In the course of rehearsal, a caption will be agreed on informally even if the other actors don't have the will or the vocabulary to discuss a scene in this manner. When someone says, "Let's rehearse the scene where she takes the ring," the caption is being announced for all to understand and agree on. You can start the ball rolling by mentioning your own idea of what happens in the scene to see if anyone else agrees or disagrees with you. It's strategic to put it in the form of a question: *You mean the scene where she practically marries him, right?*

Read the stage directions aloud

Anne has a stage direction to perform: *she spits at him.* Read it aloud at first, rather than acting it out. Understand the transaction and its role in the episode before you work up that saliva. Another useful technique is to say aloud *Anne says* or *I say* before repeating your lines. This alienates the words in rehearsal so that you can examine what is going on in the scene before you take on the responsibility of animating your role with a feeling or a point of view. In his rehearsals, Brecht sometimes had actors insert *I say* or *she says* in the middle of lines in order to alienate overly familiar speech rhythms.

Stage the tableaux first (or imagine them)

When the action of a scene baffles you, try to imagine what the audience would see when the scene begins, and what they would see when the scene ends. What *changes* between the two tableaux? A ring on your finger? How it got there is probably the episode. The moment when it changes is probably the *gest*. A director might choose to stage

---

*A common Brechtian device.

tableaux first before further work on the action of the scene. Even if that doesn't happen, you can picture the tableaux for yourself. Here's a clue for an episode: You enter the room perky and ready for a lesson; by the end of the scene you're carried out dead.

Enjoy the freedom from relentless realism

Realism is one among many styles. Experiment with others. Smash the fourth wall. Worry about externals like posture and diction. Break the illusion of character. Comment on what you're doing. Try alternate ways in rehearsal to *demonstrate* the episode, rather than enact it. Look for inconsistencies as a way to play an opposition. Use direct, even crude ways to get the episode across. You can find more subtle methods later. Expand your ideas of good taste. You can't *be* refined until you have something *to* refine.

Avoid the temptation to include motivation

It's a proud habit of many actors to include motivation in any episode, but it's not always necessary for understanding an episode, nor does it always add anything to the performance. By solving the riddle of *why*, you limit the chance the audience has to provide their own explanation—or enjoy the paradox of inexplicable behavior. Think of it this way: in an episodic performance, you provide the recipe but the audience bakes the cake—and then they complete the experience by eating and digesting the cake at home.*

Avoid the temptation to undermine episodic work with a super-task that dulls the contradictions of a role. Avoid sabotaging your ability to perform an episode by itself by hunting for what cannot be found—like Olga Knipper in her fruitless pursuit for the sources of Natalya Petrovna's whims. If you're playing Lady Anne in *Richard III* you can waste a lot of time in rehearsal trying to motivate that ring scene. *Why* does she do it? Spare yourself and others the question—it isn't your business to answer it.

Think beyond the personal

Just as you sat in the audience to watch what your role did in the context of the stage picture, try to get some distance in your thinking from the emotions of your role in the context of the episode. If the episode for the Lady Anne scene is THINKING TO DO GOOD, THE WIDOW PROMOTES EVIL, you'll need to think about the scene from a point of view other than Anne's. Revealing this aspect of the scene to yourself allows you to reveal it to the director in rehearsal, and to the audience in performance. Brecht and Piscator wanted their actors to make a habit of this awareness and use it actively to eradicate the impulse toward compassion for a role (a compassion Stanislavsky prized highly). Such awareness can be just as deeply felt as compassion. You could call it "political awareness"—Brecht and Piscator would have liked that— but you don't have to.

---

*Brecht allegedly made the charmless comment that if the actors themselves ate and digested the performance as if it were a meal, what was next presented to the audience might be better left in the toilet.

Write a letter to your grandmother

A good way to begin to analyze an episode is to describe what you are doing onstage in a letter to your grandmother, who isn't able to attend the performance:

> Dear Grandma,
> I am in a play. In the first scene I'm minding my own business, quietly working in a library, when a strange man comes in and picks a fight with me.

This kind of direct report of what you *do* while performing a role is what Brecht meant in his example of good acting (remember the actor teaching the role of Hamlet to his understudy?). PS: It's a good idea to write your grandmother anyway.

The Resemblance to Posters

A poster makes a good model for structuring a performance into episodes. Like an actor performing an episode, a poster should relay its information directly and clearly, using whatever means—graphics, pictures, text, layout, color, anything that can be printed on the paper. A poster has to be eye-catching. It has to be understandable to people, no matter who they are. It also has to be understandable to people no matter where the poster is posted: on one wall or another, by itself, or next to two other posters.

Just so, an episode needs to be understood by everyone, by itself, outside of its sequence.

Like actors playing an episode, a poster is meant to tell something, sell something, or, at the very least, relay an idea. Yes, a poster can have an aesthetic appeal. You wouldn't want an ugly or a dull one. But the aesthetic of a poster is different from the aesthetic of a realistic nineteenth-century painting in which artists placed oil glazes onto canvas, layer over layer, in order to create the illusion of depth. A poster maker can accomplish the illusion of depth by overlapping flat shapes. Episodic acting is similarly graphic and direct. It can include the nuances of depth and shading or it can dispense with them and still make its point.

The Chart

Let's return to the chart. Under the column of *Episodic Analysis* there are still some categories to be filled in.

- **Unifying image.** The unifying image is the direct graphic design of a *poster*.
- **The intended reaction of the audience.** Episodic acting encourages the audience to synthesize a story from the progression of episodes. Brecht wanted his audience *to sit in judgment of the action.*

- **The illusion of character.** *Playing the opposition* of roles is the way an actor creates the illusion of depth in character, while organizing a performance episodically.
- **Suitable playwrights.** All plays need to be clear to their audience, and in that sense all plays are suitable for episodic analysis. Some writers wrote using episodic structure, and their work is particularly appropriate for this technique: among many others, *Shakespeare, Samuel Beckett, Gertrude Stein, Harold Pinter, Caryl Churchill,* medieval playwrights, and, of course, *Bertolt Brecht.*
- **The relative theory.** *Marxism* parallels Brecht's elaboration of episodic acting, just as Freud's ideas parallel Stanislavsky's ideas of motivation. This requires some comment and elaboration before we rig up the fig leaf of an alternative theory of transactions and roles: the *psychology of transactions.*

The Social(ist) Context

Brecht's idea of acting—that behavior is commerce—borrows Karl Marx's interpretation of history as an economic process. For Marx and for Brecht, human interaction is a series of transactions: sales, trades, buy-outs, or the collapse of a deal. The idea of oppositions is also part of Marxist thinking studied by Brecht. For some people, the association of Brecht's ideas with the history of Communism has discredited their use in the theater.

The limitations of Marx

Since 1989, when the Berlin Wall fell, life under the Communist system has become the study of coprophiliacs (look it up in a good dictionary!), not actors. On the pettiest level, nobody who has spent time in Soviet countries with open eyes and a working nose can have anything too nice to say about the Communist system. No one who has experienced an entire city being routinely deprived of hot water for a month—because the hot water comes from a central communal supply—can defend the Communist system as a workable idea. When Brecht was asked why he didn't stay in Moscow after 1935, he said it was because he couldn't get sugar for his tea. He wasn't kidding.

Still, a condemnation of the Communist system does not toss out all Communist ideas any more than a child-molesting priest (or ten child-molesting priests or one hundred child-molesting priests) discredits the Christian idea of compassion or the Catholic concept of Grace. It is undeniable that the skills of cooperation should be studied, practiced, and encouraged just as much if not more than the instinct for competition and self-preservation. True, the Communist use of cooperation included cooperative murder—but then the Borgia Popes had their own scurrilous uses for the gracious Sistine Chapel, freshly decorated by Michelangelo.

Brecht prepared a parable to illustrate his own choice between Capitalism and Communism (as if those were the only options!): he was like a doctor with limited resources selecting which patient to assist—an old lecher with terminal cancer (Capitalism), or a pregnant syphilitic whore (Communism). The doctor's sympathies were with the whore. Brecht's sympathies would be with the whore for any number of reasons, but in this case it was principally because she was pregnant with hope for the future.

That's a very nice explanation, and a very good example of the smooth way that Brecht, a Communist apologist, could rationalize the system that deliberately starved to death ten million Ukrainians. Even as he was aware that Stalin's atrocities persisted, Brecht accepted a Stalin Peace Prize. The ability to hold such irreconcilable truths simultaneously is a very good example of opposition. Here's another: To the consternation of the East German authorities, Brecht put most of the prize money in a Swiss bank.

Yet, the relationship that thinking people can be expected to have to the *history* of Communism (repugnance) is not at all the relationship they can be expected to have to Brecht's ideas about *acting*—or his so-far unreachable political ideals. Brecht offers open-minded people a powerful and compassionate understanding of human behavior: that it is necessary to reform the social system to realize a person's potential. Stanislavsky, Freud, and the Protestant work ethic may place responsibility on individuals for their lives. Brecht and the generation shell-shocked by the First World War could not agree. Soldiers didn't die because they lacked enthusiasm. The poor weren't hard-up because they lacked faith, conviction, or moral standards. They were part of a bargain with the rest of society that they did not understand and could not negotiate.

As a society and as individuals, we all enter into contracts we don't recognize, yet these transactions determine our lives. That's why you might pay attention to Brecht's ideas, whatever their source. For actors, Brecht's interpretation of human behavior is applicable to rehearsal, performance, and life.

Transactional analysis

The theories of the Viennese psychologist Alfred Adler also provide a model for interpreting behavior as transactions. If it makes you feel better, you can think of transactions as Adlerian, rather than Marxist. Adler claimed that behavior has an underlying structure of barter, rather than the satisfaction of desire, as Freud and Stanislavsky would have it. According to Adler, when people meet they subconsciously assess each other and unconsciously assume mutually dependent roles. People learn roles from family and society. There, the healthy instinct for conflict between roles is reconciled by unspoken contracts that organize a mediating series of transactions. An example of a transaction agreed on by most children: *I won't shout in order to get what I want, as long as you pay attention to me.*

Adler was trained as a medical doctor and began to counsel patients in 1898, the year that Brecht was born. Adler's first clients were the tailors, acrobats, and clowns who lived in the fairground district of Vienna dominated by a Ferris wheel. Adler saw how the hard-working people he cared for were suffering from work-related diseases, both psychological and physical, and his eyes were opened to the ways in which environment, family habits, and inadequate health care caused depression and other psychological states—just as much as, if not more than, Freud's theories of repressed desire.

Adler's wife, Raissa Epstein, a forthright Russian feminist, further opened Adler's eyes to the ways in which women's behavior and mental health were affected by women's social positions. Through his wife, Adler became a personal friend of the Communist revolutionary Leon Trotsky (they played chess and took their children to the park together). Adler wrote an early paper about the psychology of Marxism. *Cooperation* became one of the keystones of his thinking—how, for example, an infant cooperates with its mother in order to be breast-fed.

Adler's ultimate rejection of the Soviet system and of Stalin's perversion of cooperation were based on first-hand knowledge: his eldest child Valentine and her husband were arrested by Stalin's secret police and disappeared, possibly because of Adler and Epstein's friendship with Trotsky. Adler's opportunities for observation, then, differed from those of Freud, who—besides having had different clients, different friends, and a much more subservient wife—had a daughter, Anna, who grew up to continue her father's life work.*

Like those who map new lands, psychological explorers are given scope by what they encounter in their lives. The same is true for the twentieth-century explorers of episodic acting, whose personal histories shaped how episodic acting was passed on, recorded, hidden—and reviled.

---

*In 1937, on the day before he died, Adler wrote his wife that he planned to go to Moscow himself to find out what had happened to Valentine. In 1945, Albert Einstein, whom Adler claimed as a follower, discovered that Valentine Adler had died in a Siberian gulag in 1942.

CHAPTER 6

THREE LIVES IN THE EPISODIC THEATER

Meyerhold in Russia

The course of three lives influenced the development of episodic acting in the twentieth century. In Germany, there were Bertolt Brecht and Erwin Piscator. In Russia, there was the great innovator Vsevolod Meyerhold, who, coincidentally, was from a German vodka-manufacturing family living in the little town of Penza, 350 miles south of Moscow. A founding member of MXAT, Meyerhold worked as an actor for Stanislavsky and was adept enough to play the central role of the young playwright Treplev in the company's landmark production of Chekhov's *Seagull*. Three years later Meyerhold created the role of the perversely contentious Baron Tuzenbach in the MXAT production of Chekhov's *Three Sisters*.

Stanislavsky recognized his protégé's brilliance early on. In 1905, after the failure of the MXAT *Julius Caesar* and other attempts at staging non-realistic texts, Stanislavsky invited Meyerhold to establish a studio in the new theater Stanislavsky was establishing outside of the Moscow Art Theater. The hope was to discover an approach to acting that would be suitable for non-realistic plays. To Stanislavsky's horror, Meyerhold, claiming to be "extending" his teacher's work, brought back external techniques Stanislavsky had spent his entire life up to then removing from the Russian stage. Stanislavsky even interrupted Meyerhold's last dress rehearsal because the lights weren't bright enough to see the actors' faces. *It goes against psychology!* cried out the Master.

Meyerhold's studio never resumed; its interruption was made permanent by the start of the first Russian revolution. Meyerhold embraced the revolt from its beginning. He became an active member of the Communist party, created plays with and for Bolshevik soldiers, and announced proudly that a new style of politically aimed acting would re-form modern man. Once the fighting subsided, Stanislavsky offered Meyerhold his old role of Treplev in the 1920 revival of *The Seagull*. Meyerhold declined. He was now more interested in directing and teaching acting than in being an actor himself.

Meyerhold searched for historical models for non-motivated acting. He studied and adapted the style and tricks of acrobats and clowns. He looked at the conventions of the ancient Greek theater, the physical craft of the Italian commedia dell'arte, and he analyzed how Shakespeare constructed dialogue, characters, and events without the formula of realism.

PLAYING EPISODES

At first Meyerhold called his work *constructivist theater*, naming it after an art movement of the time, *constructivism*. In constructivism, sculptures were constructed, like eccentric machines, from bits and pieces of other artwork and found objects. In a like manner, Meyerhold was piecing together parts of other theatrical systems. As part of his experiments, Meyerhold placed performers in the audience to explain what was happening onstage, he hung banners over the stage to caption scenes, he turned realistic dialogue into direct address to the public. He urged actors to break their performances into small units. The scenery and props of performances became tools to perform events, not illustrations of time and place.

With these and other innovative techniques, Meyerhold explored episodic acting a good twenty years before Brecht and Piscator. The word *episode*, which is Greek, passed directly into Russian. It recurs throughout Meyerhold's comments to his actors and students, peppers his essays, organizes his preparation notes, and studs his publicity announcements. For Meyerhold, structuring a play into episodes was essential to his work as a director working with actors.

As early as 1904 (when Brecht was six years old), Meyerhold noticed the phenomenon of opposition as an alternative to psychology in the theater. He wrote in an essay:

> It is natural that the rhythmical construction of a play like *Julius Caesar* with
> its precisely balanced conflict of two opposing forces is completely overlooked
> and so not even suggested [in the naturalistic theater] . . . (41)

Meyerhold's experiments with what Brecht would later call *gests* evolved from heightened physical interaction between characters at significant moments in an episode. These were codified in a set of movements called *biomechanics*, often performed by the actors in groups and applied to the performance of the entire play. Remember how classical eighteenth-century actors derived their acting poses from Greek statues? Meyerhold took his vocabulary of actors' movements from the twentieth-century aesthetic of the machine. Under his instruction, performers rotated like ball-bearings, swung their arms like hinges, and connected their bodies together like gears. The ensemble became a living machine for the performance of the play.

This embodiment of a person as part of a machine-like social group echoed avant-garde hopes in newly Communist Russia that a new and freer person—like a new and freer art—could be manufactured scientifically. However, unlike Socialist Realism, Meyerhold's approach included satire and maintained individual points of view. A basic principle of biomechanics was that the actor remain aware of his own outline within the whole stage picture. Meyerhold was eager to have the performer turn his organizing intelligence to this awareness, rather than becoming united with the role his body was performing.

Lenin rewarded Meyerhold for his early loyalty by appointing him commissar in charge of dramatic repertory and acting styles. In his new position of power, Meyerhold was Oedipally ungracious enough to snipe a little at Stanislavsky for his old-fashioned ways. But Meyerhold's challenging work baffled the peasants whose support was necessary to continue the Soviet regime. Lenin's wife wrote little notes to Meyerhold suggesting "improvements" to ensure that the factory workers and farmers who were attending performances would understand what they were seeing.

When Stalin came to power, Meyerhold was deeply in trouble. Stalin wanted an art that could be understood by peasants and he didn't want any fancy stuff, either; just good old realism allied with socialism—Socialist Realism, you could call it. (And they did, if you remember from Chapter 3.) Meyerhold protested, with predictable results. The censors wouldn't allow his productions to premiere. Stanislavsky, whose realistic aesthetic was swallowed whole by Socialist Realism, used his prestige to protect his former student as best he could, which wasn't much. In June 1939, after Meyerhold defended himself at a meeting of the directors' union, he was taken away and disappeared so completely inside a Moscow prison it wasn't even known exactly how and when he died.

It is no accident that Brecht, and not Meyerhold, became the spokesman for episodic technique. The Russian government systematically erased the record of Meyerhold's work from history. Meyerhold's writings stayed unpublished; Stanislavsky's were promoted and publicized. By the end of the Second World War, Meyerhold had become, like many Russian cultural pioneers, a whispered ghost.

Piscator began "epic" theater in an attempt to construct a German version of Meyerhold's techniques and political commitment to socialism. Brecht had seen Meyerhold's work when it was on tour in Berlin in 1930, and then later on in Moscow. But neither Brecht nor Piscator were interested in the vocabulary of a physical style, and biomechanics withered on the vine.

Meyerhold's reputation has been slowly but surely rehabilitated in Russia. Beginning in the 1960s, his writing was published, first in English, then in Russian. Although most of Meyerhold's continuing influence is as a director rather than an acting teacher, biomechanics is once again taught in Russia as well as abroad. Its practices have motivated such adherents of "physical acting" as the influential head of the International School of Theatre Anthropology, Eugenio Barba, as well as others who would fuse the energies of dance, mime, and text-driven theater. In the 1980s the Meyerhold family home was turned into a museum. Visiting the museum today, one can view the everyday articles from the house—including childhood photographs and the piano—that neighbors had hoarded (stolen?) as if they were relics of a saint.* They were subsequently returned once there was a place to display them with respect. The museum includes a large video library, photographs of Meyerhold's productions, models of the scenery, costumes (some original), and a copy of Meyerhold's death certificate next to a painting depicting him standing naked in front of a brick wall, about to be shot.

Piscator in America

Erwin Piscator wisely decided against ever actually going to the German-speaking theater he was planning for Central Asia, and so avoided arrest and murder by Stalin's

---

*The day of Meyerhold's arrest, and just before the secret police arrived, the film director Sergei Eisenstein, who had been Meyerhold's student, spirited Meyerhold's Moscow possessions to his own dacha.

agents. Many of his dedicated comrades—patiently trudging around the Central Asian plains in a wagon in the hope that Piscator would arrive—were not so lucky. When Piscator left Moscow in 1936, he went first to Paris, then took up an offer to stage an adaptation of *War and Peace* on Broadway. The production fell through and Piscator accepted another invitation, to teach at the New School for Social Research in New York City. There he organized a curriculum for professional students and child actors that emphasized the use of opposition in handling texts, and a direct, simple approach to playing the events of a scene.

Piscator was generous with his power. He was the first to hire Lee Strasberg and Stella Adler as acting teachers, although he must have been uncomfortable with some of their methods. Piscator's students went on to become influential professionals: the names claimed as alumni include Walter Matthau, Tony Curtis, Harry Belafonte, Marlon Brando, Rod Steiger, Sylvia Miles, Bea Arthur, Elaine Stritch, and Judith Malina of the Living Theatre.*

As a director, Piscator's productions—Shaw's *Saint Joan* in Washington, among them—were considered too high-minded for American audiences (Harold Clurman's opinion), and met with little success. What little other commercial work came Piscator's way he walked out on, refusing, for example, to attend the opening of his Broadway debut. He had plans for a Jewish theater in Prague and a national Mexican theater, but these projects never materialized. Like a number of German artists who came to America as refugees, including Georg Grosz, Piscator lost his impetus without the springboard of an outrage to protest. He did enjoy the creature comforts of America, among them an expensive broadcloth top coat that he wore open so that its mink lining would be conspicuous. A student called him a "talking Communist, a living Capitalist, and a practicing Fascist" (42).

Piscator's relations with Brecht during this time were problematic. Among other things, Piscator found out that Brecht had smilingly gone behind his back to secure copyrights to a property Piscator assumed was his: their successful 1928 Berlin adaptation of the Czech novel *The Good Soldier Schweyk*.† Nevertheless, in 1945 Piscator began to stage Brecht's episodic *Fear and Misery of the Third Reich* under a new title, *The Private Life of the Master Race*. When Brecht visited rehearsals, he was less than enthusiastic and Piscator quit. The exchange of letters reveals their habitual temperaments (43). Piscator's, for some reason, are written in English!

> Dear Mr. Brecht,‡
> You came late, not to say too late, and your presence didn't help to achieve results and to simplify the complications. . . . when I direct I need the time for myself without your co-directing—and when you direct you need the time without me . . . I suggest that you take over the directing, and I withdraw . . .

---

*Matthau was asked to leave, Belafonte was so miserable at the school that he left after a semester, and Brando got a job just before he was thrown out for lack of discipline.

†Piscator wanted to make a *Schweyk* movie. Brecht, who was aware of these plans, wanted Kurt Weill to collaborate on a Broadway musical version. The legal difficulties scared away investors.

‡They had known each other for over twenty years by this time.

Brecht's sunny answer:

> Dear Pis,
> The ghastly thing is that time is too short to allow one to think out theoretical disagreements.

Brecht thanks Piscator for "preventing anybody from getting the . . . impression that we have become bitter enemies." Piscator's reply, after seeing the show:

> Dear Bert:
> At different moments the other evening I wanted to jump over the footlights, come backstage, and beat you. Not because I personally felt insulted when I saw the results of this work, but at the more objective harm you have done yourself . . .

After this, they never worked together, although they acknowledged their debts to each other publicly as well as privately.

The Living Newspaper

At the time that Piscator was working in America, the United States hatched its own home-grown version of episodic acting. The Living Newspaper, a production of the Federal Theater Project, toured the United States from 1935 to 1939 and played to millions of Americans (44). The performances of the Living Newspaper theatricalized social issues—from slums (*One-Third of a Nation*) to syphilis (*Spirochete*)—with fully researched scripts and elaborate sets. More significantly, and without much theorizing, American actors were encouraged to work in a style of *reportage*; even "realistic scenes" were understood to be in the context of episodes, the way a newspaper article would quote dialogue.

America's Living Newspaper disbanded when the Federal Theater Project had its funds taken away by a Congress worried that the Project's performances of political theater led audiences to criticize the system that had allowed slums and syphilis to proliferate. Sympathy for a problem was fine, but asking questions about how to stop such problems was another thing.* The attacks on the Federal Theater Project by a so-called "House Committee to Investigate Un-American Activities" concluded—without proof, without research, and without corroboration—that "a rather large number" of Federal Theater Project employees were either members of or sympathetic to the Communist party (44). It was suspicious that the head of the Project had been in Europe attending theatrical productions—including those by Meyerhold and Piscator—and in Communist

---

*In 1928, the same thing happened to a similar group in Russia, the Blue Blouses, when Stalin decided that the only possible Communist form of acting would be Socialist Realism's embrace of Stanislavsky. What Stalin really objected to was Blue Blouses's satirical take on contemporary government policy. So it was with the Living Newspaper in America. "Satire is what closes on Saturday night" is the showbiz adage. Now you know why.

Russia, at that. One senator listed titles that "definitely bear the trademark of red Russia in their titles, plays spewed forth from the gutters of the Kremlin" (44). Among these dangerous and indecent titles was Molière's *The School for Wives.** These farcical hearings were an unnoticed dress rehearsal for what was to follow ten years later in the form of what has been called a witch hunt for phantom Communists, not just in the American theater (although there was more than enough of that), but throughout the country.

In 1951, at the height of the Congressional hunt for Communists, Piscator (who was literally a card-carrying member of the party) returned to Europe to stage plays in Germany, Switzerland, Italy, Sweden, and the Netherlands. He was considered for a number of positions at German provincial theaters, but was repeatedly rejected. Piscator was refused so many jobs in Germany that he drew up a note to himself asking whether he had lost his talent or whether his audiences had changed. In 1957 it was his fortunes that changed, and Piscator spent the next five years running West Berlin's Freie Volksbühne. There he staged celebrated world premieres of then-contemporary German plays, among them Rolf Hochhuth's *The Deputy*—refused by other theaters because of its provocative politics portraying the Vatican's relative silence during the Second World War. Piscator died in 1966 in a nursing home after a gall bladder operation, rumor had it after a heated argument with a playwright.

Like Meyerhold, Piscator's influences as a director and stage designer are more obvious and easier to write about than his influence on the actor's thinking, but his innovations in acting technique have entered history in the performances of documentary theater throughout the world. The Living Newspaper has been resurrected in America by varying political theaters. Among many other examples, there are the Living Theatre's continuing performances on the subject of capital punishment called *Not in My Name*, presented every time there is a public execution in America.

Brecht in Exile

Out of Berlin and to France, then to Sweden then to Russia then to Finland, by 1941 Brecht ended up in—of all places—Santa Monica, California. *We changed countries more often than shoes* goes one of his poems (45). Brecht had little interest in learning to speak English,† and less interest in learning about Hollywood politics. Despite good efforts from well-connected friends, he didn't get much work in California, and he didn't want to stay there.

A good story of Brecht in Santa Monica: one day a group of friends took him to see the wonders of the Pacific Coast. They drove north, past magnificent beaches and majestic trees. Brecht smoked a smelly cigar and continued to talk without looking out

---

*The committee was chaired by a Republican Texan congressman in whose district there was a "poll tax," i.e., one paid to be able to vote. It was estimated at the time that he had been elected by less than 9 percent of the electorate. The North Carolina Democrat who made the "spewed forth from the gutters of the Kremlin" remark had a similar relationship to democracy.

†Although he could read it: many books in Brecht's personal library were in English.

of the window. When they got back into town and they were nearing the Santa Monica pier, Brecht made everyone be quiet so he could pay close attention to what was going on between a crowd of sailors and prostitutes.

Aside from the forced leisure time, which bored him, the most significant thing that happened to Brecht in America was his collaboration with the English actor Charles Laughton. The two respected each other, and Brecht set about adapting his play *Galileo* specifically for Laughton to perform the leading role. Neither man spoke the language of the other, which provided a fine opportunity for Laughton and Brecht to mime the episodes and establish the *gests* of the play. It took them three and a half years. Laughton as Galileo opened in 1947 at the Coronet Theater in Los Angeles and on Broadway in New York the following year. The production was received with respect, but nothing more. Like Piscator's productions, *Galileo*'s politics were unappealing to American audiences enjoying newfound prosperity after a ten-year depression and the Second World War.

Before *Galileo* opened in New York, the House Un-American Activities Committee, ten years after it had closed down the Federal Theater Project (and no more educated than before), invited Mr. Brecht to Washington to discuss his politics with them. Brecht had rehearsed with friends before he arrived (his performance included stalling for time while puffing on a cigar), and his responses befuddled the committee (45).

FACELESS BUREAUCRAT ACTING ON BEHALF OF TROGLODYTE SENATORS ACCURATELY REPRESENTING THE POORLY EDUCATED CONSTITUENTS WHO ELECTED THEM Mr. Brecht, have you ever applied to be a member of the Communist party?

BERTOLT BRECHT No, no, no, no, no, no, never.

When asked about his marching songs, included in an American Communist songbook:

FB Did you write that, Mr. Brecht?

BB No, I wrote a German poem. But that is very different from this. (*laughter*)

The first statement is, of course, literally true. Not that Brecht joined the Communist party, but he could have become a member of the party without applying. The second statement could mean any number of things, and throughout his testimony Brecht repeated that he wrote in German and couldn't really claim to be responsible for what the committee was reading in English. Brecht's testimony is such a good example of playing an opposition that the British-born critic and heroic Brecht translator Eric Bentley adapted the transcript into a play. Parts of Brecht's testimony are performed even now at the Berliner Ensemble as part of an anthology of his writing called, in German, *Die Brecht Akte*, compiled by the American actor George Tabori.

The day after his committee appearance Brecht went back to Europe. But not to Germany, no fool he. To Switzerland, where, in 1948, he waited to see what would happen in his native country. In Switzerland he staged *Mother Courage*. While the Berlin Wall was going up, Brecht staged, again in Switzerland, an adaptation of *Antigone*, Sophocles's tragedy on the subject of personal ethics and civic responsibility. The West

German government offered him a theater. The East German government offered him a theater too,* and a paid company of actors. What do you think he did? Of course, he moved to East Germany, but he kept his money in a Swiss bank and he retained an Austrian passport.

The Berliner Ensemble

For the next eight years Brecht ran the Berliner Ensemble and staged the plays he had been brooding over in sunny Santa Monica. He entered yet another period, that of reinterpreting and adapting classic texts into epic and episodic versions: *Coriolanus*, *The Recruiting Officer*, some Molière, and others. His wife Helene Weigel, who had stayed with Brecht throughout his many infidelities, was often the leading actress in these productions.

Throughout this time the East German Communist party criticized his work for not resembling Stanislavsky's. Brecht's decision to locate to East Germany was a propaganda triumph, but his theatrical ideas proved an embarrassment to the Communist regime promoting Socialist Realism. Trying to assuage their patrons, Weigel and Brecht went so far as to claim that their work had some resemblance to Stanislavsky's, but the party hacks weren't buying it. When the Berliner Ensemble toured to Moscow, Communist party critics castigated Brecht's company for its resemblance to Meyerhold's. Of course, they didn't mention Meyerhold's name; they alluded to the "failed formalism of the twenties" (45).

The political solution was to send the theater on tour outside of the Communist orbit, like goods manufactured for foreign consumption but dangerous to keep at home. Beginning in 1943, and for almost sixty years since (and still going strong), the British-born critic Eric Bentley has championed Brecht in America, translating the plays into English and writing influential essays. He also arranged for the production of Brecht's *Private Life of the Master Race* that Piscator walked out on. Bentley was a personal friend of Brecht's, and as a young man he stayed as a house guest with Brecht in Santa Monica while *Galileo* was in rehearsal. Bentley quietly differed from Brecht in several fundamental ways. In a postscript to his *Brecht Memoir* (1989), Bentley makes the fascinating comment that his unspoken differences—he was gay, at first pacifist, then anti-Communist—actually helped Bentley to understand Brecht better than those who shared Brecht's personal values. When the Berliner Ensemble's tour of *Mother Courage* played London and Paris, Bentley was joined in his efforts by Roland Barthes in France and Kenneth Tynan in England.

Among intellectuals, the Berliner Ensemble was added to the Moscow Art Theater as a place of pilgrimage. Although Brecht's works as a writer, director, and acting theoretician were collected, printed, photographed, and translated throughout the world, his plays were not often performed in Communist countries—including East Germany—until he was safely dead.

---

*Actually, they offered him someone else's theater—which Brecht accepted while he waited for his own, the present Berliner Ensemble, to be renovated.

After Brecht died, the Berliner Ensemble continued under Helene Weigel's leadership. Apocryphal rumor has it she fired almost all the actresses, not out of jealousy, but because their primary responsibility—sleeping with Brecht—was no longer necessary. After Weigel died in 1971, the revolutionary forms of the Berliner Ensemble froze. After the reunification of Germany in 1992, the political mission of the company grew questionable and funding from the state declined. In the summer of 1999, the company decided to disband and reform with a new identity. Ironically, the Ensemble's last performances were in California.

In the year 2000, the Berliner Ensemble shifted its emphasis to premieres of texts by living German authors, although the company performs the biographical *Die Brecht Akte*, and maintains as a signature piece in its repertory Brecht's version of *Richard III* that is set—like *In the Jungle of Cities*—in Chicago, and called, after its central character, *Arturo Ui*. *Arturo Ui* at the Berliner Ensemble is performed in the Heiner Müller staging of 1964, which emphasizes the character's resemblance to Adolf Hitler. In April 2000, a performance of *Arturo Ui* held on Hitler's one hundred and eleventh birthday began outside the theater with an actor delivering a repetitive speech (written by Hitler himself) over a microphone in a Nazi-era squawk from a balcony to the street. Inside the theater, the actor in the Richard role, a popular television performer, began on all fours like a dog, barking and growling. The progression of episodes was quite clear: a wild beast rises to become a lord among men. The equivalent of Richard's scene with Lady Anne took place with the Richard character raping the widow on top of the corpse of her dead husband (not father-in-law), the widow's head between the corpse's splayed doll legs—a very clear *gest*, simultaneously funny and grotesque.

Brecht's Influence

In England

Brecht's point of view and politics were formed after the collapse of the Kaiser's Germany in the First World War. They resonated in England after the collapse of the British Empire and the reorganization of British life following the Second World War. Thus, so far, Brecht's major influence among professional actors and directors has been in England. His techniques offer new insight into the interpretation, staging, and acting of the classic texts that are the core of the British repertory system. Mindful of Brecht, British directors like Joan Littlewood and Peter Brook taught their actors the basic skills of episodic performance. Littlewood's productions, in particular, stressed ensemble work, clear *gests*, and direct address, not only in productions of Brecht's plays, but in the performances of new plays by modern British writers.

British playwrights capitalized on the abilities of British actors to perform a role within an episode just as American playwrights capitalized on the technical skills of American actors trained to perform emotional recall. Among the post-war British playwrights who wrote episodic texts with oppositional characters: Harold Pinter, Edward Bond, and Tom Stoppard. The style has been especially useful for those playwrights, like

Caryl Churchill and David Hare, who question traditional British society's assignment of roles to women, poor people, and minorities.

In the continuing struggle around the world

Episodic theater renews itself as part of social struggle in third-world countries. In Brazil and the Philippines, in Africa and India, political theaters have adapted Brecht's techniques to perform texts in indigenous as well as colonial languages. News accounts of slaughter, presentation of national heroes, and reenactments of grand historical times are performed in villages throughout the world on open ground between mud huts— with the intention of inciting political action. Approaches to theater in the Philippines (46) and in a number of African countries, among them Tanzania, Kenya, Zimbabwe, and the Union of South Africa have included episodic techniques modeled on approaches from Eastern Europe and Communist China (47).

Episodic Acting With and Without Brecht

In America

Recognized or not, episodic structure organizes such disparate American playwrights as Sam Shepard, Gertrude Stein, and Thornton Wilder. Established political theaters in America, such as the rural Bread and Puppet, the San Francisco Mime Company, and the Living Theatre (thriving since 1947; its co-artistic director Judith Malina studied with Piscator), all combine social activism with episodic acting techniques. The technique of playing episodes is taught at influential and official conservatories.

Because Brecht was a Communist, his influence was kept quiet among his Hollywood connections. When the RDF—the French equivalent of England's BBC radio— asked Charles Laughton for a quote about Brecht on the occasion of Brecht's death, Laughton dodged the interview and avoided the possibility of getting himself entangled in the House Un-American Activities Committee.

Acknowledged or not, Charles Laughton's ideas of performance had altered after his three and a half years with Brecht. The one film Laughton directed, *The Night of the Hunter* (1955), can be viewed as a checklist of episodic skills. *Opposition* organizes the acting throughout. Robert Mitchum plays a preacher who murders widows so he may use their money to praise God. *L-O-V-E* is tattooed on the knuckles of the preacher's right hand, and *H-A-T-E* on the knuckles of his left. In one sequence, the two hands wrestle with each other, *alienating* the struggle inside the hypocrite. In public, the preacher is kind and gentle with women, in private he humiliates his new wife. The couple's relationship is established by a *gest* on their honeymoon night. After the preacher humiliates his bride, he rolls over in bed facing away from her. Shelley Winters, who studied acting with Laughton, plays the bride (in the year before her performance in *A Place in the Sun*).

The characters often perform their roles reluctantly, like the hangman who washes his hands after a day's work and wishes aloud he had some other line of business. The wide-eyed Lillian Gish from the silent film *Orphans of the Storm* plays a rescuer of orphans—who packs a rifle. Almost all the shots are stagy and include crowds, families, or groups that give the individual figure significance within a social setting. The hangman's wife is seen behind the sink, disapproving of her husband's scruples. The screenplay, credited to James Agee, is an adaptation of the 1953 novel by Davis Grubb, and often incorporates tableaux. One vivid shot shows Winters sitting dead under the water with her throat slit and her hair trailing—remarkably similar to an image out of a ballad Brecht sang in a Berlin cabaret many years before. The actors (Mitchum excepted) seem to be following Laughton's direction without completely understanding what it is they're being asked to do.

To watch actors using episodic techniques with an awareness that they are doing so, study any one of the performances in Martin Scorsese's *Raging Bull* (1980), the biographical story of the heavyweight boxer Jake La Motta. Although it was shot in black and white, the film contains a few scenes presented as faded color "home movies" with the actors playing directly—but silently—to the camera: waving and mugging, obviously aware that they are creating something artificial. One character gets married, another has children, and these episodes in the story are communicated by *gests*: a ring on the hand, a baby on the lap.

The riveting performance given by Robert De Niro in the role of Jake La Motta is a dynamic opposition of self-doubt and aggression. His identity is a series of often contradictory roles: winner, loser, lover, scold, bewildered animal, cocky braggart. In the last scene, the former champion, now down on his luck, prepares for a nightclub appearance. Sitting in his seedy dressing room and looking into the mirror (his face is reflected inside a square reminiscent of a boxing ring), La Motta delivers a long monologue from Budd Schulberg's script for the film *On the Waterfront* (1954), alienating the words of the text—with what amounts to a caption—by first announcing: "Some People Aren't That Lucky."

Smoking on a cigar, De Niro recites the words to the speech in a stilted and awkward way, including *I could have been a contender*—a line made famous in *On the Waterfront* when delivered by Marlon Brando as a passionate cry. The meaning of the text and the parallel to the character's situation are inferred by the movie audience and De Niro, but not by the emotional situation of the La Motta character. The image of a boxer in a ring as a metaphor for life can, of course, be found throughout Brecht's writings on the theater (as well as in *In the Jungle of Cities*), but no direct or indirect link—not even the cigar—is necessary to explain the use of oppositions, *gests*, and alienation. After all, the use of episodic techniques in film dates back to the beginning of the medium.

In the cinema

When the invention of cinema created a new venue for acting, performers called on episodic technique to satisfy the technical demands of recording scenes on film. To begin with, the inability of the early equipment to record sound meant film scripts replaced dialogue with scenarios that described events to be performed in front of the camera, often through improvisations. The lack of sound forced actors to establish episodes clearly, without words.

An early film canister could hold only enough film to record a sequence lasting one minute. Even as late as 1949, the maximum duration of a shot was less than ten minutes. Short sections, then and now, were compiled into a sequence, but only later, after the performers had concluded their work. Directors could, did, and do ask actors to play the middle of a performance before the beginning. Working out of sequence, it was impossible for an actor to play a *through-line*; it was necessary to perform the event to be recorded by the camera as a separate unit, or episode.

As in any theatrical episodic performances, the episode of a film needs to be understood in common by an ensemble. The director, the performer, and the technicians must all agree what the point of the shot is before the film is exposed to record it. Lillian Gish worked in film until she was ninety. Remember the seven-year-old Lillian's first and only acting lesson? *Speak loudly and clearly so that everyone in the theater can hear you—or they'll get another little girl who can.* That sums up the intention of episodic acting: play so that everyone in the theater understands. Seven years old or seventy, on stage or in front of the camera, that's your job as a performer.

In the future

The demands of videotape, performance art, and rapid editing techniques continue to transform what an actor is expected to contribute to a performance. Playing episodes, cooperation within the ensemble to perform each episode, and the subordination of character to a role within an episode are the essentials of episodic acting. These reappear no matter what new venues for performance appear.

Yet there is no single written source, like Stanislavsky's, for actors to learn the vocabulary of episodic acting. Brecht's writing on the epic theater is theoretical and aimed at directors and writers much more than actors. His practical advice is sketchy and often contradictory. Along with Brecht's charts and essays in *Brecht on Theater*, the excellent critical biographies of Brecht, among them Martin Esslin's *Brecht, The Man and His Work* (1971) and *Brecht for Beginners* (1984) written by Michael Thoss, need to be combed through for something as simple as the practical application of alienation.

Any examination of Brecht and his system often drifts into a distracting discussion of the plays and the fascinating contradictions of Brecht's life. This book has fallen into the trap as well, but Brecht's life experience colors his ideas to such an extent that you need to understand that experience before you can extract or discount, say, the Marxist basis for transactions.

Although Brecht is not the only master of episodic theater, others don't offer much in print. Piscator wrote very little about his objective theater. His students and colleagues wrote less. What few books there are report on the physical productions and extol the political mission, rather than extol the reportage of the actors.* Meyerhold,

---

*The exception to this, and the fullest account, appears in John Willet's out-of-print *The Theatre of Erwin Piscator* (Holmes & Meier Publishers, 1979).

though he went so far as to set up schools to train student actors, never lived long enough to complete a technique book for performers. His ideas for such a thing can be gleaned from his collected essays *Meyerhold on Theater* (1969) and Alexander Gladkov's *Meyerhold Speaks, Meyerhold Rehearses* (1997). What has been published since is about Meyerhold's staging techniques—rather than his acting—and mostly concerns itself, understandably, with reviving biomechanics.

These chapters aim to rescue episodic acting from its history, its politics, and the lives of its founders. Episodic acting will always be around, and needs to be studied, practiced, and developed further.

One more story from Brecht's Santa Monica exile: While she was watching rehearsals for Laughton's *Galileo*, Shelley Winters noticed a German janitor picking up pieces of paper in the back of the theater and putting them in the trash. She felt sorry for him and brought him to meet her parents, who spoke German. The janitor returned weekly for Shelley's father's Friday night card game. Years later, when she went to see George Tabori's *Die Brecht Akte* in New York (where it was called *Brecht on Brecht*), Winters realized from a photograph that was hanging on the proscenium arch that the janitor was the playwright. She called her mother. "Mr. Brechstein? We always thought he was a costume jeweler." When asked what he did in the old country, Brecht had told Shelley's parents: "I made jewels for poor people" (48).*

Brecht was using an *image* to describe himself—our next subject at hand.

---

*Winters writes: "He always looked lonely and hungry" (48).

117

PART III

BUILDING IMAGES

Reading List
The Maids by Jean Genet
Yerma by Federico García Lorca
Stanislavsky in Focus (chapters 2 and 6) by Sharon Marie Carnicke

Viewing List
Dinner at Eight directed by George Cukor
Touch of Evil directed by Orson Welles

Max Ernst, detail from *Quietude*

CHAPTER 7

Masks

Olivier's Nose and Your Mother's Hat

Laurence Olivier had the good luck to be born into a time and place that recognized his talent and offered opportunities to apply it. In 1916, at the age of ten, he played Brutus in a school production in London, a startling performance that happened to be attended by the celebrated actress Ellen Terry. She wrote in her diary: "The small boy who played Brutus is already a great actor" (49). In 1972, at seventy-eight, Olivier played King Lear (on television). With nearly ninety-eight stage productions in between, he is widely admired as one of the greatest actors of his or any generation.

It was sometimes Olivier's practice to begin work on his most difficult roles by changing the shape of his nose. He also liked to rig himself out with wigs, false teeth, and putty for his forehead and chin. More than once he began the job by disguising his voice. Olivier's Othello spoke almost a full octave lower than the actor's natural pitch, an effect he worked at for several months before rehearsals began. He used what appealed to him. For the role of Richard III, Olivier based his characterization, in part, on the Big Bad Wolf from the Disney cartoon version of *Little Red Riding Hood*.

"I'm afraid I do work mostly from the outside in," Olivier said in response to an interviewer asking about his craft. He went on to say, "Perhaps I should mention what everybody's been talking about for years, and that's the Actors Studio and the Method. What I've just said is absolutely against their beliefs, absolute heresy" (50).

Olivier's heresy is any actor's healthy instinct, a child's pleasure in pretending to be someone else by putting on mother's hat. Mother's hat or rubber nose, it's playful to assume another person's character. That's why, in English, we speak about acting in a *play*, not a *depression*. The necessary prop for the game of pretending to be someone else is a mask, and although they don't cover the whole face, your mother's hat and Olivier's fake nose are both masks. In addition to his *visual mask*, Olivier's lowered pitch as Othello was a *vocal mask*. Changing the sound of his own voice helped to transform the British actor into a Moorish general as effectively as, if not more than, his three layers of black make-up.

Masks make appealing toys for children—and for actors—by offering the possibility of acting out fantasies safely and playfully. The camouflage of a mask gives you permission to shout, to rage, to love indiscriminately, to break rules without fear of punishment, or to obey rules you wouldn't ordinarily care about. A mask puts you at a distance from your actions; it is the character—not you—who rages, who flirts, who kills. The joy in this is so strong that many cultures have occasions, like Mardi Gras, when ordinarily sober people may safely act out flamboyant behavior they would never consider at any other time—once they slip on a mask.

For a professional actor, masks make powerful tools that do more than masquerade. The mask also serves to unleash hidden personality traits. Look at Olivier's nose. He couldn't. Although the actor couldn't see his own nose onstage, it nonetheless had as potent an effect on him as it did on the audience. For any actor who chooses to do so, an outer mask may evoke a yet more play-sustaining *inner mask*.

Inner masks, which we'll call *images*, have the power to transform an actor as effectively as any disguise. Some actors skip the outer masks entirely by the time they get to performance—including wigs and costume changes—and base their transformation to another person on an inner foundation. Eleonora Duse, for example, performed without make-up. Her ability to transform her height, her age, and her appearance derived from inner images, described by more than one observer as an inner flame. From 1905 to 1956, the American solo artist Ruth Draper performed without scenery, but with sufficient conviction to persuade her audiences that they were witnessing a crowded church when there was nothing onstage but the actress, curtains, and a plain chair. Draper herself needed little more than a shawl or a hat to transform from one character to another. The tradition endures. The American actress Anna Deveare Smith has played Hasidic Jews, African-American politicians, and Korean grocers with little more than a switch of her hat.

In an effort to sweep clichés from the stage, 1950s partisans of what was understood to be the Stanislavsky System (following the interpretation called "The Method," discussed in Chapter 3) were proud to exclude external masks, which they called "working from the outside in," not just during performances but at rehearsal, too. The orthodox way for a Method actor to work was to get in touch with the deep-felt memories of personal experience. From that point of view, Olivier's claim to "heresy" was true.

Of course, the alleged heresy of an external choice is just another road to inner reality. Look at the example of Sarah Bernhardt, an actress accused of so divorcing inner from outer images that it was said she could play a death scene with one hand sticking out from behind a screen and, with her other hand unseen by the weeping audience, wave hello to a friend in the wings. Sarah Bernhardt was, in some ways, the successor to the great Rachel, who had died young of consumption. Bernhardt was Jewish too, or at least her mother was a Jew, which for most Jews is what counts. As for her father, better you shouldn't ask. When it came to actresses, at least, the French were interested in classical poses, not bloodlines.

Bernhardt could stand and recite with the best of them, in a voice described as molten gold. Her body was unusually thin. She was teased about her thinness as a girl and ridiculed for it as a woman—until her own fame made being slim fashionable. Onstage, her fragility contrasted well with the volcanic energy she displayed. She had the good taste to include some stately classical gestures, but she also could—and would—abandon herself to the moment and writhe, twist, and swoon, her golden voice swooping from croak to croon. Bernhardt's technique was spine-tingling. Contemporaries compared her showmanship to Duse's realism, with a full understanding that these were rival ideas of what was great art.

Yet Bernhardt's devices were not meant to simply dazzle the audience—they were meant to dazzle Bernhardt. When she was asked why she painted henna on the palms of her hands as Cleopatra—a detail the audience would never notice—she said she did it so that if she looked at her own hands, they would be those of the Queen of Egypt. At sixty-five, with a wooden leg, Bernhardt would play the teen-age Joan of Arc* and audiences found her convincing (51). What difference did it make how old she really was? The performance of the gestures and the timbre of the voice created the illusion of character onstage, but more importantly, they convinced the lady herself that, in her own mind, she was a young girl again.

Ruth Draper once asked Eleonora Duse if Duse knew how she made herself seem larger or taller, depending on the role, something Draper herself could do without knowing how she did it. Duse laughed. Duse had asked Bernhardt, who had told her to ask Draper.† For all their differences in personal style—Draper alone onstage, Duse seemingly bare of technique, Bernhardt smothered in grandiosity—all three of them relied on the same source to power their performances: *personal inner images.*

Literary critics speak of images when they look at how words of the text set up patterns, like musical motifs. In *Macbeth*, for example, when the text mentions *clothes*, the clothes are uncomfortable. This discomfort points a clever actor to an understanding of Macbeth's guilt. (This kind of text analysis is very useful for a performer, and we will talk about it at length in Part IV: *Inhabiting the World of the Play*.) Still, an actor's use of a play is *personal*, and actors working with images must do something literary critics need not: clarify the meaning of the text by relating the words to themselves.

For now, when we refer to *imagery analysis* we are talking about an actor's internal set of images, and how an actor's idiosyncratic and personal set of images can be united with a script to yield results of great power and emotional truth. When it works, it makes for electric performances. Performers who use such images act as creative as well as interpretive artists. They arrive at rehearsals with their own sets of ideas, that is to say, the masks, external and internal, which move them to *play* in both senses of the word: as children and as mature professionals.

Ignore the playwright's images—for now

This part of the book is about the ways actors might first build their own personal images and then apply them to embody the images of the playwright and the play. Why ignore the playwright's images in order to return to them? Simply put, they are the playwright's images, not yours—at least not yet. It does happen, of course, that the words of the text will prod direct responses from your gut. If you are a lucky actor, you'll get the roles you are born to play; in preparation and performance your personal content

*The play was Emile Moreau's *Procès de Jeanne d'Arc*.

†Draper met other theater greats that month she was in Paris. In her diary, she noted that she had had a nice talk with Stanislavsky and that he was a wonderful man.

will be very rich. Interestingly, this does not necessarily happen when your life experience parallels your character's. Such a close resemblance can paralyze a performer instead of bestowing the detachment and freedom that a mask offers.

The playwright's words have the power to paralyze a performer in other ways. The beauty and complexity of the play's imagery will sometimes intimidate you so much that your own understanding seems insignificant and the play unapproachable. And, yes, there are times when you will not be moved by the playwright's images, or, if you are moved by evocative words on the page, you will often not have had the life experience (say, killing yourself, if you're playing a suicide) to grasp the playwright's ideas or the character's feelings.

In such situations, you want to try to use an image of your own to give content to what you are saying. Although Lillian Gish summarized her training as speaking so everyone could hear her, if you are going to ask twelve or twelve hundred strangers to sit in the dark and listen to you recite, perhaps you had better bring more than a loud voice to your role. You might bring something to say about the text. Better still, you might find ways the text is meaningful to you and your life, too, or the management will find someone else for whom it is meaningful. Without personal content, performances are essentially inhuman, even when they are technically proficient.

The Rosetta Stone and Images of the Play

The words of a play you do not understand, no matter how beautiful or profound, resemble rows of unreadable hieroglyphics. They will stay unreadable until you carve yourself a personal *Rosetta Stone*. What's the Rosetta Stone? In 1799, French archeologists accompanying Napoleon's Egyptian Expedition to the Rosetta arm of the Nile discovered a slab of granite inscribed with writing in two languages, Ancient Greek and Egyptian hieroglyphics. Ancient Greek was still read in Napoleon's France, thanks to monks and librarians who preserved and translated classical texts. The ability to understand Egyptian hieroglyphics, however, was long forgotten.

This stone with the same information in two languages became a key to reading hieroglyphics once the decipherers compared the hieroglyphics to the Greek. How did they know the text was the same in Greek and hieroglyphics? Because the few words they did recognize were famous names—among them, Cleopatra's*—and these names were repeated in the same place in both texts.

The process is the same for you as a performer using your own images—the language you know—to decipher the images of the play. Out in the desert of rehearsal, whipped by the hot winds of scorn, you'll be digging up your own Rosetta Stone to unearth your own key to translate the hieroglyphics of the script. Remember that no matter how beautiful the playwright's hieroglyphics might be, if you can't understand them,

---

*Not Bernhardt's or Liz Taylor's Cleopatra, but an ancestor of the Serpent of the Nile who lived 150 years earlier, in 196 BCE. A few other words that could be recognized on the Rosetta Stone in both languages were *temples, Greeks,* and the word for *him* (third person masculine pronoun). Hmmm.

neither will the audience. At first, you may make contact with only a few places—like Cleopatra's name—but eventually you will begin to translate more and more of the play.

Strindberg's Dreams

To prepare ways to use your own images in the theater, it's inspiring to learn about the playwrights for whom imagery—rather than plot or character—is at the heart of a play. At the same time that Chekhov and Ibsen were challenging nineteenth-century story-dominated melodrama with character-dominated realism, the Swedish writer August Strindberg was creating dramatic texts dominated by images. Strindberg was part of the movement toward greater realism in the theater, yet his idea of what was real was not a common one. He was convinced of the existence of vampires. He was certain that women were in a conspiracy to steal power from men. He believed that the world glowed from within with psychic energy. Ibsen kept a picture of Strindberg over his desk, and referred to the fiery-eyed Swede in the portrait as *that madman*. Strindberg did in fact spend time in a sanitarium. More than once in his life he was willing to travel across the borders of insanity in order to retrieve a vision. August Strindberg was, at times, willfully mad, just as Brecht willfully stank.

The attempt to explain human behavior as a logical mechanism, a task that fascinated actors like Stanislavsky, psychologists like Freud, novelists like Zola, and playwrights like Brecht, held no such fascination for Strindberg. Neither poses nor motivated behavior could fully satisfy the requirements of a Strindberg play like *The Ghost Sonata*, *To Damascus*, or *A Dream Play* (in which dead men walk, a castle melts into a chrysanthemum, and goddesses descend from heaven). Strindberg stated the method to his madness in his Author's Note to *A Dream Play* (52), written in 1901:

> In this dream play, the author has . . . attempted to imitate the inconsequent yet transparently logical shape of a dream. Everything can happen, everything is possible and probable. Time and place do not exist; on an insignificant basis of reality, the imagination spins, weaving new patterns; a mixture of memories, experiences, free fancies, incongruities and improvisations. The characters split, double, multiply, evaporate, condense, disperse, assemble.

That's an excellent description of the process of an actor building images of a role; any role, not just those in dream plays. You'll notice when you rehearse with images that they do not advance logically, methodically, or deliberately. In rehearsal and in performance, inner masks do indeed split, double, multiply, evaporate, condense, disperse, and assemble—just as Strindberg described.

As you build a collection of images, an illusion of character is created that is as convincing as any created by pursuing a task or playing a role in an episode. Often, creating a role by building images is a faster and bolder process than running actions into obstacles or haggling over transactions. This dynamic idea—*identity as a shifting collec-*

tion of images—echoes a theory of psychology developed by a Freudian heretic, the Swiss-born psychologist Carl Jung.

Carl Jung and Mythology

Carl Jung began as Freud's distinguished disciple, just as Meyerhold began as Stanislavsky's protégé. Jung was nineteen years younger than Freud, the older man's hope for the future in the new science of psychology. Yet, just as Meyerhold diverted the course of Stanislavsky's revolution by offering another approach to acting besides identifying needs and taking actions onstage to satisfy them, Jung offered another explanation for behavior besides Freud's identification of desire.

What Freud called Jung's "betrayal" happened by 1912, after Freud had established psychology as a discipline and had refined his definition of human motivation as the collision of desire and present circumstances. We've already discussed how those ideas parallel Stanislavsky's insistence on an actor having a task in a performance, where actions encounter obstacles. What Jung noticed and thought important—an insight later corroborated by many other psychologists—is that sometimes people behave in certain ways because, consciously or not, they are acting out an image, rather than fulfilling a desire. These images fill a pattern in a story so deeply-believed that the story can be called a *personal myth*. When adolescents, for example, smoke and drink to excess, it's because they are acting out a myth of *rebellion*. Weak people become strong under pressure because they are acting out an inner image of *strength and power*. Jung observed the same wars that Brecht observed and concluded that soldiers run off to be killed not for any logical reason, but because they are acting out a myth of *chivalry and patriotism*. Jung claimed that identifying a person's mythology of internal images explained human behavior and identity just as thoroughly as, and perhaps more than, analyzing a person's motivation, desire, or toilet training.

To take an example from a play, Hedda Gabler is a general's daughter. She issues orders to her husband as if he were a soldier; when her life defeats her she shoots herself dead using the general's pistol, the way a warrior who has lost a war might kill himself. Hedda has a man's self-assurance in a world of deferential women because her *image* of herself is *masculine*.

Jung's theories apply to the work of an actor because, for Jung, images are not isolated or self-sufficient, they are entire systems of relationships, to other people and to the world. Hedda's mythic role as General's Daughter casts Løvborg as her Incompetent Captain, and her husband as a Naïve Civilian. In real life, when people fantasize that they are persecuted, they assign other people the role of Persecutors. An actor who reinterprets the roles and events of the play according to an image is reproducing that process.

Archetypes and personae

Jung observed that people wear different masks in different situations: we are children in the presence of our parents, we are parents in the presence of our children. As peo-

126

ple make their way through their lives they acquire new and different masks, from apprentice to master, from virgin to bride. Onstage or off, these collections of masks are what we call "character."

- Woman, Temptress, Harlot's daughter, Mother, Actress, Eccentric, Romantic, Ugly Little Girl . . . *voila*: Sarah Bernhardt!
- Woman, Wife, Actress, Agitator, Survivor, Refugee, Technician, Head Wife Among Many . . . *ach so*: Helene Weigel!
- General's Daughter, Bored Wife, Romantic Lover, Town Beauty, Newlywed, Tortured Soul . . . *ja ja*: Hedda Gabler!
- Insightful Doctor, Stern Prophet, Noble Father, Trouble-making Jew . . . *oy vey*: Sigmund Freud!

When an actor creates a role by building images, he reproduces the way people collect images for "acting out" the roles of their life. Some of these roles are universal, which Jung called *archetypes* (*Woman, Wife*), some are cultural (*General's Daughter, Trouble-making Jew*), some are historical (*Romantic, Refugee*), some are professional (*Actress, Harlot*), some are personal (*Ugly Little Girl*—which was all too clearly a personal image of Bernhardt's—and *Head Wife*—who knows what Helene Weigel really thought of Brecht's philandering?). Each of us is a collection of masks, which Jung called *personae*, carved for us and by us as a result of our life experiences. The word *persona* is Latin for an "actor's mask."

Jung believed that these images were gateways to what he called the *collective unconscious*. In their own particular way, your myths and personal history echo everyone else's myths. The content of a *mother archetype* will remain the same as long as there are people, even if the form of the archetype is culturally and personally determined. Your Chinese mother urging you to eat rice is also an Italian mother passing the pasta and, yes, a Jewish mother pushing the chicken soup, because it's the same the whole world over: for mothers, Food is Love.

As an actor, you play from your own images knowing that you will connect to the archetypes of the audience. You can stuff yourself with ravioli, content that the Beijing audience watching you is relating to their own experience with wontons.

The String of Masks

The rehearsal process using images can be thought of as carving yourself a **string of masks**. You can do this by creating an outer mask (Olivier's nose) or an inner mask (Duse's flame). Either way can lead to the other and to the audience. Even the most personal and private images have the power to communicate with an audience when those images are heartfelt. Members of the audience can tell when an actor crosses a bridge to the subconscious world, and they can be persuaded, by the actor's example, to cross over on their own—to the collective unconscious. Just as the audience is meant to be sympathetic watching a performance structured by tasks, or prodded to judgment by the presentation of oppositions, an audience in the presence of deeply felt images is meant to become impassioned. Even a performer's most personal and private images can move an audience—if they are images that move the performer.

A strong image resonates with an audience, but does not necessarily echo or reconstruct itself in their hearts and minds. For example, if you care passionately about beans, it is your passion the audience will respond to, not necessarily split peas and lentils. Audience members will not always share the same image, nor should they. They will relate your passion to passions of their own.

There is a passage from Balzac's novel *Father Goriot* (1834) that gives an illustration of the power of images. An ambitious young man is listening to a father explain why he lives like a beggar so that his daughters may live like princesses:

> There was something sublime about Father Goriot; Eugene had never, till now, seen him aflame with love for his daughters. It is worthy of remark that true feeling acts like an inspiration. No matter how ordinary a man may be, whenever he gives expression to a real and strong affection, he is wrapped in an impalpable essence that alters his countenance, animates his gestures and lends a new inflection to his voice. Under the stress of passion, the dullest being may reach the highest degree of eloquence of thought, if not of language, and seems to be transfigured. At this moment, the old man's voice and gestures possessed the communicative power that marks a great actor. Are not our fine feelings the poetry of the will? (53).

"The poetry of the will" calls for performers to play with images the way poets play with words. In life, our masks are built up through experience; onstage, our images are built up in rehearsals.

Terms to Work with: Images

Image

Imagery analysis has a single term to agree on, and it's an easy one to remember: an **image**. Using this approach, the word *image* refers to a private idea you are reminded of by the script, character, line, or moment. An image is not always a picture; it can be a sound, a smell, a touch, a memory, a taste. The word itself is derived from the Latin *imago*, a root that reveals a relationship between the words *imitation*, *imagination*, and, perhaps, *magic*. For actors, an image is written as a simile. It answers the questions:

- What does this resemble?
- What is this like?
- What does this remind me of?

Some examples from scenes we've discussed so far:

- Richard III is as smooth as new suede when he makes love to Anne.
- Natalya Petrovna is as charming as the song of a bird.
- Ionesco's Professor reminds you of the sour smell of your childhood piano teacher.
- Ionesco's Pupil reminds you of the time you flunked spelling in sixth grade.
- Hedda Gabler is like a caged wolf.
- Shlink is as bitter as the sound of his name.

Images can be divided into two kinds: *fantasy* and *personal history*.

Fantasy

A **fantasy** is just that: anything you can imagine yourself being and—like the little child dressing up in Mother's hat—would like to act out. For example: animals, rock stars, super-heroes, royalty, clowns, criminals, soldiers, thieves, Hedda Gabler as a caged wolf, or Hedda Gabler as Tina Turner, or Hedda Gabler as you imagine Ibsen to have imagined her. Acting out fantasies is at the heart of an actor's experience onstage, from Olivier's nose to Anna Deveare Smith's Korean grocer.

When Stella Adler diverged from the teachings of then-accepted American understanding of Stanislavsky, it was in order to harness the instinct toward fantasy and take to heart Stanislavsky's phrase *"what if?"*: "What if I were a wolf? What if I were a general's daughter?" The impulse was kept reined to the structure of tasks by the next question: "Well, if I were a wolf—what would I do?" In class, Adler urged her students to do more than investigate their own lives; she would, for example, teach whole classes in how to behave like royalty. Her most succinct comment on the subject: "Your life is one millionth of what you know. Your talent is your imagination. The rest is lice" (54).

Personal history

Memories of your life's experiences make up the images of **personal history**. When the Professor of *The Lesson* reminds you of the smell of your piano teacher, or the events of the play lead you to remember the time in sixth grade when you flunked spelling, these are the images of personal history. Lee Strasberg urged actors to draw on personal history to identify and put into use what were called *affective memories*, a term derived from the writings of Stanislavsky and borrowed from the now-outdated experiments of the French psychologist Théodule Ribot. The theory of affective memories is that events from the past settle into the mind and body and remain capable of being accessed. It is not, as has often been assumed or taught, that an affective memory is relived. It is *remembered*, and, as a result, *emotional memories* arise that an actor can learn to access and put to use.

Sometimes personal history and emotional memory diverge. An emotional memory may change over time as the person remembering ages and gains perspective on the original experience. The theory is that emotional memories provide a lodestone of truth by returning you, like a compass pointing north, to the basic truth of your personal history. Echoing the *beads/bits/beats* brouhaha, Shelley Winters said in an interview that she always thought Strasberg was saying "effective memories" because they were always so effective (55).

Which is better—history or fantasy?

Answering this question is the basis for bitter and unending arguments. When Lee Strasberg died in 1982, news reached Stella Adler while she was in class. She asked her students to pause for a minute to pay respect. She looked at her watch as the minute ticked by. At the end of the last second she burst out, "That man has done more to ruin the American theater than anyone else."*

Emotional memories derived from your own personal history are undeniably potent. What could be more personal than what you experience first-hand in your own life? But as any psychologist or thinking adult knows, memories are *not* facts or experiences. Memories collect experience. When a net is dipped into the sea, as fine as the mesh might be, the water and a few fish will still slip away. To some degree, then, so-called "history" is *already* fantasy.

It works the other way, too, since fantasy is reality based. Our imaginations recombine experience. The mixture might be something new, but the fantasy is always an aspect of personal history. Freud famously said you are all the people in your dreams; you are certainly all the people in your fantasies.

The answer to the question of which source is better for an actor's image—fantasy or personal history—is that neither is better. Both are aspects of the same collision of experience and interpretation. Because fantasy buffers the difficulties and pain of memory, most people find it easier to start with a fantasy. If you can relate more directly to your own life, begin there. "I never travel without my diary," says Gwendolyn in Oscar Wilde's *The Importance of Being Earnest* (1899). "One should always have something sensational to read on the train."

Fantasy or personal history, the challenge is exactly the same: to translate the actor's images to the specifics of the text. When this task remains undone, criticism of images as self-indulgent and diversionary from the job of acting the play is valid. In this chapter we will explore a script using fantasy; in the next chapter we will simulate the experience of emotional memories based on personal history.

Assembling Images: Rehearsing a Scene from *The Maids*

Let's explore an actor's personal imagery rehearsing a scene from Jean Genet's 1947 play, *The Maids* (56). We're going to talk a lot more openly about images than you would ever want to in rehearsal. Images, by definition, are private and thrive on discretion.

---

*Musical theater mentor David Craig would relate this anecdote in his classes. His students now repeat it to their students.

Words can oversimplify such a complex mixture of ideas, impressions, desires, and dreams. In this way, images resemble emotions, which are also private and hard to describe or pin down with words. Yet there are techniques for an actor to structure emotions, just as there are techniques for structuring images.

First, a few notes about the play. In *The Maids*, two servants—Solange and Claire—rehearse the ritual murder of their mistress. The servants, who are sisters, take turns playing murderer or victim. The victim always masquerades as the mistress of the house, imitating Madame's affectations while wearing Madame's discarded wigs and soiled gowns. The sister performing the murderer masquerades as the younger maid, Claire. Sometimes it really is Claire, sometimes "Claire" is the older sister, Solange. But in the ritual murder, it is invariably "Claire" who kills "Madame."

One night, the rehearsals of the ritual murder conclude. The sisters attempt the genuine murder and poison Madame's tea. Despite her servants' polite insistence, Madame avoids even a sip before she gaily departs for a romantic rendezvous. We'll begin with Madame's entrance, which is midway through this one-act play.

> *A burst of nervous laughter backstage.* MADAME, *in a fur coat, enters laughing with* SOLANGE *behind her.*

MADAME There's no end to it! Such horrible gladioli, such a sickly pink, and mimosa! They probably hunt through the market before dawn to get them cheaper. (SOLANGE *helps her off with her coat*)

SOLANGE Madame wasn't too cold?

MADAME Yes, Solange, I was very cold. I've been trailing through corridors all night long. I've been seeing frozen men and stony faces, but I did manage to catch a glimpse of Monsieur. From a distance. I waved to him. I've only just left the wife of a magistrate. Claire!

SOLANGE She's preparing Madame's tea.

MADAME I wish she'd hurry. I'm ashamed to ask for tea when Monsieur is all alone, without a thing, without food, without cigarettes.

Embrace the arbitrary

If nothing comes to mind at first, don't worry, it will. Wait. It will. Images erupt spontaneously, without poking. Sooner or later the script will remind you of something. When an image comes to you, don't question if it's the best image—or hunt for its source—embrace it for being random. Whether it's a fantasy or a personal experience, either is fine. Don't derail yourself searching for real life equivalents for fantasies or a "better" fantasy. Trust that any fantasy is an image derived from your experience. It occurred to *you*, didn't it?

Preparing the role of Madame in *The Maids*, you could begin rehearsals with an image of your imperious grandmother, or Diana Ross, or Coco Chanel. Or a southern accent. Or a bad French accent. These are not Genet's images—they are too campy, too

American—but even so, if they come easily to mind, they might help bring you to your own understanding (and successful performance) of the severe irony Genet intended by having ornate baroque language issue from the mouths of dowdy servants and their chic twentieth-century mistress. The style of the production will determine in what ways your campy images are translated into performance. But you needn't begin with what you think are images "appropriate" to the style of the production. You may have no images for severe irony, the baroque phrases may freeze you in your tracks, the ritualized movements the director is wild for may confuse you. Nevertheless, let's say that the idea of Madame's laugh heard offstage makes you think of Jean Harlow in the film *Dinner at Eight* (1933) or, to use a later film as an example, Lesley Anne Warren in *Victor/Victoria* (1982): a cheap *floozy* who, despite being rigged out in diamonds and satin, broadcasts her low class every time she opens her mouth to cackle out a crude laugh. If you've smiled at the thought of this image, it might be worth a try in rehearsal.

If you've never seen *Dinner at Eight*, or if Jean Harlow leaves you cold, the image won't work for you. If it does stir you, for whatever reason, go right ahead and do your bad Jean Harlow imitation. It doesn't mean you are going to perform the role as a stereotype. It means you will *exploit a stereotype in order to explore a character*. You're not necessarily going to stop with the stereotype, you're going to begin there.

The potential to abuse stereotypes is such that it might be advisable to read the last three sentences three more times. With that in mind, please continue.

Yes, exploit clichés

The image of the *floozy*, which we've identified as Jean Harlow in *Dinner at Eight*, is a *cliché*. It comes with its own ready-made ways of walking, speaking, and emphasizing importance. Stanislavsky dismissed these ready-made characters as "stamps," meaning the image made by a rubber stamp, necessarily derivative, imprecise, and growing fainter and cruder with use. The word in Russian is pronounced *shtamp*; say it out loud to get the full sense of Slavic disgust.

Yet, when you work with images in rehearsal—especially fantasy images—these stereotypes/clichés/*shtamps* are to be explored, not squelched. Like the bad sketches that precede a drawing, or the clumsy notes a pianist hits when practicing a sonata, so too the first use of imagery in rehearsal might be crude, or halting, or just plain wrong. But images get you started; that's their usefulness. Images give momentum to rehearsals in ways that working towards a task does not. In painting, you have to start with bright color to get bright color. A careful build of pastel tones does not build to vivid color. It makes gray.

In life, it is dangerous, foolish, and demeaning to categorize people as clichés. When the Russian actor Michael Schepkin told the African-American actor Ira Aldridge that Aldridge's Othello would be more "realistic" if he behaved like a crude savage, the cultivated Schepkin was himself behaving crudely. Aldridge knew from his own experience how stereotypes transform others into objects, rather than individuals. Treated as objects, people can be manipulated without scruples or compassion.

The reason that clichés are a bad habit in life—they make it easy to manipulate the

132

image of someone else—is precisely the reason they are useful for actors using imagery in rehearsals. As a performer you *want* to manipulate images—your own as well as those of others. Aldridge sometimes followed his performances of Othello or King Lear with renditions of minstrel songs like "Jump Jim Crow." He sang these jolly banjo tunes sadly, however, and in a ridiculous dialect—a Brechtian opposition to the five acts of Shakespeare he had just performed. Aldridge would then turn to his audience and speak directly to them about the need for the abolition of slavery and respect for the African race. His performance of clichés was meant to undo clichés. In pursuit of that task, Ira Aldridge used clichés for his own purposes.

Should a rehearsal technique include as bad a habit as thinking in clichés? Yes. An actor who manipulates clichés becomes a lot more sensitive to thinking in clichés in life, much more so than someone who assigns clichés unconsciously. Lying, too, is something an actor does. So is the faking of emotions. Neither lying nor faking is much appreciated offstage, but they are work habits for actors onstage. Opera singers learn to make a sound loud enough to sail over a thirty-piece orchestra, appropriate to the vast spaces in which they work. But they do not speak as loudly when they're conversing on the phone. They don't confuse long distance with stage projection, and you shouldn't confuse the stage with life. Remember not to deal with other people in life as clichés, but do deal with the characters you are about to play in that way—at first, anyway.

We have chosen to begin with a cliché of a *movie star* as the image for Madame: Jean Harlow. There was a real woman by the name of Jean Harlow, but she was nothing like our image of her. She was an intelligent and poised young woman, a devout Christian Scientist. Audiences may have been confused about the difference between her personae on the screen and in life—but Jean Harlow wasn't. Likewise, in our own time, the thoroughly professional Goldie Hawn maintains her trademark ditzy image as a character in film and television, but she is certainly not scatterbrained when she's directing or producing the films in which she stars.

If you begin with a "Jean Harlow" or a "Goldie Hawn," what probably excites you is not the reality of their hard work in life (*"Life upon the wicked stage ain't nothing what a girl supposes"* goes Oscar Hammerstein's lyric from *Showboat* [57]), but the resonance of the images these actresses created, images you will take on for your own purposes in the text.* When it comes to working from images, for once, ignorance *is* bliss. It doesn't matter what the reality of Jean Harlow was, or any other image you pick, be it *powerful horse* (some are shy), *mighty motorcycle* (some are not), or *mysterious gypsy* (not all of them). It's precisely your misunderstanding of an image—your heightened romantic response to it—that makes it useful to you as an actor. If your idea is based on a cliché, fine, just as long as it's *your* cliché. *Your* cliché is significant to *you* because it has some connection with your life. A Chinese philosopher was walking along the riverbank with a friend. Oh, he said, looking down into the water, the fish are enjoying themselves today. You

---

*When Genet's *The Maids* was first performed in Mongolia, the performers of course had no idea who Jean Harlow was (nor Goldie Hawn, for that matter). When it was suggested that Madame was someone who pretended to be something she was not, the actress playing the role came up with her own high-pitched petulance. "The kind of girl who thinks she's a Chinese princess," she said, and chirped like a twittering bird. As rehearsals developed, so did the image, and Madame became a Mongolian girl who wanted to pass, as best she could, for Russian—with a blonde wig.

are not a fish, said his friend, how do you know what a fish can feel? You are not I, said the philosopher, how do you know what I can feel?*

True to life or not, even though you will not necessarily perform the role of Madame as a Jean Harlow-in-*Dinner at Eight* imitation, you might begin your rehearsal idea of Madame in just that way. If you haven't seen *Dinner at Eight*, do. It's funny, and you'll be able to follow what is discussed here more closely. Much more serious images could be used, of course. Madame might remind you of an overly sober woman who in private life is a drunk. Her tight-lipped severity might dissolve into a binge of emotions or a screwed-down bitterness. Still, it's a lot more playful as research, in every sense of the word, to watch *Dinner at Eight* than to study secret lushes.

> *A burst of nervous laughter backstage.* MADAME, *in a fur coat, enters laughing with* SOLANGE *behind her.*

The burst of nervous laughter backstage might begin as a high-pitched cackle associated with the *floozy* image. The fur coat, to your way of thinking, will be a white fox, something frivolous, expensive, and gauche. As Madame enters, she mocks the flowers that her maids have strewn about her bedroom:

> MADAME There's no end to it! Such horrible gladioli, such a sickly pink, and mimosa!

Here's another image for you: pointing to the stuffed vases, Madame's affected hand gestures might be like *twittering birds*. But let's cage the birds for now. In your *floozy* image, your hands can rattle with bracelets.

> MADAME They probably hunt through the market before dawn to get them cheaper. (SOLANGE *helps her off with her coat*)

Madame can drop her expensive coat on the floor. Unseen by Madame, the maid Solange can rescue it. When Bette Davis was rehearsing the film *All About Eve*, the director Joseph L. Mankiewicz—who liked to work from images with his actors—told his star that the role she was playing ". . . was the kind of dame who treats her mink coat like a poncho" (58). If you remember this story, then Bette Davis-in-*All About Eve* will be added to your images for Madame. Yes, images can change rapidly in rehearsal, from Jean Harlow to twittering birds to Bette Davis. If you were working with the image of *overly sober Madame*, she might enter more quietly, tight-lipped with disapproval at the overly gaudy flowers, and her laugh would be grim and tight. For now, though, let's stay with unadulterated *floozy*.

> SOLANGE Madame wasn't too cold?
> MADAME Yes, Solange, I was very cold.

---

*If he wasn't a philosopher he would have said: You are not me.

As *floozy*, Madame's voice will be childish and petulant as she describes her visit to Monsieur in jail:

> MADAME I've been trailing through corridors all night long. I've been seeing frozen men and stony faces, but I did manage to catch a glimpse of Monsieur. From a distance. I waved to him.

She might imitate her wave to Monsieur with her fingers folded to the palm: a *bye-bye* gesture, a little girl's gesture.

> MADAME I've only just left the wife of a magistrate. Claire!

If your image of Madame was an *imperious mature woman* (your dowager grandmother?), this line would imply that tea with a judge's wife is commonplace within Madame's social world. The image of *floozy*, however, assigns a different meaning to the same words. Harlow's character in *Dinner at Eight* convinces her thug of a boyfriend to accept an invitation to the dinner of the title in order to meet just such high-society types as a judge's wife. Such a meeting would be a social climber's gleaming trophy.

As you apply your images, the call for Claire would likewise change. From the pursed lips of an *imperious Madame*, the call might be coolly melodious. As *floozy*, Madame's call for Claire will be a nasal whine that stretches the sound into two grating syllables: *Clay-yuh!*

> SOLANGE She's preparing Madame's tea.
> MADAME I wish she'd hurry. I'm ashamed to ask for tea when Monsieur is all alone, without a thing, without food, without cigarettes.

The words "without cigarettes" will help you to establish the image of *floozy Madame*. Imagine the horror for such a Madame—not being able take a drag on a coffin nail! You might even add a loud "*The woist!*" in rehearsal.

Translate the text into the language of the image

You could have picked many other images for Madame: *icy matron, chic fashion-plate, Margaret Thatcher, Evita Perón.* Don't question why you picked this one or that one; it occurred to you, so use it. Still, it's not enough to pick one image, or even several ones. The job of an actor working this way is to *respond to the images of the text or situation with personal metaphors* (which we just did with Harlow)—and then *apply those images by reassigning a value to the rest of the specific words in the play* (which we just did with the cigarettes).

The process of responding with an image is incomplete until the rest of the play is **translated** into the language of the response. Most approaches to acting stress specificity; this approach is no different. Without such specificity, the image will be false and appliqued—sewn or glued onto the surface.

BUILDING IMAGES

To generalize is to be an idiot. To particularize is the Alone Distinction of Merit. So wrote William Blake in the margin of Joshua Reynolds' *Discourses on Art*. Like the French archaeologists discovering Cleopatra's name on the Rosetta Stone, you want to identify the points of contact between your image and the play's text, and expand from what you know to what you don't know.

It is especially important to translate the other characters and the environment into the language of your image. If Madame is your *imperious grandmother*, the unseen Monsieur is a *gentleman*. If Madame is a *floozy*, the unseen Monsieur is her *thug of a sugar daddy*. If Madame is *Jean Harlow* in *Dinner at Eight*, then Solange can be Jean Harlow's sour-faced maid in the same film. This is not necessarily the image that the actress rehearsing Solange will play, nor should you as *Jean Harlow Madame* expect the other actress to knowingly fulfil your fantasy. Each of the actors will have their own private set of images, evocative to them.

Every actor in the scene will have different images

According to the story of the play, Solange is stalling Madame while the younger maid, Claire, is in the kitchen poisoning Madame's tea. For the actress playing Solange, the image she has of herself might be nothing like a lady's maid, but, rather, a *farm woman* allowing a chicken to run around the yard before Solange seizes it and wrings its neck. If Solange is a *farm woman* preparing to kill a chicken, Madame is that chicken and her talk is just squawk. Solange might hear Madame's cry for Claire as if it were the squeal of a pig, soon to be hung as ham. Solange will maintain a butcher's professionally cool demeanor so as not to alarm the animal about to be slaughtered.

Since the actors have different images of the scene, each will see the other in relationship to that image. The quiet, methodical gestures of Solange's *farm woman* will be interpreted by *Jean Harlow Madame* as those of a crimped *spying maid*. (This parallel could work: Jean Harlow's sour-faced maid blackmails Harlow in *Dinner at Eight*; Madame's maids in Genet's play are likewise blackmailing her. Although Madame doesn't know it, Claire and Solange have sent anonymous letters to incriminate Monsieur. That's why he's in jail.)

> SOLANGE But Monsieur won't stay there long. They'll see right away that he's not guilty.
>
> MADAME Guilty or not, I shall never desert him, never. You see, Solange, it's at times like this that you realize how much you love someone. I don't think he's guilty either, but if he were, I'd become his accomplice. I'd follow him to Devil's Island, to Siberia.

If the Grade-B movie dialogue ("Guilty or not, I shall never desert him, never.") reminds you of the preening self-importance of a soap opera diva or Mrs. Siddons's "huzzing," you could change your image for Madame here. Solange might retain her image, however, calming the unsuspecting Madame before she gets too agitated to drink her poison.

SOLANGE There's no need to get panicky. I've seen worse cases acquitted.
There was a trial in Bordeaux—

MADAME Do you go to trials? You?

SOLANGE I read *True Detective*. I know these things. It was about a man.

Solange has another image here, a *crime fan* so enthused she can't conceal her expertise. To a more astute Madame, this could be a giveaway that Solange is a criminal, but *floozy Madame* or *buzzing Madame* is too besotted by her own drama to notice Solange's slip.

MADAME You can't compare Monsieur's case. He's been accused of the most idiotic thefts. I know he'll get out of it. All I mean is that, as a result of this preposterous affair, I've come to realize how deeply attached I am to him. Of course, none of this is serious, but if it were, Solange, it would be a joy for me to bear his cross. I'd follow him from place to place, from prison to prison, on foot if need be, as far as the penal colony.

If you kept up the image of the *floozy*, Madame's martyrdom is laughable, like Jean Harlow imitating Sarah Bernhardt. In Genet's play, Madame herself is playing an image here, the *tragic queen*. Towering in her high heels, it's ironic for Madame to claim she'd walk barefoot to Siberia. Notice that by casting herself as the *tragic queen*, Madame is recasting Solange as her *confidante*. At the same time, translated into Solange's language of imagery, Madame's flights of fancy are the scampers of a *nervous pig* in need of curt discipline.

Vocal masks

SOLANGE They wouldn't let you. Only bandits' wives, or their sisters, or their mothers, are allowed to follow them.

MADAME A condemned man is no longer a bandit. And then I'd force my way in, past the guards. (*suddenly coquettish*) And, Solange, I'd be utterly fearless. I'd use my weapons. What do you take me for?

SOLANGE Madame mustn't get such ideas into her head. You must rest.

MADAME I'm not tired. You treat me like an invalid. You're always trying to coddle me and pamper me as if I were dying. Thank God, I've got my wits about me. I'm ready for the fight. (*she looks at* SOLANGE *and, feeling that she has hurt her, adds, with a smile*) Come, come, don't make such a face. (*with sudden violence*) All right, it's true! There are times when you're so sweet that I simply can't stand it.

The words "I simply can't stand it" might remind you of a *sound*: the harsh voice of another cliché of a floozy. There is a very similar line in the film *Singin' in the Rain* (1952), where a screechy silent film star is taking a voice lesson and practicing to say "*I can't stand him*" with hilariously shrill flat "A's" on *can't* and *stand*. If you say Madame's lines in this way, your mouth will stretch back, and the position of your mouth, combined with the shrill pitch of your voice, will make for you a **vocal mask**.

A vocal mask is just that: a way of masking your voice. Vocal masks are created when you change your pitch, or tone, or when you place your voice differently in your throat or mouth; by stretching your lips back in a smile, for example, or lowering your chin. Olivier used vocal masks when he lowered the pitch of his voice almost a full octave for Othello and when he thinned the timbre of his sound playing Richard III. A vocal mask is different from an *accent*. Geography and class determine an accent; it can be studied with precision. Vocal masks can include accents, of course, but they don't need to be *authentic* accents, any more than a carved mask needs to be a realistic face.

If authenticity interests you, you can study technical ways to reproduce accents with some excellent Henry-Higgins-in-reverse books that instruct the reader to say *ryne*, not *rain*. In any case, if you know about accents, those associations will help enormously to carve vocal masks. Imagine a southern accent for Skinny, the henchman in Brecht's *In the Jungle of Cities*, and you have a certain approach to the character. If you know enough to specify the southern accent you'll begin to specify the role. Imagine that Skinny speaks like a native of Tupelo, Mississippi (birthplace of Elvis Presley) in a hard-nosed twangy accent. That's very different from the genteel lilt of someone from Richmond, Virginia (whence comes Robert E. Lee). Employ twangy Tupelo and you have Skinny as a *used car salesman*: insistent, humorous, and pointed in his sales pitch. Utilize lilting Virginia and you have a *gentleman salesman* Skinny, perhaps with an apologetic lifted pitch at the end of sentences, very beguiling with the customers, *very* sorry that Garga isn't taking his good suggestions.

Using a fantasy image frees you to create your own vocal masks, unrestricted by time and place. Your border-crossing Count Dracula or your inconsistent Queen's English (which will drive your speech teacher wild) are appropriate to rehearse with if they induce you to feel the sense of exotic mystery or upper-class arrogance you intend them to create—remember Bernhardt looking at the palms of her own hands?

Certain lines may suggest ready-made line readings: *"I'd use my weapons"* might make you think of the thrust-out chest of the actress Ann-Margret, known in the 1960s as "the kitten-with-a-whip," a nickname that itself might provoke an image and a sub-vocalized sound like a cat's *meow*. *"What do you take me for?"* might evoke the shrill silent film star in *Singin' in the Rain* who memorably says: *"What d'ya think I am? Dumb or something?"*

Even though the text of *The Maids* is a translation—and a British one at that, with class associations like "tay" for "tea"—the words can still give you your own ideas about which vocal masks to try on in rehearsal. The emphases of the vocal mask assign value to the words, such as Madame's "without cigarettes" or "I simply can't stand it." In the lines of Madame's entrance—"There's no end to it! Such horrible gladioli, such a sickly pink, and mimosa!"—the sharp *i*'s of *mimosa* and *sickly*, and the over-pronunciation of *gladioli* will emphasize Madame's daintiness.

Once you establish the emphases given by the vocal mask, you should rehearse with the mask long enough for it to become comfortable. As rehearsals progress, you might make a choice to alter the vocal mask. This process is often described as *dropping the ac-*

cent, but the word "dropping" is misleading. The emphases of the mask are not abandoned; rather, some aspects are kept, some are not. For example, the lilting flirtatiousness of a southern accent might be retained along with its emphasis in certain words and meanings—even though the twang and the diphthongs would be eliminated. Madame's daintiness would stay; the sharp *i*'s would go.

Work from the outside in

Physical aspects of the rehearsal or performance may trigger inner images.

> MADAME It crushes me, stifles me! And those flowers which are there for the very opposite of a celebration!
>
> SOLANGE If Madame means that we lack discretion . . .
>
> MADAME But I didn't mean anything of the kind, honey. It's just that I'm so upset. You see what a state I'm in.
>
> SOLANGE Would Madame like to see the day's accounts?
>
> MADAME You certainly picked the right time. You must be mad. Do you think I could look at the figures now? Show them to me tomorrow.
>
> SOLANGE (*putting away the fur*) The lining's torn. I'll take it to the furrier tomorrow.

In the vocabulary of Solange's *Madame-as-chicken* image, the animal about to be plucked seems ill at ease; it senses something's about to happen. As she's putting away the fur, Solange can be musing philosophically on the transient nature of life, smiling to herself at the thought that tomorrow Madame will be dead. The *feel* of that fur will evoke certain images for the actress: the luxury and cushion of Madame's life—or the fate of the animal about to be harvested for its skin. These feelings, which will be repeated in rehearsal and performance, can be a signpost (like Cleopatra's name on the Rosetta Stone) to direct your thinking.

Touch can be a very effective trigger for an actor: the heft of expensive crystal, the scratch of coarse wool. Especially evocative images come from the feel of wearing certain clothes. Helene Weigel wore her drab *Mother Courage* dress and boots from the first day of rehearsal. Genet's text for *The Maids* gives Madame an excuse to wear flamboyant costumes, which will reinforce your flamboyant internal images. If your Madame enters tightly corseted, hair piled high on her head, breasts pushed up, and hips pitched vertically due to her high-heel shoes, it's a fair guess that—woman or man—you will *feel* differently. You may not wear six-inch spikes in performance—or even in too many rehearsals—but towering precariously over the other actors will change your relationship to them.

The most obvious of outer masks to trigger an inner image is, of course, the *sight of yourself*. Dressed soberly as Solange, your hair pulled back, feet cased in flat and ugly shoes, and your collar buttoned up, you will feel like a drab lady's maid. If you look at yourself in the mirror you will *see* a drab lady's maid. There are some performers who are thrown off balance when they look in the mirror. At the sight of their own reflection, they become too critical of the differences between Jean Harlow and themselves. The vitality of their image is kept when the image is kept internal. For them, the *feel* of the clothing is more than enough to build a character.

But if staring at yourself leads to inner reflection and onstage action, don't be shy: go right ahead and stare. There are very good precedents. In the Japanese theater, actors have a special room where they go before performances just to gaze at themselves in the mirror. Stanislavsky wrote admiringly about how Salvini would spend three hours before he went on as Othello: putting on his make-up and turban in front of the mirror, then coming out to wander the stage or the wings, more and more in the image of the character by the alternation of physical and internal preparation. By the way, Eleonora Duse died in Pittsburgh because she came to the theater to prepare three-and-a-half hours before an eight o'clock performance. She had walked from her hotel to the stage door (which was locked) in a rainstorm. Once she got inside the theater, no one was there to turn on the heat and Duse caught pneumonia. (Sometimes, it's better you prepare your image at home.)

As you sit and stare at yourself in the mirror, you wait to be given an internal clue from the external, like the sculptor who looks at the block of marble in order to see the sculpture inside it. Michelangelo worked like this in stone. It's also how Eskimo carvers work in ivory. Such preparation is not free-association; rather, you are looking for a *direction* from the material. For the Eskimo it's a walrus tusk, for the performer it's your face, or your body. Looking in the mirror develops your intuitive sensitivity to the language of your images.

Stringing the masks

SOLANGE (*putting away the fur*) The lining's torn. I'll take it to the furrier tomorrow.

MADAME If you like. Though it's hardly worthwhile. I'm giving up my wardrobe. Besides, I'm an old woman.

SOLANGE There go those gloomy ideas again.

MADAME I'm thinking of going into mourning. Don't be surprised if I do. How can I lead a worldly life when Monsieur is in prison? If you find the house too sad . . .

SOLANGE We'll never desert Madame.

MADAME I know you won't, Solange. You've not been too unhappy with me, have you?

SOLANGE Oh!

MADAME When you needed anything, I saw that you got it. With my old gowns alone you both could have dressed like princesses. Besides . . . (*she goes to the closet and looks at her dresses*) of what use will they be to me? I'm through with finery and all that goes with it.

CLAIRE *enters carrying the tea.*

MASKS

A liberating aspect of working with images is that their sequence does not have to be logical in its progression any more than the scenes of a text have to follow strict chronological order for a playwright to tell the story of a play. You can begin with the afternoon, move to the dawn, and then go to the evening if those are the images that apply. In this way, working with images does resemble a dream; just as time melts, so does form. Jean Harlow can morph into Sarah Bernhardt. Your fantasy General can dissolve into a fantasy Samurai Warrior. Just as roles change from scene to scene, so too do masks. The string of masks you carve in rehearsal will have its own vocabulary. Notice it. In the example from *The Maids*, Madame is composed of *diva* images: Jean Harlow, Ann-Margret, Sarah Bernhardt, Lesley Anne Warren. Knowing that this is your language—leading ladies—you may add others. Josephine Baker? Mei Lanfang? Dustin Hoffman as *Tootsie*?

Another string might be composed of *imitations*: Jean Harlow pretending to be Sarah Bernhardt. A Mongolian woman pretending to be Russian. Ira Aldridge in whiteface as Macbeth. Laurence Olivier in black-face as Othello. Dustin Hoffman in Tootsie's red dress. The juxtaposition of masks will be intuitive, not logical or planned. As in episodic structure, image follows image without cause and effect. It isn't necessary to connect the images you are working with to one larger "guiding" image. However, it is good technique to play an image fully before moving to the next one, and to demonstrate changes in imagery so that the audience can sense, if not actually identify, the difference.

Too often in a performance an interesting image will be created in the first scene without any follow-through: the image repeats but doesn't *develop* during the course of the play. Even if you choose to play more than one image, you should develop each one somewhat before you drop it for the next one. As the Pupil of Ionesco's *Lesson* ends her tutorial, she should arrive at an image transformed from the one with which she started. The character of the unhappily pregnant Hedda Gabler who kills herself in the fourth act would be built out of images different from the images that built the character of the assured newlywed Hedda in the first act.

There is a dimension of time to images, just as there is a dimension of time to all aspects of theater. If you are working from a *scent*, for example (*sour towels* for Solange, *expensive perfume* for Madame), at what stage of the scent are you? How does the scent develop as the play progresses? A scent hits your nose, blooms, fades off, lingers in the air, and disappears—except as a memory.

Even a cliché should have some development. Are you *Bugs Bunny* at home eating a carrot? Fleeing the hunter? Outwitting the hunter? Hopping off into the distance? Or: *Jean Harlow* in the bath? On the phone? At that eight o'clock soiree? Is your *Tina Turner* playing it rough? Or taking it nice and easy? As the play progresses, images should—and will—develop and change just as Strindberg described: *the characters split, double, multiply, evaporate, condense, disperse, assemble.*

Using an image in rehearsal, even if you discard or advance past it, will add to the depth of your characterization in performance, just as preparing sketches adds depth to a finished artwork. You may find that upon reflection certain images don't really apply to a particular role or text, or are so potent to you that they can be used in other roles and in other plays. Olivier claimed to store details of observed behavior and ideas for as long as eighteen years (59). They became part of his *personal history*, the subject of the next chapter. Those partisans of the Method and Olivier had more in common than either would admit.

Let's Review Terms

images	personal metaphors that answer the question *What is this like?*
fantasy images	imaginary images that excite you to perform
personal history	images remembered from your past
translating images	converting an actor's images to the images of the text
vocal mask	a characteristic way of speaking
to string masks	to assemble a character from a collection of images

The Chart

Let's begin to fill out the chart for the techniques of *Building Images*.

- **Basic unit.** The basic unit is the *image*, the actor's personal metaphor for elements of the text including characters and events, as well as details like costume, sound, and situations.
- **Key question.** The image should answer the actor's question *What is this like?* Or: *What does this make me think of?*
- **The intended reaction of the audience.** The audience is meant to become *passionate* as they respond to a performer's image with images of their own.
- **The relative theory.** The Swiss psychologist *Carl Jung* theorized that character is made of shifting images, like a string of masks, which he called *personae*.

Notebook: Building Images

A burst of nervous laughter backstage.
MADAME, *in a fur coat, enters laughing with*
SOLANGE *behind her.*

MADAME There's no end to it! Such horrible gladioli, such a sickly pink, and mimosa! They
probably hunt through the market before
dawn to get them cheaper. (SOLANGE *helps her
off with her coat*)

SOLANGE Madame wasn't too cold?

MADAME Yes, Solange, I was very cold. I've been
trailing through corridors all night long. I've
been seeing frozen men and stony faces, but I
did manage to catch a glimpse of Monsieur.
From a distance. I waved to him. I've only
just left the wife of a magistrate. Claire!

SOLANGE She's preparing Madame's tea.

MADAME I wish she'd hurry. I'm ashamed to ask
for tea when Monsieur is all alone, without a
thing, without food, without cigarettes.

SOLANGE But Monsieur won't stay there long.
They'll see right away that he's not guilty.

MADAME Guilty or not I shall never desert him,
never. You know, Solange, it's at times like
this that you realize how much you love
someone. I don't think he's guilty either, but
if he were, I'd become his accomplice. I'd follow him to Devil's Island, to Siberia.

SOLANGE There's no need to get panicky. I've seen
worse cases acquitted. There was a trial in
Bordeaux—

MADAME Do you go to trials? You?

SOLANGE I read *True Detective.* I know these
things. It was about a man who—

(Notes for both roles,
Madame and Solange)

Madame is Jean Harlow in
Dinner at Eight.

A squeaky laugh. A cheap floozy
rigged out in diamonds and satin,
but still low class when she opens
her mouth.

Solange is the sour-faced blackmailing
maid from *Dinner at Eight*

*(Solange's image: Solange is a farm
woman allowing a chicken to run
around the yard before she seizes it
and wrings its neck)*

*(To Solange's image, Madame's cry
Claire! is like the squeal of a pig)*

without cigarettes: The woist!

Harlow miscast in a tragic role,
but gamely trying. Playing the
Tragic Queen—Sarah Bernhardt?
Solange turned into the confidante.

*(Solange's image: the gushing fan,
but Madame is too self-involved to
notice the slip)*

MADAME You can't compare Monsieur's case. He's been accused of the most idiotic thefts. I know he'll get out of it. All I mean is that, as a result of this preposterous affair, I've come to realize how deeply attached I am to him. Of course, none of this is serious, but if it were, Solange, it would be a joy for me to bear his cross. I'd follow him from place to place, from prison to prison, on foot if need be, as far as the penal colony.

Appreciating her own performance as serious actress. Childishly surprised at her serious side: God, who knew I was so deep!

SOLANGE They wouldn't let you. Only bandits' wives, or their sisters, or their mothers, are allowed to follow them.

Madame is a twelve-year-old brat

Solange as spoil-sport

MADAME A condemned man is no longer a bandit. And then I'd force my way in, past the guards. *(suddenly coquettish)* And, Solange, I'd be utterly fearless. I'd use my weapons. What do you take me for?

Madame wrinkling her face up like a thwarted child. (Solange's image: an expert) I'd use my weapons: Ann-Margret.

SOLANGE Madame musn't get such ideas into her head. You must rest.

Solange as older sister.

MADAME I'm not tired. You treat me like an invalid. You're always trying to coddle me and pamper me as if I were dying. Thank God, I've got my wits about me. I'm ready for the fight. *(She looks at* SOLANGE *and, feeling that she has hurt her, adds, with a smile)* Come, come, don't make such a face. *(with sudden violence)* All right, it's true! There are times when you're so sweet that I simply can't stand it. It crushes me, stifles me! And those flowers which are there for the very opposite of a celebration!

Madame as sulky child on a rainy day, like a little girl talking with her dolls.

I can't stand it: like the same line from Singin' in the Rain.

SOLANGE If Madame means that we lack discretion . . .

(Solange's image: the animal to be slaughtered seems to sense something's up)

MADAME But I didn't mean anything of the kind, honey. It's just that I'm so upset. You see what a state I'm in.

Like a little girl trying on hats.

SOLANGE Would Madame like to see the day's accounts?

MADAME You certainly picked the right time. You must be mad. Do you think I could look at the figures now? Show them to me tomorrow.

You must be mad: A little girl playing with a "Lady's" hat. (She would usually say, "Are you nuts?")

SOLANGE (*putting away the fur*) The lining's torn. I'll take it to the furrier tomorrow.

MADAME If you like. Though it's hardly worthwhile. I'm giving up my wardrobe. Besides, I'm an old woman.

SOLANGE There go those gloomy ideas again.

MADAME <u>I'm thinking of going into mourning.</u> Don't be surprised if I do. How can I lead a worldly life, when Monsieur is in prison? If you find the house too sad . . .

SOLANGE We'll never desert Madame.

MADAME I know you won't, Solange. You've not been too unhappy with me, have you?

SOLANGE Oh!

MADAME <u>When you needed anything</u>, I saw that you got it. With my old gowns alone you both could have dressed like princesses. Besides . . . (*She goes to the closet and looks at her dresses*) Of what use will they be to me? <u>I'm through with finery and all that goes with it.</u>

Claire enters carrying the tea.

(putting away the fur) *(Solange's image: Musing philosophically on the transient nature of life, smiling to herself at the thought that tomorrow Madame will be dead)*

I'm thinking of going
into mourning:
Like little girl playing with a black veil, a caprice. Waving her hands in excitement as if drying her nail polish. Like a new decorating scheme.

When you needed anything:
Little girl playing with a hat from a charity ball.

I'm through with finery: Like a girl playing with a nun's whimple.

(Claire's image:
the unsmiling executioner
intent on her task)

CHAPTER 8

The Language of Images

Polus and the Urn

Polus was an actor who lived in ancient Greece around the fifth century BCE, the first performer in history to be recorded as having had an acting technique. You would think he'd be better known for it. What did Polus do? He brought a funeral urn that contained his own dead son's ashes onstage with him, so that when he had to weep, he'd have something to cry about.

We think we know what lines Polus was reciting at the time: Electra mourning her brother Orestes, in iambic verse written by Sophocles. Electra's Ancient Grecian formula seems a little remote to you, you say? The verse just doesn't grab you? That's the point. It didn't grab Polus that much either, so he substituted something that did: the *emotional memory* of his dead son.

In America, beginning in the 1930s, acting teachers led by Lee Strasberg seized on substitution and emotional memory and made these techniques the foundation of honest acting, which they called the Method. Though most Method actors claim adherence to Stanislavsky (as channeled through Strasberg), the notion of identifying the sole source of onstage behavior as personal imagery provoked Stanislavsky to an angry rebuke when the same thing happened in Russia twenty years before Strasberg. As early as 1913, Stanislavsky sharply criticized one of his disciples, Vahktangov, for directing actors from a base of emotional memory into "emotional hysteria, acting in a trance, performing for themselves, not the audience" (60).

Stanislavsky's rejection of emotional memory as hysteria is similar in tone and vocabulary to Sigmund Freud's rejection of his followers' attempts to unleash hysteria under hypnosis. Both Stanislavsky and Freud were trying to create a rational system for analysis and develop a set of repeatable procedures for change. Both men disliked "inspiration" as an explanation, although both respected inspiration as a phenomenon and recognized it in themselves. Both felt that succumbing to an image or the energy released by an emotional block was a confusing diversion from the scientific, or, in Stanislavsky's case, craftsman's approach.

Strasberg was aware of Stanislavsky's displeasure. As was discussed in Chapter 3, when Stella Adler brought back criticism to Strasberg from Stanislavsky himself, Strasberg stuck to his guns—and to his Method. Over time, other acting teachers who had derived their own techniques from Stanislavsky made a point to distance themselves from Strasberg's approach and from the label of "Method" acting, similar to the way Piscator distanced himself from the term *epic theater* in order to avoid an association with Brecht.

Among Method actors, the emphases on emotional memory and personal history are variously called advancements, improvements, and adjustments of Stanislavsky's ideas. The strong tone of a good defense runs through their intolerance: *never use imitation, never begin with a cliché, never prepare in a mirror.* Due to the professional success of Method actors in America—among them Julie Harris, Paul Newman, Geraldine Page, Eli Wallach, Dustin Hoffman, Al Pacino, even Marilyn Monroe—Strasberg became famous and Method partisans spoke with the faith of convinced zealots, insisting on the uniqueness and naturalness of their school. Stella Adler students—Robert De Niro and Marlon Brando among them—who include fantasies among their personal images, are more modest about their training, which perhaps reflects that Adler taught actors to bring themselves to the role, not the role to themselves.

The clashes between the Method and other schools are the source of many good anecdotes. The best is between Laurence Olivier and Dustin Hoffman. In the one film they made together, *Marathon Man* (1976), Olivier played a sadistic dentist who was a former Nazi, and Hoffman played his hapless victim. One day Hoffman showed up on the set red-eyed and haggard. To prepare for the scene they were shooting, Hoffman had stayed sleepless and run around the block until he was as exhausted as the character he was playing. Noticing this, Olivier said, "Why don't you try acting, dear boy. It's far easier" (59). Yet when Olivier's will was read, it revealed that Olivier had bequeathed the false teeth he'd worn as Shylock to Dustin Hoffman. Having nothing to defend but excellence, Olivier could afford to be generous.

Let's examine the Method, then, denying its uniqueness (Polus did it first, two millennia earlier) but appreciating its effectiveness. In our vocabulary, the Method is a system of acting choices based on the imagery of *personal history*.

American Enthusiasm for Personal Images

Method actors claim a performer's use of personal history is so natural that all actors have done it at all times, knowingly or not. This is no more true (or false) than Stanislavsky's belief that all good actors already used his system of tasks, or Brecht's claim that Stanislavsky was staging epic theater. The desire to have one theory explain all others is one more example that, even though human behavior seems to stay the same through the ages, *interpretations* of human behavior depend on what observers have the chance to see, and when and where they see it.

American enthusiasm for images of personal experience can perhaps be understood better by considering what was happening in America during the years after the Second World War. This was the period when the Group Theatre led by Strasberg fell apart and was replaced by the Actors Studio in 1947 as a place for like-minded theater professionals to experiment with their craft.

147

Conformity and rebellion

After the Second World War ended in 1945, the United States entered a period of growth and material progress. The country was buoyed by military success, protected by superior weapons and a short-lived monopoly of the atomic bomb. The mechanical inventions of the earlier half of the century—electric power, the automobile, cinema, radio, phonograph records, and television—spread throughout the country. Foreign demand for these and other American products gave the United States political and economic influence throughout the world.

At the same time, America's expansion was shadowed by the growth of a competing power, the Soviet Union. Russia's Communist government proclaimed its own ambitions to influence the world, on behalf of the working class and poverty-stricken people left behind by capitalism's division of society into haves and have-nots. In 1949 Russia exploded its own atomic bomb, shattering America's monopoly and escalating the potential for a conflict. Arguments between the super-powers never grew beyond skirmishes and face-offs, but the threat of collision, and the possibility of nuclear destruction, created a bunker mentality in both countries.

Method acting derived from a Russian master, and its earliest American followers, like other artists and intellectuals around the world, tended to flirt with Communism in the 1930s. Whether they were naïve or delusional is a matter for debate, but their sympathy for the Soviet Union made them vulnerable in the era of Cold War politics. As early as 1939, they had seen the Federal Theater Project stripped of its funding by the innuendo of the House Un-American Activities Committee. This is one reason, perhaps, why Strasberg's followers emphasized the American—rather than the Russian—character of their technique. In Cold War America, those suspected of Communist sympathies were denied work. Those convicted of Communist party membership were jailed. The moguls of the entertainment business—enthusiastic capitalists all—understood their responsibilities as image makers and patriotically policed themselves against Communist sympathizers with industry blacklists.

The rumors of Communist oppression and the intention to spread that oppression were used to justify an uncomplaining compliance with social rules and roles, not only in the entertainment industry but in other aspects of American life as well. The postwar era remembered nostalgically for its stability was also a time of suffocating conformity. There were obvious imperfections in the American system, but attempts at reshaping society were interpreted as foreign-inspired attacks.

Most successful American plays, movies, songs, and paintings of the period catered to the majority of the audience happy to accentuate the positive aspects of growth and ignore what was ugly, ignorant, or unpleasant. In popular film, characters who broke the social rules or defied social roles came to a bad end, usually with just enough time to repent. Women who broke marriage vows or taboos of virginity were particularly doomed by plot devices to serve as examples for other women watching in the audience. The forms of mass culture that did present images of an alternative America at this time—biker movies, science-fiction films, and *film noir*—identified rebels, outsiders, and lawbreakers as losers doomed to fail or die. Sweet, positive, and altruistic characters succeeded in life because they deserved to.

In America, Method acting's reliance on the uniquely personal images of experience was attractive to those with a taste for originality. Creation of personal images had a further attraction in that the source of creativity was within the individual. This was a way for actors to make their art rebel against a conformist society and popular sentimental art.

Abstract Expressionist painters

There was a rebellion in the other arts, too, that fulfilled the American search for individuality among the rank and file. Among painters, the results were dramatic and startling. After four decades of debate in America about what to depict—Connecticut meadows or gritty slums, society matrons or prostitutes—avant-garde American artists after the Second World War chose to depict nothing at all.

"If you want to see a face, go look at one," said Jackson Pollock, the most willfully daring of them all (61). Pollock hurled, threw, dripped, and dribbled paint against his canvasses. The compositions formed were abstract. They didn't look like anything but themselves, and Pollock didn't intend them to. Other painters devised their own techniques. Franz Kline swept broad paint strokes of meaningless calligraphy across large white canvasses. Mark Rothko applied thin washes of paint to create abstract blocks of color. Although ridiculed by a public that preferred the clichés of illustrations, these painters were championed by perceptive critics and named the *Abstract Expressionists*. The traditional techniques of representational painting were unnecessary to their work. The paintings themselves were the subjects, not representations of something else. Although these artists had studied drawing and, in some cases, mastered the art of representation, they chose to create new ways to paint. "Technique is the result of saying something," Pollock said, "not vice versa" (61).

The rise of the avant-garde American jazz music called *be-bop* underscored Pollock's drive to free his art from old techniques. The word *be-bop* is a combination of nonsense syllables that refers to the bounce (*be bop!*) given to a melody, sometimes bent beyond recognition. Relatively unconcerned with the composer's intentions, *bop* musicians brought a personal response to their musical interpretations. During onstage improvisations, *bop* artists such as the trumpeter Dizzy Gillespie, or the pianist Thelonious Monk, or the alto saxophonist Charlie "Bird" Parker conversed among themselves with their instruments, developing a private musical language that was unconcerned with mass popularity or audience approval. Improvisation among jazz musicians dates back to the earliest days of jazz, but after the Second World War *bop* made improvisation central to performance, not ornamental or peripheral. These musicians' experimentation took them beyond the traditional Western scales to exotic chromatic harmonies.

But even while abstaining from traditional techniques, avant-garde painters and *bop* musicians did not diminish rigorous standards. The Abstract Expressionists often mastered traditional painting techniques before rejecting them in favor of brilliant and original methods. The *bop* musicians were accomplished and sophisticated craftsmen, and had scorn for enthusiastic amateurs. By contrast, actors who rebelled against traditional acting techniques often refused to learn their craft. They based the form of their work exclusively on the images of their experiences and ignored the discipline recommended or required by older traditions. They rebelled against elocution lessons, the practice of graceful stage movement, and the study of stage history and literature. Among some performers, personal suffering was considered an adequate enough substitute for the hard work of personal development. A revival of romantic thought ran through it all: an artist's deeply felt emotions were all that one needed to create unique, expressive forms. Everything else would follow—appropriate gestures, interpretation of lines, even diction and volume—if the actor stayed true to the expression of the impulses of passion.

This rebellion in form and process extended to rehearsals and performances that were unbound by social decorum. Actors grunted and scratched themselves. They mumbled their lines, yawned, or paused in the middle of sentences. Scratches and grunts and thoughtful pauses were a part of life and therefore were not to be excluded by anyone seeking to create truth with gestures and sounds on stage or screen. Fantasy, imitation, and clichés were rejected as copies of someone else's life.

The paintings of Abstract Expressionism didn't offer models for a performer the way Grosz's political cartoons informed the gestures of episodic acting, or Repin's nuanced social awareness shaped Stanislavsky's revelation of human relationships. Nevertheless, the *process* of Abstract Expressionism was, and is, a model for the *process* of performers using personal history. Expression begins within the painter—not with observation of the world or a technique for reproduction—just as an actor using personal history begins with the images of his own experience and memories rather than those described by the playwright.

Technology improves communication

An important factor in the rise of an actor's use of personal expression was the development of recording and broadcasting equipment. Slight vocal nuances and even subvocalizations that would have gone unheard in a theater could now contribute to a performance in film or on radio. Gestures and facial expressions that would have been unseen at a distance if they were up on a stage, could now, with the help of a close-up or a well-placed camera, become sources of strength in a performance in a film. If only an actor could *express* emotion, the camera and the microphone could do the job of communicating that expression to an audience. The ability of microphones to relay intimate expression affected other performing arts, especially popular music.

Sinatra

Strong personal expression grew not only among post-war jazz musicians, but among American popular singers as well. As great as they were, earlier popular singers like Louis Armstrong or Bing Crosby did not often offer themselves up personally in their interpretations. The next generation of American singers who reached their peak in the 1950s—Billie Holiday, Judy Garland, and Frank Sinatra are examples—sang out of their own experiences and openly identified with their lyrics, even those of standards that had been sung by hundreds of people before them. Improved microphones allowed for a more intimate tone, and singers took advantage of the opportunity to express themselves.

For an example, listen to Sinatra's 1955 album *In the Wee Small Hours,* a suite of songs describing the pain of a man going through a separation from a woman. Bob Hilliard and Dave Mann's title song is as intimate as a dramatic monologue. Sinatra's identification with the material was obvious; it was widely known that he had recently broken up with his second wife, the sultry, glamorous, and alcoholic screen actress Ava Gardner—with whom he had a famously tempestuous relationship. The titles of the songs that make up the suite are revealing:

- "Glad to Be Unhappy"
- "I Get Along Without You Very Well"
- "When Your Lover Has Gone"
- "I'll Never Be the Same"

When Sinatra was a pure-voiced boy, his early recordings of love songs had an intimate quality, but his brave self-exploration on this later album enriched the music and deepened the listener's experience. In 1955, Sinatra was forty years old and his sound was no longer sweet; his instrument was ravaged from the pain of living and all the more expressive for its imperfections. If he had been a singer of the old school and performing onstage without a microphone, Sinatra might have finessed through the rough spots, making up in volume what he had lost in quality. Even if he hadn't, the subtle tarnish and cracks in his sound would have been lost to the distance in a theater. But such subtleties and flaws are just what the microphone collects and the record preserves. On this album, without the need to project or protect himself, Sinatra reveals each self-examining song's emotional truth. The result is an affecting model for the use of personal history in a performance. Frank Sinatra could also apply personalization to other kinds of performing. The year before this album was recorded, he won an Oscar as best supporting actor for his non-singing role in the film *From Here to Eternity* (1953).

Psychological blocks

In conformist 1950s America, creativity was identified with tapping into a personal source, often of pain and anger. In acting, in music, or in painting, the creative process was one of mining the subconscious—not only to express it, but to free it from itself. A person's traumatic experiences were understood to be stored as tension that blocked feeling and free expression in the body and the brain. Often the goal of the psychologist, the artist, or the actor was to hunt down and dig into these *psychological blocks.*

A theory of uncovering psychological blocks was elaborated by another of Freud's renegade disciples, Wilhelm Reich. After much experimentation, Freud had rejected the therapeutic use of uncovering blocks. He believed that uncovered blocks could only be experienced as sensations and, ultimately, provided no more insight than hypnotic states.

151

Reich and later psychologists hoped to break down psychological blocks in order to release a flood of dammed-up emotions, which would then free patients to express themselves. The techniques developed for therapeutic breakdowns ranged from deep breathing, storytelling, sex, electroshock, hallucinogenic drugs, screaming, and, yes, hypnosis. The theory held that once blocks were removed, the true character of a person revealed itself, displaying the shadow personae (an idea borrowed from Jung) that lay behind the public and social masks, not only of the face, but of the entire body.* Suppressed and festering memories would come to the surface of awareness. Motives that had stayed dark secrets would be recognized and spoken out loud.

Popular entertainment in America was quick to exploit the idea of psychological blocks, suppressed memory, and secret personae. In films and plays, trauma victims recovered from amnesia, psychotics revealed their hidden motives, and ordinary people discovered poetic depth when psychological blocks were identified and removed. From movie thrillers to serious-minded plays, traumatic experiences provided a shorthand for understanding more complex problems.

Psychological playwrights

Even among the most celebrated American plays of the post-war era, traumatic moments stand out as significant plot devices. Post-war American playwrights included flashbacks and the recovery of traumatic experiences to explain behavior and establish character. A son's discovery of his father's infidelity in Arthur Miller's *Death of a Salesman* (1949) explains that son's lifelong failure to compete. A wife's discovery of her beloved husband's homosexuality in Tennessee Williams's *A Streetcar Named Desire* (1947) explains her subsequent nymphomania. The techniques of Method acting fulfilled the requirements to act these plays, and the emotional depth of the performers prompted writers to include passages that revealed character in flashbacks and previously repressed memories. A further incentive for an American actor to use personal images: it got you a job.

At this same time in post-war Germany, Bertolt Brecht was writing rigorously political plays. In post-war England, an entire generation of playwrights trained their eyes to observe and dramatize the decline of the British Empire. In France, a group of playwrights played with elaborated fantasy images to create what has been called the *theatre of the absurd*. In all these countries it was felt that diction, volume, and knowing your lines were still the primary skills demanded of an actor. The exclusive use of images from personal history was declared, often correctly, as self-indulgent, and incorrectly as appropriate for a limited repertory of American plays. Images based on an actors' experience can be successfully applied to embody the texts of playwrights who are not American, of course, yet who specifically use memory, flashbacks, or trauma in their writing. Method acting has much to be criticized for—especially its willful ignorance of stagecraft—but it is not true that it is limited to the American post-war psychological plays.

When relying on fantasy images, an actor's task is to use personal imagery as a

---

*With use, these masks could harden, like a callus, into what Reich called *body armor*.

Rosetta Stone to translate the requirements of a text, in addition to being heard and seen. Translating is still the challenge, and always will be, for actors using imagery.

Translating Personal Images: Rehearsing a Scene from *Yerma*

Let's explore an actor's images from personal history and identify some of the specialized terms used to describe their use as if we were rehearsing the last scene of Federico García Lorca's 1934 play *Yerma*. Lorca was a Spanish playwright and poet from the southern city of Grenada. His lifelong themes were the vast passions that erupt when natural impulses are thwarted. His four greatest plays, all set in his home region of heat-baked Andalusia, are *Blood Wedding*, *Doña Rosita*, *The House of Bernarda Alba*, and *Yerma*. Performing Lorca convincingly is one of the greatest challenges in the world repertory. Acting these texts requires a level of emotional commitment that must be believably fervent, neither melodramatic nor subtle.

Lorca invented the name *Yerma*. In Spanish, it means "barren" and it's related to the word for "wasteland." Yerma is also the title character, a woman who burns to have a child. She describes herself in the last scene of the play—the scene where she kills her husband for refusing her a child:

> YERMA I'm like a dry field where a thousand pairs of oxen plow, and you offer me a little glass of well water. Mine is a sorrow already beyond the flesh.
>
> OLD WOMAN (*strongly*) Then stay that way—if you want to! Like the thistles in a dry field, pinched, barren!
>
> YERMA (*strongly*) Barren, yes, I know it! Barren! You don't have to throw it in my face. Nor come to amuse yourself, as youngsters do, in the suffering of a tiny animal. Ever since I married, I've been avoiding that word, and this is the first time I've heard it, the first time it's been said to my face. The first time I see it's the truth.

Even translated from Spanish, without the sound reinforcing the sense, these are passionate and evocative words. If you yourself have wanted a child and that happiness has been denied you, then perhaps your entry to the role will be easier. But even if you haven't had that life experience, using images from other experiences that you have had can help you portray this character of Yerma—personalizing what being barren means to *you*, not only to the made-up character with the made-up name who speaks so beautifully.

Sense memory

> YERMA I'm like a dry field where a thousand pairs of oxen plow, and you offer me a little glass of well water.

Thirst is a common enough experience. With a little coaxing from an actor, the extraordinary thirst that Yerma compares herself to can unfold from this ordinary feeling.

BUILDING IMAGES

When in your life have you really felt parched? Can you remember the particulars of the occasion? The way the back of your throat felt, the way your tongue lay stiff and broken in your mouth? Can you recall a specific time when you were desperate for a sip of water? In childhood? Before you were seven? Before you could speak?

The specificity of the memory will increase if you investigate the experience in your memory. But if nothing comes to mind—if it has been a long time since you've been so thirsty—perhaps you might do a simple preparation by not drinking very much for several days, or drinking nothing at all for several hours. Then take a walk in the sun. Feel the sweat trickling down your forehead? Taste it. It's salty and it adds to your thirst. Feel the heat of the light on your cheekbones? Feel the dust lining your windpipe? Sit near a fountain, but don't allow yourself to take a drink. Watch the other people drinking. Notice your own feelings as you watch them satisfy their thirst.

You will begin with a cluster of sensations—the heat, the taste of your sweat—in order to build a **sense memory**. Rather than guess what the yellow dirt of Spain looks like without rain, rather than invent what it would be like to be thirsty, you will experience real thirst in order to remember the sensations and so be able to call up the experience later, perhaps when you are onstage. The hot lights of the theater might trigger the memory of the hot day when you went without water and enviously watched the fountain drinkers.

You will not, however, show up for a performance seriously dehydrated. That kind of self-manipulation is amateurish and self-defeating. If you are delirious with thirst under the hot theater lights, you may have a genuinely desperate experience that parallels Yerma's, but you won't have the strength to complete your professional responsibilities like speaking the lines, responding to cues, and positioning your gestures so they can be seen by the audience. It is this aspect of an actor's job that Olivier meant when he playfully suggested to Dustin Hoffman: *Try acting*. A genuinely exhausted actor cannot usually apply the inner image to his performance. With rare exceptions, such a performance remains its own non-translated hieroglyphic.

This may be permissible on camera, because the intelligence of a film performance is in the hands of the editor and director. Some actors' lack of stage awareness can be compensated for on a film set by the adjustment of microphones and a shift in camera angles, rather than an appeal to the performer's craft. The job of providing material to record on film can be met in a variety of ways. In the early days of film, before he made *Orphans of the Storm*, D.W. Griffith ordered pins stuck into babies to make them cry. One of the most promising young Method actresses in the early 1950s gave herself gangrene by sticking pins in her legs as a preparation for class. Baby or adult, it's better—and less painful—to be the type of actor who can *act*, not merely someone whose performance is induced or needs to be salvaged by a director, editor, and technical crew.

To continue with the scene from *Yerma*:

OLD WOMAN You make me feel no pity. None. I'll find another woman for my boy.

The OLD WOMAN *leaves. A great chorus is heard distantly, sung by the pilgrims.*

THE LANGUAGE OF IMAGES

When used appropriately, sense memory allows an actor to access a feeling and bring it onstage during the performance of the play. For example, the stage direction *a great chorus is heard distantly* could cue the memory of feelings that rise when you listen to music in church. You would expand from what you are hearing (the notes of the music) to the sense memories clustered around the sound. These might include the feel of the high straight back of the pew against your spine, the worn smoothness of the velvet pew cushion, the musty smell of the well-thumbed Bibles, or the sight of the faces in front of you, lifted in expectation to the pulpit.

These sensations—evoked by the high thin voices, and the odd bitter tones of the chorus—might evolve into an image of *serenity*. This somewhat abstract idea is composed of many sensations. You could choose from your memories a church experience that was apt. Not the time you dissolved into giggles when the overweight lady's choir robe split. Maybe the time you sang at your baby sister's communion, or attended a friend's funeral and found solace in the ritual of the ceremony.

If you haven't heard a choir lately, or ever, you can go to a church and listen to such music. How do you feel when you listen? You want to recall that feeling on stage, remembering not just the sound but the sense memories clustered around the sound. These sense memories can be triggered onstage by the sound of the music, just as the *feel* of Madame's fur in *The Maids* might trigger the fantasy images of luxury or class hatred. The theory is that working from the details of your sense memory can lead you reliably to reproduce an emotion and experience onstage. From the cluster of sensations we've labeled a feeling of *serenity* evoked by the music, you would be prompted to a feeling of peace and security:

> *A great chorus is heard distantly, sung by the pilgrims.*

Then, when you are interrupted from your genuine reverie, your reaction will be that of someone genuinely resentful that a non-believer has shattered that peace, profaning what is holy.

Yerma goes toward the cart, and from behind it her husband, Juan, appears.

YERMA Were you there all the time?
JUAN I was.
YERMA Spying?
JUAN Spying.
YERMA And you heard?
JUAN Yes.
YERMA And so? Leave me and go to the singing.

> *She sits on the canvases.*

You will not be pretending to have the shock of being interrupted from reverie, you will be experiencing reverie and such an interruption for real, and in full sight of the audience. You will not be pretending to emote, your emotion will be there, as solid a fact as the floor. This is the appropriate use of sense memory onstage, triggered by the sensations of performing the play.

Substitution

Lorca's text gives many other images to pursue for sense memories: prickly thistles, the shame of name-calling, the little glass of water. But notice that one of the most powerful—a "tiny animal" tormented by small children—is not possible with this approach. You are not a small animal. To gain access to a sense memory, you must substitute an experience of your own. This **substitution** of your own sensations for those in the script is akin to what Polus did with his son's ashes in order to cry as a sister over the death of her brother. Rather than imagining the animal's pain, the Method asks you to substitute your own.

Childhood memories are particularly useful for substitution because the experiences of a child are often dramatic. The American short story writer Carson McCullers said that any artist who survives childhood has enough material to last a lifetime. If you had an older sibling or have ever played in a schoolyard, you almost certainly have had the childhood experience of being bullied. The sensations of that experience are what you can use to put yourself in the place of the animal that Yerma describes. The name-calling that Yerma refers to might remind you of childhood name-calling. You would substitute other insults for the word *barren*. When you hear *barren*, you would respond as if you heard whatever words that initially hurt you.

Substitution can endow even the scenery and properties of a performance with significance. In a performance of *The Maids* there might not be a real sable or a string of baroque pearls onstage, but the actress playing Solange might substitute the image of those things for the rhinestones and beads she handles when she cleans up after Madame.

As with fantasy images, the actors do not need to share the same images for substitutions. These are private and personal. The actress playing Yerma might substitute a childhood memory of *torment*. If you are playing Yerma's husband, Juan, in this scene you could substitute a more innocent childhood experience: *hide and seek*.

Playing Juan, you can't help notice that the actress playing Yerma does not share your images, or join in your game. This is inevitable because while playing the role of Juan, you are preparing for a love scene, while Yerma is preparing for a murder. The frustration of not having a cooperative playmate can be substituted for Juan's frustration with his wife's unhappiness. Again, your emotion will be genuine, not feigned. You will not need to think of ways to express your frustration, you *will be* frustrated that your partner does not respond in the way you want:

YERMA And so? Leave me and go to the singing.

She sits on the canvases.

JUAN It's time I spoke, too.

YERMA Speak!

JUAN And complained.

YERMA About what?

JUAN I have a bitterness in my throat.

YERMA And I in my bones.

JUAN This is the last time I'll put up with your continual lament for dark things, outside of life—for things in the air.

YERMA (*with dramatic surprise*) Outside of life, you say? In the air, you say?

JUAN For things that haven't happened and that neither you nor I can control.

YERMA (*violently*) Go on! Go on!

JUAN For things that don't matter to me. You hear that? That don't matter to me. Now I'm forced to tell you. What matters to me is what I can hold in my hands. What my eyes can see.

Juan's inability to share his wife's image of *childlessness* is an essential aspect of the drama of *Yerma*. For Juan, a child is an encumbrance, and maybe a rival for his wife's affections. For Yerma, a child is the meaning of a woman's life. You may not feel either way about children; performing as Juan or as Yerma you can substitute something you do care about deeply in order to speak with honest passion.

Personalization

According to this way of working, everything you say and do begins with yourself. It is this insistence that the origin of a performance be personal experience—not personal fantasy or mask—that marks the Method. You can start with a substitution (the child for the animal), a sense memory (the friend's funeral), a self-induced sensation (thirst, Dustin Hoffman's sleeplessness), or an experience onstage (*I want to play a love scene but she wants to play a tragedy*), but in any of these ways you begin with *personal images*—not the playwright's, and not the character's.

Personalization is substitution made to correspond with personal history. The question to be answered is not *What is this like?* but rather *How is this like me?* This "finding the character in yourself, rather than yourself in the character" can be developed into an art. In order to create the experience onstage, instead of using fantasies or clichés, an actor can begin with self-examination of experience, and, when life experiences aren't enough to find parallels, explore further with an *improvisation* based on the script.

YERMA (*rising to her knees, desperately*) Yes, yes. That's what I wanted to hear from your lips . . . the truth isn't felt when it's inside us, but how great it is, how it shouts when it comes out and raises its arms! It doesn't matter to him! Now I've heard it!

JUAN (*coming near her*) Tell yourself it had to happen like this. Listen to me.

He embraces her to help her rise.

JUAN Many women would be glad to have your life. Without children life is sweeter. I am happy not having them. It's not your fault.

YERMA Then what did you want with me?

JUAN Yourself!

YERMA (*excitedly*) True! You wanted a home, ease, and a woman. But nothing more. Is what I say true?

JUAN It's true. Like everyone.

YERMA And what about the rest? What about your son?

JUAN (*strongly*) Didn't you hear me say I don't care? Don't ask me any more about it! Do I have to shout in your ear so you'll understand and perhaps live in peace now!

YERMA And you never thought about it, even when you saw I wanted one?

JUAN Never.

Both are on the ground.

The subject of this scene between husband and wife may be a child, but all relationships eventually have moments when partners realize that they are speaking at cross-purposes. Can you recognize yourself in the scene from those times, either in life or onstage, when *you* didn't listen to your partner?

If such a personalization seems remote, a new one can be established in rehearsal. You could do an improvisation, abandoning the script entirely, and natter along until an explosion. It could begin with something as slight as picking up your cues (*Did you hear me?*), or something as gross as suggestively lying down on the ground in expectation that your partner will join you. As the scene continues, the stage direction will gain a personal significance from your previous improvisation.

The forms of improvisation vary from nonsense syllables (a Strasberg technique), to paraphrase (an Adler technique), to wordlessness (a technique used by Stanislavsky in his later years). The aim of the improvisation, however, is to lead the actors back to the text and the demands of the play. When it does not, improvisation is a creative cul de sac—just like any other set of images not translated to the text.

Both are on the ground.

YERMA And I'm not to hope for one?

JUAN No.

YERMA Nor you?

JUAN Nor I. Resign yourself!

YERMA Barren!

JUAN And lie in peace. You and I—happily, peacefully. Embrace me!

He embraces her.

YERMA What are you looking for?

JUAN You. In the moonlight you're beautiful.

YERMA You want me as you sometimes want a pigeon to eat.

An actress playing Yerma based on her experience with sexual aggression might personalize Yerma's horror at her husband's sexual desire. The scene might remind the actor playing Juan of an experience he had seducing an unwilling, naïve girl. However, these direct personalizations may be too close to the playwright's scenario—or too close to the actors—to be understood or applied. For those reasons, or others, it may be more useful to personalize the situation by substituting something else. Personalization and substitution can obviously be combined, and often are.

The idea of personalization is a sound one. Freed from the orthodoxy of the Method, it can be used with fantasy images as well as personal history. As Shylock in *The Merchant of Venice*, Ira Aldridge's fantasy of himself as a persecuted Jew was just as personal an idea as any memory of his childhood as a black man in America.

Emotional narrative

As in work with fantasy images, it's not enough to identify an image from your past. Personal history must be elaborated before it can be applied to the text. Strasberg suggested investigating events from personal history using a technique called **emotional narrative**. The actor begins by departing from the text entirely; not just the words, but the events and the characters the text describes. The actor is instead encouraged to relate, in his own words, an emotionally charged event from his past. Led by the director or acting teacher, the emotional narrative reaches a point where the storyteller identifies emotionally with what he is describing.

Let's say that you are playing Yerma, and this scene has reminded you of the time in your childhood when you were playing with another little girl and the fun turned scary and violent. You came over on a hot Sunday afternoon to play with your friend next door. She took your doll, and you, in a hot rage, choked her until tears came to her eyes. She smashed your doll against the wall. You can still remember that sound. You grabbed your friend by the hair and shoved her head down the way she had shoved your doll. Luckily, you were interrupted by your friend's mother, who sent you home in disgrace. Remembering the sight of your scratched doll still gets you angry, even though it was damaged many years ago. As you tell the story aloud, you find your key to understanding implacable rage. In this way, Yerma's outrage at Juan's sexual overture will be personalized as parallel to your childhood outrage, when your most precious possession was treated lightly and irreverently.

159

It was not Strasberg's intention to make this exercise a performance technique. Yet, inevitably, that is what happened. The process corresponded to the then-popular psychological idea that uncovering forgotten memory would release a torrent of forgotten feelings. It was irresistible for performers to repeat the process onstage to access and reproduce emotions. But resist you must, because an emotional narrative is a form of expression, not communication. It unblocks a feeling for the person telling the story, *but it ignores the audience.*

As Strasberg led actors through emotional narratives in class, he maintained the professional distance of a therapist assisting a client in the resurrection of some long-repressed trauma. During a performer's recitation of an emotional narrative, the emotional involvement of the listener does not matter to the speaker, who is working on uncovering something inside himself. The excitement of the teacher encouraging the person remembering to go forward is not to be expected from another actor in performance. Nor would it necessarily touch an audience, because, again, this is an exercise performed without concern for the listeners' reaction. You can understand now why this valuable rehearsal technique, which does not need a partner, is an inappropriate performance technique.

> JUAN Kiss me . . . like this.
> YERMA That I'll never do. Never.
>
> > YERMA *gives a shriek and seizes her husband by the throat. He falls backward. She chokes him until he dies.*

The value of the emotional narrative is that it can take a performer to the origin of large emotions and thus provide subject matter for inner images. In the example we've worked with, the strength necessary to choke someone to death is achieved through accessing the primal rage of a child avenging her doll, just as the parched feeling of barrenness was derived from self-induced thirst.

When used purposefully, emotional narrative and sense memories are exercises to gain access to images. Substitution and personalization, when used correctly, are the ways these images are applied to the text.

Justifying: working from the inside out

To avoid the danger that an actor's fascination with private imagery might overwhelm an investigation of the text, images in the Method are never allowed to articulate their own language and forms the way a fantasy image might. Like Stella Adler, Lee Strasberg insisted that images always be yoked to tasks by what is called **justification** (because they justify the onstage behavior). The precedent for this was Stanislavsky.

In the second of the three books issued under his name in English, titled *Building a Character*, Stanislavsky describes Nazvanov—the student actor from Chapter 1 who became comfortable on the stage once he went hunting for a lost nail—now sitting in his dressing room, smearing green and grayish greasepaint onto his face, and staring into a mirror until a character emerges: The Critic. The Critic speaks in a rasping voice utterly unlike the student's own and has motives that are malicious and destructive. He is, if anything, the Spirit of Negativity.

> "[I am] the fault-finding critic who lives inside of Kostya Nazvanov. I live in him in order to interfere with his work. That is my great joy. That is the purpose of my existence." *I was myself amazed at the brazen, unpleasant tone and fixed, cynical, rude stare which accompanied it* (62).

In our vocabulary, we recognize that Stanislavsky was beginning with a fantasy image. The layer of greasepaint was an external mask, which provoked an inner image, The Critic. There is no sense memory, no substitution, no personalization; but notice that the second sentence the Critic speaks is, fortuitously, his super-task!

The technique of working from an external image is *justified* for Stanislavsky by the presence of the task: *to interfere with Kostya's work*. In other writing, Stanislavsky speaks of how, during his career as a professional actor, his inner images energized his tasks when he played Othello and Dr. Stockman in Ibsen's *An Enemy of the People*. Always, Stanislavsky's images are organized around principles of actions and obstacles.

Nowadays, we do not always believe that behavior is motivated, nor do we believe that tasks must inevitably structure performances. Separated from actions and obstacles, personal images still have a legitimate use in performance and rehearsal. If limiting your images to those derived from personal history gets you results, go right ahead and limit yourself. In practice, most actors over time use a combination of both fantasy and experience, and switch back and forth without shame.

To play Yerma, your images can begin with a real sensation of *thirst*, proceed to a sense memory of *church music*, evolve to an elaborate substitution of your *childhood trauma* over a broken doll, and still conclude with a fantasy of a *bird flying with a broken wing*. The sense memory of thirst will set off a task *to gain water*, the *serenity* of church music will have as its justification *to gain inner peace*, the *broken doll* will be one more obstacle to that peace, and the fantasy of the bird will be the fulfillment of a task. The murder will be justified as a way *to fly free of sorrow*, to an oasis of water in the parched Spanish plain.

Even yoked to tasks, the strict separation of fantasy and imagery from personal history is an aesthetic rather than a necessary choice. When the Moscow Art Theater actress Maria Ouspenskaya first settled in New York, one of the things she taught was an animal substitution exercise. Closing an eye to the implications of animal imagery (that some inner images could, indeed, begin with a fantasy experience), Method actors were encouraged to use animals to personalize images. According to the acting teacher Edward Easty, Lee J. Cobb, who played the first Willy Loman in Arthur Miller's *Death of a Salesman*, worked from an inner image of an elephant to give himself the bulk and weariness required by the role (63).

If you substitute the image of *a bird with a broken wing* for Yerma, the image of the pilgrims' choir can alter from human voices to *the sound of the other birds* calling you to join the soaring flock. Translated by the Rosetta Stone of the bird with a broken wing, your thirst will be slaked by flying away from the desert; the music will be the birds' honk or tweet. (Are you a swan? A crow? A nightingale?) The doll fantasy might become *a nest of broken eggs*, and the last image of the scene—when Yerma is discovered with the body of her husband—might become, in your mythology, the time of dawn when birds, even the ones with broken wings, rise over the fields in graceful flight. Yerma's cry will be that of a swan, honking back to the earth she soars away from.

> *The chorus of the pilgrimage begins.*

> YERMA Barren, barren, but sure. Now I really know it for sure. And alone. (*she rises, people begin to gather*) Now I'll sleep without startling myself awake, anxious to see if I feel in my blood another new blood. My body dry forever! What do you want? Don't come near me, because I've killed my son. I myself have killed my son!

> *A group that remains in the background gathers. The chorus of the pilgrimage is heard.* CURTAIN.

If you worked from an image out of your personal experience, you might personalize that cry as the sound you made when your friend's mother found you—an enemy now to your best friend—sitting on the floor with your broken doll. You might hunt down a photograph of yourself at that age, or touch a fragment of a broken doll's head before you rehearse the scene. If the shard of the doll's head is small enough, you might even carry it on to the stage with you—the way Polus carried the ashes of his son.

Let's Review Terms

the Method	a systematic use of personal images
sense memory	the cluster of sensations that when remembered induce an emotion
substitution	your experience parallels the playwright's description
personalization	the use of personal experience
emotional narrative	an event from your past told as a story in order to retrieve a sense memory
justification	the reason something happens onstage

Practical Tips for Working

Learn from Porky Pig

When the inexperienced producers at Warner Brothers first created the cartoon character of Porky Pig, they hired a real stutterer to dub the voice. Think about that. A real stutterer can't control his hesitations; if he could, he wouldn't stutter. A real stutterer can't match up his voice to the film of the cartoon character's stammer. The producers needed to hire an actor who could *simulate* the stutter, and on cue. Just so, when investigating an image in rehearsal, at a certain point you want to be in control of the image enough to match up with the words and action of the text.

Fantasy or images from personal history—you don't want to lose control. You don't want to slam your partner to the floor, you don't want to stick pins in your leg. The point of sense memory is to develop memories and sensations so that you do not have to kill someone when you play a murderer. True, when Alfred Hitchcock filmed *The Birds* he had real birds pecking at the poor actors. This kind of manipulation is available to film directors, but it is not available to stage directors or actors. Even its uses for film acting are limited.

You act AS IF you were reliving the events. You are NOT reliving them; you are remembering them. Stanislavsky put this idea of AS IF at the center of his system. When Stella Adler broke with Strasberg over his insistence on using emotional memory, she went on to stress AS IF in the use of fantasy images. You do not become enraged at your partner, you act AS IF you were enraged. If you really were reliving uncontrollable rage, you'd forget your lines and smash the face of your partner like a doll. This is not being in the moment; this is being an amateur. The ability to control what you do is what makes you a professional.

To give a voice to Porky Pig, Warner Brothers axed the real stutterer and hired Mel Blanc, a man capable of playing a gravel-voiced prospector, a wise-guy rabbit, a lisping millionaire, and, yes, a stammering pig. To do his impersonations, Mr. Blanc did not need to dress up as a pig, nor did he need to regress to a childhood state when he did stutter (since, in fact, he never stuttered as a child). In the same way that Olivier had a basso image for Othello's voice, Mel Blanc had an image of the stutter—a vocal mask. That image gave him Porky's two-steps-forward-one-step-backward character. For other characters, he imitated real people. The lisping Sylvester is a mean-spirited parody of a Warner Brothers producer who actually lisped, but here, too, Mr. Blanc did not haunt the producer's office or analyze him.

Keep a secret

Even more than with a fantasy image, care must be taken when using an image from your past not to discuss it—to keep its potency by using it only in performance. The more explicit you are in performance, the better; describing an image robs significance from the experience of acting it. An image is like the old-fashioned notion of sex or money: people who have it don't talk about it. The more private your image, the more powerful it is to keep it a secret behind the mask of your performance.

Carry a secret

Polus was on to something. Carry an object onto the stage with you that will be your hidden motor for your work. Keep it small; keep it hidden. When Edmund Kean played

163

Othello, he kept unseen Moroccan coins inside his pocket. When Paul Robeson played Othello, he wore the same earrings Ira Aldridge had worn for the role, given to Robeson by Aldridge's daughter in London—even before Robeson had thought to play the role himself. When Dustin Hoffman played Shylock on Broadway, do you think Olivier's false teeth were tucked somewhere?

Avoid trauma, don't bite off more than you can chew

Dealing with a psychological block in rehearsal is time-consuming and selfish, unless you're playing Hamlet, a character with just such a block, in which case *that* will be your metaphor. It's better to take on something smaller, or just a detail of the larger picture. An image of the last time you saw your former love is more useful than the enormity of the break-up. Similarly, with fantasy you needn't do a full-fledged impersonation, or take the time in rehearsal to perfect imitated mannerisms. Your fantasy image is meant to stir you to work on the script, not to research the exact shade of Jean Harlow's platinum blonde.

Engage, don't enrage, the director

How do you get the director to agree to this kind of work? Directors often have their own ideas of how to waste time in rehearsals. Here's a little secret: except for the very young or very inexperienced, most directors like to steal ideas that are better than their own. They can't help themselves. You as the performer just have to set a little bait for them. You say, "I'm going to try something in rehearsal today. Tell me what you like or don't like about it." This alerts the director to pay attention to what you're doing (as if the six-inch heels and Tina Turner leather miniskirt aren't eye-catching enough). Establish a way for you and your director to communicate ideas on how to translate your images to the text and you will have a partner for your work.

What you're not going to do is say, "I think she's a little bit like Tina Turner. Am I really thinking that?" Or: "I'm going to do a Tina Turner imitation today. Sit back and enjoy it." You don't want to be talking about fantasy images, you want to be acting them out.

What happens when an image goes dry?

The question always comes up: what happens when an image goes dry? After four weeks of performing from the memory of your grandfather, the idea of Gramps isn't doing a thing for you and onstage you're beginning to wonder what you'll have for dinner after the show. Should you switch the image? That's hard to do at first without disrupting the performance. It's helpful to begin with a *detail* from the image, a small close-up: Gramps's walk, his accent, his wink. Remember that externals are steps to get to the internal truth and recall what Gramps means to you as a vital image of, say, piety and fear of God. Try an associated image: Gramps's friend Sam, or the sound of the surf at Gramps's beach house, or the smell of Gramps's cheap cologne called Florida Water.

Any of these might work. Here is where sense memory is useful. Expand the image to all the senses. It's not unlike enlarging the circle of concentration, although in this case the mind extends to the image, not to the circumstances onstage.

Work on images when you're not in a play

The creation of a personal mythology—discovering and investigating your own set of masks—is something that you can do when you're *not* in a play. If there are photographs from your past or in some book that move you, save them. Copy them. If certain music moves you, keep a list. That may sound cold, but it isn't. Take advantage of music's ability to trigger emotions. You'll have your own images that make you cry, or giggle, or sway your hips. There are other possible triggers: scents, certain sounds, certain objects, even mimicry, if the way you mimic combines outer observation and inner imagery.

Over time you will see that you have patterns. You enjoy Barry White, the "Buddha of the Boudoir." *There's* an image to investigate. Pictures of the ocean turn you on. The patterns might give you a clue to what else to investigate: a rhythm and blues concert, a trip to the sea? Maybe there's something about the deep sound of Barry and the deep blue sea that make you think of—your Norwegian grandfather. Vikings might interest you, which might lead you to Cousteau documentaries and a visit to a meat locker to experience extreme cold. Just don't stay too long.

Transforming and type actors: *Touch of Evil*

Does cultivating your own images mean you will begin to play the same kind of character for every role—and end up as a *type actor* who trades on personality? It's not a bad life. Mae West made a very good career for herself playing the same character over and over again, but she herself knew she couldn't stretch it to fill every role that was offered to her. Recognizing her limitations, she turned down such plum roles as Norma Desmond in *Sunset Boulevard*, Mrs. Levi in *Hello, Dolly!* and any number of characters in various Tennessee Williams plays. Does that make her a lesser artist? No, it makes her a specific one—with the self-knowledge of a working professional.

On the other hand, *transforming actors* use their self-knowledge in other ways. Even if you are the kind of actor who changes from role to role, you can only begin with your own personal history and your own fantasies. Stage-trained (and, so far, unwilling to return) Meryl Streep's ability to change herself is the subject of jealous parody. She is famous for her vocal masks, but she also disguises herself with wigs, make-up, and costumes. Her range has limits, but she has no identifiable "type."

Robert De Niro is an actor who often transforms *within* type—gaining weight to play a boxer in *Raging Bull*, learning to play the saxophone for the musical *New York, New York* (1977)—but he still keeps within a range of the masks he has discovered inside himself, made up of controlled rage and outbursts of violence. In film, De Niro's passion for experiencing the life of someone other than himself led him to insist, very early in his career, that he lie in a grave when the character he was playing was dead. De Niro hoped the camera would record the dirt being shoveled over him, covering his face. Shelley Winters, who was playing his mother, was graveside, bawling hysterically (intent on an emotional memory?). When she realized it was De Niro and not a dummy in the grave, she stopped the scene, genuinely worried for De Niro's safety (64).

There's nothing wrong with being a personality actor if you can manipulate that personality to the role. To create a myth of yourself and then play it onstage successfully requires artistry—and hard work. Sometimes the mask can explain and amplify the role—think of Whoopi Goldberg and Robin Williams in their film roles. Sometimes a mask can obliterate the role—look at the grossly overweight Marlon Brando in Francis Ford Coppola's film *Apocalypse Now* (1979). Coppola, a film director who loves actors, tried to make a metaphor between the self-indulgence of Brando and the decadence of the role he was playing. But Brando was no longer self-aware enough to make it work.

Don't complain that type-acting is by definition narcissistic and unrelated to acting as the art of human relationships. Yes, many performers stop at this step. They reach a plateau where they create a voice and an image for themselves, and then apply them as a mask to whatever role they happen to be doing. The rest of the actors can drop dead behind them and they wouldn't know until they realized there's no one to give them their cue. If you plan to be a legend and an icon, try stretching your talent—and perhaps your acclaim—and have your mask take the story and the other actors into account.

Let's look at some transforming and type actors in the 1958 film *Touch of Evil*, directed by Orson Welles. It's a black-and-white B-movie made relatively quickly (forty-two days) and cheaply (for less than $900,000). The film is most famous for its opening sequence, an unbroken three-minute tracking shot that follows a ticking bomb across the Mexican border and into a seedy southwestern town. The story of the film is the investigation of the explosion. Orson Welles himself acted the role of a corrupt border town sheriff.

Welles was trying to work on time and on budget. His previous inability to do so had led to his banishment from the studio system; he had not directed a Hollywood film for ten years before *Touch of Evil*. Taking advantage of the B-movie limitations, Welles created a spiky, unsettling visual style and made highly dramatic use of sound. During production he was busy fighting with his producers; thus preoccupied, he left his actors alone to do what each did best. They were a colorful collection of individuals, and they each did their best differently.

For purposes of comparing performance techniques, this film is ideal, practically a documentary. In 111 minutes you get to watch a practiced *transforming actor* (Welles), a shameless *type actor* (Marlene Dietrich), eager *Method actors* (Dennis Weaver, et al.), and cliché-spinning *professionals*, 1950s vintage (Charlton Heston and Janet Leigh).

The most compelling is Welles, who creates a complex portrait of a brutal and greedy tyrant. More than a touch of evil, he's a bloated bag of lies. In all his roles, onstage or on screen, Welles used fantasy images to transform himself. Here, in good health at the age of forty-two, he put on a false nose, padded himself to grossness, and flattened his accent to gravel. His unflattering make-up gave him the look of a dried-up drunk studded with gin blossoms. From entrance to exit there is nothing of Orson Welles to be seen; he is submerged in the character. The role itself is a collection of masks: *crusty professional, fallen alcoholic, cunning manipulator, desperate liar, corrupt policeman*. For all the exciting camera work, the dramatic action of *Touch of Evil* is in Welles's performance as he changes from one mask to another. The uncovering of his corruption and his loss of face are moving and complex. As the dying sheriff lies on his back panting out his life, we mourn for him.

Marlene Dietrich plays his old Mexican flame; or rather, she plays Marlene Dietrich. Oh, the character has another name—"Tanya" (not very Mexican)—but it's the same Dietrich persona from many other films, other masks of herself strung together: the *jaded tart* of a frontier bordello (*Destry Rides Again*), combined with an *enervated siren* (*The Blue Angel*), and a *world-weary fortuneteller* (*Ramona*). Dietrich's German accent stays marvelously intact in Mexico, and she is accompanied just as miraculously by a player piano that cranks out something very much like her Berlin signature song, "Lili Marleen." As Tanya, Dietrich shamelessly plays to type, and though her mannerisms are appropriate for the role, they create no illusion of another person.

Besides type and transforming actors, *Touch of Evil* is chockablock with other 1950s acting styles. Charlton Heston and Janet Leigh play naïve Americans lost south of the border. Heston plays a Mexican district attorney who speaks accent-free English—and whose make-up leaves him looking as if he'd been dipped in milk chocolate. Other than the greasepaint, Heston makes no attempt to transform to Hispanic; even his Spanish has an American accent. But never mind, he's good at what he does, playing a cliché image of the period: the 1950s *leading man of integrity*.

Janet Leigh, playing his wife, acts a 1950s *innocent blonde leading lady* (don't tell Dietrich), lost in a (Communist-infiltrated?) third world of not-very-nice people. The innocent-blonde and man-of-integrity roles are built of images that fulfil the B-movie and *film noir* stereotypes. The cornball dialogue sounds genuine coming out of their mouths, in a way it wouldn't from "believable" characters.

Touch of Evil also boasts a collection of young stylish actors, among them a motorcycle gang led by Mercedes McCambridge as a leather-jacketed female version of the motorcycle rebels played by more famous Method men like Brando and James Dean. Dennis Weaver plays a young "eccentric" motel owner, improvising and pausing—and grunting, giggling, and twitching. The would-be Method-acting gang's wide-eyed portrayal of drug-induced euphoria is as entertaining as Janet Leigh's wide-eyed stupefaction at meeting impolite people, although certainly not as fascinating as when Dietrich gives the fat old sheriff a languorous glad-eye. Welles squints a lot in his shots; so convincingly that you'd swear it's a real rogue sheriff shoved in front of the camera. Of course, it isn't. Welles had been just as convincing the year before, on Broadway as King Lear.

And look who is playing the blustering Mexican gangster "Uncle Joe." It's Akim Tamiroff, an actor from Stanislavsky's Moscow Art Theater. What was his task? To get a job. Was his Armenian accent an obstacle? Not in this case: it was an opportunity to substitute the rolled *rrrr*s of Russia for those of a Spanish vocal mask.

Collage

When actors place image on image, a useful analogy for performing is the art of *collage*. In creating a collage, an artist takes already-formed objects—or already-formed pictures—from other sources and places them together in order to produce an effect, an image, greater than the sum of the parts. The word *collage* was coined to describe the work of a group of artists called the *Dadaists*, whose response to the First World War was to create art as an illogical combination of the wreckage of civilization. The name *Dada* was chosen at random, and appealed to the group because it had no meaning. The Dadaists assembled theater events, too—what we now call *performance art*—without plot, without logic, and without characters. Words, if used at all, were part of an assemblage of images.

The word "collage" could be used especially to describe the work of Max Ernst, an older German member of the group, whose fertile imagination invented new techniques of assemblage and the creation of images.* Among many other ways of arriving at a new image,† Ernst cut out images from catalogs, engravings, newspaper advertising, and book illustrations and arranged them together in startling and evocative ways. In a collage by Ernst called *Quietude*, a fashionably dressed man leans back in an upholstered armchair, bobbing on the surface of stormy waves. A woman's left arm and talon-like hand lift up from a ripple below him. The man's legs cross nonchalantly at the ankles and stretch above the water. Behind him, a tower erupts, shrouded in a column of water that blows off into a spray. In the black and white print, the spray looks like leaves, or flames, or vapor. The man's eyes are closed. Is he oblivious to what is around him? Is he thinking of all these things? What is the curious bent rod to the right of the armchair, with what looks like an eye on its handle? The chair is from an advertisement, the sea is from another source, probably an engraving or a book illustration. Where do the woman's arm and the mysterious rod come from? As with an actor's combination of images, the impact of a collage is greater than the sum of its individual parts.

Ernst resisted creating a codified set of images, and enjoyed the mystery and illogic of his connections. Other collage artists, though, created entire and consistent vocabularies of images, with their own Rosetta Stones of meaning. One of the greatest artists with a vocabulary of images was the New York sculptor Joseph Cornell. Cornell assembled objects inside boxes: glass shards on blue velvet, an antique doll crushed behind a curtain of twigs, a parrot against a whitewashed wall or above a coil of wire, an owl in a dirt-encrusted box. Like an actor investigating his own mythology, Cornell built *systems of associations*. Owls, connected to darkness, were the opposite of parrots, which were connected to the sun. A viewer need not share these particular associations. The art objects are evocative for each viewer's dark forest (a child lost in the woods), bright hopes (a parrot chattering in the sun), or shattered dreams (cracked glass).

In the same way, an actor assembles images—fantasies or personal experiences—without explanation. Roles, once assembled, are compositions that have their own meanings. Remember our collage for *Yerma*? It was built up of a free mix of personal and fantasy images:

---

*Ernst once staged a Dada event in a men's room.

†In 1941, at a bookshop in New York City, Ernst held an exhibition and displayed a new technique: a canister on a string with a hole punched in the bottom. Paint was poured in and the dripping canister swung above a canvas. Jackson Pollock, who was watching, was so taken with the notion of drip painting that Ernst created a painting named for Pollock, *Young Man Intrigued by the Flight of a Non-Euclidean Fly*. The painting was originally named *Abstract Art, Concrete Art* a few years before the "Abstract" painters called themselves by this title.

- great thirst
- a gospel choir
- childhood name-calling
- marital nagging
- sexual aggression
- a smashed doll's head
- attacking a friend in a childish rage
- a bird with a broken wing
- a nest of broken eggs
- a flying swan
- a piece of eggshell

The Chart

Let's return to the chart. There are still some categories to fill in for *Building Images*.

- **Illusion of character.** Collecting a *string of masks* creates the illusion of character for an actor building a role with images.
- **Dramatic action.** Dramatic action happens with the *change from one mask to another*.
- **Unifying image.** The unifying image is a *collage*, where images are placed together to make evocative combinations.
- **Suitable playwrights.** Plays that include a playwright's strong imagery are best acted when an actor's imagery is equally strong. The fantasy images of *Strindberg, Genet, Pirandello,* and *Samuel Beckett* need to be translated into a performer's own, as do the heightened psychological images of *Tennessee Williams, Eugene O'Neill,* and *Federico García Lorca.*

Responsibility—Not Just Response—to the Words of the Play

In the television series *Saturday Night Live,* the sadly short-lived comedienne Gilda Radner played a character who was a television commentator named Emily Litella. This opinionated older lady would offer stinging responses to the problems of the day. "What's all this fuss I keep hearing about violins on television?" she would ask provocatively. Or: "What's all this fuss about Soviet Jewelry?" Given a topic, Emily would rattle on: "Now, if they only showed violins after ten o'clock at night the little babies would all be asleep and they wouldn't learn any music appreciation . . . I say there should be more violins on television and less game shows! It's terrible . . ." until someone would point out that the issue was *violence* on television, not *violins*. Soviet *Jewry,* not Soviet *Jewelry.* Emily would invariably end her commentary with an abrupt: "Never mind!"

As an actor, you're meant to have a responsibility, not just a response, to the words of the play. No matter how deeply you personalize your images, if you don't bother to understand what you are saying, your worked-up feelings are as pointless as Emily Litella's.

169

BUILDING IMAGES

On the simplest level, as an actor you're responsible for knowing your lines and not rewriting them because you can't remember them. On the next level, you're responsible for understanding what the words you say and listen to mean. There is no excuse for bewildering the audience because you yourself are confused. Emily had plenty of images to use when she defended "violins on television." The final responsibility, once you do understand what you are saying, is to communicate that understanding to an audience while you're performing.

When you work from images, the responsibility of communicating your ideas involves some choices about style; in other words, the images of the production. Before those choices can be made, when different actors with strong individual images get together in rehearsals, it's often a shock: the *Bride of Frankenstein* strides alongside somebody's *Aunt Bessie* and meets up with—*Barry White*.

If you and the director like the theatricality of dueling images placed together, you can create a collage-like performance style for the production of the play. The Wooster Group and the American director Richard Schechner do just that, freely combining images to create theatrical montages of style. It is a delicate balancing act between two aspects of a production, aspects well described by the French playwright Jean Cocteau in a preface to his scenario for a 1936 dance-drama called *The Eiffel Tower Wedding*:

> The action of my piece is pictorial, though the text itself is not. The fact is that I am trying to substitute a "theater poetry" for the usual "poetry in the theater." "Poetry in the theater" is a delicate lace, invisible at any considerable distance. "Theater poetry" should be a coarse lace, a lace of rigging, a ship upon the sea. *Wedding Party* can be as terrifying as a drop of poetry under the microscope. The scenes fit together like the words of a poem (65).

When a performer's images are most effective, they translate the "poetry in the theater" to "theater poetry." Approaching a script, that is your responsibility: to transform the text into a performance.

The danger is that the theater poetry will out-shout the poetry in the theater and that the text will be lost, or adjusted to fit the dramatic action defined by the switch of masks. Badly done, this is not so much translation as adaptation, and frequently involves cuts in the text, transpositions, and additional writing.

The conventional technique is to slowly, slowly translate the specifics of your images into the words of the play, and in doing so, create a consistent world for the production of the play. If the image for Hedda Gabler is a *wolf locked in a cage*, in the world of Victorian Norway the bars of the cage transform into the laces of a corset. If you're setting *In the Jungle of Cities* in Chicago, you'll want more than a vocal mask, you'll want an accurate Chicago accent. Your image for Madame in *The Maids* might be Jean Harlow, but in the world of a Parisian flat there will be a mirror to stare at instead of a movie camera. Yerma's sexual frustration will be defined by the standards of ultra-Catholic southern Spain; it wouldn't be compared to thirst, but to the unnatural cravings of a dipsomaniac. More ways to inhabit the world of the play? For that you need a *world of the play analysis*, which is, fortunately, the subject of the next chapter.

PART IV

INHABITING THE WORLD OF THE PLAY

James Gillray, detail from *King of Brobdingnag and Gulliver*

CHAPTER 9

COMPARISON

Gulliver's Conclusion

When Lemuel Gulliver—the hero of Jonathan Swift's 1726 novel *Travels into Several Remote Nations of the World*—is shipwrecked on the island of Lilliput, he wakes on the Lilliputian beach surrounded by an army of men six inches tall. Gulliver tries to be considerate under the circumstances, but his tiny hosts consider him gross, dangerous, and loud. Gulliver wins the Lilliputians' confidence only after he butts into their wars, after which they consider him the greatest prodigy ever seen. Granted permission to return to England, Gulliver sails from tiny Lilliput and, shipwrecked once again, lands up on the island of Brobdingnag, where the locals are giants twelve times his size. Although Gulliver acts with dignity with the Brobdingnagians, they hold him in their hands and poke at him like he is a doll. Hiding from a monstrous dog by huddling in a forest of grass blades, Gulliver concludes that ". . . nothing is great or little otherwise than by Comparison."

Is Gulliver big or small? Dainty or gross? It depends on where he is. We could ask similar questions of the plays we've studied so far and reach similar conclusions. Is Hedda Gabler's suicide an act of desperation or triumph? Does Richard III excite or repulse Lady Anne? Does Madame of *The Maids* think she's beautiful or ugly? When the Pupil dies at the end of Ionesco's *Lesson*, is she happy or sad? Answers to these questions can be found by looking at each play as a whole—just as Gulliver was defined by which island he happened to find himself on.

The text of a play is just such an island of meaning and—like tiny Lilliput or gigantic Brobdingnag—a world of its own with its own standards and measures. Like Gulliver, actors inhabiting the world of the play do so in an environment—created or implied by the script—that frames, explains, restricts, amplifies, motivates, and organizes the action of the play and the identity of its characters. A *world of the play analysis* is an investigation of this environment and how it can organize and motivate rehearsals and performance.

The customs of the country

World of the play analysis begins with a strategy for discovering the *rules* of any play. As an actor inhabiting the world of the play, if you understand its rules you'll know who you are, you'll know the meaning of your words and your actions, and, most importantly, you'll know how to survive or fail in that world—and in performance. Think of

173

it as a way to learn the customs of a foreign land you're visiting. You don't have to conform to those customs, of course, but you should know the local laws of etiquette.

Knowing the rules for one play won't help you learn the rules of another. The modest gestures and quiet tones that could make a performance of *Hedda Gabler* believable and effective would have no such effect when used for performances of Lady Anne from *Richard III* or Madame of *The Maids*. Yerma's passion for children has no place in *In the Jungle of Cities*. In order to analyze the world of any play systematically, it helps to look beyond acting techniques to other disciplines—artistic and scientific—that investigate human relationships.

Cultural Anthropology

Seeing a pattern

A good model for world of the play analysis is the social science of *cultural anthropology*. A psychologist might study why you cry at the news of your son's birth; a cultural anthropologist studies why you went to buy cigars and a blue blanket. As an actor inhabiting the world of a play, you should know why you're crying *and* why the blanket is blue. Like actors, cultural anthropologists examine behavior, relationships, emotion, and purpose. And like actors analyzing the world of a play, cultural anthropologists analyze the *context* of behavior, man-made and natural. Predictably harsh winters, for example, might prompt a tribe's trek every autumn to a warmer pasture, establishing a tradition of tent-living. The culture carried along inside those tents would include pots, pans, and prejudices. This culture might reward aggression, punish originality, prize certain colors, or eroticize the sight of a woman's ankles.

The first principle that world of the play analysis borrows from cultural anthropology is *to respect each world, like each culture, separately*. Put into use for actors this means: *The world of the play is its own measure. It isn't gauged by any other.* This is the idea taught by the German-American anthropologist Franz Boas. According to Boas, all aspects of human behavior are relative, without fixed meaning, to be understood and judged in terms of their relationship to the culture as a whole. One culture is not superior to another, neither primitive, barbaric, nor civilized. From one place to another, there is no such thing as "common sense," even when it comes to what would seem like obvious common sense: *don't kill yourself*. As one anthropologist observed:

> We might suppose that in the matter of taking life all peoples would agree in condemnation. On the contrary . . . Suicide may also be a light matter, the recourse of anyone who has suffered some slight rebuff, an act that occurs constantly in a tribe. It may be the highest and noblest act a wise man can perform. The very tale of it, on the other hand, may be a matter of incredulous mirth, and the act itself impossible to conceive as a human possibility. Or it may be a crime punishable by law, or regarded as a sin against the gods (66).

This insight can point the way to an actor's interpretation. Hedda Gabler's suicide should be evaluated within the world of the play; it shouldn't be judged according to its value in our world, or even Ibsen's. Hedda kills herself in a world where painful endurance—no matter what—is an expected way of life. When the last character who speaks (a judge, significantly) hears that Hedda has killed herself, he says, "People don't do such things." Hedda's offstage pistol shot is her last defiance of what is expected from her. Suicide within the world of *Hedda Gabler* can be considered an act of strength, not weakness (although there are other interpretations, of course). In the pitiless world of Brecht's *In the Jungle of Cities*, survival at any cost is the highest good; suicide, for whatever reason, would be an act of failure and defeat. These may or may not be the values of the audience members, or the playwright, or even of the onstage characters. They are the values of the world in which the play takes place.

Ruth Benedict's Model

That quote about suicide was written by a student of Franz Boas—a quiet, shy woman who always wore the same dress for class when she was Boas's teaching assistant at Barnard College. On those occasions when she had to speak to the class on her own, she was often awkward, but as one of her later students described: "between the 'uh' and 'ah' often came a bombshell of light which changed everything" (67). Her name was Ruth Benedict, and she theorized that each culture had a central idea that organized that culture like a "personality writ large." This is the second theory of cultural anthropology to adapt for use in an actor's analysis of a play: *the rules of the play make a pattern.*

When one value is held highest, others are less important by comparison, and this configuration adds up to the characteristics of a consistent world. In Shakespeare's *Richard III*, pity and scruples are not as important as self-conviction and aggression. A deformed hunchback double-crosses his allies, arranges the murder of his brother and best friends, orders the death of children, and seduces the widow of a man he has killed. In our world, Richard is a wretch; in his own world he is the King. When playing such a role, it doesn't help to condemn Richard or even to investigate his motives; it helps to understand him in the context of the world in which he is set.

Ruth Benedict's theory offers an actor a good understanding of how such a wretch could become King. Her first and most influential book, *Patterns of Culture* (1934), summarized years of research, thinking, and comparative analysis. Boas, by the way, wrote the introduction. For each of the cultures she examined, Benedict claimed to have identified a pattern that influenced the way tribe members perceived and lived in the world. Individuals, of course, rebelled or fit in, but they all measured themselves by the local standards, and within the accepted pattern. Like the physical dimensions of Gulliver's hosts, this cultural pattern or configuration determined identity and meaning.

Benedict's first field studies were among the Zuni communities of the American southwest, a people who valued sobriety and inoffensiveness above all other virtues. They disliked charisma. If he had been born in a Zuni pueblo, someone like Richard III would have been hung by his thumbs as a witch. Five years later, Benedict was startled to find that the Pima Indians—near neighbors of the Zuni who lived in the same desert conditions—thought that conflict and ecstasy were the essence of existence. Had someone like Richard III lived among *them*, where fighting was the highest of virtues, he would have thrived (although he probably would have been despised for his relentless opportunism).

In organizing her field research, Benedict did not rank the two tribes as better or worse, but respected them as systems of their own. She labeled them as *Dionysian* and *Apollonian*, based on which value the group held highest: ecstasy or calm. These labels were borrowed from an essay about Greek tragedy by the German philosopher Friedrich Nietzsche. Later, Benedict added a dour group of South Pacific Islanders—called the Dobu—as a third example of a psychological frame of mind, which she called *paranoid*. Richard III would have been quite at home among the Dobu. Benedict writes:

> The motivations that run through all Dobuan existence are singularly limited
> . . . All existence is cut-throat competition, and every advantage is gained at
> the expense of a defeated rival . . . The good man, the successful man, is he
> who has cheated another of his place (68).

In the pattern of Richard III's world, a ruthless man is characteristic and admirable, just as in the Dobu's world. Richard's butchery is therefore exemplary, not monstrous. This is the third principle to be taken from cultural anthropology: *A role should be characterized within the context of the play*. In Brecht's *In the Jungle of Cities*, savagery is normal, reticence a disease. Garga's mildness would be praised among the Zuni. But among the Dobu, Garga, like all people "of sunny, kindly disposition who like work and like to be helpful," would be considered "silly and simple and definitely crazy" (69).

Even before *Patterns of Culture* was published, Benedict wrote an article for the *Journal of General Psychology* that urged psychologists and psychiatrists to encourage tolerance for less-usual types in our own culture, since ideas of normal and abnormal were relative. In 1937, Karen Horney, an American psychoanalyst directly influenced by Benedict, also challenged the accepted theories of psychology to redefine "normal" and "abnormal" as particular to culture. According to Horney (who wished her name to be pronounced *Horn-eye*), there was no one biologically inevitable psychology—as Freud had claimed. There was, for example, no inevitable women's envy of men, there was no inevitable rivalry with one's father. These were the definitions of the society in which Freud lived, where men were powerful, women were not, and winning a competition was the goal of life. In a society where women were powerful, there would be and was envy of men for women. In a society that endorsed compromise, fathers and sons would have less competitive relations.

Horney's acceptance of Benedict's theory of a culture as "a personality writ large" was and is unusual. Among most other scientists, Benedict's theory is controversial. Her labels "Dionysian" and "Apollonian" are subjective and interpretive, by definition unscientific. Like stereotypes, they reduce complex and dynamic forces to a single word: *serene, ecstatic*, or *paranoid*. Another complaint is that Benedict did not sufficiently take into account that cultural patterns are always changing, and a cultural environment rarely, if ever, has clear origins or borders. Yet the criticisms of Benedict's theory as science reinforce its perhaps more appropriate application to the analysis of the world of a play. A play *is* finite in time and space: it begins and ends. Its borders are marked by a curtain or a raised platform or a line drawn on the ground. It has a limited number of people to compare. Its sources are generally known, and the subjectivity of an organizing image like *Dionysian* or *ecstatic* is exactly what an actor is looking for to galvanize his performance.

Significantly, Ruth Benedict was partially deaf, and grew deafer as she grew older. Like Stanislavsky watching Duse perform in Italian, or Brecht watching Mei Lanfang perform in Chinese, wherever Benedict went she paid close attention to what her subjects did, separately from her grasp of what they were saying. Her built-in deference to the foreign culture being observed set up a habit of observation that was antithetical to the aloof and distanced protocol of other researchers. In order to read lips, she needed, like an actor, to understand the *emotional images* of the speaker with whom she was trying to communicate.

Reading Shakespeare in context

The similarity of Ruth Benedict's methods to an actor's is not a coincidence. In 1946, two years before she died, in her last speech as President of the American Anthropology Association, Benedict revealed that her insight of how meaning changes from culture to culture had been shaped by reading Shakespeare criticism. The texts written by Shakespeare, she explained, had been known and performed for four centuries; from her own reading of each era's critics she had learned how each era read very different meanings into the same words. Criticism, she wrote, also taught techniques for studying symbols and arranging what seemed like a writer's free associations into patterns (70).

At the same time Benedict was reading Shakespeare criticism and organizing *Patterns of Culture*, critics of Shakespeare were lining up new systems of criticism that closely paralleled Benedict's ideas. In 1930, the British critic G. Wilson Knight laid out the new guidelines in *On the Principles of Shakespeare Interpretation*:

1. We should first regard each play as a visionary unit bound to obey none but its own self-imposed laws.
2. [We should] . . . relate any given incident or speech either to the time-sequence of the story or the peculiar atmosphere, intellectual or imaginative, which binds the play. . . . we should not look for perfect verisimilitude to life, but rather see each play as an expanded metaphor . . . It will then usually appear that many difficult actions and events become coherent and with the scope of their universe, natural (71).

Following G. Wilson Knight's lead, a very influential essay with the sarcastic title "How Many Children Had Lady Macbeth?" was published in 1933 by another British critic, L.C. Knights. Knights considered any modern search for a Shakespearean character's motivation as further evidence of a reluctance to master the words of the play—as inadequate a method for explaining the meaning of these roles as the Victorian era's sentimental biographies that invented answers to the essay's title question. Knights declared that Shakespeare's texts only made sense when one started with "so many lines of verse on a printed page. . . ." The key to understanding the plays, Knights wrote, was "the unique arrangement of words that constitutes these plays" (72).

For example, in Chapter 7 it was pointed out that when clothing is mentioned in *Macbeth*, it is associated with an image of clothing borrowed—or stolen—from someone else. Other associations in *Macbeth* cluster around this same idea of false or unnatural appearance. The play begins with witches described as women who have men's beards. "Fair is foul," they say at the end of the first short scene. Macbeth, too, announces as he enters, "So fair and foul a day I have not seen."

Similar images throughout the five acts of *Macbeth* build what Shakespeare critics called a *recurring theme* of the play: unnatural nature, named within the play itself as *equivocation*, a lie passed off as the truth. If she had observed this in a field study, Ruth Benedict would have called this recurring pattern the "personality writ large."

An actor answering the question *Is Macbeth a bad man or a good man?* should do so in the context of the play. Within the world of equivocation, Macbeth can be understood to have equivocal motivations and obstacles. The smiling traitor, the trusted nobleman who kills his King—like a woman with a beard or a day simultaneously fair and foul—Macbeth is a living mix of opposites: a good man who does bad things.

Meaning in the world of *Macbeth* also depends on the form in which the characters speak. Here, as in the other plays written in iambic pentameter by Shakespeare, "natural" speech is poetry with ten syllables to a line. Ten-syllable lines tap out a base rhythm, as in the unsuspecting King's appreciation of the place where he is to be killed:

This / cas / tle / hath / a / plea / sant / seat; / the / air (10)
Nim / bly / and / sweet / ly / re / com / mends / it / self (10)

Set against a norm of ten syllables, deviations of fewer and more syllables are significant, and often characterize the speaker as disturbed in some way—even a harmonious character like Ross, here describing the King's murder:

Thou / seest / the / hea / vens, / as / troubl / ed / with / man's / act, (11)
Threat / en / his / blood / y / stage: / by / the / clock / tis / day, (11)
And / yet / dark / night / strang / les / the / trav / el / ing / lamp. (11)

The lines are overloaded with syllables because the speaker is overcharged with emotion. Among plays by Shakespeare, *Macbeth*, with its central theme of distortion, is one of the texts with the most frequent distortion of the verse pattern: many lines of nine, eleven, twelve, and thirteen. Audience members are not tapping out the number of syllables with their feet, but the repetition, like the beat of music, sets up a visceral response when the "normal" rhythm is broken. Anything an actor might try is set within this rhythm and variation. An actor concentrating on inner imagery to the exclusion of such technical considerations will sabotage the possible effect of psychological motives or motivated behavior.

Read according to Knight and Knights, the text called *The Tragedy of Macbeth* is its own unique system of meaning. That system is made up of words that are configured around recurring themes. The character called Macbeth, or any character in the play, can only be understood against the grid of those words. From criticism or from anthropology, then, we can borrow similar concepts to define the world of the play.

Terms to Work with: The Rules of the World of the Play

The world of the play

The **world of the play** includes the specific environments within which the play is set and performed, the form in which the play is written, and the rules that measure the behavior of characters set within the world. World of the play analysis considers the play as a whole. If you want to approach your work with a world of the play analysis, it helps to look at all the scenes of the play, not just the ones you are in. Look at all the roles, not just your own. Only when the rules for the play are understood can a role, specific behavior, or episode be understood.

Other disciplines use different terms to describe a similar idea: in psychology, the word is *gestalt* (from the German word meaning "configuration"); in anthropology, the words used in place of Ruth Benedict's *pattern* can be *cultural configuration* or a *culture* among other cultures. Besides being simpler, the word *world* has a history that recommends its use—which has nothing to do with land or territory. *World* comes from the language called Old German, and is made up of two words: *wer*, meaning "man" (as in "werewolf"!), and *ald*, as in "age" or "time." Literally *wer-ald* mean "man time" or "era." In literature it is called the *worldview* or, as in the title of E.M.W. Tillyard's excellent book: *The Elizabethan World Picture*. As we have in other chapters, let's agree to call the idea by the same name and move on.

Also, as in other chapters, the world of the play is an interpretation. Barren, Yerma can be seen as pathetic in a world where women are meant to have children. Barren, Yerma can be seen as a heroine in a world where women are meant to have children, so strong in her purpose that she is willing to kill what stands in her way. There is no single interpretation, although there are useful ways to look for answers in order to establish a set of *rules*.

The rules and patterns of the world of the play

The **rules** of the world of the play organize the behavior and the environment in that world. The rules do not govern, they are a measure. Not everyone conforms. A big mistake—and a common one—is to think that every character you play is wise, beautiful, strong, and a winner. No. World of the play analysis allows you to measure your character against other characters and to define weakness or strength in an active relationship with other characters. Not everyone is as beautiful as you are, or as intelligent—but then again, your intelligence might count for nothing in the world, just as Gulliver's didn't when the King of Brobdingnag picked him up and examined him like an insect.

Once you define the rules of the world of the play, you can identify a **pattern** of behavior governed by those rules. The pattern is the consistent configuration of behavior in the play; it is the context, the system of meaning within which roles are characterized. World of the play analysis identifies and collects details of behavior and dialogue in order to relate them to deeper patterns embedded in the text.

The Ten Questions

How can you begin defining the rules of the world so that you can begin to identify the play's patterns? The rules of the world are derived, at first, from the answers to **ten questions**. You can, should, and will ask more questions than ten. You can refine and clarify your vision by adding three more questions at every rehearsal and performance, but, to begin, answer at least these ten. They need not be asked in this sequence. If you want, you can notice that the questions are in categories that correspond to anthropological study. You don't have to notice that. Just answer the questions.

Here are the ten questions with quick answers—all of them interpretations, not absolutes—from the scenes we've already analyzed for tasks, episodes, and images.

- **In the world of this play, what is beautiful and what is ugly?**
  In the world of *Hedda Gabler*, traditions are beautiful, innovations are ugly. In the world of *The Maids*, artifice is beautiful, to be plain and unadorned is to be ugly.
- **In the world of this play, what is strong and what is weak?**
  In the world of *Richard III*, sureness of purpose is strong, doubt is weak. In the world of *Yerma*, instinct is strong, the rules of society are weak.
- **In the world of this play, what is wisdom and what is ignorance?**
  In the world of *In the Jungle of Cities*, knowing how to undermine your rival is wisdom, ignorance is believing in compromise. In the world of *The Maids*, wisdom is understanding that reality is a manufactured façade, ignorance is accepting things for what they seem to be.
- **In the world of this play, what is skill and what is ineptitude?**
  In *In the Jungle of Cites*, cunning is a skill, compassion is ineptitude. In *The Maids*, skill is the ability to tell a convincing lie; when you get caught lying you're inept. (Notice that wisdom and ignorance are states of mind, skill and ineptitude are things you do.)
- **In the world of this play, what is common and what is elite?**
  In the world of *Richard III*, civilians are common, warriors are elite. In the world of *The Lesson*, Pupils are common, Professors are elite.
- **In the world of this play, what is polite and what is not polite?**
  In the world of *The Lesson*, it is polite for the Pupil to obey the Professor. It is not polite to be too smart. In the world of *Hedda Gabler*, it is polite to suffer in silence. It is not polite to shoot yourself dead. (Notice that the difference between polite and elite is that polite depends on *what you do*, elite is *who you are*.)

- **In the world of this play, what is good and what is evil?**
  In the world of *Yerma*, it is good to have a child, it is evil to be barren. In the world of *Hedda Gabler*, convention is good, eccentricity is evil.
- **In the world of this play, how do people survive?**
  In the world of *Richard III*, people survive by lying, deceiving, outwitting, and back-stabbing. In the world of *Hedda Gabler*, people survive by hard work, narrow vision, and aping conventional morals. Hedda does not survive, but her husband and her friend live after her.
- **In the world of this play, how do people improve?**
  In the world of *The Lesson*, the Pupil improves by obeying the Professor—even if that means dying. In the world of *Richard III*, people improve by killing their rivals.
- **In the world of this play, how do people win or lose?**
  In the world of *Yerma*, you win by having a baby. This is not a world of adoption, abortion, or planned parenting. In the world of *The Maids*, people win when they meld illusion with reality. In *The Maids*, people lose when they're stuck with their plain, banal lives. In the anti-romantic *In the Jungle of Cities*, you lose if you fall in love.

There will be some overlap and repetition in answering the ten questions, but not as much as you would think. In some worlds, strong is not beautiful (*Richard III*), polite is not elite (*In the Jungle of Cities*), and skill is not wisdom (*Yerma*). Notice that for Hedda the world is ugly; for her husband George and his Aunt Juju, it is beautiful. George, who has a conventional mind, is a survivor; Hedda, who embraces originality, is doomed. Richard III is ruthless, a virtue in his world; his prey, Lady Anne, for all her "virtues" in other worlds, lacks common sense in this one.

Notice also that answering the ten questions helps direct and define the results of previous approaches already used to investigate scenes. The glamorous image Madame has of herself is foolish and self-deluding. Out of her finery, Madame is as common and as ugly as her maids, although she doesn't know it. The episode of Richard seducing Anne is reinterpreted as theft: on his way to steal the throne, Richard steals a dead man's wife. Hedda's motivation is revealed as defiance, and her flirtation with Mr. Løvborg is motivated by rebellion against society, rather than sexual attraction.

Finding Answers to the Ten Questions: Analyzing *Desire Under the Elms*

Let's answer the ten questions in our analysis of a scene from Eugene O'Neill's 1924 *Desire Under the Elms* (73) and see how the behavior in the scene can then be interpreted. Later, we'll look at ways that this scene can help with the interpretation of other scenes in the play, and how knowing the rules of the world of the play will structure rehearsals.

Eugene O'Neill was the first American to receive a Nobel Prize for literature. He based the text of *Desire Under the Elms* on an ancient Greek myth—the story of Phaedra's unrestrained love for her stepson Hippolytus. The same subject was already the source for two other famous plays: *Hippolytus* written by Euripides in 428 BCE in Greek verse and *Phèdre*, written in 1677 by Jean Racine, who set the story in rhyming twelve-syllable French couplets, called *alexandrines*. O'Neill set his American stepson/stepmother love story in Vermont in 1850. The play is written in a rural New England dialect, which makes it difficult to read. It makes it difficult to translate, too, but that hasn't stopped the play from taking its place in the world repertory. In 1999, there was a production in Belgrade; in the 1980s it was performed in Mongolia. There have been productions in Russia since the 1920s.

This excerpt is from the fourth scene of the first act. The stepmother has yet to enter. The section we'll look at begins with two characters O'Neill added to the story, Simeon and Peter, two other sons from the father's previous marriage.

> SIMEON *and* PETER *stare at the sky with a numbed appreciation.*

PETER Purty!

SIMEON Ay-eh. Gold's t' the East now.

PETER Sun's startin' with us fur the Golden West.

SIMEON (*staring around the farm, his compressed face tightened, unable to conceal his emotion*) Waal—it's our last mornin'—mebbe.

PETER (*the same*) Ay-eh.

SIMEON (*stamps his foot on the earth and addresses it desperately*) Waal—ye've thirty year o' me buried in ye—spread out over ye—blood an' bone an' sweat—rotted away—fertilizin' ye—richin' yer soul—prime manure, by God, that's what I been t'ye!

PETER Ay-eh! An' me!

SIMEON An' yew, Peter. (*he sighs—then spits*) Waal—no use'n cryin' over spilt milk.

PETER They's gold in the West—an' freedom mebbe. We been slaves t' stone walls here.

SIMEON (*defiantly*) We hain't nobody's slaves from this out—nor no thin's slaves nuther. (*a pause—restlessly*) Speakin' o' milk, wonder how Eben's managin'?

The play itself will define its world—and in direct words

When spoken aloud and acted onstage, the words of the text set out the rules that govern the world of the play. Often, those rules are established directly. A character will announce that *this is beautiful, this is strong,* and *this is my idea of good.*

- "Fair is foul and foul is fair," say the witches in *Macbeth*, and they're not kidding.
- "It's better to know which is more important, a pound of fish or an opinion," Shlink announces in *In the Jungle of Cities*.
- "People don't do such things," says the Judge at the end of *Hedda Gabler*.

COMPARISON

In this scene from *Desire Under the Elms*, some statements are made:

- The sky is pretty.
- People are manure to the earth.
- There's no use crying over spilt milk.

From this, it's not too complicated to begin to answer some of our questions:

- In the world of *Desire Under the Elms*, the sky and the earth are beautiful. Men are not beautiful, they are manure.
- In the world of *Desire Under the Elms*, it is polite to conserve your emotions: compress them, numb them, control them. It is rude to waste them.

Although these statements are made by individual characters, they hold true for the entire play. Similar statements are made in earlier scenes as well as in later scenes.

The historical period and setting help establish the rules

Although he was writing in 1924, O'Neill set his play in 1850, in New England. Life in that place at that time was tied to the land. The soil was rocky, difficult to farm, and yielded few rewards. Labor was hard and unforgiving. There were few emotional outlets. Church-going was orderly and dull, New England churches no longer the places of ecstasy or torment they had been a hundred years earlier.

In 1848, far from the Atlantic coast, gold was discovered out West, free for the panning out of California's rivers. The chance to strike it rich was a direct challenge to the Puritan work ethic, an alternative to hand-to-mouth subsistence picking rocks out of the Connecticut soil. Going to California meant abandoning life as it was known: those who chose to stay East accepted a life of hardship.

Also, in 1850 the argument over slavery was building to the Civil War, which would erupt a decade later. It was a point of pride with New Englanders that they were free men, not slaves, who owned the land they worked. This pride in possession compensated for their back-breaking work. Peter and Simeon realize that they'll never own the farm they've been working, so they're leaving New England. Eben, the third son (in the role of Hippolytus), is happy to do both his and his brothers' chores; he thinks of the farm as his eventual inheritance. His stepmother Abbie (in the Phaedra role) will explain that she married Eben's father, Ephraim, so she wouldn't have to work for someone else. In other plays—and worlds—working for someone else is not the horror it is made out to be here. With these ideas in mind, a few more questions can be answered:

- In the world of this play, it's bad to be owned by someone; it's good to be free.
- In the world of this play, there's freedom in the West. The play takes place in the East, by inference the land of servitude.

PETER They's gold in the West—an' freedom mebbe. We been slaves t' stone walls here.

SIMEON (*defiantly*) We hain't nobody's slaves from this out—nor no thin's slaves nuther. (*a pause—restlessly*) Speakin' o' milk, wonder how Eben's man-agin'?

PETER I s'pose he's managin'.

SIMEON Mebbe we'd ought t'help—this once.

PETER Mebbe. The cows knows us.

SIMEON An' likes us. They don't know him much.

PETER An' the hosses, an' pigs, an' chickens. They don't know him much.

SIMEON They knows us like brothers—an' likes us! (*proudly*) Hain't we raised 'em t' be fust-rate, number one prize stock?

PETER We hain't—not no more.

SIMEON (*dully*) I was fergittin'. (*then resignedly*) Waal, let's go help Eben a spell an' git waked up.

PETER Suits me.

They are starting off down left, rear, for the barn when EBEN *appears from there, hurrying toward them, his face excited.*

Notice that the rules of the world are established not only from what the characters say, but also from what they do—their behavior. From these lines and the behavior associated with them, we learn more:

- In the world of this play, people survive by doing their chores and by serving a hard master.
- In the world of this play, it is impossible to win. You can only escape.

Understand that the historical period is a rendering of the playwright's—what the writer understands and what the writer selects to include in the action of the play. O'Neill's 1850s America is his own creation, like Shakespeare's Rome or Brecht's Chicago, and not a historical reality. In 1850, not too far from the setting of this play, Herman Melville wrote home to his friends in New York that he was finishing *Moby Dick* on sweet Berk-shire grass. The New England grass is certainly not sweet in *Desire Under the Elms*.

The time and place in which the play was written help to establish the rules

The environment in which the play was written is often more important for a world of the play analysis than the period in which the play is set. Think of the different versions of "Cleopatra." Bernard Shaw's witty Egypt defines a very different Cleopatra from Shakespeare's romantic Egypt. Claudette Colbert's Cleopatra and Elizabeth Taylor's and Sarah Bernhardt's are all very different too, reflections of the fashions in the world that created them. Think of Liz and Dick's 1960s *La Dolce Vita* version or Colbert's 1932 soigné evening gowns and Art Deco cruise on Cecil B. DeMille's glassy Nile.

COMPARISON

When *Desire Under the Elms* was written in 1924, traditional American values were as challenged as they had been in the 1850s. During the 1920s, American women voted for the first time. Sexuality was more openly expressed, especially in popular dance and in the movies, where a new female character, the "vamp" (short for vampire), modernized the late-nineteenth century's fear that a woman's sexuality would steal a man's power.*

The most significant challenge to America's traditional values was the new popular science of psychology: Sigmund Freud's theory that behavior was a function of sexual desire, especially repressed desire. Because Freud's theories explained the dynamic of American repression and predicted its inevitable end, they appealed especially to American intellectuals. *The old God is dead*, wrote O'Neill, *and what can take his place?* The answer for many people was the psychology identified by Freud as universal, among them the daughter's inevitable desire for her father and hatred of her mother, called the *Electra complex*. The *Oedipus complex* was Freud's theory of a similarly inevitable competition between father and son for the mother's love.

These complexes resonated with many Americans as explanations for the conflict between generations and changing social patterns. O'Neill used the Electra complex for his 1932 retelling of Greek myth in American images, *Mourning Becomes Electra*. In *Desire Under the Elms*, he added the Oedipus complex to the ancient story of Phaedra and Hippolytus and insisted on a motivation not to be found in the original: that the stepson was consciously stealing the stepmother from the father.

SIMEON Waal, let's go help Eben a spell an' git waked up.

PETER Suits me.

> *They are starting off down left, rear, for the barn when* EBEN *appears from there, hurrying toward them, his face excited.*

EBEN (*breathlessly*) Waal—har they be! The old mule an' the bride! I seen 'em from the barn down below at the turnin'.

PETER How could ye tell that far?

EBEN Hain't I as far-sight as he's near-sight? Don't I know the mare an' buggy, an' two people settin' in it? Who else . . .? An' I tell ye I kin feel 'em a-comin', too! (*he squirms as if he had an itch*)

PETER (*beginning to be angry*) Waal—let him do his own unhitchin'!

SIMEON (*angry in his turn*) Let's hustle in an' git our bundles an' be a-going' as he's a-comin'. I don't want never t'step inside the door agen arter he's back. (*They both start back around the corner of the house.* EBEN *follows them*)

EBEN (*anxiously*) Will ye sign it afore ye go?

PETER Let's see the color o' the old skinflint's money an' we'll sign.

---

*You can see vamps flouncing about in *Orphans of the Storm*. They're the lascivious party girls with black rings of make-up around their eyes that give them the appearance of raccoons. Not a bad image for Madame in *The Maids*.

They disappear left. The two brothers clump upstairs to get their bundles. EBEN *appears in the kitchen, runs to the window, peers out, comes back and pulls up a strip of flooring in under stove, takes out a canvas bag and puts it on the table, then sets the floorboard back in place. The two brothers appear a moment after. They carry old carpetbags.*

Another change in American society in the 1920s that O'Neill was sensitive to was the redefinition of American values into increasingly material terms. The Protestant idea that God rewards hard work was harnessed by the growing and persuasive field of advertising to convince the public that the accumulation of bought and sold objects could improve a person's soul. "The business of America is business," said Calvin Coolidge, the taciturn American president at the time (who, not coincidentally, was from New England). O'Neill wrote that it disgusted him to think that the progress of the human race was now to be measured by the acquisition of material goods.

EBEN (*puts his hand on bag guardingly*) Have ye signed?

SIMEON (*shows paper in his hand*) Ay-eh. (*greedily*) Be that the money?

EBEN (*opens bag and pours out pile of twenty-dollar gold pieces*) Twenty-dollar pieces—thirty of 'em. Count 'em. (PETER *does so, arranging them in stacks of five, biting one or two to test them*)

PETER Six hundred. (*he puts them in bag and puts it inside his shirt carefully*)

SIMEON (*handing paper to* EBEN) Har ye be.

EBEN (*after a glance, folds it carefully and hides it under his shirt—gratefully*) Thank yew.

PETER Thank yew for the ride.

SIMEON We'll send ye a lump o' gold fur Christmas. (*A pause.* EBEN *stares at them and they at him*)

PETER (*awkwardly*) Waal—we're a-goin'.

SIMEON Coming out t' the yard?

EBEN No. I'm waitin' in here a spell.

Another silence. The brothers edge awkwardly to door in rear—then turn and stand.

SIMEON Waal—good-by.

PETER Good-by.

The bag of gold is a prop from a melodrama and is meant to be misleading. In the world of this play, people do not get rich or improve their lives with money. The characters *think* they improve by accumulating wealth, but by the play's end they learn that none of that has worth. In the last scene, Ephraim Cabot, the father, claims that he too will go to California, but the gold he saved to pay for such a trip is gone and he is forced to live his life in the hard way God wants him to.

- In the world of this play, it is common to work the soil, to pay attention to traditional values. It is elite to ignore them.
- In the world of this play, it is skill to squeeze money out of rocks. It is inept to give money away or let it be stolen.

The author's value system

Sometimes a playwright will organize the world of a play with his own systematic insight into life. Some playwrights really worked at their systems like philosophers. You may recall from Chapter 7 that the Swedish playwright August Strindberg held the belief that the world was organized into vampires and their victims. So when you're acting in a play by Strindberg, it's good to ask: *Am I the vampire or the victim? Do I survive by sucking the life force out of people around me, or am I the person who is being drained?* Strindberg also believed that there was an ongoing war between the sexes. He further held that women naturally bonded against men and met in secret to discuss strategy. Now, whether it's true or not isn't the point. Strindberg wasn't creating a mirror, he was creating an energy-charged world of his own imagination that, yes, did have some relationship to corseted nineteenth-century Scandinavian sex roles.

Similarly, the American playwright Tennessee Williams created an imaginary landscape inhabited by noble losers and virile survivors. It helps to know that, to Williams, losing was noble, not shameful. It's equally useful when playing the murderous *Maids* to know that being a criminal was glamorous to their creator, Jean Genet.

Of necessity, a playwright has a vision of the world as relationships between people, and often a playwright will have a vision that he has developed from play to play. That doesn't mean that all of a playwright's plays have the same value systems, but some playwrights seem to be visiting the same imaginary world repeatedly. In the many plays O'Neill wrote within the decade, his return to the structure of a Freudian pattern is consistent, especially his dramatic use of tension between public behavior and the unexpressed subconscious. In *Desire Under the Elms*, as in his other plays, a system of values is set out directly by statements and stage action. Here is O'Neill's description of Ephraim Cabot's abandon during a square dance from later in the play:

CABOT (. . . *suddenly, unable to restrain himself any longer, he prances into the midst of the dancers, scattering them, waving his arms about wildly*) Ye're all hoofs! Git out o' my road! Give me room! I'll show ye dancin'. Ye're all too soft! (*He pushes them roughly away. They crowd back toward the walls, muttering, looking at him resentfully*)

FIDDLER (*jeeringly*) Go it, Ephraim! Go it.

He starts "Pop, Goes the Weasel," increasing the tempo with every verse until at the end he is fiddling crazily as fast as he can go. CABOT *starts to dance, which he does very well and with tremendous vigor. Then he begins to improvise, cuts incredibly grotesque capers, leaping up and cracking his heels together, prancing around in a circle with body bent in an Indian war dance, then suddenly straightening up and kicking as high as he can with both legs. He is like a monkey on a string. And all the while he intersperses his antics with shouts and derisive comments.*

CABOT Whoop! Here's dancin' fur ye! Whoop! See that! Seventy-six, if I'm a day! Hard as iron yet! . . .

The undeniable effect of this onstage is the establishment of another rule: *In the world of this play, under a veneer, the savage power of the body is strong. Civilization is weak.*

Acknowledged or not, an author's insight is affected by the circumstances of his life, and it's useful to know those circumstance when determining the rules of the play. Be careful here. In defining the author's value system, it is a mistake to interpret the play as a symptom of the playwright's life. However, if we examine *Desire Under the Elms*, Eugene O'Neill's personal life does organize this play—and every other play he ever wrote that contained father and son characters.

EBEN Good-by.

They go out. He sits down at the table, faces the stove and pulls out the paper. He looks from it to the stove. His face, lighted up by the shaft of sunlight from the window, has an expression of trance. His lips move. The two brothers come out to the gate.

PETER (*looking off toward barn*) Thar he be—unhitchin'.

SIMEON (*with a chuckle*) I'll bet ye he's riled!

PETER An thar she be.

SIMEON Let's wait'n'see what our new Maw looks like.

PETER (*with a grin*) An' give him our partin' cuss!

SIMEON (*grinning*) I feel like raisin' fun. I feel light in my head an' feet.

PETER Me, too. I feel like laffin' till I'd split up the middle.

SIMEON Reckon it's the likker?

PETER No. My feet feel itchin' t'walk an' walk—an' jump high over thin's—an'. . .

SIMEON Dance? (*a pause*)

PETER (*puzzled*) It's plumb onnateral.

SIMEON (*a light coming over his face*) I calc'late it's 'cause school's out. It's holiday. Fur once we're free!

PETER (*dazedly*) Free?

COMPARISON

In life, O'Neill's father was the actor James O'Neill, who began his career with the potential to become a master of classical roles, but out of constant fear of poverty limited himself to repeating the same successful swashbuckling role from the melodramatic play based on the Dumas novel *The Count of Monte Cristo*. O'Neill's mother was a soft person and a drug addict, easily swayed by her stingy husband. O'Neill blamed his father for his mother's drug addiction, and rebelled against his family by running off to sea as a sailor. Wraith-like mothers are part of the O'Neill mythology. So are skin-flint fathers associated with the word "stinking"—a combination unforgettable to anyone who knows O'Neill's masterpiece *Long Day's Journey into Night* (published 1956), a play with two sons, a wraith-like mother, and a stingy father.

"You stinking old miser!" The younger son Jamie, who has tuberculosis, hurls these words at his father, who is deciding whether to send Jamie to a cheap state-run sanatorium. "To think when it's a question of your son having consumption, you can show yourself up before the whole town as such a stinking old tightwad!" (74). *Long Day's Journey* is a family saga so frankly autobiographical that O'Neill wrote the play with tears streaming down his face.

> JAMIE (*trying to control his sobs*) I've known about Mama so much longer than
> you. Never forget the first time I got wise. Caught her in the act with a hypo.
> Christ, I'd never dreamed before that any women but whores took dope! (74)

Defying one's father and then *cursing one's father* are major actions in the world of *Desire Under the Elms*, or any O'Neill play. The playwright spent his whole life writing about these subjects, setting them in worlds where:

- It is skill to be hard, it is inept to be soft.
- Mothers are soft, fathers are hard.
- Freedom is so rare it is practically unimaginable.

O'Neill's ideas are specific to his life. In playing a son or father or mother in one of his plays, it is important to understand that these family roles make up a system, like a mythology. Your memories of your own father are probably not those of Eugene O'Neill's. For O'Neill, the pride of a father is that of possession, not love. It is promiscuously sentimental to work yourself up about dear old dad until you first understand what it means to be a dad in the world of the play.*

---

*Ruth Benedict has something pertinent to say about this in *Patterns of Culture*: "Without the clue that in our civilization at large man's paramount aim is to amass private possessions and multiply occasions of display, the modern position of the wife and the modern emotions of jealousy are alike unintelligible. Our attitudes toward our children are equally evidences of this same cultural goal. Our children are not individuals whose rights and tastes are casually respected from infancy, as they are in some primitive societies, but special responsibilities, like our possessions, to which we succumb or in which we glory, as the case may be. They are fundamentally extensions of our own egos and give a special opportunity for the display of authority. The pattern is not inherent in the parent-child situation, as we so glibly assume. It is impressed upon the situation by the major drives of our culture, and it is only one of the occasions in which we follow our traditional obsessions" (75).

The conventions of the text

O'Neill restlessly tried different dramatic forms and theatrical conventions to return to the theme of repression and desire. In his play *The Great God Brown* (1925), two different actors wore masks to express different aspects of the same character. In *Strange Interlude* (1926–1927), characters spoke their subtext directly to the audience as "interior monologues." In *Lazarus Laughed* (1925–1926), there is a masked chorus with, according to O'Neill, the "seven general types of character," including the "Self-Tortured" and the "Introspective." In *Desire Under the Elms*, with the rich source material of the Hippolytus story and the intimidating examples of brilliant verse treatments by Euripides and Racine, O'Neill applied the New England dialect he had used earlier in his Pulitzer Prize-winning *Beyond the Horizon* (1920).

The homely language is the equivalent of the bleak physical landscape. The flat tones of the characters are as much a part of the world as the stones of the earth or the animals in the barns. O'Neill's tin ear—a serious problem in other texts (to which his foreign admirers are happily deaf)—contributes to the consistent pattern of the world of the play. According to the aesthetics of our world, O'Neill's lines can seem ludicrous, especially the use of *ay-eh* for "yes," said in flat tones like the *moo* of a cow:

> ABBIE I—I killed him, Eben.
> EBEN (*amazed*) Ye killed him?
> ABBIE (*dully*) Ay-eh . . .

And a few lines later:

> EBEN Not—not that baby!
> ABBIE (*dully*) Ay-eh!

The division between passion and the poverty of passion's expression reinforces the pattern of repressed emotional characters in a repressed world. The effect is to evoke emotion by what is not said and to characterize emotional expression as stingy.

Despite its seeming poverty, the dialect used by O'Neill has rules and its own riches. In the climax of the play, when Eben decides to suffer along with Abbie, she says what is laughably trite:

> ABBIE (*forcing a smile—adoringly*) I hain't beat—s'long's I got ye!

But notice that the dialect forces a line reading. The overly familiar and lovesick "So long as I got YOU" is impossible, since *ye* cannot be extended that way. The emphasis must be placed on *got*: "So long as I GOT ye." This reinforces that, in the world of this play, possession is a much stronger value than love. O'Neill could have written the line as *yew*, a form he uses a few lines before:

EBEN . . . I'd suffer wuss leavin' ye, goin' West, think' o' ye day an' night, being out when yew was in—(*lowering his voice*) 'r bein' alive when yew was dead.

The forms of language used in any play can be examined for structure. Verse drama, of course, is written to dramatize the structure of speech. In Racine's 1676 version of the same story, speech on stage is in the form of twelve-syllable rhyming couplets. The rule is that a thought ends with the end of a line. When Racine's stepmother, Phèdre, fails to complete her thought—five times in a row!—it's a signal that she has lost her mind and can no longer control herself. Here is a description of the celebrated French actress Rachel (from Chapter 2) performing the role in Russia:

> Rachel begins with full voice the tale of her criminal love. Soon the words, the couplets, as if driven by the thought, begin to run as incredible, barely audible speech. . . . In mid-monologue, Phèdre, giving herself up totally to a single thought, loses self-consciousness and is almost beside herself. Her lips tremble, her eyes blaze with a maniacal fire, a gesture becomes insanely expressive, that ghastly whisper goes on the whole time, and the words run on, filled with agonizing truth (76).

O'Neill gives his stepmother a wild cry, which set among the *ay-eh*'s, flies free:

ABBIE Don't ye leave me, Eben! Can't ye see it hain't enuf—lovin' ye like a Maw—can't ye see it's got t'be that an' more—much more—a hundred times more—fur me t'be happy—fur yew t' be happy?

From these and other speeches we can deduce one more rule: *In the world of this play, to be happy is desire's defiance of morality.*

The conventions of the production

The physical production and the director's concept also affect the meaning of performances, as anyone doomed to stand onstage trapped in a stupid costume or buried under a ton of scenery can tell you.

The original production of *Desire Under the Elms* was staged in a cut-away house designed by Robert Edmond Jones, based on a sketch by O'Neill. This setting had realms as well as rooms. Upstairs, there were the father's room and the son's room. The stepmother had the power to see through those walls, just as she had the power to move from father to son. The kitchen and the parlor were downstairs. Early in the play, the parlor was established as the dead mother's realm. The stepson brought his stepmother into the parlor to meet his dead mother, who haunted the place. When the long-closed parlor window shade was rolled up, and later, when the glass in the same window was shattered, these were understood by the audience to be the desecration of a tomb.

Other aspects of the production's scenery added meaning. In a play where walls are essential and proper for restraint, protection, defense, and identity—a broken wall and an open gate are significant as a breach in the social order.

> SIMEON The halter's broke—the harness is busted—the fence bars is down—the stone walls air crumblin' an' tumblin'! We'll be kickin' up and tearin' away down the road!
>
> PETER (*drawing a deep breath—oratorically*) Anybody that wants this stinkin' old rock-pile of a farm kin hev it. T'ain't our'n, no sirree!
>
> SIMEON (*takes the gate off its hinges and puts it under his arm*) We harby 'bolishes shet gates, an' open gates, an' all gates, by thunder!
>
> PETER We'll take it with us fur luck an' let 'er sail free down some river.

When Simeon and Peter lifted the gate, the pattern of the play was announced again: *Gates will be abolished by the sons of the father who put them there.*

Other aspects of a production can and do contribute to the pattern of the world. Costume in the world of *The Maids* and music in the world of *Yerma* are good examples. Up until the early 1800s, actors portraying Othello on the London stage wore a British general's redcoat, stressing both the role's military rank in the pattern of the play and the virtue of obeying orders. The London actor William Macready (remember how his Macbeth had instigated riots?) wore a turban and pointy shoes as Othello, which set up a pattern of the exotic Orient with its associations of menace and mystery. Ira Aldridge played the same role in what looked like a Greek chiton with a cape, placing his Othello in line with other classical heroes. In the eyes of his European audiences, Aldridge also wore the mask of his skin. So did the black actor Paul Robeson, born ninety-one years after Aldridge, who played Othello to acclaim in London and on Broadway in the twentieth century. To the audiences watching Aldridge and Robeson, the sight of a black man among white men would create a different pattern: an Othello strong enough to defy a racist world by loving a white Desdemona, yet weakened by his isolation from the rest of society. In Aldridge's case, such isolation would have been heightened since he alone spoke English onstage while the actors around him spoke another language. This was also the case for Tommaso Salvini, who played Othello in a turban and spoke Italian while American actors performed around him in English.

As you see, casting can affect meaning. Consider the possible implications for a modern American audience if, in a production of *Desire Under the Elms*, the stepmother was played by an African-American woman. In 1850, this would indicate a remarkable strength of will on the part of the father; it might also demonstrate his attitude toward his wife as a possession. Two more rules, then, derived from the conventions of specific productions:

- In the setting of *Desire Under the Elms*, the kitchen is the common area; anyone may come there. The parlor, where the dead are laid out, is the elite area. Only those who respect the dead may enter.

- In the New England world of *Desire Under the Elms*, it is uncommonly rare to be of African descent. An African-American woman cast as Abbie brings to the role the connotations of a freed or runaway slave—or, perhaps more significantly, the rarity in 1850 of an African-American born free.

The Play Will Create Its Own Categories for Rules

Any play will have a unique set of values that configure its pattern. Fertility in *Yerma*, rococo elegance in *The Maids*, and correct speech in Shaw's *Pygmalion* are all issues of importance in their own plays, but unimportant or nonexistent in other plays. In *Desire Under the Elms* there are meaningful categories of birth mother/stepmother, freeman/slave, hard/soft. Other aspects of the production contribute meanings to the play: dance is mean-spirited, the parlor is a haunted tomb, and rock and stone stud the earth and stick in men's hearts.

Notice also that the characters' *names* are part of this pattern. In the New Testament, *Peter* (which means "rock") is the name given by Jesus to the fisherman with the Hebrew name of Simeon. By virtue of their names, O'Neill's Peter and Simeon share the same character, and in more ways than one. O'Neill's Peter and Simeon can be understood as two more lumps of stone on Ephraim Cabot's farm. Ephraim, according to the Old Testament, means "God hath caused me to be fruitful in the land of my affliction."

Let's review the interpretation of the rules for *Desire Under the Elms*:

- The sky and the earth are beautiful. Men are not beautiful; they are manure.
- The savage power of the body is strong. Civilization is weak.
- Wisdom is knowledge that the world is hard. It is ignorant to think there's an easy out.
- It's good to be hard; it's bad to be soft.
- It is skill to squeeze money out of rocks; it is inept to give money away, or let it be stolen.
- It is common to work the soil and to pay attention to traditional values. It is elite to ignore them.
- It is polite to conserve your emotions: to compress them, numb them, control them. It is rude to waste them.
- People survive by doing their chores, by serving a hard master.
- People improve by suffering.
- It is impossible to win. You can only escape, by death or emigration to a new country, in this case California.

For the actors playing Simeon or Peter, the scene where they leave is a departure for Paradise. There is no information given about what subsequently happens to them. In real life, the journey to California was hard. But in *Desire Under the Elms*, the journey is out of the picture, beyond the frame. It's as if Simeon and Peter have died and gone to heaven. In the context of the world of the play, these characters are allowed a happy ending—because they are escaping the hard, tragic life of their father and brother.

One Scene Helps You Interpret Another

Even before the main characters of the play arrive and the plot begins, our analysis of the early scene with Simeon and Peter supplies rules that help define the rest of the text. When later events in the play do occur—the stepmother kills her child, the father discovers his money has been stolen, the stepson decides to accept punishment with his lover—the characters' behavior can be understood more clearly by measuring that behavior in the context of the play, rather than by assigning it arbitrary significance as episode, image, or task. The stepmother kills her son because in the world of this play a child is primarily a possession, and more so, desire is so strong that it subverts even the "natural" love a mother is supposed to feel for her child. The father learns that his life savings have vanished, but the loss does not destroy him; it sets him on to more hard work, which is his survival skill. The stepson accepts punishment because, in this world, life is hard, softness is an illusion.

> EBEN I'd suffer wuss leavin' ye, goin' West, think' o' ye day an' night, being out when yew was in— (*lowering his voice*) 'r bein' alive when yew was dead. (*a pause*) I want t' share with ye, Abbie—prison 'r death 'r hell 'r anythin'! (*he looks into her eyes and forces a trembling smile*) If I'm sharin' with ye, I won't feel lonesome, leastways.
>
> ABBIE (*weakly*) Eben! I won't let ye! I can't let ye!
>
> EBEN (*kissing her—tenderly*) Ye can't he'p yerself. I got ye beat fur once!
>
> ABBIE (*forcing a smile—adoringly*) I hain't beat—s'long's I got ye!

In the world of the play, Abbie and Eben are losers. Cabot, the father, is the one with skill and knowledge to survive. His comment on that last bit of dialogue:

> CABOT Ye make a slick pair o'murderin' turtle doves! Ye'd ought t' be both hung on the same limb an' left thar t'swing in the breeze an' rot—a warnin' t'old fools like me t' b'ar their lonesomeness alone—an' fur young fools like ye t' hobble their lust. . . .

At the end of the same speech, when Cabot realizes he's lost all his money, he says:

> CABOT . . . God's lonesome, hain't He? God's hard an' lonesome!

From this, we can infer another rule of the play: *In the world of this play, people improve by suffering. They may not win or lose except by death.* We may disagree about God in our world, but we cannot argue about it in the world of O'Neill's play. Here, under the elms, Cabot is stingy, ugly, hard, powerful—and wise.

Let's Review Terms

world of the play	the place where the action of the play takes place
rules of the world	what organizes the behavior and the environment
pattern	a more or less consistent configuration of words and action in the play
the ten questions	answering them defines the rules

In the world of this play, what is beautiful and what is ugly?
In the world of this play, what is strong and what is weak?
In the world of this play, what is wisdom and what is ignorance?
In the world of this play, what is skill and what is ineptitude?
In the world of this play, what is common and what is elite?
In the world of this play, what is good and what is evil?
In the world of this play, what is polite and what is not polite?
In the world of this play, how do people survive?
In the world of this play, how do people improve?
In the world of this play, how do people win or lose?

The places to find answers to the ten questions:

- The play itself
- The time and place
- The playwright's system of values
- The form of the play
- The form of the production

The Chart

- **Basic unit.** The given norms of *behavior and form*.
- **The relative theory.** Ruth Benedict's ideas of *cultural anthropology* are a model for a world of the play analysis.
- **Key question.** *What are the values of the play?*

CHAPTER 10

PLAYING BY THE RULES—OR NOT

Learning the Rules

Like Gulliver sailing from one island to another, let's reevaluate how an actor inhabits the world of the play by the measure of a different time and place—the baroque age of seventeenth-century France.

One thing that never changes from age to age is the difficulty of starting a theatrical career. In 1643, in hopes of becoming a professional actor, twenty-one-year-old Jean-Baptiste Poquelin renounced his right to succeed his father as upholsterer to the King. Upholsterer to the King was not a bad job to come into: the furniture-obsessed Louis XIV was next in line. Despite his enthusiasm for the stage, Jean-Baptiste Poquelin's professional beginnings were disastrous. *He acts with his eyebrows*, sniffed a certain Mademoiselle Poisson in her *Memoirs* ("Miss Fish," her name translates to in English) (77). Poquelin spoke too quickly, too harshly. His voice was so strained he was prone to hiccups. The company he formed with the more experienced Béjart family went bankrupt. He was sent to jail. His father paid his debts and bailed him out. Like Stanislavsky, Poquelin eventually changed his name to save his family embarrassment. From then on he was known as Molière (77).

For the next thirteen years, the Paris-born Molière toured the French provinces, mostly in the south. His acting improved through repetition, observation, and hard work—and by contact with another member of the company, the Italian actor Tiberio Fiorelli. Fiorelli was best known for playing the popular commedia dell'arte character Scaramouche with startling physicality. Onstage, Fiorelli could freeze his body in the midst of frantic action and fall silent. Molière was a good pupil of Fiorelli's and learned, among other things, restraint. He even improved his diction, although his rubber face and eyebrows remained irrepressibly mobile.

Nevertheless, the improvements in his craft gained Molière status, and after five years of touring he became the manager of his troupe. In 1658, the company had the opportunity to play a double-bill for the King in a little room at the Louvre. The tragedy they performed was forgettable, but Louis laughed at the farce, written by Molière, entitled *The Doctor in Love* (*Le Docteur amoureux*). *Monsieur*, the King's cross-dressing brother, liked the troupe so much he gave them his patronage.

Molière had fifteen more years to live. During that time he wrote and staged over thirty-two texts: comedies, farces, satires, and interludes for pageants. He had the wit to include his own eccentricities in the characters he wrote for himself—often that of a man blinded to common sense by enthusiasm and subject to various manias for money, religion, status, or a complacent wife.

Although better known to history as a playwright, Molière was nevertheless first and last a performer. In 1673, he was carried off the stage after having had a fit while playing a hypochondriac, a role he wrote to include his unstoppable cough (a malady that had replaced his hiccups). He died a few hours later, before he had time to renounce his profession, as was the custom necessary to receive holy rites. In death, as in life, Molière was bound within the rules of his society. The parish priests refused to bury him until the King intervened.

Playing by the Rules

Molière wrote no books explaining his craft, yet when Louis requested that Molière dramatize a rehearsal, the playwright-actor complied with the play *The Versailles Impromptu* (1663)—in which the playwright depicted himself rehearsing the actors of his company. He criticizes them for not following the ways of other troupes, and in doing so he reveals his own skills by comparison. Other actors paused unnaturally before beautiful passages of verse, from which we can conclude that Molière's actors spoke according to sense, not effect. Other actors were impossibly cast as young people when they were old, from which we can deduce that Molière's company were cast appropriately to type. Other actors ranted and raved in order to show off their voices; Molière's actors were more subtle.

To their contemporaries, Molière's actors were refreshingly unaffected in performance—even when they spoke in twelve-syllable rhymed couplets and acted love scenes facing the audience, not each other. When they played fops and aristocrats, actors of Molière's era took to the stage teetering on high-heeled shoes, corseted at the waist, and topped by powdered wigs. They wore little pads stuck under their tights to make their legs look fashionably plump. For purposes of decorum, they held their arms parallel to the stage floor, so that the lace on their cuffs didn't droop. They placed their feet in ballet-like positions, the legs turned out from the hips, the better to display those lovely calves.

There were people who sat watching these performances who were themselves teetering on heels, corseted, powdered, bewigged, and padded. They took lessons to fence and dance, and considered their own movements to be cultivated and graceful, not affected. Our contemporary manner of movement, devoid of harmony and lace cuffs—on or off a stage—would have seemed barbarous to them.

A world of the play analysis is obviously necessary for actors preparing to perform a text as stylized as Molière's, if only to be able to make sense of the baroque behavior and arcane references. Yet simply copying the flamboyant details and gestures of Molière's period will not create dramatic action for an actor. Analyzing the world of the play involves something other than copying exotic physical styles. This is recognized, by the way, even among the members of Molière's troupe—which endures three hundred years later. Now called the Comédie Française, the troupe proudly retains and passes down even the improvisations of the original performers. But the actors recognize that these tricks are the outer and not the inner substance of their inheritance.

Breaking the Rules

The value of a world of the play analysis for the actor doesn't lie in its ability to reproduce history or imitate reality, but in its ability to create meaning. The words and behavior seen and heard in a play by Molière, as in any other play, are dramatically significant because they establish dramatic actions and human relationships. Hedda Gabler is an *outcast*, Shlink is an *instigator*, and Molière's impostor Tartuffe is a *hypocrite*—despite the style of performance. As long as the words of the play stay as they are, and the dramatic situations they call for are performed, a pattern of relationships will emerge in production. For example, in the 1660s love scenes were sometimes played with both partners facing the audience. Following the guidelines set out in the previous chapter, a world of the play analysis might interpret such a stage convention as a rule: *In the world of this play, the public display of emotion is more important than the emotion itself.* Other scenes, with other displayed emotions, will then be understood within this pattern.

Against the measure of the world of the play, onstage behavior becomes dramatic action when it *disrupts the pattern already established*. For example, let's look at scenes we've already analyzed. When the Professor stumps the Pupil, this event has dramatic significance because it contrasts with the Pupil's quick and ready answers to previous questions. When Yerma defies her husband, it has dramatic significance in light of her previously passionate resignations to God and her husband's will.

Onstage behavior also becomes dramatic action when it represents a *return to the status quo that has been disrupted*—the slaughter of the unstoppably perverse Richard III, the punishment of Abbie and Eben after their desire oversteps New England conventions, or the arrival of the King's messenger who restores justice in *Tartuffe*.

Molière understood about disrupting patterns. He even wrote about it in a petition to the King, in which he defended *Tartuffe* against charges of blasphemy:

> The comic is the outward and visible form that nature's bounty has attached to everything unreasonable, so that we should see, and avoid it. To know the comic we must know the rational, of which it denotes the absence, and we must see wherein the rational consists . . . incongruity is the heart of the comic . . . it follows that all lying, disguise, cheating, dissimulation, all outward show different from the reality, all contradiction in fact between actions that proceed from a single source, all this is in essence comic (78).

A world of the play analysis identifies the dynamic between what Molière calls the rational and the unreasonable. Bewigged or not, the play's patterns will assign certain onstage events significance as dramatic action, just as a melody assigns value to certain notes. Actors preparing and rehearsing a role in any play should understand the meaning of their behavior and dialogue within those patterns. Guided by this understanding, which is the product of rehearsal and private preparation, episodes will be reinterpreted, tasks will lose and gain priorities, and images will form new and varied constellations as sense memory or fantasy.

The Rules of the Strange and the Familiar

Preparation for a role in a stylized play like *Tartuffe* inevitably suggests the need for a world of the play analysis, if only for the technical reasons of articulating the verse and making sense of the lines. As we've noticed in *Macbeth* and *Richard III*, the language of a verse play is significant in its form and content. As retorts and rejoinders, the exchange of words is essential to the action. Even in translation, it is important that the audience understands every spoken syllable. A vocal technique different from the one you would use for O'Neill's nuanced *ay-ehs* is required to deliver rhymed couplets or blank verse. Performing a play like *Tartuffe* often also requires studying and practicing stylized gestures. If performing in period dress, you will need to learn how to move in the costumes without tripping or ripping—one more specialized skill, like vocal technique, required to act the text and inhabit the world of the play.

Yet, each text of Molière's plays configures its patterns differently: the mania for religion is not the same as the mania for money or for a quiet spouse. Although they come from the same sources in time and space, each of Molière's plays has a distinctly different world, just as individuals from the same era had distinctly different personalities. There should be no blanket "Molière style" with which to smother creativity among the actors or the differences between texts.

By the way, too much concern for period detail can divert a performer's attention from the search for the more significant pattern of the whole text. It is the pattern of *behavior and words*, not exotic details, that a world of the play analysis tries to identify and apply in rehearsals and performance. Once again, Ruth Benedict's insights in the field of anthropology—that anthropologists struck with the oddness of foreign customs lose sight of the cultural patterns that make such exotica understandable—can point the way to improve an actor's process.

Like social anthropologists turning their attention from the unsmiling Dobu Islanders (remember them?) to modern society, let's now examine ways to develop the world of the play by rehearsing a scene—not from *Tartuffe*, but from Neil Simon's *The Odd Couple* (1965) (79). A familiar and relatively modern comedy can better illustrate, with less distractions than a baroque period piece, how any play can be better rehearsed and performed by applying world of the play analysis.

A comedy like *The Odd Couple* calls for actors to master the technique of getting an audience to laugh, but a comic technique is simply a collection of arbitrary tricks if applied to a play without respect for the meaning of the text, even a play as seemingly obvious in its meaning as *The Odd Couple*. Neil Simon's text isn't just a collection of jokes. The play is about something, and world of the play analysis helps to identify what that subject matter is. To dramatize the subject matter, *The Odd Couple* displays a pattern of behavior and dialogue as strong and distinctive as O'Neill's *Desire Under the Elms*. World of the play analysis can help you identify that pattern, and then playfully use that knowledge to support other techniques and approaches to acting—including the ones that get laughs.

Analyzing the World of *The Odd Couple*

Begin your preparation by yourself

World of the play analysis can begin as you read the play alone at home, and perhaps after you've look at related background material suggested by the setting of the text and the circumstances of its writing. If you have no copy of the script, you'll have to begin preparation after you've heard the script read aloud. Your interpretation will change as you rehearse, of course. Still, preparation you do by yourself will help you begin rehearsals with some idea—even if mistaken—of what you are saying to other people. This way you can make sure you don't resemble Gilda Radner's deaf television commentator who got herself worked up defending violins on television, until she realized the topic was *violence* on television. Never mind. A good way to begin is by answering the ten questions listed in the previous chapter.

This chapter reviews practical ways to apply a world of the play analysis to rehearsals. In order to proceed to those skills, let's agree on the premise of an interpretation. You may come up with different answers to the ten questions, but you can apply them in the same ways. It doesn't matter which interpretation you choose, as long as you can demonstrate its validity by speaking the words of the play—since those are the words you share with an audience.

Neil Simon wrote *The Odd Couple* between 1964 and 1965. The story concerns two men, estranged from their wives, who share an apartment in New York City. Felix is compulsively neat, Oscar is a slob. The new bachelor roommates recreate the circumstances of their marriages. Their individual habits, which drove their wives to separate from them in the first place, now drive the guys to distraction and to a new separation—from each other. Productions of the play have been very successful. The original production of *The Odd Couple* ran on Broadway for years, and in 1968 Neil Simon adapted his script into an equally popular movie.

In order to begin with a premise, then, here are answers to the ten questions about the world of *The Odd Couple*:

- *In the world of this play, what is good and what is bad?* The answer to this question is an excellent example of how values in the play as a whole redefine the values of any single character. Being neat is good for Felix. Being a slob is good for Oscar. Within the play, neither one extreme nor the other is good. Being too neat is bad, being too casual is bad. What is good is the middle, reasonability. What is bad is extreme.
- *What is beautiful and what is ugly?* Friendship and sharing are beautiful. Selfishness is ugly. The love between two friends is what is most beautiful in this play.

- *What is ignorance and what is wisdom?* Ignorance in this play is sticking to your guns, wisdom is knowing when to give in. Wisdom is graceful submission and apology.
- *What is polite and what is not polite?* The etiquette of the play is that of the middle class of the mid-1960s. Good manners are soft and gentle; bad manners are loud, outspoken, and gruff. Contained is polite, messy is rude. Felix is polite. Oscar is rude. But polite is not always good, nor is rude always bad. Common sense overrides manners in this world.

The play takes place in Felix's apartment, where the men's buddies gather once a week to play poker. These poker-playing pals are the real barometer of reasonability throughout the play. Even the "regular guys" think Oscar's lack of housekeeping is extreme. Before Felix tidied it up, Oscar's refrigerator had been broken for two weeks. One of the poker players claims to have seen milk standing in there—and it wasn't even in the bottle.

- *How do people survive?* By compromise. This is the secret for the play's success with middle-class audiences; it establishes the middle road as the road to achievement. That doesn't make it a bad play. It doesn't make it a good one, either. It might explain its popularity.
- *How do people improve?* By reaching the golden mean, by getting along with their neighbors.
- *How do people win or lose?* They don't. This is a play where the characters interact but don't change their relative positions, and it is for that reason that it could be so skillfully adapted into a television series. The series ran from 1970–1975, 114 half-hour treatments of the same characters' relationship—none of them written by Neil Simon (who thought the idea of an *Odd Couple* television series odd).

Onstage or on screen, Felix and Oscar don't win or lose. They go on being extreme, and then compromising for the sake of love between friends—until the next chance for selfishness arises. That is why the situation is funny: whenever the friends break the rules, eventually they are forgiven and return to the bosom of the partnership. No matter what the characters do, they end up the same way, with the possibility of renewed happiness.

After effortlessly completing the first two acts of this play, Simon had trouble writing the third and final act. Perhaps the reason is that the pattern of the action is repetitive. As it reads now, at the play's end Felix is about to return to his wife and Oscar is beginning to reconcile with his wife over the phone. But in our hearts we know it won't happen. Two television series and a film sequel later, it still hasn't happened. Back to our questions:

- *In the world of this play, what is strong?* What is common to all men—love wins out over the individual. The needs of the group are stronger than the desires of the individual.
- *What is common and what is elite?* Married men are elite, single men are common. Single women are elite, married women are common. In *The Odd*

Couple, we meet relatively few elite people. The class distinctions in the play are few, and for a reason: the unspoken assumption is that we're all basically middle-class. This reflects the mid-1960s American worldview.

- *What is the ultimate skill?* Bargaining. Knowing how to negotiate. Giving enough away, but still having your own.

So a pattern is established that structures the behavior of the play: *Selfishness gives way to love between friends. The highest good is friendship and compromise.*

The Odd Couple is set in the era in which it was written: New York in 1965. The text includes jokey references to New York neighborhoods, which implies that its audience shared an understanding that Rockaway was far away (it's a beach, several miles from the center of Manhattan); and that the Upper West Side faced the coastline of New Jersey. The year 1965 was a "middle year," a period of American history when the country stood tall, confident in itself. John Kennedy had been gone long enough for Lyndon Johnson to be measured in his own right as President of the United States—reelected the year before by a landslide majority. Counterculture challenges to that majority—like the Black Power movement, the Sexual Revolution, and hippies—were thunder on the horizon, if perceived at all. The small concerns of middle-class life (too neat or too messy?) could take on dramatic metaphor without touching on politics. Part of the pleasure of the play for contemporary audiences is that it offers an oasis of such petty concerns.

On a personal level, Neil Simon was just under forty years of age when he wrote *The Odd Couple*, and he was still with his first wife. He had his second big success on Broadway two years before with *Barefoot in the Park*, and the optimistic and happy *Odd Couple* is influenced by that perspective. Simon's later plays—after a few flops and a few more wives—are neither as sunny nor as funny (deliberately). They reveal introspection gained from experience.

Now, you may disagree with the above interpretation. You may offer other ideas: that the play is a version of Neil Simon's two aspects, *the nerd* and *the adventurer*—described by the playwright in the introduction to the collection of his first plays. You may disagree that compromise is the highest good in *The Odd Couple*; you may say that integrity is the highest good, and point to examples in the text. You may demonstrate that love wins out in the end. You may comb through Neil Simon's many generous interviews in which he has answered questions about *The Odd Couple* to prove that the playwright contradicts every answer given to the above ten questions. It doesn't matter. Choose what you want, and let's begin to rehearse the play applying whatever set of rules you've defined for the world of the play. For now, accept these answers to the ten questions as a premise from which to proceed.

Apply the rules to tasks, episodes, and images

Let's look at a scene from the second act, when Felix has arranged a date for himself and Oscar with the Pigeon Sisters, two British ladies who live in the same building. These comic siblings announce their own meaning: not Pidgeon like Walter, but pigeon like coo-coo pigeons. When Oscar goes in to get drinks for the coo-coo sisters, Felix is left to entertain them.

> FELIX *turns and faces the girls. He crosses to a chair and sits. He crosses his legs nonchalantly. But he is ill at ease and he crosses them again. He is becoming aware of the silence and he can no longer get away with just smiling.*

FELIX Er, Oscar tells me you're sisters.

CECILY Yes. That's right. (*she looks at* GWENDOLYN)

FELIX From England.

GWENDOLYN Yes. That's right. (*she looks at* CECILY)

FELIX I see. (*Silence. Then, his little joke*) We're not brothers.

CECILY Yes, we know.

FELIX Although I am a brother. I have a brother who's a doctor. He lives in Buffalo. That's upstate in New York.

GWENDOLYN (*taking a cigarette from her purse*) Yes, we know.

FELIX You know my brother?

GWENDOLYN No. We know that Buffalo is upstate in New York.

FELIX Oh! (*he gets up, takes a cigarette lighter from the side table and moves to light* GWENDOLYN'S *cigarette*)

CECILY We've been there! Have you?

FELIX No! Is it nice?

GWENDOLYN Lovely.

> FELIX *closes the lighter on* GWENDOLYN'S *cigarette and turns to go back to his chair, taking the cigarette, now caught in the lighter, with him. He notices the cigarette and hastily gives it back to* GWENDOLYN, *stopping to light it once again. He puts the lighter back on the table and sits down nervously. There is a pause.*

Felix's *task* is *to put the girls at ease*. His *obstacles* are his own clumsiness and physical awkwardness. A reference to the world of the play orients Felix's tasks more precisely. Within the pattern of the play, Felix's desires are invariably connected to and balanced against Oscar's. Here, the balance works like this: Felix would prefer to stay home and clean; Oscar wants some excitement and maybe a little fling. Oscar is divorced and available for other women; Felix is separated, not yet divorced, and very much attached to his family. Felix's task in entertaining the coo-coo sisters is to keep them in a good mood until Oscar returns with their drinks. An additional obstacle to Felix's task is the ladies' interest in Felix, which flusters him.

World of the play analysis also identifies *opportunities* to fulfill tasks. According to the manners of 1965 middle-class America, pious girls neither smoke nor drink. If the aim is to find willing partners for Oscar, the opportunities in the scene are identified by the fact that the ladies are smoking and waiting for alcohol to be served. These girls are *swingers*, out for a good time.

> FELIX Isn't that interesting? How long have you been in the United States of America?
> CECILY Almost four years now.
> FELIX *(nods)* Uh huh. Just visiting?
> GWENDOLYN *(looks at* CECILY*)* No! We live here.
> FELIX And you work here too, do you?
> CECILY Yes. We're secretaries for Slenderama.
> GWENDOLYN You know. The health club.
> CECILY People bring us their bodies and we do wonderful things with them.
> GWENDOLYN Actually, if you're interested, we can get you ten percent off.
> CECILY Off the price, not off your body.
> FELIX Yes, I see. *(He laughs. They all laugh. Suddenly he shouts towards the kitchen)* Oscar, where's the drinks?
> OSCAR *(offstage)* Coming! Coming!

World of the play analysis will also redefine *episodes* and the value of *transactions*. Felix and the girls trade social gestures. The world of this play defines this as the exchange of polite, not very intrusive, personal information. Felix offers clichés, which entail little: "I have a brother in Buffalo." The Pigeon sisters offer innuendoes, which entail a good time, if not a good deal: "People bring us their bodies and we do wonderful things with them." Felix will not pick up on the girls' innuendoes or successfully light Gwendolyn's cigarette because he will not trade his politeness for what they are offering. The actors playing the sisters need to understand this in order for the episode to make sense. The exchange of the cigarette is an incomplete *gest*, because it is a failed exchange.*

> CECILY What field of endeavor are you engaged in?
> FELIX I write the news for CBS.
> CECILY Oh! Fascinating!
> GWENDOLYN Where do you get your ideas from?

---

*World of the play analysis helps clarify episodes we've identified in previous chapters. The episodes that accumulate during *In the Jungle of Cities* are all better understood within the context of the play. If we agree that the pattern of life in Brecht's vision of Chicago is a pitiless contest for survival, the episode's caption, PEACEFUL MAN DRAWN INTO VIOLENT STRUGGLE TO SURVIVE, can be refined by a world of the play analysis to THE VICIOUS SNAKE ATTACKS THE SLEEPING MONGOOSE. A similar reorganization of *Richard III* takes place when you understand that the episodes in which the hunchback appears all undermine the natural order of who is King of England—until the final episode where the natural order rises up and obliterates Richard. One of the captions we've already arrived at for Act I, scene ii, KILLER HUNCHBACK PITCHES WOO TO VICTIM'S WIDOW, could be further refined to THE IMPOSTER KING STEALS THE WIFE OF A HERO.

FELIX (*he looks at her as though she's a Martian*) From the news.

GWENDOLYN Oh, yes, of course. Silly me . . .

CECILY Maybe you can mention Gwen and I in one of your news reports.

FELIX Well, if you do something spectacular, maybe I will.

CECILY Oh, we've done spectacular things but I don't think we'd want it spread all over the telly, do you, Gwen?

They both laugh.

The *images* of a text are major components of the world of the play. British accents might evoke *stuffy formality* to you. In *The Odd Couple*, British means *swingers*, not crumpets and tea. The names of the girls wink at this change from prim to permissive: Gwendolyn and Cecily are the names of the proper young ladies in Oscar Wilde's *The Importance of Being Earnest*. In 1965, to a Broadway audience savvy enough to laugh at jokes about Rockaway, London meant Mod London and Carnaby Street, the source of raised hemlines, lowered morals, and libertine behavior. America may have been standing tall in 1965, but London was swinging. So, if you're playing one of the Pigeon sisters, you'd better find something that works for you to swing before you get yourself buttoned up in the image of a prim British maiden.

Notice how the characters form a composition

The two Pigeon Sisters are virtually identical giggling twits—or are they?

CECILY Oh, we've done spectacular things but I don't think we'd want it spread all over the telly, do you, Gwen?

They both laugh.

FELIX (*he laughs too, then cries out almost for help*) Oscar!

OSCAR (*offstage*) Yeah, yeah!

FELIX (*to the girls*) It's such a large apartment, sometimes you have to shout.

GWENDOLYN Just you two baches lives here?

FELIX Baches? Oh, bachelors! We're not bachelors. We're divorced. That is, Oscar's divorced. I'm *getting* divorced.

CECILY Oh, small world. We've cut the dinghy loose too, as they say.

GWENDOLYN Well, you couldn't have a *better* matched foursome, could you?

FELIX (*smiles weakly*) No, I suppose not.

GWENDOLYN Although technically I'm a widow. I was divorcing my husband, but he died before the final papers came through.

FELIX Oh, I'm awfully sorry. (*sighs*) It's a terrible thing, isn't it? Divorce.

GWENDOLYN It can be—if you haven't got the right solicitor.

CECILY That's true. Sometimes they can drag it out for months. I was lucky. Snip, cut and I was free.

FELIX I mean it's terrible what it can do to people. After all, what is divorce? It's taking two happy people and tearing their lives completely apart. It's inhuman, don't you think so?

CECILY Yes, it can be an awful bother.

GWENDOLYN But of course, that's all water under the bridge now, eh? Er, I'm terribly sorry, but I think I've forgotten your name.

FELIX Felix.

GWENDOLYN Oh, yes. Felix.

CECILY Like the cat.

FELIX *takes his wallet from his jacket pocket.*

The characters in a play acquire meaning by *comparison* with each other. Oscar is the messy one, Felix the neat one. If Gwendolyn is the taller sister, Cecily becomes the shorter (or is it the other way around?) The New Yorkers are the locals, the standard; the British girls are the outsiders, exotic, and available. The audience understands these differences and identifies characters by comparing role to role, as if the roles formed a **composition.**

The Odd Couple has been adapted for a number of situations, but regardless of the changes in circumstances, the dynamic composition of the characters remained the same. In Portugal, there was a television series, not a dubbed version of the American show, but one with a Portuguese setting and characters. In 1982–1983, an American television version was set among middle-class African-Americans. In 1985, Neil Simon himself wrote a new stage version with female characters in the leading roles named Olive and Florence; the Pigeon sisters converted into the Costazuela Brothers from Barcelona, Spain. Again, in all of these variations the essential composition of characters remained the same: divorced people of the same sex live together, one neat, one messy. The scene we are examining here appears in all of them. A date is arranged for a possible good time, which Felix/Florence ruins.

In other plays we've examined, the contrast in characters sharpens their identity. In *Desire Under the Elms*, Simeon and Peter are the older, duller sons who escape their father's hard rule. Eben, by way of contrast, is the younger, brighter son who challenges his father. In *Hedda Gabler*, the composition of characters is essential to establish that Hedda is a misfit in the world she inhabits. Ibsen mentions that Hedda's old schoolmate, Thea, has healthy, thick blonde hair—the better to point up Hedda's thinning, dark hair and general ill health.

The relationships between the roles can make much more of a setting for the play than any walls. Think of the composition of *The Maids*: the mistress-who-is-to-be-killed, the elder-maid-who-arranges-the-killing, the younger-maid-who-does-the-killing. In *Yerma*, the happy women with children who surround Yerma contrast with the barren Yerma's misery.

As for the two Pigeon sisters, the playwright offers some clues for differences: one had a happy marriage that turned sour, the other had a marriage that was always bad. But more importantly, if you are one of the actors playing these roles, your individual character will be established by how you play against your "sibling": *I'm the slow one, she's the fast. I'm the blonde, she's tastefully gray.* Or, the two of you can agree that there are no differences and you're both the same—like the Rockettes. If the two sisters are played as amusingly identical, that too is based on rules. You'll both be blonde or both be gray, and certainly you'll speak with the same British accent.

Playing (and rehearsing) by the rules

Just as the play will suggest new categories for value, it will suggest new ways to rehearse. If you agree that the Pigeon sisters resemble each other, then you will need to rehearse that resemblance. In *The Maids*, the maids imitate Madame. The actresses who play these three roles will have to rehearse the gestures, tones, and other traits they mean to share as Madame.

Other plays will suggest certain skills that you'll need to master in rehearsal. In *The Lesson*, the speed at which the characters speak is a crucial dynamic that indicates the Pupil's ability to dazzle and the Professor's ability to baffle. Rehearsals could very easily take place with a metronome marking an accelerating beat or music underscoring the scene with ever-quickening tempi. This is the director's business to suggest, but even if the director doesn't do anything so creative, *you* can—on your own. You could also practice certain things, like speaking more rapidly, and apply them to rehearsal.

The skills required of one play, of course, are not those required of another. The precision of a Vermont accent for *Desire Under the Elms* will not really help in the Upper West Side milieu of *The Odd Couple*—but the quick delivery of vaudevillian comedians would be well worth studying, copying, and stealing.

The rules of conduct for *The Odd Couple* are that of *social politeness*, which might be gleaned from an etiquette guide from the period. During polite conversation, when a subject is brought up, it should be followed up by the listener, however inanely:

> FELIX I have a brother who's a doctor. He lives in Buffalo. That's upstate in New York.
>
> GWENDOLYN Yes, we know.
>
> FELIX You know my brother?
>
> GWENDOLYN No. We know that Buffalo is upstate in New York.

Polite conversationalists find points of common interest:

> FELIX We're divorced. That is, Oscar's divorced. I'm getting divorced.
>
> CECILY Oh, small world. We've cut the dinghy loose too, as they say.

Sadness and negativity should be unmentioned, or turned positive:

FELIX It's inhuman, don't you think so?

CECILY Yes, it can be an awful bother.

GWENDOLYN But of course, that's all water under the bridge now, eh?

There are other, unspoken rules: when you're with someone you're interested in, you don't talk about your ex-wife. Felix takes out pictures of his children, and praises his ex-wife to the skies. The girls gamely follow along:

FELIX (*taking pictures out of his wallet*) That's her, Frances.

GWENDOLYN (*looking at the picture*) Oh, she's pretty. Isn't she pretty, Cecily?

CECILY Oh, yes. Pretty. A pretty girl. Very pretty.

FELIX (*takes the picture back*) Thank you. (*shows them another snapshot*) Isn't this nice?

GWENDOLYN (*looks*) There's no one in the picture.

FELIX I know. It's a picture of our living room. We had a beautiful apartment.

GWENDOLYN Oh, yes. Pretty. Very pretty.

CECILY Those are lovely lamps.

FELIX Thank you! (*takes the picture*) We bought them in Mexico on our honeymoon. (*he looks at the picture again*) I used to love to come home at night. (*he's beginning to break*) That was my whole life. My wife, my kids—and my apartment. (*he breaks down and sobs*)

CECILY Does she have the lamps now too?

FELIX (*nods*) I gave her everything. It'll never be like that again. Never! I— I— (*he turns his head away*) I'm sorry. (*He takes out a handkerchief and dabs his eyes.* GWENDOLYN *and* CECILY *look at each other with compassion*) Please forgive me. I didn't mean to get emotional. (*trying to pull himself together, he picks up a bowl from the side table and offers it to the girls*) Would you like some potato chips?

CECILY *takes the bowl.*

It wouldn't be a bad idea to read a 1965 Emily Post *Guide to Good Manners* and try to apply its rules to the day's rehearsal.

Other plays have harsher, more life-crushing rules of etiquette. Lorca identified Yerma's central problem as the inflexible, life-denying institution of marriage. Practice holding your spine rigidly in emulation of the properly brought-up Spanish villager (who carries water from the well in a bucket balanced on her head), and you will gain an appropriately austere posture for Yerma. The rules binding Hedda Gabler, we know, drive her to kill herself. In rehearsing any of these scenes, it is very helpful to understand how the social environment restrains the action, or permits it to fly free—like Simeon and Peter once they lift up the gate.

Breaking the rules is dramatic action

Once the audience is accustomed to the rules of the pattern, they will feel that any behavior or words that break the rules are dramatic actions. In *The Odd Couple* that can mean losing your temper; in *Macbeth* it can mean speaking with twelve beats to a ten-syllable line.

When rule-breaking is punished, the pattern of the play can be called *tragic*. In classical tragedies like *Oedipus the King*, rule-breaking is followed by the obliteration of rule-breaking characters as individuals; when the pattern resumes, the rule-breakers are folded back into the group. Often definitions of tragedy apply the rules of offstage morality, or philosophy, which ends up excluding, say, Arthur Miller's *Death of a Salesman* as tragic, because the story does not conform to an idea of ancient Greek responsibility. True, the salesman of the title, Willie Loman, doesn't break the rules of his world; Miller's play is not about that. What the play is about is the way the system of Willie's life flouts the rules of nature, which overwhelm Willie, and everyone around him, as he grows old. In the same way, Richard III's evil ways and Macbeth's ambivalent wrongs are overwhelmed when the natural order of the world—the rightful succession of King—rises up and reasserts itself.

When rule-breaking is forgiven, the pattern of the play can be called *comic*. Often, a comic plot is a series of errors that lead to the correct answer. The characters are secretly obeying the pattern they seem to flout. In classic comedies, very often the character's rule-breaking attacks that world's definition of the role the character is supposed to play. Respectable fathers turn fools, servants talk back to the masters they are meant to obey, pious leaders prove hypocritical, heroes prove cowardly, women take on men's roles. By the end of the play, the behavior that challenged the pattern is forgiven, or, in some cases, leads to a rearrangement of the pattern. Sometimes the pattern of the play is revealed to be different from what was previously thought, and the hero who seemed to be so ridiculous was secretly on the right track to revealing a new aspect of the world.

A performer should understand the pattern of the play enough to say whether it's comic or tragic. Interpretations such as Hedda Gabler's heroism will be supported by the framework of the play. Interpretations that try to emphasize the tragic loneliness of the two expatriate Pigeon Sisters will be undermined by the pattern of the play. In a comedy like *The Odd Couple*, breaking the rules is funny, and then forgiven.

GWENDOLYN You mustn't be ashamed. I think it's a rare quality in a man to be able to cry.

FELIX (*puts a hand over his eyes*) Please. Let's not talk about it.

CECILY I think it's sweet. Terribly, terribly sweet. (*she takes a potato chip*)

FELIX You're just making it worse.

GWENDOLYN (*teary-eyed*) It's so refreshing to hear a man speak so highly of the woman he's divorcing! Oh, dear. (*she takes out her handkerchief*) Now you've got me thinking about poor Sydney.

CECILY Oh, Gwen. Please don't. (*she puts the bowl down*)

GWENDOLYN It was a good marriage at first. Everyone said so. Didn't they, Cecily? Not like you and George.

CECILY (*the past returns as she comforts* GWENDOLYN) That's right. George and I were never happy. Not for one single, solitary day.

> *She remembers her unhappiness, grabs her handkerchief and dabs her eyes. All three are now sitting with handkerchiefs at their eyes.*

As an actor, it is important you break the rules without calling attention to yourself or winking at the audience that you know better. Usually, the character breaks the rules without thought to the consequences:

FELIX Isn't this ridiculous?

GWENDOLYN I don't know what brought this on. I was feeling so good a few minutes ago.

CECILY I haven't cried since I was fourteen.

FELIX Just let it pour out. It'll make you feel much better. I always do.

GWENDOLYN Oh, dear; oh, dear; oh, dear.

> *All three sit sobbing into their handkerchiefs. Suddenly OSCAR bursts happily into the room with a tray full of drinks. He is all smiles.*

OSCAR (*like a corny M.C.*) Is ev-rybuddy happy?

The episode is organized to recognize that the rule is being broken. The *gest* here is everybody sobbing into their handkerchiefs, which is translated into the world of the play as FELIX RUINS OSCAR'S CHANCE TO MEET NEW WOMEN. Certainly this is how *Oscar* understands the event, and for once, the audience is meant to understand it in the same way.

Satisfy the audience by following the rules

An audience is satisfied when the pattern of the play is completed, in the same way that they can be satisfied by the completion of a melody while listening to music. In order to achieve this connection to your audience, you can use your understanding of the pattern to shape the through-line of your tasks, organize the progression of your transactions, or channel the transformation of your images.

There is the possibility for the audience to feel deep satisfaction at the end of *The Maids*, for example, because the servants who have been rehearsing the murder of Madame finally realize their dream of killing someone—even if it's Claire in the place of Madame. There is a similar satisfaction possible at the end of *Richard III* when the usurping monster is finally stopped. As a performer, your shaping the pattern of actions gives the audience an understanding of the significance of events: Hedda's suicide, the Pupil's death, Anne's seduction. Although the rules of a world are often announced, the consequence of rule-breaking is more often demonstrated with behavior and reactions. In a comedy, there is a particular pleasure in seeing how, through a chain of errors, the rule-breaking character ends up following the rules after all:

OSCAR (*like a corny M.C.*) Is ev-rybuddy happy? (*then he sees the maudlin scene. FELIX and the girls quickly try to pull themselves together*) What the hell happened?

FELIX Nothing! Nothing! (*he quickly puts his handkerchief away*)

OSCAR What do you mean, nothing? I'm gone three minutes and I walk into a funeral parlor. What did you say to them?

FELIX I didn't say anything. Don't start in again, Oscar.

OSCAR I can't leave you alone for five seconds. Well, if you really want to cry, go inside and look at your London broil.

FELIX (*he rushes madly into the kitchen*) Oh, my gosh! Why didn't you call me? I told you to call me.

OSCAR (*giving a drink to* CECILY) I'm sorry, girls. I forgot to warn you about Felix. He's a walking soap opera.

GWENDOLYN I think he's the dearest thing I ever met.

CECILY (*taking the glass*) He's so sensitive. So fragile. I just want to bundle him up in my arms and take care of him.

OSCAR (*holds out* GWENDOLYN'S *drink. At this, he puts it back down on the tray and takes a swallow from his own drink*) Well, I think when he comes out of that kitchen you may have to.

The pleasure in this is that Felix, by doing everything wrong as a host, has outshone Oscar, who has been doing everything right.

By yourself again, look at all the incidents at once

When the incidents of the play are looked at all at once, a pattern will emerge. This technique was identified as **spatial analysis** by the Shakespeare critic G. Wilson Knight. It can be used by a performer to review and reorganize what has taken place in rehearsals. All the scenes in *The Maids* can be seen as variations of the same murderous episode; all the tasks of *The Lesson* can be seen as variations of the same obsessive super-task; all the descriptions of *Desire Under the Elms* can be seen as variations of the same stony imagery. All episodes in *The Odd Couple* can be seen as variations on the act of finding a way to give in, to meld the extremes. Any task of Felix's is balanced against a task of Oscar's. The images of the characters are complementary; they bring out each other by contrast. By recognizing what is the same throughout those plays, you can begin to create for your performance what is distinct, because what is distinct is a *variation* within the pattern. Bring your understanding to rehearsals as a way to further refine your choices.

Let's Review Terms

dramatic action	a significant breach in the rules
tragic pattern	when rule-breaking is punished
comic pattern	when rule-breaking is forgiven
composition of characters	characters are defined by comparison to other characters
spatial analysis	to look at all the events of the play as if they happened at once, in order to define a repeated pattern

Notebook:
Analyzing the World of the Play

Following the rules:
Felix is there is to keep
the girls interested in Oscar—
Breaking the rules:
—but not in himself!

FELIX *turns and faces the girls. He crosses to a chair and sits. He* <u>crosses his legs</u> *nonchalantly. But he is ill at ease and he crosses them again. He is becoming aware of the silence and he can no longer get away with* <u>just smiling</u>.

<u>crosses his legs</u>: Legs crossed, at the ankles, not like a woman or an effeminate man. Important to register that he is attracted to the women, not oblivious to them (and attempt to seem *strong)*

<u>just smiling</u>: To *survive* in this situation, but not to improve or to win

FELIX Er, Oscar tells me <u>you're sisters</u>.
CECILY Yes. That's right. *(she looks at* GWENDOLYN)
FELIX From England.
GWENDOLYN Yes. That's right. *(she looks at* CECILY)
FELIX I see. *(*<u>Silence</u>. *Then,* <u>his little joke</u>*)* We're not brothers.
CECILY Yes, we know.

<u>you're sisters</u>: The safest thing for him to say (he knows this already) *(Skill)*

<u>Silence</u>: The worst thing that can happen, during conversation *(Bad!)*
<u>his little joke</u>: It's *smart* to think of something amusing to say to put them at ease.
(*Skill* in finding a subject that is noncommittal)

FELIX Although I am a brother. <u>I have a brother</u> who's a doctor. He lives in Buffalo. That's upstate in New York.
GWENDOLYN *(taking a cigarette from her purse)* Yes, we know.
FELIX You know my brother?

<u>I have a brother</u>:
Filling the gap *(Polite)*

GWENDOLYN No. We know that <u>Buffalo</u> is upstate in New York.
FELIX Oh! *(he gets up, takes a cigarette lighter from the side table and moves to light* GWENDOLYN'S *cigarette)*

<u>Gwendolyn smokes</u>: A loose girl! Oscar will like that (single and available, a *rare bird,* this Pigeon)

<u>Buffalo</u>: Not very interesting *(Inept)*

213

CECILY We've been there! Have you?

FELIX No! Is it nice?

GWENDOLYN Lovely.

> FELIX *closes the lighter on* GWENDOLYN'S *cigarette and turns to go back to his chair, taking the cigarette, now caught in the lighter, with him. He notices the cigarette and hastily gives it back to* GWENDOLYN, *stopping to light it once again. He puts the lighter back on the table and sits down nervously. There is a pause.*

FELIX Isn't that interesting? How long have you been in the United States of America?

closes the lighter on her cigarette: Felix's proximity to the girls arouses and startles him. He doesn't want to be aroused, so he doesn't look too closely into Gwendolyn's eyes, which is why he makes the mistakes. *(Weak, polite, inept)*

Not really listening, although it's important to keep the appearance that he is deeply interested. Most important to keep a look of interest on his face. *(Polite)*

CECILY Almost four years now.

FELIX *(nods)* Uh huh. Just visiting?

GWENDOLYN *(looks at* CECILY*)* No! We live here.

FELIX You work here too, do you?

CECILY Yes. We're secretaries for Slenderama.

GWENDOLYN You know. The health club.

CECILY People bring us their bodies and we do wonderful things with them.

GWENDOLYN Actually, if you're interested, we can get you ten percent off.

CECILY Off the price, not off your body.

FELIX Yes, I see.

four years/just visiting: It's *inept* to reveal he's not paying attention to what they say.

Slenderama: The name is trendy, so are they—beauty! And Oscar will like this! *(Good!)*
bring us their bodies: Not picking up the innuendo, not hearing it *(Ignorant)*

> *He laughs. They all laugh. Suddenly he shouts towards the kitchen.*

FELIX Oscar, where's the drink?

OSCAR *(offstage)* Coming! Coming!

He laughs: The laugh of the girls clues him into the risqué nature of the joke *(Knowing)*

Suddenly he shouts: The delayed reaction to the sexual offer, *losing his own cool* (by shouting) suddenly *wise to what's going on.* Afraid that he has compromised himself, Felix calls for help. (*Surviving,* just barely—with the help of his friend: the highest good)

Practical Tips for Working

Let the artwork of a period shape your thinking

Being familiar with art from the periods in which a play is set or created will shape your ideas as a performer. Remember that the forms of art in any era have a range as distinct as personalities and social classes. Picture the differences between seventeenth-century baroque painting praised at court and the French folk art that flourished during the same time—each practiced by a very different group of artists and appreciated by a very different public.

Listen to the music. The music of a period is as telling as a heartbeat. American jazz groups touring to Berlin inspired the steady pounding drums of Brecht's city-jungle; Viennese elegance drifting through the Scandinavian out-lands provided the lilting waltz of Hedda Gabler's dancing days (and Henrik Ibsen's, too). Not every character will enjoy the same music. In *The Odd Couple*, the radio dial probably swings between Felix's classical station and Oscar's sports reports before it settles on what they both can agree on—Gershwin, perhaps. Definitely not rock and roll, since connotations of sexual freedom are outside of this world. Not country and western, either. New Jersey is as far west as this world reaches. If you can feel what an intrusion country and western music would be in this Upper West Side apartment, you already have a sense of the borders of the world of *The Odd Couple*—as well as that world's lack of a frontier.

Learn the moves. From Japan to France, the national theaters that specialize in evoking long-gone worldviews conduct rehearsals that are often accompanied by period music. Sometimes, actors learn dance steps and movements even before they learn their roles or the lines of the play. If theater tells the story of human relationships, social dances are the poems of human relationships.

Learning to dance a minuet is an excellent introduction to the court of Louis XIV, where proper display was the highest of virtues. Like all court dances, the minuet was performed by a group that faced the King. The formation seen by Louis was more important than the individual steps or the expression of an individual dancer. The men's legs were turned out from the hips to make a good impression; a woman displayed her rank and position by what hung between her legs—literally: stitched on the wide front of her dress was her family's coat of arms. In life, as onstage, flirtations between dancers took place with partners looking straight ahead, not at each other.

Other physical activities shape a worldview. The hard work of farming a poor soil instills the patience and resignation designated as superior values in the world of *Desire Under the Elms*. For plays set or written in England during the early 1700s—when gentlemen studied fencing—an actor could appropriately use dueling terms such as *attack*, *counter-thrust*, *retreat*, and *parry* to evaluate the way characters exchanged their cutting remarks.

Pay attention to what you (and other characters) are wearing. Clothing, shoes, and underwear disclose the conventions of any time and place, including a play's. Big hips, little waists, white skins, dark skins, big feet, little feet—all have had different worth in different places and times. In performance, corsets, push-up bras, padded

215

shoulders, and pointy shoes all mold the body, for better or worse, according to changes in the rules of beauty. Shoes, from cowboy boots to satin slippers, are literally the "under-standing" of a character.

While he was writing *Yerma*, Lorca was also at work on a play called *Doña Rosita*, the story of a fifteen-year-old girl (Rosita), affianced in 1900, who remains faithful to the lover who abandoned her. In 1925, at the age of forty,* Rosita accepts that her fiancé will never return and that she has become a spinster. The demise of Rosita's world, a pattern organized around the central value of hope, can be understood by following the parade of hats worn by the ladies who visit Rosita over the three acts of the play. The hats of 1900, when Rosita is fifteen, look like luxuriant flower gardens. The hats of the second act, when Rosita is thirty, are still flamboyant, but are set on a more structured frame. The last set of hats, from 1925, are felt flapper caps worn close to the head—reduced in line in the same way the characters are reduced in all the other circumstances of their lives.

Look around you. The spaces in which people live will necessarily shape their view of the world, and their behavior. The gilded salons of Molière's settings induced an aristocratic hauteur that would be deflated by the squat dark furniture chosen by Auntie Juju to fill Hedda Gabler's salon. Neil Simon writes in his memoirs that the idea for *The Odd Couple* took shape when he could picture the apartment in which the play was set—complete with its dying goldfish and bachelor-pad mess. With this flash of inspiration came the comic possibilities of finicky Felix's housecleaning disrupting Oscar's squalor.

Look at artwork. The visual arts lend a period its shape and forms. Experience of the visual arts will do the same for you, widening your vocabulary of gestures and poses so that they may become specific to the world of the play. The chunky woodcuts of Shakespeare's day parallel the crude vigor of representation in Elizabeth's England, onstage and off. Rigaud's famous portrait of Louis XIV—note the fashionable stance of the King's thigh toward the viewer—was stamped on Molière's actors and audiences as the proper way to display themselves. After the First World War, Georg Grosz and Brecht revealed to weary Berliners that they were not alone in feeling like animals. More than that, Grosz's savage etchings and Brecht's plays gave their public a vocabulary with which to express their intuitions.

Read something other than the play. Your grasp of the conventions of a world created by a play can be strengthened by reading other plays, poetry, fiction, or contemporary newspapers (if there were any) from the time and places the play was written or set. A good trick is to look at the popular works of the period that are now considered to be dated. You can apply the Spanish theory that says the second-rate literature of a culture reveals more about that culture than the first-rate literature (which is, by its excellence, not bound by the specifics of its time and place). If you're preparing to play Jean Genet's maids, better read *True Detective* magazines; Solange and Claire say they do.

The non-dramatic texts written by playwrights are particularly helpful to under-

---

*The dates for *Doña Rosita*'s setting are confusing. The published text gives as a subtitle: *A Tale of 1900 Grenada*.

stand the worldview of their plays. Chekhov's short stories are a wonderful introduction to his compassion and irony. Brecht's poetry is very beautiful, and offers an insight into his heart. Shakespeare was working on his sonnets while he put sardonic sweet nothings into the mouth of the hunchback Richard III.

What to do without a full script

World of the play analysis considers the play as a whole, but this is impossible when actors are handed their lines and their cues—and nothing more. This was and is still common practice in Eastern Europe. At the first rehearsal, The Leader—the director or author—reads the entire script out loud while the cast listens intently. Then the actors receive their sides (pages with only their scenes on them) and get no more chances to learn about the rest of the play until late in rehearsals, when the whole play is rehearsed in sequence. The claim was and is that this saves paper. The other claim is that an ensemble needs to be sensitive to each other, and over time will have learned to play off each other. Maybe. Maybe it has more to do with the idea that only the Leader can know the whole plan; everyone else learns to do their own job and not worry about the purpose.

For whatever excuse, all too often film scripts give the actors only the words of the scenes they are in, and sometimes only the cues. Keeping actors ignorant reinforces the authority and intelligence of the director, casting director, and producer. It's sad but true: working in a film, you will often not have the materials to prepare yourself to enter the world of the performance. In a play, if you don't have a full script, you can derive clues from your costume, the settings, and especially from what the other actors are doing. Simeon and Peter's scene in *Desire Under the Elms* sets the rules for the world of the play, even before the plot begins and the main characters of the story enter.

Work within the world of the production

The physical aspects of a production—lighting, scenery, costumes, the architecture of the theater—assign meaning to your acting, and you should learn to play within the measure of those circumstances. You'll especially want to understand how the physical production makes you stand out—or disappear. There is a play by Samuel Beckett, *Happy Days* (1961), in which a woman sits up to her waist in a pile of sand. Although she's immobile, she is alive; she still has her memories and counts them among her blessings. After an intermission the audience returns to find the same woman now buried *further* up to her neck in sand and still counting her blessings. "Another happy day!" she chirps (80). Her clichés, which would be trite in the world of the audience, are, by the measure of the sand, the forceful weapons of a hero bravely fighting off resignation and death.

The specifics of the production, even those that can't be seen, can also organize *images* you use, even the most personal images of yourself and others. In the film version of Edward Albee's *Who's Afraid of Virginia Woolf* (1966), Elizabeth Taylor, after years of being treated as a beautiful object to be photographed, delivered the performance of her lifetime because she had a chance to use her self-knowledge of her own image—and the public's response to that image—within the world of the production. That world was established when Taylor and her real-life husband Richard Burton were cast as husband and wife in the film. The Burtons' reputation as a decadent royal pair, given to tempestuous battles and impetuous love, provided Taylor (and her public) a powerful Rosetta Stone for translating what it meant in the world of a small New England college campus to be a college president's daughter who drunkenly argues in public with her husband, demeaning him for not being the head of his own department.

Perform with the logic of absurdity

Samuel Beckett, the author of *Happy Days*, is the most important of a group of playwrights, who, in the years immediately after the Second World War, created a body of work set in surreal worlds divorced from identification with specific times and places. Perhaps this is a response to the nationalism of the two World Wars and the Cold War after: when people have nothing in common, perhaps the one thing they do have in common is what is strange to all of them.

Beckett, who was Irish, wrote his plays in France and in French, but translated them into English himself. He is usually considered to be an English writer. Eugene Ionesco, the Romanian author of *The Lesson*, wrote in French, and conceived his most famous play, *The Bald Soprano* (1950) (81), from the dialogue found in an English-language primer. This is the first line of that play, spoken after the clock strikes seventeen:

> MRS. SMITH There, it's nine o'clock. We've drunk the soup, and eaten the fish
> and chips, and the English salad. The children have drunk English water.
> We've eaten well this evening. That's because we live in the suburbs of
> London and because our name is Smith.

This is not a realistic England, and it isn't meant to be.

In 1951, the British critic Martin Esslin categorized these plays as the *theater of the absurd*. The word *absurd* does not justify erratic and arbitrary onstage behavior. The rules within such plays are absurdly different from the rules among the audience, but nevertheless they are rules for the behavior of the characters. We've already examined a scene from Ionesco's *The Lesson* for tasks and obstacles, and discussed the logical outcome of absurdly unquestioning obedience.

The texts of Samuel Beckett's plays create dramatic landscapes with rules consistent enough to have resulted in an adjective, *Beckettian*, that describes the similarities of the blasted wastelands in which the plays are set and the behavior that takes place in those landscapes. Grim humor often serves as a survival tactic. Discussing the Beckettian view seen out the window of a featureless room in Beckett's *Endgame* (1957) (82), two characters exchange the following lines:

> HAMM Is it night already then?
> CLOV (*looking*) Gray. (*louder*) Gray! (*louder*) GRRAY! (*whispers in his ear*)

HAMM Did I hear you say gray?
CLOV Light black.

Beckett resisted translating his landscape to recognizable settings. In 1984, when the American director Joanna Akalitis tried to place *Endgame* in a New York City subway station, the playwright protested and asked his lawyers to close the production.

Other playwrights have created alternative worlds meant to lie adjacent to recognizable settings, populated by the clichés of a national character. Harold Pinter in England, Luigi Pirandello in Italy, Jean Genet in France, Peter Handke in Germany, Slawomir Mrozek in Poland, Edward Albee and Sam Shepard in America—all have created texts that evoke worlds in which the façades of a benign national identity are revealed as fronts for a sinister parallel world. Actors performing in these plays are meant to act in such a way as to convince the audience that the parallel world behind the façade is *also* a norm and a reality, not just a disruption or an illusion.

The illusion of reality—onstage and in films

Sometimes a play, like the reflection in a mirror, gives the audience the impression of a real world. Remember Hamlet's instructions to the actors he hires?

> . . . the purpose of playing, whose end, both at the first and now, was and is,
> to hold, as 'twere, the mirror up to nature . . .

> *Hamlet, Act III, scene ii*

Follow Shakespeare's image through and think carefully about what mirror-makers do: they put silver on the back of glass, or polish steel to brilliance, or use some other technique to create a reflection of reality. They don't hold up an empty frame. They don't polish *glass*, or paint *steel* from behind. They use the techniques specific to the medium in which they work.

Techniques for creating a convincing illusion vary from play to play, just as they do from mirror to mirror. The realistic world of *The Odd Couple* has every one of its characters unrealistically deliver comic zingers with deadpan regularity. The realistic world of *Hedda Gabler* requires unrealistic eloquence of speech. The realistic world of *Desire Under the Elms* restricts the actor to an unrealistically limited vocabulary. Actors performing in these realistic plays must identify the specific skill—comic timing, fine speaking, or plain speaking with a hint of repressed passion—that is necessary to make their unnatural behavior seem believable within the frame of the individual play.

Creating these illusions of reality for an actor requires submersion in the world of the play, which, at its best, will result in the transformation of an actor's accent and physique into elements of the production. This work is familiar from film. It is fascinating to watch the work of Robert De Niro throughout his long career. For *Bang the Drum Slowly* (1973), De Niro traveled south to learn that region's way of life and speech; for *Taxi Driver* (1976), he worked twelve-hour shifts in a cab. The next year, for *New*

York New York, he learned to play the saxophone. The year after that, to prepare for *The Deer Hunter* (1978), he spent weeks among Ohio Valley steelworkers. Most famously, for his performance two years later in *Raging Bull* (discussed in Chapter 6), De Niro worked out for months in a boxing ring and gained fifty pounds to play heavyweight fighter Jake La Motta at different stages in his life, from lean and mean contender to bloated ex-champ.

Within the rules of the world of *Raging Bull* (much of which takes place among Italian immigrants), blondes are elite. La Motta marries a blonde. A quarreling wife is common; La Motta gives his wife plenty of reasons to quarrel with him. Winning is beautiful, losing is ugly. Ignorance is thinking you can become champion without the help of gangsters. Wisdom—something La Motta never seems to acquire—is knowing how to get along with the powers that be. Sexual jealousy is a sickness; sexual desire, healthy. Within the rules of the boxing ring, flab is not just ugly, it's *bad*. A trim belly is good; a fast right hook is better. To swing out is inept, to wait for the time to land a blow is skill. Getting hit in the head is all in a day's work.

Speaking in an interview of how his research and preparation shapes his performances, De Niro has said:

> There was a scene in *Raging Bull*—one of the scenes where I went back to the corner after knocking somebody down. I was doing too much because I didn't know what to do, and it was the first fight scene that we shot. I was jumping up and down a little too much. When you see actual fighters, they do that. But they also just wait in the corner. It's like anything else. In the beginning you learn the rules, and then you realize that the rules are there to use or not to use and that there are millions of different ways of doing something (83).

Include the audience

Though the audience doesn't necessarily share the rules that structure the onstage world, they should appreciate, if not always understand, the *significance* given in the world of the play to behavior and action. In order to shape the audience's perception, onstage reactions become as important as actions to establish these values.

For example, Molière's world can be reproduced onstage with some degree of accuracy. But no research can resurrect the original audience for whom red heels were the height of fashion and Louis XIV a living presence to be feared. How an actor portraying an onstage courtier *reacts* to the presence of the King, however, will convey to a modern audience Louis's life and death powers.

An odd problem arises when the audience thinks they understand what's going on, but do not. Neil Simon has noted that his plays do better in other countries of the world than in England—because in other countries the plays are translated idiomatically. In England they are performed in the original language, of course, but the British audience does not value or react to American idiom in the same way as an American audience. As the British comedian Benny Hill used to say: "What is this thing *called*, Love?"

When the audience can be led to share the rules of a long-gone period, texts that seem impossibly dated can spring to life within the *rules of the era*. A good example of how this can succeed is the story of Sarah Bernhardt's 1903 revival of Jean Racine's play *Esther*, written in 1689.

In 1689, Racine had been retired from the stage for twelve years. His retreat was prompted by the religious powers at the French court who had persuaded Louis to shun the playwright. Racine's sympathetic portrayal of a sexually eager woman in *Phèdre* was denounced as a bad influence on the morals of the country. At the suggestion of the King's pious consort, Madame de Maintenon, Racine took up a subject from the Bible. He chose the story of Esther rescuing her people from the wicked plans of an evil courtier, and wrote a play on this theme to be performed at a convent girls' school—Madame de Maintenon's favorite charity.

When Bernhardt revived the play in 1903, she reproduced the conventions of the original production. Actresses played all the roles, including the men, as if they were school girls. What brought the world of the play into focus was the presence in the audience of actors portraying the aristocrats, Louis XIV among them, who had condescended to view the original production (84).*

Esther is not a great play, but its world of simple, heartfelt truth triumphing over evil-minded politics was understood by and moved its audiences—in Racine's day and in Bernhardt's. Sarah herself played the Persian King of the production as an awkward adolescent girl with an obviously fake beard. Her voice broke and her beard slipped, but she did her best. This performance is a good example of how to create a convincing illusion by working within the conventions of a world. In 1903, when she was playing this adolescent "King," Bernhardt was fifty-nine.

The Chart

- **Unifying image.** The world of the play acts as a *frame* to organize behavior onstage so that it becomes significant form.
- **Dramatic action.** Dramatic action is a *breach in the rules of the world*.
- **The intended reaction of the audience.** The aim of the performer is to *transport the sensibilities of the audience* to the onstage world, so that they feel, if not always understand, the disruptions and returns to the pattern of the play.
- **The illusion of character.** The illusion of character is understood in *the context of the world*; a role is characterized as part of a *composition* of other characters and the environment.
- **Suitable playwrights.** World of the play analysis is particularly useful when preparing to work on texts written by playwrights whose worldview is distant from our own in time and place: *Molière, Oscar Wilde*, the Restoration playwrights; also, authors who create alternative and artificial worlds: *Beckett*,

---

*The description of the production in Cornelia Otis Skinner's book *Madame Sarah* is well worth reading—although she does get the date of *Esther* wrong.

Ionesco, all verse plays, including *Shakespeare*; and playwrights who seem to be creating a world that they repeatedly visit: *Tennessee Williams, Genet, Pinter, Strindberg*, and *O'Neill*.

Is There a Right Way to Do It?

Is Bernhardt's reproduction of *Esther* the only way to stage that play? Was Samuel Beckett right—morally right, aesthetically right—to want to close down a production of his *Endgame* set in a New York subway station? Is there a *correct* world for some plays, a world inextricably bound to an appropriate style intended by the playwright or the age in which the play was first presented?

The answers to these questions have to do with property, not just propriety. Beckett's lawyers insisted that he owned and controlled the world of the play just as much as he owned the legal rights to its text. "National" theaters worldwide make similar claims to their nation's literature as their rightful heritage, and regard foreign interpreters as trespassers who lack respect, authenticity, and shame. In various theaters and schools from Paris to Tokyo, actors who enter the profession take on a lifelong submission to the discipline of preserving and passing on theatrical traditions. Once they dictate the rules laid down by their models, these schools reward continuity, not originality, and demand single-minded devotion to a closed system. In India it's a flexed foot, in France it's a hand parallel to the stage, among the Maoris it's a wagging tongue, in Japan it's a hidden thumb. These all have meanings within their separate styles. Very often, after years of repetition, the shape of an actor's body changes: hips spread, fingers fold back, toes curl—on their own.

Such sincere dedication demands respect, just as sincere religious beliefs demand respect, even if one doesn't share those beliefs. Traditional theaters cater to audiences trained to appreciate the nuances of their limited vocabularies. Sometimes a play needs more distance from its original style to make its worldview felt by an audience with a different orientation. That different point of view can be an advantage. A Buddhist parable points out that, although they are very close to the eyebrows, the eyes cannot see the eyebrows; only another pair of eyes has the necessary distance.

A living playwright is certainly entitled to prevent the meaning of his words from being perverted, if only out of respect. Yet, if the script is open to only one interpretation—the playwright's—it probably won't survive its author's death, if it lasts that long. Of course, there are undeniable close affinities with the style of a production and the world of the play. Yet even a "national" style interpreting a "classic" text changes from era to era, just as the images of nations change. Stanislavsky's interpretations of Chekhov altered when Russia came under Communist rule and aesthetics, even though the texts stayed the same and the style remained realistic.

The script evokes the world of the play, but only when the text intersects with the shifting points of view of living actors who transmute words into dramatic action. That is the subject of the next chapter: *the dramatic action of a shifting point of view.*

PART V

TELLING A STORY

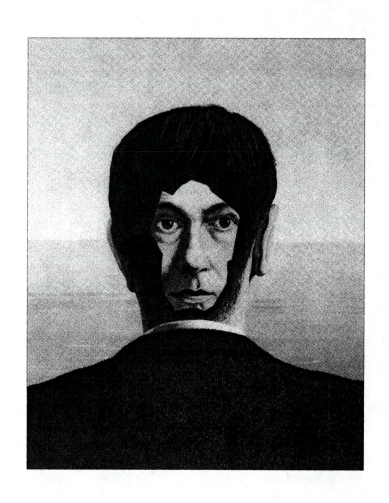

Reading List
Iphigenia in Aulis by Euripides
Buried Child by Sam Shepard
Stories from other plays cited as examples are included in the text

Viewing List
Long Day's Journey into Night directed by Sidney Lumet

René Magritte, detail from *The Glass House*

CHAPTER 11

STORYTELLING

In the Theater of the Audience's Mind

Telling stories dates back to the caves. Telling stories in plays probably dates back to the Greeks, and has persisted ever since. When that prototype Method actor Polus (Chapter 8) tottered out onstage in 511 BCE carrying his dead son's ashes in order to mourn Orestes, the audience was prepared to sob along with him because another character in the play had previously told the story of how Orestes died in a chariot race. When Helene Weigel first caught Brecht's eye, she was delivering the Servant's speech in *Oedipus the King* that describes the death of Jocasta, the hero's wife and mother. When the fifteen-year-old Sarah Bernhardt auditioned for the Paris Conservatory, she forgot to bring a copy of the scene she had prepared. Since no one could feed her cues, she told a story instead, and her rendition of a children's fable about two pigeons was so moving that her auditioners' initial giggles gave way to open tears (85).

Classic, romantic, or modern—storytelling persists in theatrical tradition because in all times and all places it renews its contributions to the performance of a play. Stories told as performances depict dramatic action that the stage could not otherwise depict: ungodly horror, the glory of the gods, a battle at sea. Stories told in the course of a play refine the actor's expression of thought and memory. Stories told onstage expand the audience's vision to include what individual characters cannot see, or understand, or want known—even about themselves. Be it soliloquy or gossip, revelation or panorama or report, the action of a play doesn't stop or even pause when a character onstage tells a story; the action proceeds, but on a different plane.

Yet, storytelling braided into the action of a play is not always subject to the same rules as impersonation. An actor telling a story onstage can use a technique specific to storytelling, a technique different from any he might employ while acting out a role in a scene. Since Shakespeare's soliloquies offer performers and audiences such a wide range of action, vision, and personal investigation, they will be considered separately, in Chapter 13.

Storytelling as Illusion

Onstage—as opposed to in a living room or a courtroom—storytelling is an illusion. You are not really remembering what happened; you are not really reporting what can be seen offstage. What's happening offstage? The actors are flirting with each other in the wings, or playing cards, or staring into their dressing room mirrors, or sipping from flasks. Whether reminiscing, reporting, or delivering a message, an actor tells a story onstage so the audience can picture what's being described.

That bears repeating (so that you can repeat it too): *An actor is telling a story so the audience can picture what the story describes.*

The power to place an image in other people's minds, and to make that image vivid enough to arouse listeners to emotions of their own, is rightly called *casting a spell—spell* being related to the German word *spiel*, for "story." Radio plays, bedtime stories, ghost stories, erotic stories—any of these are familiar examples of how a storyteller can make a listener turn the mind into an amphitheater, a boudoir, or any place the action described is occurring. Casting a spell is much more wonderful than deep-felt reminiscence; the whole value of a story, on the stage and in life, is that a story transcends the personal and becomes a form of shared vision, wider than an individual's. This magic is repeated onstage whenever a story is told. Yes, it helps to have a vision of what you are describing, but even performers who believe in their visions as spiritual revelations have to share their insight with the congregation.

The Advantages of Storytelling: From Aeschylus to Sam Shepard

Past and present, and in all cultures, playwrights have returned to storytelling in the course of a play because telling a story offers a heightened dimension with which to express dramatic action. In the West, telling stories has been part of theater from its historical origins. Let's review a few texts from the Western repertory that we can use later as examples.

A vision that exceeds the possibilities of life

The Persians (86) was written by the Greek playwright Aeschylus in 472 BCE. It describes events that occurred eight years before the play was written: the defeat of the vast Persian navy by the small ships assembled from the Greek city-states. There is no battle shown onstage; it is described. The scene takes place at the court of Persia. A chorus of old men and the Queen wait to hear news from the front. A Messenger arrives. He describes a rout:

> MESSENGER At first by its huge impetus
> Our fleet withstood them. But soon, in that narrow space,
> Our ships were jammed in hundreds; none could help another.
> They rammed each other with their prows of bronze; and some
> Were stripped of every oar. Meanwhile the enemy
> Came round us in a ring and charged. Our vessels heeled
> Over; the sea was hidden, carpeted with wrecks
> And dead men; all the shores and reefs were full of dead.

226

Then every ship we had broke rank and rowed for life.
The Greeks seized fragments or wrecks and broken oars
And hacked and stabbed at our men swimming in the sea
As fishermen kill their catch inside a net.

The Persians

If you begin to prepare your performance of this text by identifying *tasks*, as described in Chapter 1, you will have begun your own losing battle. What is the Messenger's task in telling this story of the disastrous Persian defeat to the Persian Queen? He doesn't have any other than *to tell the story*, and, through his efforts, bring the naval battle onto the stage.

To do the job, it helps to have the episode told, not shown; the Messenger's report can depict what no single person could possibly have seen. Hacked or hacker, each participant in the battle would have been caught up in the immediate experience. Not even if you climbed a mast could you have seen the vast Persian fleet run aground. Told as a story, onstage, the historic Battle of Salamis gains a focus it never had in life.

The clarity of distance—emotional and physical

The physical distance needed to comprehend a panorama has a parallel in the psychological distance needed to comprehend outsized emotions. *Oedipus the King* (87), written by Sophocles around 430 BCE, reaches its climax when the queen, Jocasta, hangs herself and Oedipus, her son, tears out his own eyes. These events are described by a Servant of the Queen's, a role played so effectively by Helene Weigel that Bertolt Brecht wrote about her performance for years after.

> SERVANT What happened after that I cannot tell,
> Nor say how the end fell, for with a shriek
> Oedipus burst on us; all eyes were fixed
> On Oedipus, as up and down he stalked,
> Nor could we mark her agony to the end.
> For striding back and forth "A sword!" he cried,
> "Where is my wife, no wife, the teeming womb
> That bore a double harvest, me and mine?"
> And in his frenzy some divine power
> (No man nor woman, none of us who watched him)
> Guided his footsteps; with a terrible shriek,
> As though someone beckoned, he crashed against
> The folding doors, and from the hinges forced
> The wrenched bolts and hurled himself within.
> Then we saw the woman hanging there,
> A running noose was twisted round her neck.
> But when *he* saw her, with a maddened roar

> He untied the cord; and when her wretched corpse
> Lay stretched on earth . . . what followed was horror.

Oedipus the King

If you begin preparation for this speech using the approach of playing an *episode* described in Chapter 5, the question of what is happening onstage can only have one answer: the episode is THE SERVANT TELLS A STORY. What the audience watches onstage is how the speaker is transformed by telling her story. Brecht described how Weigel went from stern pronouncement to begrudging respect to conventional grief to submission. The transaction of the episode is between the speaker and the audience. Brecht puts the transaction as *hear me out / and now you may weep*.

On the simplest level, any story that is an episode has as its transaction: *if the audience pays attention to the speaker / they will hear the story and follow the action of the play*. This is particularly true for the climax of *Oedipus the King*, which would be much more difficult for the audience to understand if they, and not the Servant, witnessed the sights of a suicide by hanging and a man gouging out his own eyes. For most, if not all the spectators, disgust would overwhelm most other responses.

In Greek tragedy, horrors are very often described rather than shown. Potentially vivid theatrical events—the moments you think would attract a playwright to source material in the first place—are usually left offstage. An irreligious king is torn apart by a mob of zealots, a mother kills her children, a wife kills her husband: in Greek tragedies, all these are described after the fact, the better for the action to proceed in the theater of the spectators' minds.

Greek playwrights also used stories to bring the glory of the gods onto the stage. In another play by Sophocles, *Oedipus at Colonus* (88), written forty years after *Oedipus the King*, the hero is assumed by Heaven. How? Again a Messenger speaks:

> MESSENGER The man was gone, he vanished from our eyes;
>   We saw only our king whose upraised hand
>   Shaded his eyes as from some awful sight,
>   That no man might endure to look upon.
>   A moment later, and we saw him bend
>   In prayer to Earth and prayer to Heaven at once.
>   But by what doom the stranger met his end
>   No man except Theseus knows.
>   For there fell
>   No fiery bolt that split him in that hour,
>   Nor whirlwind from the sea, but he was taken.
>   It was a messenger from heaven, or else
>   Some gentle, painless cleaving of earth's base;
>   For without wailing or disease or pain
>   He passed away—an end most marvelous.

Oedipus at Colonus

Actors telling stories in ancient tragedy can penetrate the depths of horror or ascend to the heavens—all with the playwright's words.

Closer than in life, and behind the façade

In classic ancient comedies, storytelling took on a form it would anywhere, be it Greece or Rome or Albuquerque: *gossip* about the neighbors. As gossip, an actor can tell an audience what is really going on behind the façades of respectable homes.

Prologues set the scene for the audience, explain the background of the plot, and reveal the secret lives and lies of the characters. Despite their name, these Prologues could happen even after the play had started, the better to puncture pretense. *The Braggart Soldier* (*Miles Gloriosus*), written in 205 BCE by the Roman playwright Plautus (89), begins with a dialogue between an obsequious underling and a vainglorious soldier. The flunky can't help but praise his commander's valor, good looks, and success with women. After the soldier and his yes-man exit, out comes a slave, Palaestrio, who explains to the audience just whom and what they've been watching.

> PALAESTRIO This is the city of Ephesus. That soldier who just left for the forum is my master, a stinking shameless blowhard, full of lies and lechery. He says all the women chase after him—actually, wherever he goes, the ladies crack up at the sight of him. You noticed most of the hookers around here have twisted mouths. That's so they don't laugh in his face.
>
> *The Braggart Soldier*

The gossip, often from a slave or a woman, sets out the comic confusion of conventional roles in Roman society: the mighty soldier is a jerk, the respected old senator is randy, his submissive wife is a shrew, his heir a fool, his daughter a ninny, and his slave insubordinate (and usually freer than any citizen). The listening audience for the original productions of these plays shared a world in which slaves and women were excluded from official power; onstage gossip was a way for women and slaves to exercise the force of their own power, by sharing their knowledge of the ruling class in all its hypocrisy.

The collaboration of the audience

In Europe, the dramatic tradition of telling stories ran from the Greek theater to the Roman to the theater of the Middle Ages, which adapted its stories from the Bible and its form of direct address from sermons. Medieval performances were often staged for a faithful illiterate. The story of the scene—and its moral significance—were often repeated to the audience before, during, and after performances.

During the European Renaissance that followed the Age of Faith, attention focused on individuals, rather than categories or moral allegories. There was renewed curiosity, even delight, in the world's variety. Zoos and botanical gardens were established, and portraits were painted to emphasize character and idiosyncrasy, rather than classical beauty or social rank. There was an interest in the drama of individual experience on stages as well, often expressed as stories. There was also a curiosity in the marvels of the past or faraway places, and this, too, could be satisfied on stage with stories that brought the fabulous (a word derived from the Latin *fabula*, or "story") to view. Shakespeare described Cleopatra's barge. Marlowe described the inaccessible Central Asian city of Samarkand. The prolific Spanish playwright Calderón de la Barca described the exotic wilderness of Poland (seen from Spain, Poland seems exotic).

The limited resources of small stages without scenery presented special challenges for playwrights who hoped to present the wonders of history. The events to be dramatized could span decades and, like the naval battle at Salamis, involve a cast of thousands. For Shakespeare, this resulted in a story *about* storytelling, which was probably first delivered by the playwright himself to an audience standing around him, like spectators at a fight:

> CHORUS . . . can this cockpit hold
> The vasty fields of France? Or may we cram
> Within this wooden O the very casques
> That did affright the air at Agincourt?
> O, pardon! Since a crooked figure may
> Attest in little place a million;
> And let us, ciphers to this great company,
> On your imaginary forces work.
> Suppose with the girdle of these walls
> Are now confin'd two mighty monarchies,
> Whose high upreared and abutting fronts
> The perilous narrow ocean parts asunder:
> Piece out our imperfections with your thoughts;
> Into a thousand parts divide one man,
> And make imaginary puissance;
> Think, when we talk of horses. That you see them
> Printing their proud hoofs i' th' receiving earth;
> For 'tis your thoughts that now must deck our kings . . .
>
> *Henry V, Prologue*

This is a basic principle of storytelling on stage: the conversion of words to dramatic action is a *collaboration* between the performer and the audience. The listeners must participate in order for the story to unfold. The performer must present the story in such a way that the listeners can participate.

If we were to approach the Prologue from *Henry V* by building *images*—the technique described in Chapters 7 and 8—the images described in the speech would be more important than any images the speaker might have of himself as the Chorus. In fact, the Chorus says as much. He asks the audience to forget where they are and who is speaking in order to picture in their minds the ocean, the heroes, and the brave horses. The images are the images of the story, and they are evoked in the act of collaboration between speaker and listener. Without the listener, they have no effect.

STORYTELLING

The images of the story are also ineffectual without the speaker—as voice-over. When Laurence Olivier filmed his 1945 *Henry V*, his biggest problem in the adaptation was how to treat these Chorus speeches. When horses, soldiers, and oceans could be filmed, wouldn't that erase the need for descriptions? Olivier's solution was to start his film with an actor onstage, in a replica of Shakespeare's Globe Theater. This device illustrated perfectly that Shakespeare had written a speech with the power to transport the attention of an audience from reality to vision—a power not unlike a camera's power to command a movie audience's focus and attention. The actor telling a story is presenting—like a camera—close-ups, long shots, or panoramas.

The inner life revealed

Actors speaking Shakespeare's soliloquies can do something a camera cannot: pierce to view the inner life of a role. These stories report the *private thoughts* of a character, which contrast with—or complement—the same character's *public behavior*. A memorable graphic version of this idea is a picture painted in gouache by the Belgian artist René Magritte in 1939. It shows the back of the head and shoulders of a man contemplating the ocean. The man's hair on the back of his head is parted, revealing a pair of eyes, a nose, and a mouth—the better to tell us what he might be contemplating in front. The painting is titled *The Glass House*, which is not as opaque a title as it would seem, or off the subject of acting either. The title is reminiscent of the story of Comus, the Greek god of mockery, who was unhappy that humans had no glass in their chests—the better for Comus to observe humans' whims.

In his novel *Tristram Shandy*, written in 1776, Laurence Sterne commiserates with Comus. If people were transparent, then all that the god or the writer (or, for that matter, any artist) would need to do to view or display a man's character was pull up a chair and watch:

> But this, as I said above, is not the case of the inhabitants of this earth; our minds shine not through the body, but are wrapt up here in a dark covering of uncrystalized flesh and blood; so that if we would come to the specifick characters of them, we must go some other way to work (90).

The man who seems to reveal his thoughts in Magritte's painting is as good as housed in glass. Just as transparently, characters in Shakespeare's plays report to the audience on their *inner* character.

Even committed villains turn out to have compunction, of sorts. The unscrupulous Richard III is alone with the audience when, waking from a nightmare, he admits his ambivalence:

RICHARD Alack, I love myself. Wherefore? For any good
   That I myself have done unto myself?
   O, no! Alas, I rather hate myself

For hateful deeds committed by myself!
I am a villain: yet I lie, I am not.

Richard III, Act V, scene iii

Macbeth's introspection is part of his ambiguity, a brave man heroically facing up to the consequences of his cowardice.

MACBETH I have liv'd long enough: my way of life
Is fall'n into the sear, the yellow leaf;
And that which should accompany old age,
As honor, love, obedience, troops of friends,
I must not look to have . . .

Macbeth, Act IV, scene iii

While Shakespeare's soliloquies give actors access to a character's self-awareness, Molière's comedies include introspection as an opportunity to demonstrate the character's self-delusion. The story of a young bride seduced by a young man once the bride's elderly husband leaves town was familiar to Renaissance audiences from the improvisations of the Italian commedia dell'arte. This well-known scenario also occurs in Molière's *The School for Wives* (91), written in 1662, the year the playwright himself married a much younger woman. But Molière includes the episodes *within a story*: they are not shown, they are told.

The storyteller is Agnès, the young bride, who informs her older husband Arnolphe (played by Molière in the original production) just what has happened while Arnolphe was away:

AGNÈS It's the most amazing story you ever heard.
I was sewing, out on the balcony, in the breeze,
When I noticed someone strolling under the trees.
It was a fine young man, who caught my eye
And made me a deep bow as he went by.
I, not to be convicted of a lack
Of manners, very quickly nodded back.
At once, the young man bowed to me again.
I bowed to him a second time, and then
It wasn't very long until he made
A third deep bow, which I of course repaid.
He left, but kept returning, and as he passed,
He'd bow, each time, more gracefully than the last,
While I, observing as he came and went,
Gave each new bow a fresh acknowledgement.
Indeed, had night not fallen, I declare
I think that I might still be sitting there,

232

And bowing back each time he bowed to me,
For fear he'd think me less polite than he.
ARNOLPHE Go on.
AGNÈS Then an old woman came, next day,
And found me standing in the entryway.
She said to me, "May Heaven bless you, dear,
And keep you beautiful for many a year.
God, who bestowed on you such grace and charm,
Did not intend those gifts to do men harm,
And you should know that there's a heart which bears
A wound which you've inflicted unawares."

The inner life of the character is revealed in this scene by the way the storyteller interprets what has happened. The events Agnès describes are different from the actual episode: THE YOUNG BRIDE DOESN'T KNOW SHE HAS BEEN SEDUCED. The audience takes pleasure in picturing this seduction while at the same time witnessing the rubber-faced husband's barely suppressed wrath and the naïve bride's seeming artlessness.

The past brought to the present in memory

Storytelling endures in the realistic theater, tucked within the framework of *memory*. As twentieth-century playwrights relied on the theory that past events explain present behavior, it became increasingly important to include memories onstage. No one has done this more consistently and effectively—or more beautifully—than the American playwright Tennessee Williams. The Mississippi-born playwright's southern heritage granted him direct experience of a culture haunted by memory and stories—the memory of losing a war, the stories of a long-gone glory.

In Williams's first important play, *The Glass Menagerie* (1944) (92), a character named Tom (the playwright's own nickname) walks onto the stage, like the Prologue in Plautus, and announces:

TOM The play is memory. Being a memory play, it is dimly lighted, it is sentimental, it is not realistic. In memory everything seems to happen to music. That explains the fiddle in the wings.

From the opening speech, the audience is alerted that the realistic style of performance is an illusion that can be returned to or abandoned: *I am the narrator of the play, and also a character in it.*

Tom does take part in scenes; he also addresses the audience directly in monologues, all of them stories told from a point in time many years after the action of the play. There are memories within the scenes themselves, too, and they develop the dramatic action as strongly as dialogue or direct address. Amanda, the mother who dominates the family of *The Glass Menagerie*, has a fabled past, a fable she is glad to remember:

> AMANDA One Sunday afternoon in Blue Mountain—your mother received—
> *seventeen!*—gentlemen callers! Why, sometimes there weren't chairs enough
> to accommodate them all . . .
> TOM How did you entertain those gentlemen callers?
> AMANDA I understood the art of conversation!

In this scene, Tom is not in the same room as his mother, Amanda, although Amanda speaks as if he were. As her story proceeds, Tom gives his cues, according to the stage direction: *as though reading from a script**—which is to say, not as emotionally involved as if he were fully in the scene. As Amanda continues her memory, the stage direction asks that:

> TOM *motions for music and a spot of light on* AMANDA. *Her eyes lift, her face
> glows, her voice becomes rich and elegiac.*

The story-telling actor separated from the scene by lighting, staging, or music is meant to transport a listening audience to the places he is describing. Williams used these techniques throughout his long career. The emotional range of the device can be as delicate as the violin-scored elegies in *The Glass Menagerie* or as melodramatic as the drums and cymbals in *Suddenly Last Summer* (1958). The latter is a single dramatic action comprising an entire play: the telling of a forbidden tale, itself a symbol, with cymbals. That awful pun is the least of the horrors in *Suddenly Last Summer*, which concludes with a twenty-minute monologue that climaxes, like a Greek tragedy, with the story of a man ripped to pieces by a mob.

One of the most powerful of memory stories occurs in Williams's *A Streetcar Named Desire* (1947) (94). The stage direction suggests that the speaker, Blanche, sit at a window sill, looking out. What it doesn't say, because it was considered too crass to mention, is that Blanche sits in the window so she may tell the story directly to the audience, while maintaining the realistic style of the performance.

> BLANCHE . . . When I was sixteen, I made the discovery—love. All at once
> and much, much too completely. It was like you suddenly turned a blind-
> ing light on something that had always been in shadow, that's how it struck
> the world for me. But I was unlucky. Deluded.

The speech is long. When the story it tells moves to a casino dance hall, the music Blanche remembers begins to play in the distance.

> BLANCHE We danced the Varsouviana! Suddenly in the middle of the dance
> the boy I had married broke away from me and ran out of the casino. A few
> moments later—a shot! I ran out—all did!—all ran and gathered about the

---

*These are the techniques of epic acting. Williams was a student at Piscator's Dramatic Workshop. After his first play was staged on Broadway, Williams asked to become Piscator's secretary. He was turned down; Piscator thought it more important for Williams to work on his own, although Williams did contribute to Piscator's 1942 staging of *War and Peace* (93).

terrible thing at the edge of the lake! I couldn't get near for the crowding. Then somebody caught my arm. "Don't go any closer! Come back! You don't want to see!"

The storyteller is, yes, sometimes reliving what she describes; the stage directions ask that she sway and cover her face, a gesture echoing what she would have done when she saw the body of her husband. But the storyteller does not remain in a state of emotional recall. Like Tom's monologues in *A Glass Menagerie*, the story is told from a vantage point several years later, when the character speaks with experience, not horror or shock.

> BLANCHE And then the searchlight which had been turned on the world was turned off again and never for one moment since has there been any light that's stronger than this—kitchen—candle . . .

A performer handed the gift of a Williams story to deliver has the chance to relive the events described, but also to plant in the audience's mind a scene that motivates the character's unending hunger for love. It is important that the audience picture that scene, even as they empathize with the character's pain or the emotional memory of the actress who is performing. Empathy and understanding are also the responsibility of the other actor onstage (playing Mitch, Blanche's would-be suitor) who, once Blanche has finished her tale, returns Blanche to the realistic world of the play by giving her a hug. Blanche stares at Mitch vacantly—her speech has lost any task related to him—until she too returns to the realism of the scene and, as the playwright asks, *huddles, sobbing in his embrace.*

Establishing the character in the world of the play

Among other playwrights, the American author Sam Shepard offers actors speeches that reveal how the roles they play acquire significance within the world of the play. This is done through descriptions—literally—of landscape, but also through moments of self-awareness. Such self-discovery would seem to be too private to enact. But, like the glory of the gods depicted by the Greeks or the introspection of Shakespeare's heroes, *self-discovery as storytelling* can be presented by an actor with precision and grace. This is from Shepard's Pulitzer Prize-winning play *Buried Child* (1978) (95):

> VINCE (*pause, delivers speech front*) I was gonna run last night. I was gonna run and keep right on running. I drove all night. Clear to the Iowa border. The old man's two bucks sitting right on the seat beside me. It never stopped raining the whole time. Never stopped once. I could see myself in the windshield. My face. My eyes. I studied my face. Studied everything about it. As though I was looking at another man. As though I could see his whole race behind him. Like a mummy's face. I saw him dead and alive at the same time. In the same breath. In the windshield, I watched him breathe as though he was frozen in time. And every breath marked him. Marked him forever without him knowing. And then his face changed. His face became his father's face. Same bones. Same eyes. Same nose. Same breath. And his father's face

changed to his Grandfather's face. And it went on like that. Changing. Clear on back to faces I'd never seen but still recognized. Still recognized the bones underneath. The eyes. The breath. The mouth. I followed my family clear into Iowa. Every last one. Straight into the Corn Belt and further. Straight back as far they'd take me. Then it all dissolved. Everything dissolved.

Buried Child is the story of the mysterious relations between a father, mother, and their two sons who live in a farmhouse similar to the cut-away rooms of O'Neill's *Desire Under the Elms*. Significantly, the upper story is unseen, just as the family's motives and desires are obscure. Vince is the only grandson of this family, and he hasn't seen them since he moved away from home. Now, he has returned, and he's brought his girlfriend along to meet his relations. But none of the family seem to recognize Vince or know who he is. In an effort, perhaps, to re-enter family life, Vince agrees to run an errand for his grandfather. Vince drives off, but takes so long to return that suspense builds with the possibility that he may have run away, leaving his girlfriend behind. This speech follows Vince's forceful return, which resembles an invasion when he rips through the screened porch and into the family home. The story itself is the revelation that, in the world of the play, Vince has fought his way back home for the highest good: to find his place in the family line.

Terms to Work with: Four Elements of Storytelling

No matter the play, an actor preparing to tell a story onstage should break a text down by separating four elements: *events, character quotes, descriptions,* and *story apparatus*. Each offers different opportunities for an actor and, if identified, each may be used in its own way to propel dramatic action.

At first, it helps to concentrate on answering the question of *HOW does the story mean?* before you go on to the equally important question of *WHAT does the story mean?* Working this way, you will begin by identifying the structure of the story before you decide on its meaning or interpretation.

In a better world, this could be called structural analysis, but let's use the term *narrative analysis* because the words *structural analysis* drag along implications—sometimes contradictory—piled on by linguists, anthropologists, psychologists, and literary critics. From Russia to Prague to Paris to Cambridge, Massachusetts, *structural analysts* of behavior, language, and culture have built up specialized vocabularies, none of them so far helpful to actors.

But at least one idea out of the structural analysis of literature is worth a performer's notice. In the late 1960s, a French critic named Jacques Derrida identified a process of separating a text into its parts—*deconstructing* is the jargon used—in order to recognize that meaning was relative and dependent on the reader—no matter what the intentions of the writer. Deconstructed, no text has a meaning without an organizing interpretation. Applied to a script, a performance text is broken down with an understanding that its meaning is subject to the way it is performed. This is the key concept for an actor to borrow from structuralism and deconstructivist theories.

STORYTELLING

For an actor to apply these concepts, it is necessary to rescue them from history and self-imposed obscurity by using clear, concise words in rehearsal and performance. Once more, let us agree to use a common vocabulary and proceed to the work of analyzing a variety of performance texts—by focusing on the aspects of a story that an actor can separate.

Event

An **event** is an episode that is described, not acted out. It is action that can be understood in and of itself, separately from its sequence. Events are the backbone of a story. A performer should usually begin preparation to tell an onstage story by first identifying events.

- I ran from the casino (from *A Streetcar Named Desire*).
- I saw a young man under my balcony (from *The School for Wives*).
- Our enemy sunk our ship (from *The Persians*).

Here is a sequence of three events from *Oedipus the King*: *We broke into the room. I saw the Queen. She was hanging from a rope.* Here is a sequence of two events from *Buried Child*, and in the words of the playwright: *I could see myself in the windshield. I studied my face.* Events are what you would like the audience to understand as happening—so that they may enact an episode in their mind's eyes. The events of the story, for the audience and for the performer, are understood in the sequence in which they are told, which is not always the sequence in which they happened.

Label events in the same way that you would label episodes. It helps to use complete sentences with subjects, verbs, and objects: *I walked into the room. I saw the woman. She saw me.* You can leave out the adjectives and the adverbs if you like. Answer the question: *Who did what to whom?* or *What happened?* In some cases the label will answer the question *What is happening now?* but the form of the answer is the same: a complete sentence.

The difference between an event and an episode is that an event is *described* and an episode is *enacted*. A sequence of events and their telling can very often become an episode onstage. For example, the sequence of events related by Agnès—*I was minding my business. I was distracted by a handsome young man. An old woman came to see me the next day*—create the episode: THE YOUNG BRIDE DOESN'T KNOW SHE HAS BEEN SEDUCED. Notice again that the episode is understood by the audience and the actor, but not necessarily by the character.

Character quotes

Stories often, though not always, include characters, including yourself, who act and speak in the course of the events. When a storyteller assigns a voice or gestures, or otherwise identifies a role within a story, this is a **character quote**:

- Then somebody caught my arm. "Don't go any closer! Come back! You don't want to see!"
- She said to me, "May Heaven bless you dear / And keep you beautiful for many a year."

237

After you identify the events, you should identify the quotes. Answer the obvious questions: *Are there characters quoted? Who is quoted? How can the audience understand who these characters are?*

You can demonstrate how characters speak most simply by speaking in voices distinct from your own. The technique of quoting will be as familiar as telling a joke. Here's one from Samuel Beckett's *Endgame* (96):

> NAGG (*raconteur's voice*) An Englishman, needing a pair of striped trousers in a hurry for the New Year festivities, goes to his tailor who takes his measurements. (*tailor's voice*) "That's the lot, come back in four days, I'll have it ready." Good. Four days later. (*tailor's voice*) "So sorry, come back in a week, I've made a mess of the seat." Good, that's all right, a neat seat can be very ticklish. A week later. (*tailor's voice*) "Frightfully sorry, come back in ten days, I've made a hash of the crotch . . ."

There are more complications over details. Nagg ends his joke:

> NAGG Well, to make it short, the bluebells are blowing and he ballockses the buttonholes. (*customer's voice*) "God damn you to hell, Sir, it's indecent, there are limits! In six days, do you hear me, six days, God made the world. Yes, Sir, no less, Sir, the WORLD! And you are not bloody well capable of making me a pair of trousers in three months!" (*tailor's voice, scandalized*) "But my dear Sir, my dear Sir, look—(*disdainful gesture, disgustedly*)—at the world—(*pause*) and look—(*loving gesture, proudly*) at my TROUSERS!"

A character quote can be used even when there is no speech to quote in order to color emotionally the seemingly neutral *she says*, or a description of a character in a story:

> PALAESTRIO If you noticed, most of the hookers around here have twisted mouths. That's so they don't laugh in his face.

It's almost impossible not to say these lines without puckering up your mouth to demonstrate (and quote) the girls' attempts to keep a straight face.

The personification of characters within the story can be done with character-specific gestures or *physical quotes*; for example, the tailor's loving gesture toward his perfect trousers. A character quote does not have to be a fully embodied voice or pose; you can use very little. Even a shrug, if set up, will convey information about who is who. You can use a lot of details the first time a character is quoted, and fewer as the character reappears. Or the other way around: the character quote can build from slight details to a full personification. The only thing that's essential is that the audience knows who is speaking, especially if there are multiple voices and characters.

Sometimes, the character called *I* can be quoted, since *I*'s relationship to the speaker is not always direct. You may be describing yourself at an earlier age, or in a fantasy, or in an emotional state different from the one you are in while you are telling the story: "I was gonna run and keep right on running" is told by a narrator who has stopped running and returned to tell the story. The *I* of "I made the discovery—love" is different from the *I* of the experienced Blanche.

Within a character quote, a performer can apply actions to complete a task as well as utilize obstacles, transactions, and images. Set within a story, character quotes can display virtuoso realistic acting, but character quotes, like roles in episodes, shouldn't overwhelm the audience's understanding of events.

Descriptions

Descriptions are the words of a story that help the audience picture the events. Descriptions give meaning to action and behavior because they help to establish the world of the play, as it is presented in the story:

- Never stopped raining. Never stopped raining once.
- The sea was hidden, carpeted with wrecks / And dead men; all the shores and reefs were full of dead.
- The bluebells are blowing . . .

Descriptions can reflect the point of view of the character or of the narrator. They can set the emotional tone of the scene. Think of creaking doors, the dark of a corridor, the bright light of the heavens. All can be made to contribute to dramatic action with an image, but *not* by playing an action or a transaction.

Story apparatus

Story apparatus consists of the words in a story necessary for grammar, narrative devices, or the conventions of storytelling; conventions that call attention to the story as story:

- It's the most amazing story you ever heard . . .
- What happened after that I cannot tell . . .
- Think, when we talk of horses. That you see them . . .
- Well, to make it short . . .

The most frequent words of story apparatus are probably *she said, he said*. These can be made to do many things onstage. Among other things, they can give a story its bias or they can render the passage of time. The mechanical elements *she said, he said* can be inflected with a point of view. Agnès in *The School for Wives* continues her story:

AGNÈS "You say I've wounded somebody?" I cried.
"Indeed you have," she said. "The victim's he
Whom yesterday you saw from the balcony."
"But how could such a thing occur?" I said;
"Can I have dropped some object on his head?"

Coloring the words "said" and "cried" will demonstrate *how* the quoted character did the saying. We hear these nuances in life when we listen to speakers, even when they are trying to be even-handed and impartial.

The words of story apparatus can be organized by tasks because they do have a job: *to make the story clear to the listeners*. The words of story apparatus can be thought of as transactions, too: *pay attention now / and you'll learn the important part*.

Each of the structural elements of a story presents its own options for an actor. Character quotes allow you to apply actions; descriptions do not. Character quotes and descriptions allow you to bring images to your preparation; story apparatus will not give you as much of a chance. Story apparatus will allow you to execute a task; events will not. This is not a matter of blind obedience to the writer's intentions; it is acceptance of the difficulty inherent in setting water on fire.

Analyzing a Story from *The School for Wives*

> AGNÈS It's the most amazing story you ever heard.

The story apparatus in this speech prepares Agnès's listeners—her husband Arnolphe and the audience—for what follows. These words can be given a task: *to get Arnolphe's help in explaining this mysterious stuff*, or *to share the wonder of an interesting day*.

> AGNÈS I was sewing, out on the balcony, in the breeze,
>   When I noticed someone strolling under the trees.

This is the only description in the text we are examining here, but it does set the emotional tone of what follows: breezy, carefree, and comfortably at home. The event described, which the audience, but not necessarily the character, is meant to understand: *I was minding my own business*. This is followed by the next event: *I was distracted by a handsome young man*.

> AGNÈS It was a fine young man, who caught my eye
>   And made me a deep bow as he went by.
>   I, not to be convicted of a lack
>   Of manners, very quickly nodded back.
>   At once, the young man bowed to me again.

There is the possibility of a character quote here by imitating the gesture of the young man's bow. There is also the possibility to quote yourself winking at the young man's advances. The next event: *His behavior confused me*.

> AGNÈS I bowed to him a second time, and then
>   It wasn't very long until he made
>   A third deep bow, which I of course repaid.
>   He left, but kept returning, and as he passed,

STORYTELLING

The next event: *I did the best I could to make sense of it.*

> AGNÈS He'd bow, each time, more gracefully than the last,
>   While I, observing as he came and went,
>   Gave each new bow a fresh acknowledgement.
>   Indeed, had night not fallen, I declare
>   I think that I might still be sitting there,

The words "I declare" are a little bit of story apparatus:

> AGNÈS . . . I declare
>   I think that I might still be sitting there,
>   And bowing back each time he bowed to me,
>   For fear he'd think me less polite than he.
> ARNOLPHE Go on.

Arnolphe is not telling a story, and his behavior may have the task *to control his emotions*, whether those emotions are fear, anger, or jealousy. His line can also be thought of as a transaction: *I'll keep my temper / you'll tell me what happened.* Meanwhile, the next event: *The next day, I learned what had happened*:

> AGNÈS Then an old woman came, next day,
>   And found me standing in the entryway.
>   She said to me, "May Heaven bless you, dear . . ."

This is a character quote and would be quite effective spoken in a very sweet and concerned voice. The image could be *a warning from a nun.*

> AGNÈS "And keep you beautiful for many a year.
>   God, who bestowed on you such grace and charm,
>   Did not intend those gifts to do men harm,
>   And you should know that there's a heart which bears
>   A wound which you've inflicted unawares."

To accomplish the task, the speaker will need *to warn, to protect, to twist, to seduce.* The frame of Agnès telling the story will prevent her from accurately quoting the old woman's real task: *to plant a seed of disquiet* in Agnès.

It is the work of another role to make the episode, and not just the events, clear:

> ARNOLPHE *(aside)* Old witch! Old tool of Satan! Damn her hide!

Arnolphe's lines might be said directly to the audience with the task *to warn the listener* not to trust what Agnès says about the old woman. The lines could also be considered part of the transaction with the audience: *In order to hear more / I will keep my thoughts to myself and the audience—but not my wife.*

AGNÈS "You say I've wounded somebody?" I cried.
    "Indeed you have," she said. "The victim's he
    Whom yesterday you saw from the balcony."
    "But how could such a thing occur?" I said;
    "Can I have dropped some object on his head?"

Agnès quoting herself can be done in such a way that the audience understands Agnès is an innocent girl who believes what she is told. The little scene between Agnès and the old woman will be organized by the old woman's task *to alarm the naïve girl* and Agnès' task *to apologize*. The image for the quote (and the episode) could very well be the innocent Marilyn Monroe of *Some Like It Hot*—or any other attractive woman unaware of the effect she has over men. If you like to use emotional memory, here's the place to do it: substitute a time from your past when you have made a social mistake unknowingly. The episode understood by the audience, but not the character: A MAN SEDUCED AGNÈS (AND SHE STILL DOESN'T REALIZE IT).

Let's Review Terms

To review: When you have a story that is supposed to stage the events it describes in the mind's eye of the listener, you should begin by separating four different elements.

events	episodes described in the story
character quotes	speaking or behaving in such a way as to identify characters who act or speak in the events of the story
description	the environment described in the story
story apparatus	words used as technical aspects of telling the story

The Chart

- **Appropriate playwrights.** It is appropriate to use these techniques whenever a story is told onstage. It is especially useful for plays by authors who rely on storytelling, rather than enactment, to create dramatic action on stage. These include the Greek playwrights, *Shakespeare, Bertolt Brecht, Tennessee Williams, Sam Shepard, Caryl Churchill,* and many others.
- **Intended reaction of the audience.** The audience is meant to *participate* in the creation of the action. By picturing it in their mind's eye they contribute to the dramatic events of the play.

Filling in the rest of the chart for a *Narrative Analysis*—illusion of character, dramatic action, key question—must wait. Separating the structural elements of a story is only part of the performer's task in preparing a story to be performed. There is more to be done, more questions to be answered.

CHAPTER 12

DRAMATIC ACTION AND
ILLUSION OF CHARACTER

The Point of a Point of View

That cheerfully vulgar movie star Mae West, who wrote her own material, was brought to court several times for obscenity, but never in any trial could judge, juror, or prosecutor point to a single lascivious line. The Assistant District Attorney for the County of New York at Miss West's 1926 trial for performing, writing, and producing a play called—rather pointedly—*Sex* charged that "Miss West's personality, looks, walk, mannerisms and gestures made the lines and situations suggestive" (97).

Disappointed perhaps that Miss West did not demonstrate her belly dance (or what the prosecutor called her "danse du ventre"),* the jury nevertheless agreed with the assistant D.A., and at the height of her stage fame Mae spent eight days in the ladies' ward with two days off for good behavior. Even back in her vaudeville days, when she sang a little ditty called "The Cave Girl" (dressed in a leopard skin and, as she put it, singing the spots off it), Mae would conclude her act with a speech to the audience: "It isn't what I do, but how I do it. It isn't what I say, but how I say it, and how I look when I do it and say it" (98).

Once again, learn from Mae West: when you tell a story in a play, the illusion that you are someone other than yourself is created by the way you tell the tale. What you are talking about is not as important as how you talk about it. Not only do you have the power to characterize yourself in this way, the elements of a story—its events, character quotes, descriptions, and the apparatus of its telling—all change meaning depending on the **point of view** with which you present them to the audience. (In later years, Mae West used to end her act by reciting "Mary Had a Little Lamb"—with suggestive pauses.)

As another example of the way character can be revealed, think of an audience listening to a marriage announcement being read aloud by:

- the mother of the bride
- the bride's ex-boyfriend
- the girl who had a crush on the groom in high school

---

*Miss West hotly claimed these were innocent contractions of her abdominal muscles, an exercise learned from her athletic father.

- the groom's ex-wife
- the wedding editor at the newspaper who notices several grammatical mistakes
- the groom's mistress
- a radio announcer who doesn't know these people
- the bride

Change not a word, yet the meaning of the words will change with a change in perspective. Like Mae and Mary's lamb, an actor establishes character in storytelling by the intersection of the story and a point of view.

Points of View: Rehearsing a Monologue from *Buried Child*

Not every story has a characterized narrator. Some stories work without one: the description of the naval rout in *The Persians*, for example, reports the defeat without evoking a specific role or emotional reaction for the narrator. Storytelling without a characterized storyteller is common in Eastern theatrical traditions. There is also the genre in modern Western drama, called *Story Theater,* in which actors tell stories and recite stage directions and descriptions without any illusion that they are anything but performers. The use of story apparatus—*she said, then it happened, one day it happened*—further identifies Story Theater performers as actors, not characters.

Story Theater occasionally has its uses for a characterized monologue, but not often. The switch from enactment to narrative offers a wide range of expression, and has been used successfully to stage novels as sweeping as Dickens's *Nicholas Nickleby* and John Steinbeck's *The Grapes of Wrath*. But when the choice is made to characterize the narrator, there are usually four categories of points of view from which to choose. Each requires the collaboration of the audience to establish the illusion that the speaker is a person distinct from the story-telling actor.

Identification

When the narrator **identifies** with the story being told, the words of the text are meant to be understood as a faithful description of the speaker's emotional state, and the actor is meant to use the power of images to persuade the audience that the description is true.

> VINCE I could see myself in the windshield. My face. My eyes. I studied my
> face. Studied everything about it. As though I was looking at another man.
> As though I could see his whole race behind him. Like a mummy's face.

If the actor playing Vince identifies with the lines, he will take the time to recreate the moment of being transfixed by his own reflection. If successful, Vince's rapture will be understood by the audience much more clearly than if the actor were sitting onstage under a spotlight in a rolled-on car seat and gripping one of those cliché fragments of a steering wheel. It helps that the speech is written in the first person, using the word *I*.

But *I* doesn't always have to be present for there to be identification. The feeling of exaltation in communion with one's family will be understood by the audience in this description without the use of the word *I*—if the actor chooses to make it so.

> VINCE And then his face changed. His face became his father's face. Same bones. Same eyes. Same nose. Same breath. And his father's face changed to his Grandfather's face.

Emotional identification with the story can extend to the act of speaking itself. This story is being told by someone who ran away from his home and his roots. The act of speaking is the act of rejoining them.

> VINCE I followed my family clear into Iowa. Every last one.

The statement is a vow of commitment. The actor's sincerity will persuade the audience that the story he is telling—about his feelings—is accurate and true, and that he has returned.

Bias

When the narrator speaks with **bias** about the story being told, the audience is meant to synthesize the meaning of the text and the narrator's point of view to establish for themselves the character of the narrator and the nature of events. Skepticism, sarcasm, favoritism, outrage, and shame are all attitudes with which to tell a biased story. The audience should understand the narrator's bias, although they don't have to agree with it.

The story from *Buried Child* begins with the following lines:

> VINCE I was gonna run last night. I was gonna run and keep right on running. I drove all night. Clear to the Iowa border. The old man's two bucks sitting right on the seat beside me.

This part of the story can be told in such a way that we know the speaker thinks running is useless. In life, the emotions evoked by memory don't necessarily repeat what the person felt at the time it happened. Vince's adolescent rebellion is spoken of by a more mature man. The way Vince tells the story now tells the audience who he has become since the events described.

A critical narrator speaks with bias in description, character quotes, events, and even story apparatus. When the presumably English Chorus of *Henry V* describes the French, he does so critically. So does the servant who describes his master's excesses, or the villain describing the hero—or a good deed.

The bias of criticism isn't always negative. An actor can tell a story biased with approval. When Brecht noticed Helene Weigel performing the Servant's speech from *Oedipus the King*, what struck Brecht was the Servant's grudging admiration for death, in opposition to her concern for her mistress. Agnès's understanding of her story in

245

The School for Wives is at odds with what she is describing, and even if she doesn't know it, the audience does, and it characterizes her point of view as naïve (although this naïveté might be an equally characteristic pose on the part of the ingenue).

Distanced point of view

When a story is told with a **distanced** point of view, the storyteller tries to keep personal bias out of the story. When stories are written in the third person, the performer may speak with the distance of an uninvolved observer, even ludicrously, as when a cheery television announcer reports a disaster.

A distanced point of view can even be used for stories that are written in the first person using the word *I*. When an actor speaks of intimate details with the objectivity of a third-person point of view, this invites the audience to create the illusion of a character for the speaker. The audience tends to assign motives for objectivity: the speaker is in shock, or callous, or forgiving, or that much more heroic for facing the truth about himself. This would be the case if Vince switched from identification to a more distanced point of view at the end of his story:

> VINCE I followed my family clear into Iowa. Every last one. Straight into the
> Corn Belt and further. Straight back as far as they'd take me. Then it all
> dissolved. Everything dissolved.

The building rhythm of the lines "Straight into the Corn Belt and further. Straight back as far they'd take me" suggests *identification*, and the changed rhythm of "Then it all dissolved"—as well as the new event and subject matter—suggests a distanced approach on the last words: "Everything dissolved."

In the same speech from *Buried Child*, there are passages of *description* that are told very naturally from a distanced point of view.

> VINCE I drove all night. Clear to the Iowa border. The old man's two bucks
> sitting right on the seat beside me. It never stopped raining the whole time.
> Never stopped once.

If that same distanced point of view was applied to the whole speech, the audience would still understand the events of the story, but would probably not gain as much insight into the character of the speaker. Sometimes a distanced point of view is meant to supplement the illusion of character, in the same way a Cubist painter shows the profile of the same face that's being depicted head-on. Such a use of a distanced point of view—essentially a report to the audience from the actor—can be used to isolate behavior and call attention to it outside of its context, the process Brecht called *alienation*.

Brecht was a master of using a distanced point of view to describe highly emotional situations. In his early play *Drums in the Night* (1922) (99), a young girl, pregnant and engaged, tells her ex-boyfriend what has happened while he was away in Africa soldiering:

ANNA In the beginning you were with me a long time, your voice was still fresh. When I went down the hall, I brushed against you, and out in the meadow you called me from behind the maple tree. Even though they wrote that you'd been shot through the face and buried two days later. But then one day it was different. When I went down the hall, it was empty, and the maple tree didn't speak. When I stood up from bending over the wash trough, I still saw your face, but when I spread the washing out on the grass, I didn't see it, and all that time I didn't know what you looked like. But I should have waited.

The whole story, start to finish, can be told icily, with as distanced a point of view as possible. Let the audience assign the emotions here, and they will. You could even smoke while you said it.

There is no episode (since nothing changes onstage) until the soldier, Kragler, speaks:

KRAGLER You should have had a picture.

ANNA I was afraid. Even with my fear I should have waited, but I'm no good.
Let go of my hand, everything about me is bad.

If Kragler says his line gently, tenderly feeling sorry for Anna, the episode will become HE FORGIVES HER. If he is angry at himself, the episode will be something else. If he is as distanced as Anna, the episode will wait until he lets go of her hand, which will then become the *gest*.

Projection

When an actor telling a story **projects** onto the audience a response that influences the telling of the story, the audience is cast in a role and both the speaker and his listeners are characterized. This can happen in a realistic play when the convention of the fourth wall allows the audience to be addressed as, say, a crowd or a school-room of students. In less realistic plays, soliloquies and prologues and asides may be openly spoken to the audience as audience. When the audience is effectively cast as a partner, a relationship of tasks and actions—or transactions and *gests*—now extends beyond the fourth wall to establish interaction between performers and listeners.

Although the script doesn't specify it, some of the lines from the speech we are looking at from *Buried Child* could be delivered directly to a *characterized audience*.

VINCE His face became his father's face. Same bones. Same eyes. Same nose. Same breath. And his father's face changed to his Grandfather's face. And it went on like that. Changing. Clear on back to faces I'd never seen but still recognized. Still recognized the bones underneath. The eyes. The breath. The mouth.

The actor playing Vince could look at the audience members as if they were the faces he described. He could establish a line of them in the audience, one behind the other. For each face he could attempt the task *to find myself*. His obstacles would be the change in noses and eyes and other features; the action would be *to search each face* until he did see some resemblance. The conclusion of the task, his reunion with his ancestors, is dictated by the words of the text; whatever the audience's real response, the response necessary for the story would be projected by the storyteller onto his listeners.

In life, the reactions of the audience shift and change, just as any other partner's do. It is the actor's choice to interpret the audience's changing reactions as approval or disapproval, and sometimes, in the absence of spectators, to imagine that someone is reacting. Improvisers can change what they say to respond to the audience. Performers who honor the words of the text by speaking them as written can still alter *the meaning* of those words in order to respond.

Sometimes the audience can be coaxed into playing their part. Sometimes they offer themselves a little too enthusiastically. When Stanislavsky played Dr. Stockman in Ibsen's *An Enemy of the People* in 1904, the play's protests against corrupt authority were recognized by the Russian audience as references to their own country's sorry politics. The Tsar's censor sat backstage at every performance to make sure that only an approved and censored script was spoken. The production opened in St. Petersburg on the night of a massacre in that town, and during the performance the audience broke into pandemonium. In character as Dr. Stockman, Stanislavsky had lines to say like "I'll cry out the truth from every street corner! The whole country will learn what's happened!" The stage was low, and there was no orchestra pit; hundreds of spectators reached across the footlights to shake hands with Stanislavsky, as if he were Dr. Stockman. Some audience members jumped onto the stage and embraced him (100).

But Stanislavsky understood that the task of his role was *to search for truth*. Any popular acclamation was an obstacle to the actor and to the character he played. The admiration of the crowd, characterized in this way, was such a living presence that it egged Stanislavsky on to speak the words of the text with fury and purpose.

> "You are mistaken, you are animals, yes animals," I said to the crowd at the public lecture in the fourth act of the play, and I said this truthfully and sincerely, for I was able to assume the viewpoint of Stockman himself. And I found it pleasant to say this to feel that the spectator, who had begun to love me in the role of Stockman, was excited and angry at me for the tastelessness of arousing my enemies with too much sincerity (101).

As an active partner, as a listener who deduces motivation, or as a spectator convinced by passion, the audience collaborates with an actor telling a story to create the illusion of character.

The Shifting Point of View

While telling a story, a **shift in the point of view** is dramatic action. When any actress playing Amanda in *The Glass Menagerie* warms herself with the memory of her girlhood ("*seventeen* gentlemen callers!"); when the actor telling the tale of the tailor in *Endgame* cracks himself up laughing ("and look, Sir, at my trousers!"); when *An Enemy of the People*'s Dr. Stockman turns on the crowd; then the episode onstage is that *change* in the storyteller. This is not always the progression of the events described.

Just as every story told onstage doesn't necessarily have a characterized narrator, not every story has a dramatic action. If there is a progression of events with no change in the teller, that might be dramatic if the events described were interesting. But it is not active. This can be exactly what is called for in, say, a bulletin or a report. Here the dramatic action is meant to be in the audience's mind, not in the performance of the play.

This is the difference between reciting and acting. When dramatic poetry is recited, the words themselves will evoke pictures for the audience to animate. This lack of dramatic action sometimes happens during performances of arias in operas. The progression of music is, for some listeners and singers, theater enough. Sometimes, when an actor achieves an unvarying emotional tone, there is no action, just emotion. This is permissible in a film performance, which can be edited to create action by alternating the point of view of the camera, if not the speaker.

To identify a change or changes in the point of view onstage, it helps to look at what is different about the narrator at the beginning of the story compared to the narrator at the end. The question to ask is: *What happens to the teller while telling the story?*

The most familiar shift in point of view, due to the conventions of realism (not life), is when an actor begins with a *distanced* point of view and moves slowly in degrees to *identification*, ultimately reliving the event at the moment of its description. There are many other possibilities, however. Let's look again at the text from *Buried Child*:

> VINCE (*pause, delivers speech front*) I was gonna run last night. I was gonna run
>   and keep right on running . . .

The speaker begins with a biased point of view: what a foolish thing it was to try to run away. Then the point of view shifts to a more distanced observation. The *I* of the story is seen objectively, without bias.

> VINCE I drove all night. Clear to the Iowa border. The old man's two bucks
>   sitting right on the seat beside me. It never stopped raining the whole time.
>   Never stopped once.

Emotional identification begins. The *I* is the speaker, reliving a past event. This is by no means the only way to interpret these lines, but let's choose it as a way to quote behavior.

> VINCE I could see myself in the windshield. My face. My eyes. I studied my face. Studied everything about it. As though I was looking at another man. As though I could see his whole race behind him. Like a mummy's face. I saw him dead and alive at the same time. In the same breath. In the windshield, I watched him breathe as though he was frozen in time. And every breath marked him. Marked him forever without him knowing. And then his face changed.

Emotional identification could continue here, or as discussed above, the actor could *project* the story onto the audience. The faces lined up behind each other would be cast as the generations of ancestors.

> VINCE His face became his father's face. Same bones. Same eyes. Same nose. Same breath. And his father's face changed to his Grandfather's face. And it went on like that. Changing. Clear on back to faces I'd never seen but still recognized. Still recognized the bones underneath. The eyes. The breath. The mouth.

The actor could interpret the audience's reaction as distrust, followed by acceptance. Emotional identification could return to a declaration:

> VINCE I followed my family clear into Iowa. Every last one. Straight into the Corn Belt and further. Straight back as far they'd take me. Then it all dissolved.

The story could now be told from a more distanced point of view that would parallel the events of the story: *Everything dissolved*. The episode: VINCE REJOINS HIS FAMILY. The events, baldly put, are:

- *Vince ran away from home.*
- *As he drove, he studied his own face.*
- *He had a vision of himself as part of a family line.*
- *He returned home.*

The dramatic action of the story is the change in the point of view:

- Biased point of view: *I was gonna run . . .*
- Distanced observation: *Never stopped raining . . .*
- Emotional identification: *I could see my face . . .*
- Projected story onto the audience: *My father's face . . .*
- Emotional identification: *I followed my family . . .*
- Distanced point of view: *It all dissolved . . .*

The change in the speaker is from scorn to acceptance. This, of course, is an interpretation, and other interpretations are possible. What stays the same are the events, and the episode itself.

Some playwrights dictate changes in the point of view while stories are being told. In Eugene O'Neill's *Strange Interlude* (102), the characters speak their thoughts aloud. Here are the stage directions the playwright set down for a single character thinking aloud for the first three pages of text:

- *His voice takes on a monotonous musing quality, his eyes stare idly at his drifting thoughts*
- *He smiles*
- *His face has become sad with a memory of the bewildered suffering of [an] adolescent boy*
- *He shakes his head, flinging off his thoughts*
- *He sighs—then self-mockingly*
- *Then self-reassuringly*
- *He grins torturedly*
- *His face suddenly full of an intense pain and disgust*
- *Mocking bitterly*
- *Impatiently*

A performer who abides by these stage directions accepts O'Neill's attempt to make dramatic action out of the shift in the point of view. It almost works, but the play is nine acts long and the running time usually exceeds the patience of an audience. The gossip goes that when the script was first produced, the producers begged O'Neill to make cuts. He was very resistant. One day he called them up to say that he had figured out a way to cut an hour and a half from the performance. They were very happy, until O'Neill told them his idea was to cut the lunch and dinner breaks.

In O'Neill's masterpiece, *Long Day's Journey into Night*, the climax of the play is the mother's story of how she came to leave her school and marry. In order for this long speech to be logically included in the realistic style of the play, it is framed as an opium-induced regression to an earlier identity. O'Neill specifies that Mary begin listlessly and that her voice take on a young quality as she moves further into her tale. Because he is writing a realistic play, O'Neill must explain this transformation as the effect of the narcotic. Explained by medicine or not, the metamorphosis is magical and powerfully moving: out of the body of a life-shattered old woman rises a young girl filled with hope.

In the film version of *Long Day's Journey into Night* (1962) directed by Sidney Lumet, the body of the speech is performed by Katharine Hepburn in one long take. The camera echoes her drifting romantic point of view by slowly ascending high above the room. From close-up to panorama, the camera lifts back from the actors' faces, to the table where they sit, to the shadowy room, until at last the shot widens so far that what is seen on screen resembles what an audience member would see watching a play, not a film, in a theater. The actors are dwarfed by the black surround, no longer providing information to illustrate the scene; the audience must concentrate on the words being spoken to picture what is being described.

Then, when Hepburn speaks the last line, the camera cuts to a sharp and startling close-up so as to parallel the reversion in the storyteller's point of view from hope to experience. Usually in a film monologue like this, footage would be pieced together and therefore unreliable as evidence of a performance, but Sidney Lumet wanted the film *Long Day's Journey into Night* to resemble a stage play in process as well as technique.* The actors had three weeks' rehearsal, the shoot was short—less than forty days—and most generously, it was filmed in sequence, Hepburn's monologue included.

As convoluted as a plot, or as simple as a fall off a cliff, movement of the point of view creates dramatic action, which distinguishes storytelling in a play from recitation.

Let's Review Terms

point of view	the storyteller's reaction to the story being told
distanced point of view	the storyteller remains impartial while telling the story
identification	the storyteller emotionally identifies with the story being told
biased point of view	the storyteller comments on the story being told
projection onto the audience	the storyteller characterizes a listening audience
shift in the point of view	a change in the storyteller's attitude as the story is told

The Chart

- **Basic unit.** The *event* and the *point of view* are the basic units in storytelling.
- **Illusion of character.** The illusion of character for a storyteller is the *intersection of point of view and the story*.
- **Dramatic action.** A *shift in the point of view* of the storyteller creates dramatic action.
- **Key question.** There are two key questions for telling a story onstage: *What am I describing?* and *What's my point of view about it?*
- **Unifying image.** The unifying image of telling a story is the *film camera's use of different angles* to show the same event or object.

---

*Although Lumet couldn't resist adding a reverb to Hepburn's voice to heighten the sense of distance. Hepburn derived her mannerisms for this performance from an image of her own mother.

- **Relative theory.** A model for storytelling onstage can be derived from the theories of *literary deconstruction* that the meaning of a text is determined by the reader—and creative actor.

Switching from Acting to Storytelling: Rehearsing a Scene from *Iphigenia in Aulis*

You don't need to restrict narrative analysis to monologues; the techniques used to tell a story can be applied to scenes. Certain playwrights give an actor artful possibilities to switch from narrative to demonstration. Some of the greatest opportunities are in texts written by Shakespeare, Brecht, and Euripides, the third of the great Greek playwrights. Let's use as an example a scene with two long stories from the last play Euripides wrote, *Iphigenia in Aulis* (103).

The play takes place during the Trojan War. The Greek fleet is stalled in Aulis, becalmed on its way to Troy and waiting for a wind. Agamemnon (pronounced a-ga-MEM-non) is the elected commander of the fleet. He has agreed to sacrifice his daughter Iphigenia (if-e-je-NY-a *or* if-e-je-NEE-a) in order to convince the gods to send a wind to move the fleet. But Agamemnon has thought more deeply about killing his own child and has sent a letter to his wife telling her not to come with Iphigenia. Agamemnon's brother, Menelaus (me-ne-LAY-us) has confiscated the letter and is outraged that Agamemnon has gone back on his word. Before the play starts, Menelaus's wife Helen has run away with a Trojan prince. It is to recapture Helen from Troy that the Greek fleet led by Agamemnon is assembled in Aulis. Each brother accuses the other of a conflict of personal and political interests.

The example is long and difficult to read—which is the reason to read it. The impulse otherwise is to cut so much talk, because the performer (or director) does not understand how it can be made dramatic. Be patient. The first time you read a story this complicated is similar to a first rehearsal when dialogue is obscure and the character of the roles unknown. To save time and energy at rehearsals, narrative analysis can—and should—start with the actor at home. In rehearsal you can test your ideas, revise them, refine them, abandon them if they don't work, and try others. As before, what follows is one interpretation of the scene; other interpretations are possible.

The scene begins with the brothers confronting each other over the letter Agamemnon has tried to send to his wife, taking back his promise to sacrifice his daughter.

AGAMEMNON So, you have broken the seal [of my letter] and read it. It was not for your eyes.

MENELAUS Yes, I read it. I know your secrets and your shame. You will regret it.

AGAMEMNON Gods above! The arrogance of the man! Where did you way-lay my messenger?

MENELAUS I was waiting for your daughter to come here from Argos.

AGAMEMNON Why?

MENELAUS Because I felt like it. I am not your slave.

AGAMEMNON This is an outrage. Am I not to be master of my own house?

MENELAUS Not when you are a cheat and a liar, when you slither your way into everything.

AGAMEMNON You talk to me of cheating and of lying. You! I hate a facile, quick tongue.

First identify episodes and events

The backbone of a story—and a scene—is *what happens*. As you read the text, establish episode and event first, and, in separating storytelling from enactment, distinguish between episodes shown onstage and events that are described.

The episode is MENELAUS CATCHES HIS SUCCESSFUL OLDER BROTHER IN THE WRONG. The dialogue can be played for tasks and actions. Agamemnon's super-task will be *to save his daughter's life*; his first task will be *to brush off his brother's accusations*. The obstacles will be *the oath* he swore before and *the letter* in his brother's hand. Menelaus's super-task will be *to repossess his wife*. The obstacle will be *Agamemnon's compunction* about sacrificing his daughter. Menelaus's action will be *to rebuke Agamemnon*, which will run up against the next obstacle, the *successful politician's poise*.

MENELAUS And I hate a devious, quick mind.

Menelaus could say this to Agamemnon, but he could also say it to the audience, *projecting* onto the listeners the identity of Greeks. The original audiences for this play were accustomed to personal address. They were the same group who voted on political issues of state and to whom speakers pleaded with sentiments similar to the lines of the play. Menelaus's task here could be *to persuade the listeners* to agree with him. The obstacle would be *their respect for Agamemnon* as their commander.

What follows is story apparatus. It reveals the speaker's bias for the story that is to follow. It also sets up the beginning of the episode: HOT-HEADED MENELAUS PROMISES NOT TO PUSH HIS ARGUMENT. The words of the story apparatus have a task too: *to expose his brother in public*.

MENELAUS You know neither justice nor honesty. I will prove your guilt. No lies, my brother! No quick denials. You cannot bluff your way out of this. Listen to me. I will not be too hard on you.

This is followed by an event: *When Agamemnon wanted to be elected commander, he bribed the Greeks with condescension.*

MENELAUS Do you remember your past ambitions? To be leader of the Greeks against Troy? You pretended to be reluctant. But in your heart you

254

longed for it. And to get it you groveled. You shook everyone by the hand. Your doors were open to all who wished to enter. You spoke to everyone, whether they wanted to listen or not. You were nice to everyone. You wanted to be popular. You wanted no rivals.

After events are established, you can assign character quotes

Character quotes relate to events as roles in an episode. Once the event is established, if the text allows, you may add a character quote. Even if there are no spoken words to quote, as is the case here, you could quote: "You shook everyone by the hand. Your doors were open to all who wished to enter. You spoke to everyone, whether they wanted to listen or not. You were nice to everyone" demonstrating with an outstretched hand and plastered-on smile the behavior of a solicitous and oily politician. Notice that within the quote, you have the task of getting elected by the voters. The character quote of the concerned politician Agamemnon switches here to the biased narrator Menelaus, whose task is *to mock his brother.* Bias can be established by the way "nice" is spoken.

The second event is announced: *When Agamemnon got what he wanted, he was his same old standoffish self.*

> MENELAUS But then when you were made commander-in-chief, you changed your tune. You abandoned all your old friends. You were inaccessible. You locked your doors. You rarely appeared in public.

After episodes and events, identify the changes in point of view

Because the dramatic action of telling the story is created by a change in the point of view, once events and episodes are clarified, the next step is to see how the perspective of the story changes. Here, Menelaus shifts from speaking to Agamemnon to speaking to the audience. This will be a powerful dramatic action; Menelaus's task will still be *to win the listeners to his opinion,* just as he would in a political debate. First, he speaks to his brother.

> MENELAUS Brother, a good man does not change when he gets on in the world.

Then Menelaus might speak to the audience:

> MENELAUS That is precisely the time when his friends ought to be able to count on him, when his power and success allow him to do more for them than ever.

Story apparatus follows:

> MENELAUS This is my first point, my first reproach—your lack of character.

255

TELLING A STORY

Story apparatus often has a task; here it is *to alert the listeners* to the pattern of Agamemnon's wrongdoing. Framed by this biased point of view, the next event is stated: *A crisis came and Agamemnon was paralyzed.*

> MENELAUS Then, when the Greek army came here to Aulis and we were denied a favoring wind, you became the lowest of the low. This injunction of the gods filled you with fear. The Greeks shouted at you, demanded that the fleet turn back, that you put an end to this futile delay.

Within the quote, establish tasks or transactions

The event sets the stage in the audience's minds for the character quote that follows, developed slowly—first face, then voice.

> MENELAUS One could see the distress on your face. You could not bear the thought of not launching your thousand ships, of not filling the fields of Troy with the cries of war. So you came to me. "What shall I do? How can I get out of this?" You were afraid of losing your command, losing the glory.

Rather than play bewildered—a vague state of emotion—it will help the character quote ("What shall I do? How can I get out of this?") if it is an action—*to beg*—done to fulfil a task: *to rescue his command.* The quote can also be organized as a transaction: *Agamemnon will humble himself, even ask advice / if Menelaus will help him.*

> MENELAUS Then Calchas [the head priest] spoke. You were to sacrifice your daughter. Only then would the Greeks be free to sail to Troy. You were quick to make promises. And your heart smiled. No one forced you to do what you did next. You cannot say that. You sent word to your wife that your daughter was to come to Aulis and be married to Achilles. That was the pretext you devised. And now?

Story apparatus helps to establish the point of view

The story apparatus—"And now?"—reinforces the bias that these events add up to the pattern of Agamemnon's duplicity. The speaker loses his temper, which is a change in the point of view from distance to identification:

> MENELAUS And now? You have been caught red-handed. You have changed your mind and sent a different message.

A quote follows. In some translations it is a direct quote: "I am no longer . . . prepared to be my daughter's killer." It might be more effective, in this translation, to display the words with a distanced bias, even distaste, rather than to directly quote them:

> MENELAUS You are no longer prepared to be your daughter's killer.

If the speaker addressed the rest to the personified audience of Greeks, a new task—
to egg his listeners on to condemn Agamemnon—would organize the story apparatus that
follows:

> MENELAUS I cannot be more blunt. This is the same heaven that bore witness
> to your oaths.

The obstacle for Menelaus is that *the audience doesn't take sides*. This could anger
him, and the dramatic action would be his increasing identification with what he is
saying:

> MENELAUS Think! You are not unique. Many a man has worked hard to gain
> power. And many a man has lost that power in shame. Sometimes it is the
> fault of the people. They do not understand the complexity of power. But
> just as often it is the man himself who is incompetent and fails to protect
> the interests of the people.

The telling of the story should be an episode

So that an episode happens onstage and not just in the minds of the audience, a change
should come over the speaker as he tells his tale. Here, Menelaus, who began speaking
with a promise to remain calm, loses his temper: YOUNGER BROTHER LOSES HIS TEMPER
AT SUCCESSFUL OLDER BROTHER. What he says next is petty and pointed:

> MENELAUS My tears are for Greece. She planned an action steeped in
> glory. Now she must suffer the mockery of barbarians. All because of
> you and your daughter. It is not courage that makes a great leader or a
> great general. It is intelligence. A man who has half a brain can be gov-
> ernor of a state. But a commander-in-chief must be blessed with intel-
> ligence.

Still speaking to the audience, personified as the Greek army, Menelaus might choose a
task *to arouse the Greeks to strip his brother of command*. The obstacle will remain that the
army respects Agamemnon—and has lost respect for Menelaus.

You can refer to the world of the play

This play is set on a battlefield. The rules of the world of this play are those of army
life. Self-control is strength, losing one's temper is weakness. Status is based on rank,
but also on public displays of strength. A public display of spite will lose Menelaus status. Loyalty—including loyalty to one's family and loyalty to one's brother—is ranked
as a high good in this play.

> CHORUS When brothers fight and anger and recrimination fly between them,
> there is only sorrow.

The single line of the Chorus, if it is not to become a throw-away line, should be given importance as an episode: THE CHORUS BALANCES THE ATTACK ON THE COMMANDER WITH THE RULES OF THE WORLD.

The Chorus is a group of women come from another city to watch the Greek fleet. This is not a matter of opinion or costume; the Chorus Leader identifies herself to the audience in direct words: "I have come to the shore and the sands of Aulis . . . from Chalcis, my city . . . to see this fleet." It's possible to direct this scene so that Agamemnon and Menelaus are trying to persuade the Chorus, not the audience, but this might make the leaders of the Greek army look silly, as if they were playing to groupies from another town. It might be more dramatic if it is the audience, personified as the Greek army, who must be convinced.

Even so, the response of the Chorus needs to be given weight as its own episode, and in the role of judge. What is the morality of keeping a bad promise? What is the morality of abiding by a bad treaty? The use of dueling stories helps Euripides keep his evaluation of morality open-ended, unfinished, and relative. Euripides presents several points of view, none correct, echoing the erosion of values at the time he was writing.

The one thing the playwright does insist on is that the old certainty of a single narrative is gone. Euripides tells another version of Iphigenia's story in his play *Iphigenia in Tauris* (104), which includes this speech:

> ORESTES Even the gods who claim to see the future are as blind as we.
> In heaven, as on earth, confusion reigns.

> *Iphigenia in Tauris*

Iphigenia in Aulis was Euripides's last play, written and staged during a Civil War so corrupting that a contemporary historian recorded that even "words had to change their ordinary meaning and take that which was now given them" (105). The lines in the play that question the meaning of honor, loyalty, and truth echo a contemporary political debate—contemporary then and contemporary now.

The telling of the story can be dramatic action

Agamemnon's reply to Menelaus sets his story against his brother's, but even more, sets his own calm point of view against his brother's hot-headedness. The story apparatus is tempered with a deliberately distanced point of view.

> AGAMEMNON Now it is my turn to criticize you. I will be compassionate, not
> arrogant. I will show you the respect due a brother.

Even his address to the audience advises temperance.

DRAMATIC ACTION AND ILLUSION OF CHARACTER

AGAMEMNON Compassion springs from a good heart.

The original audience for *Iphigenia in Aulis* would have understood, and, by force of habit, participated in the evaluation of Menelaus and Agamemnon's opinions. Caught up in their own ongoing civil war, they were voting on policies after public discussions not unlike those in the play—including debates on honoring bad promises. Directing these lines to the audience, telling the stories rather than enacting them, will return a structure to the text of *Iphigenia* that makes the play in performance dramatic and interesting.

As a distanced narrator, Agamemnon will not use character quotes to describe his brother and establish the event: *Menelaus began all this because he couldn't keep his wife at home.*

AGAMEMNON Tell me first why you are so angry. You are short of breath, your face is flushed. Why? Who has done you wrong? What do you want? Do you desire to win yourself a good wife? I cannot help you there. You had no control over the one you had. *You* made the mistakes. Must *I* pay for them? *I* do not have an adulteress for a wife. You talk of my ambition. But it is not *that* which torments you. No. You long to hold a beautiful woman in your arms. Discretion and common decency mean nothing to you. Your passions make you grovel. You have become an evil man.

Agamemnon will try to persuade the audience that he is acting for impersonal reasons, not just to save his daughter's life.

AGAMEMNON If I have the intelligence to undo a previous mistake—am I to be called a fool? You are the fool. You lost a faithless wife and now you want her back—be the gods willing.

The story that follows alternates its focus between Menelaus and the listening army. Speaking to his brother, Agamemnon's task will be *to rebuke Menelaus*; speaking to the audience, Agamemnon will appeal to the common sense of people in a similar crisis—as was true when the play was first performed.

AGAMEMNON Think back. The suitors who pursued Helen swore all manner of oaths to her father. But *you* won her hand. Not through strength or virtue but by the help of a goddess—the goddess of Hope. You want an army? Conscript the suitors! Be their general! They were fools before, why not now?

A shift in the point of view takes the distanced Agamemnon to identification with what he is saying:

AGAMEMNON But the gods are not fools. They know when an oath has been sworn under duress and when a promise is evil.

TELLING A STORY

As identified storyteller, using the word *I* and identifying with it emotionally, Agamemnon can speak passionately here, and with great force.

> AGAMEMNON I will not kill my child. Why should you, with no concern for what is right, take vengeance on a worthless wife and live a life of happiness and success while I am forced to weep unending tears for my sins, my unjust unconscionable sins against my own child? I shall say no more. I have been brief and to the point. If you will not see sense, that is your choice. But I must follow my conscience and do what I must do.

Agamemnon, for at least this part of the play, joins other characters written by Euripides who defy conventional loyalty and denounce the honor of war as dishonorable. The speaking of the lines is the *gest* of an episode:

AGAMEMNON PUBLICLY GOES BACK ON HIS PROMISE

The Chorus tries to stay neutral, balancing the alternative points of view.

> CHORUS Your words have changed—for the better. You now refuse to harm your child.

But Menelaus is hot-headed. To his mind, the listeners are either for him or against him.

> MENELAUS Then I am alone. I have no friends.

Rather than say this line sarcastically or reproachfully to the Chorus—would Menelaus really be that concerned over the opinion of some women from Chalcis?—it might work just as well to say it to the audience. Menelaus will be just as biased but without the added blinders of pettiness. The scene then switches from storytelling to dialogue.

> AGAMEMNON Not true. Simply stop destroying the friends that you have.
> MENELAUS Are you our father's son!? Prove it!
> AGAMEMNON We should be brothers in virtue, not in sin.
> MENELAUS If you *were* my friend, you would share in my misfortunes.
> AGAMEMNON Brother, you hurt me. If you chastise me, do it with some good in mind.
> MENELAUS Are you abandoning Greece in its pain?
> AGAMEMNON Greece, like you, is the victim of some god.
> MENELAUS Revel in the power of your crown. Betray your brother. I shall make new plans and other friends.

DRAMATIC ACTION AND ILLUSION OF CHARACTER

The world of the play this scene is set in is one caught up in a civil war. The text was written during a civil war. To call someone a traitor within this world is provocative. The scene of dueling stories is meant to provoke the audience to question who is right. The episode: THE HOT-HEADED MAN IS FURIOUS THAT THE CHORUS DOESN'T SIDE WITH HIM. At this point in the play a Messenger arrives to announce that Iphigenia has arrived.

The text alternates between personal attack, moralizing, the story of Helen, and the personal emotions expressed while saying all this. To play the text with fourth-wall realism motivated by accomplishing tasks and encountering obstacles would prompt the cutting of long passages that seem not only un-dramatic but anti-dramatic. Analyzing the stories as stories, not just dialogue, reveals a vital way to act the scene. The speeches become dramatically active by shifting points of view. Shifting from storytelling to dialogue, the actors playing Menelaus and Agamemnon have different ways to establish character and action.

The scene can be broken apart by:

- Setting aside portions of the scene for direct address to the audience (Menelaus appeals to the Greeks for support).
- Playing the scene "realistically" (Menelaus attacks his older brother).
- Telling stories for their description of events (Menelaus demonstrates how his brother lied).
- Telling stories for their own value as episodes (MENELAUS LOSES HIS TEMPER).

The notebook pages that follow demonstrate how the stories from *Iphigenia in Aulis* can be broken down and integrated with other ways of working, including objectives and episodes. Although it isn't included in the notes, it would be possible to add work from images as well for the poised Agamemnon and the hot-headed Menelaus. From a study of the characters' words and the time the play was written, an actor could define a world of the play for *Iphigenia in Aulis* that is as equivocal as *Macbeth*'s. The highest good in this world is keeping your word. Only Iphigenia, who willingly sacrifices herself at the end of the play, seems to live up to that ideal. But is Iphigenia's sacrifice worthwhile? The playwright does not give a definite answer.

The history of the production reflects that ambivalence. Euripides died before the play could be produced, and it was staged by his nephew, who seems to have added a different ending. At the last minute, just as Agamemnon is about to plunge a knife into his daughter, Iphigenia disappears and a ram appears in her place. Of course, this doesn't happen onstage. Even Euripides's nephew had the good sense to describe such a miracle, rather than show it in a scene.

Notebook:
Applying Narrative Analysis

AGAMEMNON So, you have broken the seal and read it. It was not for your eyes.

MENELAUS Yes, I read it. I know your secrets and your shame. You will regret it.

AGAMEMNON Gods above! The arrogance of the man! Where did you waylay my messenger?

MENELAUS I was waiting for your daughter to come here from Argos.

AGAMEMNON Why?

MENELAUS Because I felt like it. I am not your slave.

AGAMEMNON This is an outrage. Am I not to be master of my own house?

MENELAUS Not when you are a cheat and a liar, when you slither your way into everything.

AGAMEMNON You talk to me of cheating and of lying. You! I hate a facile, quick tongue.

MENELAUS And I hate a devious, quick mind. You know neither justice nor honesty. I will prove your guilt. No lies, my brother! No quick denials. You cannot bluff your way out of this.

Listen to me. <u>I will not be too hard on you.</u> Do you remember your past ambitions? To be leader of the Greeks against Troy? You pretended to be reluctant. But in your heart you longed for it. And to get it you groveled. You shook everyone by the hand. Your doors were <u>open to all who wished to enter.</u> You spoke to everyone, whether they wanted to listen or not. You were nice to everyone. You wanted to be popular. You wanted no rivals.

EPISODE: MENELAUS CATCHES
HIS OLDER BROTHER DOING WRONG

Agamemnon's task:
to save his daughter
Action: *to brush off Menelaus*
Obstacle: his brother has proof

Menelaus's task:
to repossess his wife
Action: *to slap Agamemnon into action*
Obstacle: his brother's poise

Menelaus's Story:
P.O.V. Projected to the audience, personified as the Greek army.
Task: *to persuade the army*
Obstacle: their respect for their commander

Story apparatus:
<u>I will not be too hard on you.</u>
Revealing his task, *to expose his brother in public*
Event: *When Agamemnon wanted to win election, he bribed the Greeks with condescension*

Quote: <u>. . .open to all who wished to enter,</u> solicitous and oily

But then when you were made commander-in-chief, you changed your tune. You abandoned all your old friends. You were inaccessible. You locked your doors. You rarely appeared in public. Brother, a good man does not change when he gets on in the world. That is precisely the time when his friends ought to be able to count on him, when his power and success allow him to do more for them than ever. <u>This is my first point</u>, my first reproach—your lack of character.

> Event: *When Agamemnon got what he wanted, he was stand-offish as usual*

> Change in P.O.V.: <u>This is my first point</u>
> Projected to the audience, still to persuade them, by demonstrating his good will. Coldly, in order to prove he's impartial

<u>Then</u>, when the Greek army came here to Aulis and we were denied a favoring wind, you became the lowest of the low. This injunction of the gods filled you with fear. The Greeks shouted at you, demanded that the fleet turn back, that you put an end to this futile delay. One could see the distress on your face. You could not bear the thought of not launching your thousand ships, of not filling the fields of Troy with the cries of war. So you came to me. "<u>What shall I do? How can I get out of this?</u>" You were afraid of losing your command, losing the glory.

> Story apparatus: <u>Then</u>
> Task: *to point out the pattern of wrongdoing*

> Event: *Crises came, Agamemnon was paralyzed*

> Quote: "<u>What shall I do? . . .</u>"
> Task?: *to beg, to rescue,*
> Transaction?: *I'll humble myself / you'll help me*

<u>Then</u> Calchas spoke. You were to sacrifice your daughter. Only then would the Greeks be free to sail to Troy. You were quick to make promises. And your heart smiled. No one forced you to do what you did next. You cannot say that. You sent word to your wife that your daughter was to come to Aulis and be married to Achilles. That was the pretext you devised.

> Story apparatus: <u>Then</u>
> Pointing out again that this is the pattern of Agamemnon's duplicity

> Event: *Agamemnon agreed to sacrifice his daughter so the ships could sail*

> Event: *Agamemnon has gone back on his word*

And now? You have been caught red-handed. You have changed your mind and sent a different message. <u>You are no longer prepared to be your daughter's killer.</u>

> Quote: <u>You are no longer prepared to be your daughter's killer.</u> Display the words, don't quote them.
> P.O.V. held at a distance, with distaste.

I cannot be more blunt. <u>This is the same heaven that bore witness to your oaths.</u> Think! You are not unique. Many a man has worked hard to gain power. And many a man has lost that power in shame. Sometimes it is the fault of the people. They do not understand the complexity of power. But just as often it is the man himself who is incompetent and fails to protect the interests of the people. <u>My tears are for Greece.</u> She planned an action steeped in glory. Now she must suffer the mockery of barbarians. <u>All because of you and your daughter.</u> It is not courage that makes a great leader or a great general. It is intelligence. A man who has half a brain can be governor of a state. But a commander-in-chief must be blessed with intelligence.

CHORUS When brothers fight and anger and recrimination fly between them, there is only sorrow.

AGAMEMNON <u>Now it is my turn to criticize you.</u> I will be compassionate, not arrogant. I will show you the respect due a brother. Compassion springs from a good heart. Tell me first why you are so angry. You are short of breath, your face is flushed. Why? Who has done you wrong? What do you want? Do you desire to win yourself a good wife? I cannot help you there. You had no control over the one you had.

You made the mistakes. Must *I* pay for them? *I* do not have an adulteress for a wife. You talk of my ambition. But it is not *that* which torments you. No. You long to hold a beautiful woman in your arms. Discretion and common decency mean nothing to you. Your passions make you grovel. You have become an evil man. If I have the intelligence to undo a previous mistake, am I to be called a fool?

This is the same heaven that bore witness to your oaths:
Change in P.O.V.: Identifying more, less distant.

Change in P.O.V.:
<u>My tears are for Greece</u>
Task: *to egg on the listeners*
Obstacle: *they don't take sides*

<u>All because of you and your daughter:</u>
EPISODE: MENELAUS LOSES HIS TEMPER (Note: in the world of this play, losing your temper is weak and makes you lose status)
Task?: *to arouse the Greeks to strip Agamemnon of his command*

The Chorus's Story:
To balance the attack with the rule of respect due to the commander

Agamemnon's Story:
Story apparatus:
<u>Now it is my turn to criticize you</u>.
Task: *to establish his objectivity*
(In the world of this play, calm brings honor)

Event: *Menelaus began all this because he couldn't keep his wife at home*

Change in P.O.V.: Alternating between two tasks: *to scold his brother* and *to appeal to the audience*, personified as people in a similar crisis (when the play was first performed)

You are the fool. You lost a faithless wife and now you want her back—be the gods willing. Think back. The suitors who pursued Helen swore all manner of oaths to her father. But *you* won her hand. Not through strength or virtue but by the help of a goddess—the goddess of Hope. You want an army? Conscript the suitors! Be their general! They were fools before, why not now? But the gods are not fools. They know when an oath has been sworn under duress and when a promise is evil.

I will not kill my child. Why should you, with no concern for what is right, take vengeance on a worthless wife and live a life of happiness and success while I am forced to weep unending tears for my sins, my unjust unconscionable sins against my own child?

I shall say no more. I have been brief and to the point. If you will not see sense, that is your choice. But I must follow my conscience and do what I must do.

CHORUS Your words have changed—for the better. You now refuse to harm your child.

MENELAUS Then I am alone. I have no friends.

AGAMEMNON Not true. Simply stop destroying the friends that you have.

MENELAUS Are you our father's son!? Prove it!

AGAMEMNON We should be brothers in virtue, not in sin.

MENELAUS If you *were* my friend, you would share in my misfortunes.

AGAMEMNON Brother, you hurt me. If you chastise me, do it with some good in mind.

MENELAUS Are you abandoning Greece in its pain?

AGAMEMNON Greece, like you, is the victim of some god.

MENELAUS Revel in the power of your crown. Betray your brother. I shall make new plans and other friends.

Event: *The Greeks kept their oath* (Biased P.O.V.: And they were fools to do it)
Change in P.O.V.:
Alternating between two tasks:
to scold his brother and
to appeal to the listeners

Change in P.O.V.:
I will not kill my child. Increasingly less distanced and more identified with what he is saying
EPISODE: AGAMEMNON PUBLICLY GOES BACK ON HIS PROMISE

Story apparatus:
I have been brief, to temper the army and his brother

EPISODE:
THE CHORUS STAYS IMPARTIAL

EPISODE: THE HOT-HEADED MAN IS FURIOUS THAT THE CHORUS DOESN'T SIDE WITH HIM
Agamemnon's task:
to calm his brother
Obstacle: Menelaus's passion

Menelaus's task:
to shame his brother
Obstacle: Agamemnon won't take the bait and stays serene

Practical Tips for Working

Spare us your feelings, limit your emotional recall

During the relatively short time that realistic dramas have been performed realistically, stories told onstage have been interpreted as aspects of one character's relationship to another. According to these rules, when there is no one else onstage, actors telling a story are meant to establish an emotional relationship with themselves. The character's task is *to release the memory* of what is being described; obstacles include anything that blocks those memories, including personal inhibitions. Among actors who find a parallel with in-character storytelling and Lee Strasberg's emotional recall exercises, successful narrators overcome those blocks and arrive at the emotional state described in the story.

The search for a private image to parallel the story being told propels actors to unlock their personal histories. It doesn't always happen. Not even storytelling during psychoanalytic therapy—from which emotional recall exercises derive—can reliably reproduce an emotional state from the past. In therapy, as in performance, the process is undependable, which makes it a daring choice to try and get away with onstage.

When emotional recall works it can be thrilling, and for all the wrong reasons. It's easy for the drama of a performer accessing the past to distract the audience from the action of the play. When an actor's pathology floods the text with a wash of emotion, the audience can't help but notice the performer is elated or terrified—or working hard to get that way—but what has happened to the character or the plot of the play is drowned in oil.

From the audience's side of the stage, self-manipulation isn't dramatic, it's just selfish. Emotional recall during storytelling is very selfish, not only because it ignores the needs of the audience and the intentions of the author; it reduces the other actors to props and the lines of the play to Muzak on your solo elevator ride to catharsis.

There are legitimate ways to contain storytelling within the fourth wall: the telling of the story can itself be a task, as it is when storytelling defies authority or tries to stir other characters to action. Yet, when the task is *to defy* or *to seduce* or *to alarm* by telling a story, a performer is returned to the technical problem of how storytelling is different from enactment (and very different from emotional memory, which has no task but self-exploration).

Strasberg intended to restrict emotional recall exercises to the classroom or rehearsal hall, but, inevitably, emotional recall seeped into performance technique. Emotional recall does have its uses in film, since self-involved performances can be compensated for with interspersed reaction shots of other actors. But unlike watching a film, what the audience sees onstage cannot be selected from one successful performance among twenty failed ones. When self-indulgent emotional recall isn't confusing or boring an audience at the expense of the story, the search for personal metaphors as a stage technique exhausts the patience of the other actors and saps the progress of rehearsals.

DRAMATIC ACTION AND ILLUSION OF CHARACTER

Remember, don't relive

Emotional memory is undependable and it's selfish. It's also baloney that emotional re-call is always true to life. When a criminal tells his tale, or a victim gives testimony, or a long-married couple look through their wedding album, they usually do not relive past events. They *remember* them. That's very, very different. On any given episode of *Court TV* you can witness for yourself something not unlike the following:

> DISGRUNTLED HOUSEWIFE (*coldly*) I hit him with the bottle three times. (*pause, thinking*) No. Four. Then he moved over to the bed and . . . (*pause, small smile*) No. It was a couch. Yes. Yes, it was a couch.

Or, visiting your happily married friends:

> LONG-MARRIED WIFE LEAFING THROUGH WEDDING ALBUM (*warmly*) Look, dear, there's that photograph of your Aunt Matilda. (*pause, small frown*) But wait. Who is that man with her? That's not Uncle Bob. Who is that?

The process of remembering has its own successes and failures. How many times did Disgruntled Housewife smack him? Who was Matilda dating before she met Bob? What seemed hot then (the disco-fever sideburns on Aunt Matilda's beau, the Housewife's feeling of getting even with the creep) is going to be remembered coldly now, and vice versa. The success of remembering has its own tasks and its own emotions when those tasks are accomplished—or encounter an obstacle.

> DISGRUNTLED HOUSEWIFE (*calmly*) It was *four* times I hit him. (*pause for thought, followed by smile*) No-o-o . . . It was three.

What makes you laugh now may be exactly what embarrassed you years before. What you laughed at years earlier might embarrass you now.

> LONG-MARRIED WIFE LEAFING THROUGH WEDDING ALBUM Oh, yes! (*laughing*) I remember, it's that man she hit over the head with a bottle! My, that was embarrassing! (*laughing more*) I nearly died of shame!! (*giggling*)

Have the telling of the story be an episode

Try to make the telling of the story be an episode. Have the audience notice that some-thing has changed by the time you conclude your story. This is especially true of stories told as songs. Otherwise, the music blankets the drama and the song is a pause, not a continuation of the dramatic action.

A physical change in the storyteller—like the character of Edgar in *King Lear*, who transforms himself onstage into a beggar—will tell the audience that the story has dramatic significance as an episode. The environment can be changed in the telling of a story, too.

Learn from Mei Lanfang's sleeves

The arms of Mei Lanfang's traditional costumes ended in long-hanging sleeves. The great Chinese actor waved them like water to illustrate a description, set them in the air to flutter like a dove, let them hang over his hands, or rolled them back in character. They could be scenery, commentary, characterization—even birds. You might not have long-hanging sleeves, but anything else you might carry on with you to the stage—costume, prop, make-up—and anything you might find on the stage, scenery and lighting included, can be used to relay the event to the audience.

Imagine a retired general in a rest home fighting his old battles again—over lunch. He uses his salt and pepper shakers as enemy cannons, the folded napkin as a sand dune. The fork and the knife are two wings of the army—until the water glass gets in the way. The general's lunch table has a meaning of its own: it's the battlefield. The water glass can spill and the napkin can unfold in order to represent the blowing away of the sand dune.

In the general's storytelling, if the napkin is the last brave soldier, when the general puts the napkin back in his pocket, the soldier dies, or retreats. When the general crushes the napkin, he crushes the soldier. In all of these actions the general has the possibility of rendering the passage of time through his pace and rhythm.

It is important to think that as an actor telling the story, you have the same relationship to the props and costumes as a puppeteer to a puppet show. Onstage, you can use a table, a chair, a salt-shaker, or your handkerchief—even the sleeve of your costume—to tell the story.

Simplify character quotes

A word of caution. Too much impersonation during a character quote defeats the purpose of the story. It's supposed to be different from enactment; it need not be a detailed impression. Simpler character quotes invite the audience to participate in fleshing out the character.

Take advantage of the stage's freedom by thinking of a film's freedom

As storyteller, you have control over the audience's perception. You can send them flying over the seas or burrowing into the head of the villain. Use this power to present events the way a film editor combines camera angles to create a sophisticated, multi-dimensional approach when depicting a scene.

Novels also make a good model. Eighteenth-century writers structured their novels as collections of letters from different people describing the same events. If you like a challenge, you could look to a novel written in the twentieth century: *Hopscotch* by the Argentine writer Julio Cortázar, first published in Spanish in 1963. *Hopscotch* turns a shift of view into the playful game of the title.* The first fifty-six short chapters can be read in order and the book be done with. Or, as Cortázar suggests in a "Table of Instructions," the reader may begin with Chapter 73, jump back to Chapters 1 and 2, leap forward to chapter 166, back to Chapter 3, and skip over to 84, in a pattern that concludes with Chapter 131—hopping backward from Chapter 155 between 64 and 123. . . . Of course, you could read the chapters in the order that they're printed or in an order of your own.

It is with the art form of the twentieth century—the cinema—that the alternation of points of view achieved greatness as a narrative technique, complete with a history and vocabulary of its own. From the beginnings of the epic cinema—D.W. Griffith's *Intolerance* and Abel Gance's *Napoleon*—the permutations of shifting points of view have revealed a new way to conceive of human relationships, including character and the meaning of behavior.† Relativity is not just a theory of Einstein; it is the worldview of our time as surely as motivation was the worldview of Stanislavsky and Freud.

Learn from Mae West . . . to pause

While telling a story, you control time—for the events and for the audience. Your listeners can hang on your every word or be left behind. Mae West's trick was to pause in order to give her audience time to receive the performance and think about what they'd just been told. It's a good way to make sure listeners understand and have time to react. The audience is your partner in the creation of the illusions of character and dramatic action, and they need time to do their work. Give them that time.

Don't speed up for a long story out of a fear that the audience will lose interest over time. It works the other way around. You'll lose them if you go too fast, because they won't have time to take in the significance of events, character quotes, and descriptions. Take your time, make your points. Just as the passion you have for an image transfers to the audience, so too will your interest in a story get the audience interested as well.

There are exceptions

Some stories are told without dramatic action or character or events. Recitations, for instance, have no character and often no dramatic action. Some reports keep a distanced point of view that does not change. Therefore, the report itself is not a dramatic action but part of a larger action. Unvarying emotional display has the same effect: static by itself, but useful in a larger design.

Not every story is important for the information value of its words. Sometimes a story is meant to be like birdsong; the sound of a speaker is intended to sooth, to seduce, to baffle. Sometimes the action of simply *speaking* is significant, as in Beckett or Ionesco.

Rayuela in Spanish.
†Griffith derived the use of close-ups alternating with longer shots of the same scene from techniques used by Dickens in his novels.

When asked, interrupt realistic behavior with storytelling

Sometimes a director or an adventurous playwright will ask a performer to juxtapose storytelling techniques within detailed realistic scenes. This use of mixed techniques resembles a Cubist painting with a composition impossible to view in life: the bottom of a bottle, the hole in a guitar, the profile of a wineglass—all these curves in contrast to the checkered pattern of a tablecloth as seen from above. Working like this onstage, an actor separates narrative lines from dialogue and tells the story of the scene directly to the audience. When the behavior of a role is held up for such a discussion, the contrast between the character's thoughts and actions are set out as sharply as the wineglass against the checkered tablecloth.

In some Cubist paintings there are real objects—scraps of newspaper, wallpaper, a train ticket—pasted onto the canvas next to a splat of paint. The Spanish Cubist Juan Gris could fake wood grain so well that he fooled the eye—next to his convincing "wood" he'd paint an obviously splotchy spread of polka dots. Such a dynamic and exciting juxtaposition of techniques can be used in acting to similar effect, when a narrative approach to dramatic text is combined within a "realistic" scene.

It is difficult to volunteer storytelling techniques unless the director agrees. Certain directors encourage actors to mix narration with enactment: in America, Richard Schechner and Anne Bogart (among others); in Western Europe, Ariane Mnouckine and Peter Brook; in Eastern Europe, Lev Dodin and Jerzy Grotowski; in Japan, Suzuki. For some directors—and litigious playwrights—it is disrespectful to the text and the author's intentions.

Onstage narration is neither off-putting nor strange in the middle of a scene. The best known example (so well known as to be unnoticed) is the use of an *aside*. An aside's switch from the dramatic to narrative establishes a personal relationship of confidence with the audience. In no way does an aside diminish the illusion of a character being created; on the contrary, it reinforces the characterization. If the style or the aesthetics of the production permit the liberty, storytelling techniques woven into the texture of a realistic scene enhance characterization and dramatic action.

Storytelling Within Enactment:
Rehearsing a Scene from *The Three Sisters*

Let's look at the last scene from Chekhov's 1904 play *The Three Sisters* (106)—a text with a history of being performed rather than narrated—for the possibilities of storytelling. As a creative artist, as well as an interpretive one, an actor can choose to include storytelling even in texts that seem to require enactment exclusively. Proust, speaking about "realism," says the real problem with "realism" is that, over time, it teaches us to mistake its formulae for reality.

Irina (pronounced e-REE-na) and Olga are two of the three sisters who live in a provincial town. Anfisa (An-FEE-za) is their old nurse, whom they still call by the childish name of Nana. Vershinin (Ver-SHEEN-in) is an army officer in love with the third sister, Masha (who is not in this scene). The play, in part, is about the way hope withers with time. The sisters have hoped to escape provincial life and go to Moscow. Vershinin and Masha have hoped for a true love together, outside of their marriages to other people.

This is the day Vershinin's division of soldiers, the central point of the sisters' lives, is leaving town. The scene occurs in the last act of the play, in the garden of the sisters' family house, now taken over by their sister-in-law. The first three acts have taken place indoors; now the sisters are sitting outside in the garden, which is intruded on by outsiders. The shift in the scene from indoors to outdoors would support a change in point of view for the speakers, turned out of their home, crowded in the garden, with nowhere to turn but the audience. Throughout the play, characters crowd in on each other. Deeply felt confidences are poured out to whomever happens to be in the room. Here, out in the garden, that pressure might force those confidences toward the listening audience.

> *Two street musicians, a man and a girl, play on the violin and harp;*
> VERSHININ, OLGA, *and* ANFISA *come out of the house and listen in silence*
> *for a moment;* IRINA *approaches.*

> IRINA Our garden's like a public thoroughfare; people keep walking and driving through it. Nurse, give those musicians something.

Why can't Irina split the focus of her lines and announce to the audience, not her nurse, that the garden is overrun? Because this is not the style that Stanislavsky used when he directed the play? Chekhov himself objected to the realistic style of Stanislavsky's direction in letters to Meyerhold, who played the important role of Tuzenbach for Stanislavsky in the original production.

> ANFISA (*gives money to the musicians*) Go along and God bless you, good people. (*the musicians bow and leave*) Poor things! You don't go around playing like that if you're well-fed.

The old nurse Anfisa will, at first, retain the focus of the scene onstage when she speaks to the onstage musicians, although her comment about them might be made to the audience. Another choice might be that Anfisa is unaware of the audience until they laugh at her comment. Notice that, in the scene that follows, she calls the sisters by their childhood names: Arisha, Olyusha, and Mashenka.

> ANFISA (*to* IRINA) Good day, Arisha! (*kisses her*) Ee-e, little one, what a life I am having! What a life! What a life!

It is possible to justify the repetition of the words "What a life!"—often obscured in translation by one emphatic sentence, rather than two—by performing them in two different ways: the first as a declaration to Irina, the second as a report to the audience.

TELLING A STORY

There's even a characteristic task to be found: Old Anfisa would enjoy a chance to boast to and tell her story to a crowd.

> ANFISA What a life! What a life! Living at the high school in a government apartment with Olyusha—that's what God has granted me in my old age. Never in my life have I lived like this, sinner that I am . . . A big government apartment, a whole room to myself, my own bed. All at government expense. I wake up in the night and—oh, Lord, Mother of God, there's not a happier person in the world!

Storytelling doesn't take away from the reality of Anfisa as a character; it increases the illusion of character by allowing her to tell her listeners about her new life. The next part of the scene might be left as observed behavior. Vershinin is speaking of the army division:

> VERSHININ (*looking at his watch*) We shall be leaving directly, Olga Sergeyevna. Time to be off. (*pause*) I wish you everything, everything . . . Where is Maria Sergeyevna?
> IRINA She's somewhere in the garden . . . I'll go and look for her.
> VERSHININ Please be so kind. I must hurry.
> ANFISA I'll go look for her, too. (*calls*) Mashenka, aa-oo! (*goes with* IRINA *to the rear of the garden*) Aa-oo, aa-oo!
> VERSHININ All things come to an end.

If Vershinin speaks "all things come to an end" to the audience, the switch from enactment to storytelling will create its own dramatic action. It will be as if the soul of the character is speaking, having left the body of the role. Vershinin tells the audience that his hopes are gone; that there will be no love affair with Masha—not even a satisfying goodbye. He's announcing other dreams in the play are coming to an end as well.

Speaking these lines to the audience can also make it appear that the actor has stepped *out* of the role, alienating—in Brecht's terms—the meaning of the lines so that they comment on the action of the play itself, which is now coming to an end. If such a decision is made to alienate the lines—the actor and not "Vershinin" speaking them—the dramatic effect will be striking and harsh. The words are the announcements of the episode, now told as an event: ALL THINGS COME TO AN END.

Said to the audience from the point of view of the role, however, the words offer up Vershinin's response to a number of finales: the end of his affair with Masha, the end of the army in the three sisters' life, and the end of the play itself. The other actors onstage don't have to pretend they don't notice that Vershinin is speaking to the audience. They can react—in character, or not—as if the thought that their dreams have ended had passed through all their minds and stirred up various responses. The words "all things come to an end" will now hover over the "realistic" scene that follows.

The return to enactment after narration can be very moving. This way, the audience has had a chance to appreciate, judge, and sympathize with the *web of relationships.* The characters act heroically, because they are pressing on despite knowledge of their inevitable failure. Openly including the character's—or the actor's—understanding of the end of the role as part of the performance will create an understanding of the characters among the audience that exceeds observation.

> VERSHININ Here we are parting. (*looks at his watch*) The town gave us a sort of lunch, we had champagne, the Mayor made a speech, I ate and listened, but in my heart I was here with you . . . (*looks around the garden*) I've grown attached to you.

Olga could emphasize the event by asking her question to the listening audience.

> OLGA Shall we meet again some day?
> VERSHININ Probably not. (*pause*)

Vershinin's comment would be funny as story apparatus told to the audience.

> VERSHININ My wife and the two little girls will remain here for another month or two; please, if anything happens, or if they need anything . . .
> OLGA Yes, yes, of course. You needn't worry. (*pause*) By tomorrow there won't be a single officer or soldier in town; it will all be a memory, and for us, of course, a new life will begin . . . (*pause*)

Olga's faith can be established by the way she tells this story to the audience, and established just as strongly, if not more so, than if she said the same words to Vershinin. It won't deny emotion to the scene by ripping the web of relationships between characters that is claimed to be the basis for the audience's interest. Narration engages the audience in a different way, by letting them play the scene in their minds.

> OLGA Nothing ever happens the way we want it to. I didn't want to be a head-mistress, and yet I became one. It means we are not to be in Moscow . . .

In telling this story, does Olga identify with the *I* in her story? Maybe. Or is she emotionally distanced, speaking as if the *I* was a third person? Does she laugh? Maybe. To whom is Olga saying "Nothing ever happens the way we want it to"? Why not address it to a projected audience? How is such an audience characterized? Should the audience be characterized as modern-day Russians, who might cry at such a sentiment?

There are many examples of familiar texts written to combine narration with performance that are now performed without narration, because the "realistic" style of the twentieth century has obscured the memory of other approaches. The most significant are the stories written by Shakespeare, called *soliloquies*, the subject of the next chapter.

CHAPTER 13

SHAKESPEARE'S SOLILOQUIES

A **soliloquy** is a speech said by an actor onstage and alone. This is not the same thing as being onstage and alone and speaking to yourself. By being loud enough to be overheard, even in a soliloquy, performers acknowledge the presence of a listening audience and their obligation to communicate—not just express themselves like introspective songbirds spied on in the woods.

In a soliloquy, the story of a role's inner thoughts and feelings is told with a characterization projected onto the audience; a characterization that reflects the speaker. In short, you address the audience as if they were an aspect of yourself. This is what distinguishes soliloquies from Shakespeare's prologues, epilogues, and choruses, in which actors frankly address the audience as audience.

An actor performing a soliloquy is still meant to report to the audience, not muse. As the Greek God Comus is supposed to have pointed out—and the British novelist Laurence Sterne repeated—people aren't made of glass. If an artist invites an audience to enjoy the inner drama of a role, there must be some way to expose that inner drama to common sight. Actors performing Shakespeare's soliloquies speak directly to describe and demonstrate what's going on beneath the surface of the role.

Playing a soliloquy without acknowledging the audience is one of many conventions well-meaning actors have applied to speaking Shakespeare's words during four centuries of performance history. Sliding an invisible fourth wall between a speaker and listeners is not just an interpretation; it is something more intrusive. Over time, such additions to an artwork obscure that they are additions and become mistaken for the artwork itself. This is true not only for plays, but for other forms of art to which meanings have been added over time. A good example is the story of a once famous classical Greek sculpture called *Zingara*—Italian for "gypsy woman," which is what the statue depicts.

Zingara was highly praised during the seventeenth century and still quite popular in the eighteenth and mid-nineteenth centuries. Connoisseurs wrote at length about the cunning gypsy expression "on the lookout for dupes" (107). The work was especially valued among scholars as evidence of gypsies during the classic period of the Greeks and Romans. Edmund Gibbon, the celebrated author of *The Decline and Fall of the Roman Empire* (1776–1788) wrote of the statue's "true character of impudence and low cunning suitable to a fortune-teller" (108).

The *Zingara* had been in the collection of the Italian Borghese family for at least a century and a half when, in 1807, Prince Camillo Borghese sold it to his brother-in-law,

Napoleon Bonaparte. Napoleon added this prize to the collection at the Louvre, where it was affectionately known as "La Petite Bohémienne." At first. Today, the *Zingara* is deposited at Versailles and languishes in obscurity—its "gypsy" character is more fraud than any fortune-teller's.

The marble section of the work is, without a doubt, fourth-century Greek, but it depicts nothing more than folded drapery. The bronze "gypsy" head, hands, and feet were stuck on to the ends of the marble over fifteen-hundred years after it was first carved—by a French sculptor working on Borghese orders. If you need an image for *cunning*, don't think of the statue; think of the expression on the Prince's face after he sold the thing to Napoleon.

When you treat an Elizabethan soliloquy as a chance for spied-on soul-searching, you are doing the same thing as adding the gypsy's head, changing and obscuring the meaning of the original. Even though the convention of talking to yourself may have been accepted for a hundred and fifty years, like the smiling Italian prince, you are selling a false bill of goods.

If you reread the soliloquies written by Shakespeare with an eye to their storytelling opportunities, you will see storytelling well supported by the text. Like other stories told onstage, performing a soliloquy to an audience can be an episode by itself. The way a soliloquy is told onstage will characterize the speaker's role, and a shift in the point of view of the narrator will create dramatic action. Shakespeare's particular use of storytelling has further opportunities for characterization and action, as we'll see.

Share Your Thoughts with the Audience: Rehearsing *Romeo and Juliet*

Let's start with a speech made overly familiar by its excellence:

> ROMEO But, soft! what light through yonder window breaks?
>
> *Romeo and Juliet, Act II, scene ii*

To whom is Romeo talking? We all know—having seen the speech parodied endless times, even by the Flintstones—that Romeo is supposed to be deep in contemplation, talking to himself. But the words the character speaks are not contemplative; they are an over-eager, one-sided conversation. The listening audience is characterized as a friend with whom the would-be lover shares his confidence, or, in Romeo's case, lack of confidence.

When this scene was first staged, the role of Juliet was played by a boy. There was no scenery, there were no lighting effects. It was daytime at the Globe Theater. In order to set the scene, the actor playing Romeo first had to tell the audience who was who and what was what. So the soliloquy began with an announcement of the event: *That's supposed to be the girl I love, and it's supposed to be night, and she's supposed to be radiantly beautiful in the moonlight.*

TELLING A STORY

Shakespeare put it much better:

ROMEO It is the east, and Juliet is the sun!

Now that that's been made clear, Romeo can speak to Juliet, although at a distance, please, and from a *distanced point of view*, according to the poetic conventions of the time.

ROMEO Arise, fair sun, and kill the envious moon,
    Who is already sick and pale with grief,
    That thou her maid art far more fair than she:
    Be not her maid, since she is envious;
    Her vestal livery is but sick and green,
    And none but fools do wear it; cast it off.

The point of views *shifts* as Romeo identifies with what he describes:

ROMEO It is my lady; O, it is my love!
    O, that she knew she were!

The unsure way the story is told characterizes Romeo with an adolescent blend of boldness and uncertainty. The events are described—

ROMEO She speaks, yet she says nothing.

—but the storyteller is unsure what the events signify. Is it an invitation for him to approach?

ROMEO What of that?
    Her eye discourses, I will answer it.

As he lurches forward—and balks—Romeo makes an excuse to the audience for his shyness:

ROMEO I am too bold; 'tis not to me she speaks.

If he cannot talk to her, he can at least talk *about* her. The description that follows sets a scene in the theater of the audience's mind. The actor and the character—and the playwright—enjoy their fantasies more by sharing them.

ROMEO Two of the fairest stars in all the heaven,
    Having some business do entreat her eyes
    To twinkle in their spheres till they return.

Like someone telling a riddle, Romeo sets up a question for his listeners.

276

ROMEO What if her eyes were there, they in her head?

He can answer his own question, and brag some more about the girl he would like to have as his lover.

> ROMEO The brightness of her cheek would shame those stars,
>   As daylight doth a lamp; her eyes in heaven
>   Would through the airy region stream so bright
>   That birds would sing, and think it were not night.

It's a lot more fun to brag to other people than to yourself. Speaking this lush poetry to himself would characterize Romeo as self-absorbed, in love with his own ability to make metaphors. The character is interpreted as such whenever he's shoved behind the fourth wall. But as a story told to an audience, the point of view demonstrates the narrator's exuberance and characterizes both roles at once.

Although the boy playing Juliet enacted the scene by moving his hand, it was the actor playing Romeo who told the audience what that movement meant and how much it moved him to watch it.

> ROMEO See how she leans her cheek upon her hand!

Romeo is now intimate enough with the listening audience to reveal his desire.

> ROMEO O, that I were a glove upon that hand,
>   That I might touch that cheek!

Saying the words of this soliloquy, any actor playing Romeo is meant to generously share the hopes, dreams, and fears of the character. Even his famous opening lines— "But, soft!"—don't have to be said to himself. They can be directed to the audience as a command: *Shhh! Be quiet. Don't scare away the girl in the window.*

When Romeo's doubts and hopes and desires are reported directly to the audience, the soliloquy is active and vigorous, not pensive or meandering. Don't talk to yourself unless you have to. It's a lot easier, and a lot more interesting, if you talk to someone else. Yes, of course, talk to Juliet in her balcony. But talk to the matinee ladies in *their* balcony, too. Unlike Juliet, the ladies in the balcony will announce the episode for you. "Oh, look," they will say to each other (and anyone else within earshot). "He wants to be with her and he's afraid to act on it. So young!"

Telling the Audience What They Already Know: Bottom from *A Midsummer Night's Dream*

One special feature of Shakespeare's soliloquies is that sometimes a character describes a scene after it takes place. When an audience has already seen what the character describes, they can better assess the storyteller's point of view—and collaborate to characterize the role of the speaker.

After Richard III pledges his love to Lady Anne, as soon as Anne leaves and Richard is alone onstage, the actor playing the role gets to crow out his version of what just happened and show himself off as an eager hypocrite and shameless liar.

> RICHARD Was ever woman in this humor wooed? . . .
>   I'll have her; but I will not keep her long.
>   What! I, that kill'd her husband and his father,
>   To take her in her heart's extremest hate;
>   With curses in her mouth, tears in her eyes,
>   The bleeding witness of my hatred by;
>   Having God, her conscience, and these bars against me,
>   And I no friends to back my suit withal,
>   But the plain devil and dissembling looks,
>   And yet to win her, all the world to nothing!
>   Ha!
>
> *Richard III, Act I, scene ii*

The audience has just witnessed for itself the hypocritical love scene Richard describes. After he tells the story, the cunning and cruelty of his role is reinforced.

An actor describing a scene after the fact can reveal a role's motives as well as character, but description can also reveal that the character is lost to the meaning of what he describes. In *A Midsummer Night's Dream*, the Queen of the Fairies is bound by a spell to make love to a man so low his name is Bottom—a dolt with the magically added ugliness of an ass's head. The audience is shown their grotesque courtship and lovemaking, as well as the scene when the Fairy Queen abandons the sleeping Bottom in disgust and returns to her fairy kingdom. Alone onstage, Bottom ends his sleep with a start, thinking he is where he was when last awake: at a rehearsal for a play.

> BOTTOM (*waking*) When my cue comes, call me, and I will answer . . .
>
> *A Midsummer Night's Dream, Act IV, scene i*

Shakespeare has characters wake with a start and blurt words to the air in other plays as well, the better to distinguish that the rest of the lines are spoken directly to the audience and not to the air. Once Bottom understands he is alone, he stops looking around the stage for the other actors and tells the audience what it already knows:

> BOTTOM I have had a most rare vision.

The audience has seen this vision. The question is, what will Bottom say about it? What will he remember? How will he describe it?

> BOTTOM I have had a dream, past the wit of man to say what dream it was.

Not very articulate, is he?

> BOTTOM Man is but an ass if he go about to expound this dream. Methought I was—there is no man can tell what. Methought I was, and methought I had—but man is but a patch'd fool, if he will offer to say what methought I had.

The joke, of course, is that he was an ass. He knows it, the audience knows it, the audience knows he knows it, and now the audience knows more: that Bottom is too proud to admit he was an ass. You may interpret his hesitations to mean that his erotic adventure is too embarrassing—or stimulating—for him to talk about. Either way, how he tells the story is weighed by the audience's knowledge—not the character's ignorance—to characterize Bottom as ass or prude or lecher.

Bottom's inability to describe or appreciate what he has experienced reveals the limits of his understanding and expression, and in turn tells the audience who Bottom is. The description that follows tells the audience still more: Bottom is a *blowhard*.

> BOTTOM The eye of man hath not heard, the ear of man hath not seen, man's hand is not able to taste, his tongue to conceive, nor his heart to report what my dream was.

Not just a blowhard, he's a show-off, too:

> BOTTOM I will get Peter Quince to write a ballad of this dream. It shall be call'd Bottom's Dream, because it hath no bottom; and I will sing it in the latter end of a play, before the Duke . . .

The character of Bottom is reinforced by the way he tells his story, especially because the audience knows from the play that his visit to the fairy kingdom offers sumptuous possibilities for description.

Establish Dramatic Action by What Happens to You as You Tell the Story: Don Armado from *Love's Labour's Lost*

Speaking a soliloquy is itself a dramatic action and can often be an episode with a beginning, middle, and end. Romeo talks himself out of saying hello; Bottom talks himself from ass to playwright. For five acts (and four and a half hours), Hamlet talks himself in and out of revenge. In various comedies, Shakespeare gives various characters soliloquies to talk themselves in and out of love. Here is a Spanish knight from *Love's Labour's Lost* doing just that:

DON ARMADO I do affect the very ground, which is base, where her shoe, which is baser, guided by her foot, which is basest, doth tread.

Love's Labour's Lost, Act I, scene ii

In order for the speech to be an episode, or to have a dramatic action, something has to change. Here, the change is the speaker's attitude to love. If an actor starts this silly soliloquy with a swooning "I do affect the very ground," the episode has begun at its conclusion and the role has no room for action.

In order to create an onstage episode, Don Armado must first try to talk himself out of love. His description of the girl is biased against her. He would like to disgust himself—and the audience—with the baseness of the girl. When that doesn't work, he switches to more logical objections. He has made an oath not to fall in love:

DON ARMADO I shall be forsworn—which is a great argument of false-hood— if I love . . .

Logic is not strong enough, either, to defend Don Armado from his feelings. His resolve wavers and his point of view *shifts* as he asks the audience to consider other great heroes who have fallen in love; heroes as strong and as wise as even Don Armado himself.

DON ARMADO Yet Samson was so tempted—and he had an excellent strength; yet was Solomon so seduced—and he had a very good wit . . .

The drama here is the change in Armado's feelings and his intentions as they weaken in opposition to what he describes. At last the Spanish knight admits "Cupid's butt-shaft is too . . . much odds for a Spaniard's rapier." Despite his supposed bravery in battle, Don Armado submits to Cupid:

DON ARMADO . . . his disgrace is to be called boy; but his glory is to subdue men.

In the course of the soliloquy, Don Armado changes his mind and announces the episode himself, although with a little fanfare first:

DON ARMADO Adieu, valour! rust, rapier! be still, drum! for your manager is in love . . .

Next is the *gest*, the act of the soldier saying the words:

DON ARMADO Yea, he loveth.

The point of view has moved from disgust to submission. Like Romeo and Bottom, Don Armado knows it's more fun to tell people about such an experience rather than keep it to yourself. He finishes with a promise to write poetry. Here, you can go right ahead and talk to the air. Talk to yourself, too. It's meant to be ridiculous.

> DON ARMADO Assist me, some extemporal god of rhyme, for I am sure I shall turn sonneteer. Devise, wit; write, pen; for I am for whole volumes in folio.

By the way, on the rare occasions when a character does speak to the air, Shakespeare often includes the word *fool*. Cressida, a Trojan princess almost as silly as Don Armado, reproaches herself for speaking her thoughts out loud in the middle of a love scene with Troilus: "See fools, why have we blabbed?" Why blab? The better to play an episode.

The Episode Involves a Change in the Relationship to the Audience: *Richard III*

When a soliloquy implies a partner, an episode will evolve onstage between the actor and the projected partner. Some soliloquies have interaction with the audience as complex as in a scene. At the beginning of *Richard III*, the villainous title character enjoys the presence of the audience, and projects onto them the character of fellow rogue. Throughout the play Richard projects the crowd's approval when they laugh at his jokes—even about murdering a child. "So young and wise, they say, do never live long," he says about the boy princes he plans to have killed.

At the end of the play Richard discovers that the audience has turned on him. Like Bottom, he wakes from a dream and speaks to himself:

> RICHARD Give me another horse—Bind up my wounds—
> Have mercy, Jesu! Soft!—

> *Richard III, Act V, scene iii*

The beginning, "Have mercy, Jesu," is said to the air. Enjoy it! Richard has been dreaming of a battle:

> RICHARD —I did but dream.
> O coward conscience, how dost thou afflict me!

Yes, he could be speaking to himself, but read a little further. It makes more sense that he is speaking to the audience, personified as *his conscience*.

> RICHARD The lights burn blue. It is now dead midnight.
> Cold fearful drops stand on my trembling flesh.

For whose benefit does Richard describe this? To reassure himself that he is in bed?

That the lamp is blue? That it's late? Doesn't it make more sense that he says these things, like the actor playing Romeo, so that the audience may picture them?

> RICHARD What do I fear? Myself? There's none else by.

If the lines are said to the audience, personified as his accusing conscience, then the actor playing Richard may play the role of defender.

> RICHARD Richard loves Richard; that is, I am I.
>   Is there a murderer here? No—yes, I am.

No—yes, I am? Do you want to say this to yourself by flinging your head from side to side? Wouldn't you rather say this to members of the audience on whom you *project* the role of your attackers?

> RICHARD Then fly. What, from myself? Great reason why—
>   Lest I revenge. What, myself upon myself!

Now you can confess to the audience:

> RICHARD Alack, I love myself. Wherefore? For any good
>   That I myself have done unto myself?
>   O, no! Alas, I rather hate myself
>   For hateful deeds committed by myself!
>   I am a villain—

Now you can defy the attacking audience:

> RICHARD—yet I lie, I am not.

If you feel you must, speak to yourself here. The word *fool* would indicate you could.

> RICHARD Fool, of thyself speak well. Fool, do not flatter.

Nevertheless, Shakespeare's words return you to a vision of the audience stretched out in front of you:

> RICHARD My conscience hath a thousand several tongues,
>   And every tongue brings in a several tale,
>   And every tale condemns me for a villain.

It is much more dramatic to see your condemning judges sitting in rows than to talk to yourself. Quote them:

> RICHARD Perjury, perjury, in the high'st degree;
> Murder, stern murder, in the dir'st degree;
> All several sins, all us'd in each degree,
> Throng to the bar, crying all "Guilty! guilty!"

The point of view switches here. What it changes to is a matter of interpretation. The audience seems to listen with pitiless indifference.

> RICHARD I shall despair. There is no creature loves me;
> And if I die no soul will pity me:
> And wherefore should they, since that I myself
> Find in myself no pity to myself?

If you choose a distanced point of view, Richard will be describing himself coolly and dispassionately. The effect will be chilling, and the episode will become RICHARD FACES UP TO DAMNATION. If you choose to identify the speaker with the emotion he describes—despair—then the effect will be pathetic as Richard tries to pry pity from his listeners. The episode will become VILLAIN BEGS FOR PITY.

Next comes a description, very bare, of what the audience has already witnessed in the scene before.

> RICHARD Methought the souls of all that I had murder'd
> Came to my tent, and every one did threat
> To-morrow's vengeance on the head of Richard.

This simple statement of fact implies a more distanced point of view, and a change toward the audience, as if Richard had appeased his conscience by admitting his loss of faith. He is calm now, able to tell a story and continue the rest of the play—without fear.

Here is the line of roles projected onto the listening audience, and to which Richard responds with roles of his own.

- Consoler/Frightened Dreamer: *I did but dream*
- Intimidator/Defiant Hero: *O coward conscience, how dost thou afflict me!*
- Attacker/Defender: *Is there a murderer here? No—yes, I am*
- Confessor/Sinner: *Alack, I love myself. Wherefore? I am a villain*
- Judge/Accused: *Several sins . . . Throng to the bar, crying all "Guilty! Guilty!"*
- Indifferent Friend/Despairing Friend: *There is no creature loves me*

Grant Richard some courage and call the episode RICHARD FACES UP TO DAMNATION. The transactions will follow a pattern of trading an admission of weakness for calm. The *gest* will be spoken at first—"I myself find in myself no pity to myself"—until, in rehearsal, the actor can devise some behavior to establish the transaction. When Olivier played the role, he faced his enemies like a snarling animal and practically spat. If you remember, one of his images was the Big Bad Wolf.

Continue a Relationship with the Audience: *Macbeth*

The character of the speaker will be reflected in the characterization of the audience. Bottom speaks to an audience as dumb as he is, Richard to an audience as pitiless as himself, Don Armado to fellow knights. Different characters within the same play will personify the audience differently. Edmund in *King Lear* speaks to fellow rogues, his brother Edgar in the same play speaks to compassionate friends.

There is a continuing relationship each time the character addresses the audience. It is as if the audience was a consistent character, like any partner in a play. This happens most with Shakespeare's villains—Richard III, Edmund from *King Lear*, Iago from *Othello*. They all begin speaking with great familiar ease to their audiences, a convention borrowed from medieval morality plays in which the Devil likewise boasted of his powers. Unlike the morality plays, where the dynamic was one-sided, as in a sermon, the exchange between villain and listener in a play by Shakespeare develops as a progression, almost a subplot all its own.

Look at the relationship between Macbeth and his audience. Through all five acts, the audience is the murderer's one true friend to whom he can be honest, even in defeat. At first Macbeth makes furtive contact, done on the sly in the middle of a scene with onstage friends:

MACBETH My thought, whose murder yet is but fantastical,
    Shakes so my single state of man, that function
    Is smother'd in surmise, and nothing is
    But what is not.
BANQUO Look, how our partner's rapt.
MACBETH (*aside*) If chance will have me King, why, chance may crown me
    Without my stir.

Macbeth, Act I, scene iii

When the time comes to murder, he hopes to persuade the audience to approve:

MACBETH If it were done when 'tis done, then 'twere well
    It were done quickly . . .

Macbeth, Act I, scene vii

On his way to commit the murder, Macbeth famously sees and speaks to an imaginary dagger hovering before him. Yet, even as he speaks to the air, Macbeth describes his hallucination to the audience:

MACBETH Mine eyes are made the fools o' the other senses,
    Or else worth all the rest. I see thee still;

And on thy blade and dudgeon gouts of blood,
Which was not so before. There's no such thing:
It is the bloody business which informs
Thus to mine eyes . . .

Macbeth, Act II, scene i

When the same speech resumes, Macbeth shares a vision with his listeners:

MACBETH Now o'er the one half-world
Nature seems dead, and wicked dreams abuse
The curtain'd sleep; witchcraft celebrates
Pale Hecate's offerings; and wither'd murder,
Alarum'd by his sentinel, the wolf,
Whose howl's his watch, thus with his stealthy pace,
With Tarquin's ravishing strides, towards his design
Moves like a ghost.

The point of view expands from the personal to the universal, exactly the opposite direction a point of view usually moves—from distanced narration to emotional identification—when stories are told in a "realistic" play.

By Act III, Macbeth is King, and the audience is still the confidante to whom he may admit the truth of his new status, and his dislike of his other old friends:

MACBETH To be thus is nothing;
But to be safely thus—our fears in Banquo
Stick deep; and in his royalty of nature
Reigns that which would be fear'd.

Macbeth, Act III, scene i

The character of Macbeth is that of an introspective man who wishes his nature to change to unthinking action. The transformations in his character are told to us as much as shown to us:

MACBETH . . . from this moment
The very firstlings of my heart shall be
The firstlings of my hand. And even now,
To crown my thoughts with acts, be it thought and done:
The castle of Macduff I will surprise;
Seize upon Fife; give to the edge o' the sword
His wife, his babes, and all unfortunate souls
That trace him in his line.

Macbeth, Act IV, scene i

As Macbeth describes the scene to follow, the boy playing Lady Macduff, like Juliet with Romeo, would have simultaneously taken his place onstage with Macbeth's description. One of the reasons the brief scene with Lady Macduff is often cut is that it takes more time to bring the "castle of Macduff" on and off stage than it does to play the scene. It's unnecessary, though, to have a castle onstage; the actor's description of his intentions will suffice.

By the play's end the role is characterized by the heroic and unsparing way Macbeth faces up to the consequences of his crimes:

> MACBETH I have liv'd long enough: my way of life
>   Is fall'n into the sear, the yellow leaf;
>   And that which should accompany old age,
>   As honor, love, obedience, troops of friends,
>   I must not look to have; but, in their stead,
>   Curses not loud but deep, mouth-honor, breath,
>   Which the poor heart would fain deny and dare not.
>
> *Macbeth, Act V, scene iii*

From furtive aside to brutal honesty, Macbeth's continuing intimacy with the audience allows an actor to reveal aspects of the role that are otherwise difficult if not impossible to express.

Combine Techniques

In plays written by Shakespeare, Brecht, Chekhov, or Euripides, narrative analysis can be used in conjunction with the other forms of analysis described in previous chapters. The telling of a story may itself be an episode, character quotes may include Stanislavsky's tasks, and descriptive passages will depend on images. World of the play analysis helps organize the meaning of it all. Yet, even if a narrative analysis includes other methods, storytelling has a distinctive feel of its own because it relies on the audience to play the scene in their heads and so combine the different techniques of representation.

To return to the metaphor of Cubism, a Cubist painter juxtaposes a realistic drawing of the side of a glass with the abstraction of an emblem, such as the hole in the guitar, placed next to the patterns of faked (though convincing) wood grain and pasted-on wallpaper. Out of combined techniques and skills, a new beauty is formed.

Translate those painting techniques by your Rosetta Stone of acting techniques: the realistic drawing is the equivalent of a likeness constructed by tasks and actions, the hole of the guitar is an image, the wallpaper fragment evidence of the world of the play. Placed together, they create a satisfying composition like an actor's episode, and within the frame they combine to tell the story of the table top. If a painter can do all that with what the French call *nature morte*—not just still life, but *dead* life—think of what you can do to bring life to a story onstage.

PART VI

COMPARING, CHOOSING, AND COMBINING APPROACHES

René Magritte, detail from *Clairvoyance*

CHAPTER 14

COMPARING APPROACHES

Different Methods Yield Different Results

Different approaches to a role result in different performances. The outcome of any one approach will vary from performer to performer, and some approaches can mimic or reproduce the effects of others. But, generally, there will be characteristic distinctions. Each of the five approaches of acting we've examined in this book will reproduce a distinct tone, require a certain set of skills, and mandate a period of time necessary for mastery. Each invites an audience to participate in a characteristic relationship with the performers as well. Each approach will have limitations—some intended, some hotly denied.

Differences between rival acting techniques have been striking enough to incite riots. If you remember from Chapter 2, a mob in nineteenth-century New York went into a fury arguing that an American actor's romantic posturings, rather than a British actor's stiffly classical poses, were images best suited to portray the vigorous character of Macbeth. In another town, that same British actor, William Macready, was playing Hamlet, and partisans of American acting made their views known by tossing onto the stage (during the Rosencrantz and Guildenstern scene) half the raw carcass of a dead sheep (109). In 1930s Russia, an early advocate of the Socialist Revolution in the arts, Vsevolod Meyerhold, was shot dead for attacking the monopoly of Socialist Realism onstage.

A more pleasantly memorable contest between approaches to acting could be described as the War of the Camellias. This happened when the refined Italian actress Eleonora Duse chose to perform a few of the same roles as the grandiloquent French diva, Sarah Bernhardt. Among those roles was Bernhardt's most popular: a dying courtesan known as Camille (for her love of those extravagant flowers). Both actresses were undeniably superb in the role. They were undeniably different in the role as well, but both had confidence enough in their craft to invite comparisons.

It was on Bernhardt's crafty invitation that Duse came to Paris in the spring of 1897 to play at the Théâtre de la Renaissance—a theater Bernhardt owned (110). During Duse's Camille, Bernhardt sat prominently in a box and crooned in pleasure. Her fellow French audience members were less enthused—at first. Duse's work was subtle, quiet, and smooth. It hid its craft. Even sitting in the audience Bernhardt called attention to herself. Bernhardt's tubercular heroine was famous for dying onstage in a glorious death scene, but Duse didn't even cough, not once during the whole play.

289

By the final curtain, Duse had won over the French audience, for which Bernhardt never forgave her. Bernhardt's acting was compared to "an army with banners, instantly perceptible and triumphantly sweeping all before it. Duse was the still small voice which gradually, but all the more powerfully, undermined all resistance, and at last penetrated to the very heart of the audience" (111).

Actions and obstacles are quiet and smooth

Like Duse's work, an actor's use of an inner structure of tasks and actions is meant to achieve a performance with a deceptively dull finish. The craft necessary deliberately hides itself. Meyerhold used to say there are certain kinds of theater that act like Borgia poison: they take hold before the person swallowing them knows what's happening. Stanislavsky's system of tasks and actions—gleaned, in part, by watching Duse perform—is that kind of theater. The technique guards against stylization as unreal, avoids direct address as bad taste, considers awareness of an audience a distraction, and uses "cartoon-like" and "caricature" as words of severe criticism (and, in Meyerhold's case, an excuse for execution).

Weaving actions with obstacles—the necessary skill called for by this technique—takes time to establish in rehearsal. Working this way, an actor's performance must include the reactions of other actors, especially as obstacles, and these effects cannot be predicted or simulated. They are arrived at after repetition, rethinking, and refinement.

The collision of action and obstacle hopes to provoke an instant sympathetic response from an audience.* For film performances, playing a task to the camera dependably establishes a relationship as if speaking to another person. It also, when necessary, provides a trustworthy technique to use when the presence of the camera is to be ignored—by concentrating one's attention on actions and obstacles. All the films mentioned in this book provide examples of both uses of the technique. Typical are the scenes in Sidney Lumet's *Long Day's Journey into Night* that record what is usually stage dialogue as opposite sides of a conversation, alternately told to the camera.

The aim to have a stage performance taken for life itself, rather than artifice, has meant that working exclusively with a through-line of actions and obstacles often hits an obstacle itself when applied to stylized plays—Shakespeare's, for example—where characters are presented in a deliberately stylized way. Another drawback: ignoring the audience has a tendency to shut out the public. When the actor is oblivious to the need to keep the audience's attention, the pace of his performance can drag and the dynamics of the play can sag. Duse herself was criticized for her "air of listlessness" and acting in all her roles as "a guardian angel half asleep at her post over humanity" (112). Bernhardt wrote in her *Memoirs* (still shocked, perhaps, by the cough-less Camille): "Eleonora Duse is more an actress than an artist . . . she puts on other people's gloves, but puts them on inside out" (113).

---

*Still, whatever their response, sympathizers are usually meant to stay unnoticed, sitting on the other side of an impenetrable, if invisible, barrier.

Episodes are broad and sharp

Performances established by episodes tend to be bold and graphic, easily communicated to an audience, easily photographed. Working this way, performers may call attention to their craft. Bertolt Brecht—who codified a system of playing episodes that called for dynamic oppositions, transactions, and crucial *gests*—noted with approval the nonchalant excellence of the Chinese actor Mei Lanfang, smiling at his own prowess while performing a *gest* that turned the long sleeves of his costume into a sign for passing clouds.

Working this way, cartooning, caricature, and direct address are all apt—as long as they clarify the episode onstage to the audience. Because the aim of episodic playing is communication, there is little danger that one will get lost in self-expression. Once established in rehearsal, episodes are quickly and easily repeated; it is an approach almost always used to fit an understudy into an ongoing production. It works well for episodic television, too, where the usually slight material would be burdened by detailed psychological preparation. The pace brought about by using this approach is usually workmanlike: brisk and sharp.

Sometimes the broad simplifications of episodic technique turn gross; sometimes the cartoon results obscure the subtleties of a script or situation. When *gests* lose their function and cease to identify a transaction or establish a role in an episode, they can end up exploited by a ham for self-aggrandizement. When one aspect of an opposition overwhelms the other, the amalgam of oppositions can result in a muddle, rather than a mystery. When oppositions are balanced and *gests* are connected to the episode, performances are memorable and strong.

An episodic approach avoids psychological understructure, which makes it limited for plays that require subtext—Brecht himself never asked his actors to perform Chekhov. Meyerhold had the actress known as "The Russian Duse," Kommisarzhevskaya, play *Hedda Gabler* as a series of Egyptian-derived poses and alienated monotones. The misguided result doesn't encourage further exploration.

For one example of a well-balanced opposition in a film, look at the scene in *The Night of the Hunter* when the executioner talks of going into another line of business, even as his wife disapproves in the background. For another, study Robert De Niro's performance throughout *Raging Bull*, or look at Francis Ford Coppola's *The Godfather* (1972). Marlon Brando is an affectionate grandpa in one scene, a cold killer in another. The omnipotent Godfather's power is always used apologetically; Brando's hands lie folded and calm as he orders someone shot. Brando is a Stella Adler-trained actor, but one of his first jobs was playing in a *Twelfth Night* that Erwin Piscator supervised.

Onstage, the homely reality of episodic performances—that a group of people are play-acting—unabashedly invites the audience to consider human relations for their beauty, their form, their meaning, and the craftsmanship of their execution by performers. This kind of acting isn't meant to be taken for reality, just as a Cézanne still-life isn't meant to be mistaken for a blotchy photograph of fruit. Like the separated colors of an Impressionist painting that are meant to be blended in the eye of the beholder, the dynamic opposition of an episode in performance is meant to be completed by an audience piqued to resolve the contradictions.

When realistic behavior is performed as a quote within an episode, it is made to seem strange—alien—set as it is within a frankly theatrical context. The English language connotations of the word *alienated* have led to a misunderstanding that the public watching alienated acting is meant to stay cold, themselves alienated. Wrong. The audience members watching a well-played episode are meant to sit emotionally involved—but not identified with—the situation they are asked to witness and judge.

Images are persuasive and appeal to emotions

When an actor's source for playing is an image (a fantasy mask or a personal memory), what results has the potential to become the most compelling performance of all. Inner images make a performance seem to glow; such performances are often described as if a light shone from inside the actor. The audience sits rapt, mesmerized. The technique to achieve this can be innate or developed in class; it cannot be worked up within the time constraints of a rehearsal period, and actors who rely on images must already have the craft to reliably reproduce results.

When images work best, the performance of the play is a significant event in the performer's life; and the audience intuits that the actor is working out some personal issue or living out a long-wished-for fantasy. Driven by impulsive force, the text in performance takes on a powerful immediacy and an arresting tone of unpredictable pacing and irregular dynamic changes, which, having been executed, seem inevitable and secretly rhythmic. Sometimes the connection is obvious. When Ira Aldridge played Shylock, it was obvious to all that the classical poses and elocution cloaked the black actor's identification with the persecuted Jew.

On film, an exclusive use of inner images provides splendid material to be photographed and then reshaped by the editor and director. A stage actor, though, has no such control over such a performance.

An exclusive use of inner images will often have technical failings, usually of speech, but when caught up in their own corresponding images, the public can be persuaded to ignore or forgive poor craft. Screen actors exploit this effect when they go onstage to perform plays for which they have no gift other than an admirable ambition and personal identification. Film records a few such failures: watch Marlon Brando stumble through the role of Marc Antony in *Julius Caesar* (1952). He does look the part. John Gielgud, who played the title role, reports that on the first day they met, Brando invited Gielgud to record one of the Antony speeches on a tape-recorder in his dressing room. "He had tapes of Maurice Evans and John Barrymore and three or four other actors, and listened to them every day to improve his diction" (114). Gielgud gave some suggestions and was startled to see that Brando explicitly followed them the next day. Bravely, Brando was trying to cram the effects of years of training and experience into the few weeks of a film shoot. It was impossible, and he often lost his voice. Such technical work as speaking verse or pacing a succession of episodes requires at least some channeling of impulse into a form.

On the other hand, exclusive reliance on form has its own limitations, as when an outer image tries to mask an inner hollowness. The passion of executing something with skill or the ham's enthusiasm for showing-off can be contagious enough to corrupt an audience into a willing accomplice. George Bernard Shaw, who was a partisan of Duse's, described Bernhardt's splendor in this way:

> She is beautiful with the beauty of her school and entirely inhuman and incredible . . . instead of imposing on you, she adds her own piquancy by looking you straight in the face and saying, in effect, "Now who would ever suppose that I am a grandmother?" (115)

Dietrich's warmly familiar performance as a Teutonic floozy in *Touch of Evil* is done with just this same enthusiasm and a self-appreciative wink. Olivier's Othello was criticized for its self-appreciation—and it did not help the performance for Lord Olivier to say in an interview just before *Othello* opened that his life's work was "to lead the public towards an appreciation of acting so that they will come not only to see the play but to watch acting for its own sake." A critic wrote of the results: "*Othello* [is] a kind of bad acting of which only a great actor is capable . . . Sir Laurence can move every muscle at will—I regret he could not move me" (116).

When the concentration and skill needed to complete outer images fails to compensate for a lack of inner content, then showmanship falls flat; the collapse often brought on by rote repetition. This happened to Eugene O'Neill's father, who as a young actor had the talent to be a great Iago and the potential to grow into an American Lear. He instead bought the rights to a blockbuster hit based on the novel *The Count of Monte Cristo* and spent the next thirty years playing the same role for over six-thousand performances—including climactic scenes from the play in vaudeville (where, by the way, Bernhardt performed climactic scenes from Racine's *Phèdre* [117]). In *Long Day's Journey into Night*, Eugene O'Neill drew on his father to create a similar actor named James Tyrone (118). Late in the fourth act, when family secrets are spilling, the old man has this to say about himself:

> TYRONE I've never admitted this to anyone before, lad, but tonight I'm so heartsick I feel at the end of everything . . . That God-damned play I bought for a song and made such a great success in—a great money success—it ruined me with its promise of an easy fortune. I didn't want to do anything else, and by the time I woke up to the fact I'd become a slave to the damned thing. . . . I'd lost the great talent I once had through years of easy repetition, never learning a new part, never really working hard . . . Yet before I bought the damned thing I was considered one of the three or four young actors with the greatest artistic promise in America.*

---

*Freudians would, perhaps, trace the source of the elder O'Neill's behavior to a traumatic experience he had when playing Jesus for an 1879 production of the *Passion Play*—a production in which the producer, David Belasco, had a live flock of sheep onstage. Strangers would sink to their knees when they met O'Neill on the street, and it seems they weren't kidding.

At their best, technical performances meld outer images with inner to create something viscerally unforgettable. Performing this role of James Tyrone in *Long Day's Journey into Night*, Laurence Olivier, in his last stage role, stood precariously balanced on the edge of a table, teetering on the brink of falling in order to change a light bulb—giving an unforgettable image of the man's stinginess, willing to risk death for a few cents. Having gripped the audience's attention, Olivier then nonchalantly stepped backward and landing gracefully on his toes. The stunt took some practice, but it was fueled by bitter memories of his own parsimonious father. Olivier said: "I didn't have to invent his eccentricities. I knew them all" (119).

The concentration and commitment necessary to perform outer images communicate themselves to the audience as surely as an inner image. When such commitment is lacking—or unappreciated by the audience—the response is slack and the performance dull. The time necessary to perform outer images, of course, depends on the difficulty and the experience of the performer. Olivier spent almost a year lowering the pitch of his voice in order to create his vocal mask for Othello; preparations for *Long Day's Journey* were also unusually long: four weekly readings, followed by seven weeks of rehearsals (120).

World of the play analysis transforms actors

A rigorous approach to playing a role using world of the play analysis transforms a performer, often to the point of the performer not being recognizable. The craft goes beyond disguise; it calls for skills of inner organization and conviction. To play Marc Antony, Marlon Brando agreed to be tricked out in a toga and a very Roman haircut, but he had little other connection with the world of Julius Caesar or Shakespeare's version of it. In fact, Brando felt so silly he used to tuck a cigarette behind his ear. But when Brando auditioned for his role as the Godfather he stuck cotton in his mouth and had himself filmed in grainy black-and-white, as in a home movie. People who saw the footage liked it very much, but wondered if the old Italian guy could act. He could.

Extreme reliance on a world of the play approach has the danger of losing the audience, as various traveling troupes have discovered while performing in front of foreign audiences who do not share the vocabulary of gestures or stage conventions, much less a common language. This was the case among Mei Lanfang's students when they toured to New York. The skill needed to perform the Beijing opera is undeniable; it is also, for the moment, unappreciated in the West. The problem can be solved when the audience, too, is characterized in the world of the play. The original cast of *Tony 'n Tina's Wedding* used world of the play rules both as the backbone for their improvisations and for enfolding the audience's participation into the action of the play. During Sarah Bernhardt's revival of Racine's *Esther*, an actor playing Louis XIV sat in the audience to effectively recast the public as courtiers.

World of the play analysis can be done in advance of rehearsals and continue to be applied during rehearsals, as well as in performance, as it folds new information into the mix. The resulting performance will usually hide the necessary craft, the point being to identify the character with the actor by placing both in the context of the world of the play. On stage, such an approach reinforces the dictates of the script, and focuses work within the ensemble to pay attention to what it is collectively creating.

The challenge in this approach is to internalize the rules of the world in which you have been set. Enthusiastic faking doesn't work too well. When an amateurish teenage Shelley Winters crashed the auditions during the national search for *Gone With the Wind*'s Scarlett O'Hara, she dressed herself in a Brooklyn girl's idea of a southern belle and drawled out a Brooklyn girl's idea of a—kinda sorta—southern accent. The producer and the talent scout laughed, but the director (George Cukor) had the generosity to sit Winters down and suggest that she get some speech lessons (121). A few years later, when Winters—by that time a starlet in Hollywood—asked to audition for *A Place in the Sun*, she was told she was too glamorous to be taken seriously as a factory girl. But Shelley Winters knew the world of striving workers; in her own way, she was such a person herself. Her hair dyed bottle-brown, dressed in her sister's drab clothes, Winters sat waiting for an hour in the lobby for her interview—opposite the director who was waiting for *her*. When the director, George Stevens, realized that the girl he was staring at was a transformed Shelley Winters, he eventually offered her the part, but insisted he be allowed to photograph Winters in this drab persona. She agreed, of course. Her sister loaned her the clothes for the movie, too (121).

Storytelling brackets technical difficulties

The craft to tell a story onstage requires understanding, repetition, and memorization rather than the more traditional skills of other acting techniques: impersonation and emotional commitment. Technical demands for performers telling stories increase as speeches grow long, when the action requires a shifting point of view, or when there is a call for skillful character quotes. The tone of a story told onstage will depend on the tale being told; the dramatic effect of the story will be a mutual creation between teller and audience. The separation of performer in storytelling from the material coaxes audience members to enliven the text and events for themselves.

Storytelling as an exclusive technique is an enduring art form with a long history and heritage held in common by all continents: from the African *griot* to the Australian dream master to the Siberian shaman to the bards in European countries. Frequently in the history of storytelling the most celebrated performers are blind, and the performer's reliance on inner sight seems to inspire the audience to stage the events in a vision of their own.

The distance between performer and story allows an unskilled actor some refuge and excuse for limitations in craft. Character quotes can be minimal and still be dramatically effective. A story with a heightened emotional task can be very effectively performed by putting the storyteller's point of view, emotionally, in the third person, rather than reliving in horror or ecstasy what is described. There is a discipline to keeping oneself cool, and it isn't easy, either. Brecht described how Helene Weigel chose to maintain a taut tension with her listeners while describing the horror of the Servant's speech in *Oedipus the King*.

295

She announced the death of her mistress by calling out her "dead, dead" in a wholly unemotional and penetrating voice, her "Jocasta has died" without any sorrow but so firmly and definitely that the very fact of her mistress's death carried more weight at that precise moment than could have been generated by any grief of her own . . . it became plain to even the most emotionally punch-drunk spectator that here a decision had been carried out which called for his acquiescence (122).

For Greek classics, and the plays written by, among others, Shakespeare, Brecht, and Sam Shepard, storytelling techniques are inescapable. More often then not, the nature of the material undermines other approaches. When storytelling is used inappropriately, it becomes arch, too distanced from the material to be anything more than a false pose of naïveté. Bad children's theater is full of such over-explained and over-articulated performances; so is the musical comedy stage. Stories on screen are sometimes piped in as voiceover, and this distancing effect can also make telling a story ridiculous. The most conventional form for telling a story in a film is a close-up. A more sophisticated example is Katharine Hepburn's final speech as the mother in the film of *Long Day's Journey into Night*, where director Sidney Lumet uses the change in camera angles to amplify rather than disguise the work of the actress as she changes her point of view.

Ignorance Is Not Bliss—It's Ignorance

Single-minded devotion

In order to pass on a heritage of excellence, some schools of acting require single-minded devotion—despite the reality that there are many ways to approach a performance. The zealous gurus of India demand that their students' toes point upward; jealous Method teachers prefer to rely on personal history for images and look suspiciously at any other source. Like orthodox religions that permit no flirtation with other gods or experiments with sin, pure-minded schools of acting demand that a performer's creativity flow through a single conduit.

The aim of perfecting craft is laudable, and distractions are many in learning any technique, but it is important to remember that the founders and great practitioners of acting theories are more often than not synthesizers, not purists. Helene Weigel griped that the younger actors who were trained in Brecht's Berliner Ensemble didn't use observed behavior for their *gests*; she herself had gotten an idea for *Mother Courage* by copying someone she saw walking on the street (123). Shelley Winters's reliance on the inner images of the Method is famous; her use of dress-up and outer images supports that work. Olivier's tics as Tyrone were based on emotional memories of his father. The American actress Eva Le Gallienne had the privilege of watching Duse in the wings for many performances and was astounded to discover that what seemed like spontaneous response to situations was repeated every night the same way and with the same intonations. "Never had I seen such virtuosity concealed" (124). Frustrated rehearsing *A Month in the Country*, Moscow Art Theater actress Olga Knipper, at Stanislavsky's urging, abandoned actions and obstacles for an episodic approach.

Take advantage of opportunity

Like Weigel or Olivier, or any of the other actors mentioned in the text, when you create your own synthesis and choose what works for you, you will become a mature performer and an artist in your own right. You will have the confidence, like Duse, to compare yourself to Bernhardt; you will have the bravado of Brando to incorporate Gielgud's suggestions; you will develop the pragmatism of Olga Knipper to use what works. Close-mindedness will prevent you from benefiting from what other people can give you, and over time, it will limit your expertise and freeze a supple response even in your chosen approach. Choosing more than one method is not a sign of weakness; it can be a sign of strength. There is a passage in the Koran that can be translated to say, in the voice of the Creator:

> I could have made one religion. I am, after all, All-Mighty, but I chose to have many paths, so that they might compete with each other for works of goodness.
>
> *The Koran, The Table, 5:49*

Just so, as you gain strength in your craft and confidence in your choices, let the many approaches to acting compete for works of goodness.

CHAPTER 15

CHOOSING AN APPROACH

There are three factors to consider when choosing an approach to perform a role in a play: your own abilities, the nature of the text, and the time available for rehearsal. Of course, the text sets out the challenge of a terrain to be crossed. You can't walk on water no matter how fast you can run; you will sink and drown in syllables if you try to recite Shakespeare's verse as if it were everyday conversation. To go under water, it helps to have scuba gear. Excuse the forced image, but finding tasks and the actions to accomplish them will help you dive into Strindberg. No matter what the terrain, it is *you* who are crossing it. If you can't swim, you'd better take a boat—and avoid diving. To switch images, no matter what a composer has written on a page, a pianist can't play down to the fifth octave below C major or sustain a single note the way a violinist or a singer might. As an actor, you are your own instrument; start with your instrument's capabilities.

Start with Yourself

Outside of class, use what works for you

In your professional work, use what you know you can do. There will be certain techniques you are naturally adept at or will have learned to perform well. With these approaches you can establish a base from which to set out on unforeseen adventures.

Class is the time to exploit your weakness and expand your range with exercises and experiments that build character—*your* character, not the character in the play. Rehearsal process is also a time for experiments, but experiments of a different kind, using the craft you can command rather than skills of which you are unsure. By the time you are collaborating with other people, you should have something you can reliably contribute. That's what makes you a professional rather than an amateur. When Neil Simon's *The Odd Couple* was first produced, the gruff, hangdog actor Walter Matthau was asked to play the role of the gruff, messy Oscar. Matthau read the script and liked it so much he refused to take part unless he could invest in the production. He then asked to be considered for the overly neat Felix—so that he might demonstrate his range. Do that with someone else's play, Neil Simon said. For his play he wanted what Matthau could dependably do well; that's why they were hiring him. That's why you will be hired, too.

Not every actor will be good at the same thing. It is self-sabotage to compare yourself with other actors' skills. If you come from a volatile emotional background, you may find it easy to access emotional images in order to cry or laugh at will, but episodes and transactions may initially baffle you. Ignore them and rely on the other actors' ensemble work to point out the episodes. Your contribution to the ensemble will be to polish the *gest*—once it is identified—with the force of your personal images. If you have a knack for discovering episodes and an instinct for performing them, that is what you will bring to the process—your own process and everyone else's, including the audience's.

Understand the limits of your method

Recognize your own limitations and craft and compensate with what you do well. For some performers it is difficult to arrive at personal images, except in private, if ever at all. If such images are a torture for you to find, don't torture yourself, use another approach. You don't need to feel inadequate as an actor because you don't work from personal images. And you don't need to discuss what you're not doing. If you play an episode, work at a task, or add a fantasy image—and shut your mouth about your lack of emotional recall—chances are partisans of the Method will never know the difference. They will probably think you are keeping mum about your traumatic past in order to preserve its efficacy onstage.

There is a contagious nervousness in watching something done badly or in an unsure manner. This is intentional in street performances like juggling, where a few dropped bowling pins are meant to build sympathy for the performers among the gathering crowd, as well as build suspense: those flaming wands they're tossing in the air might fall too, and set the performers on fire. While acting in a play, however—even on the street—such fumbling distracts from the action and calls attention to the actor, not the role. Turning their weaknesses to strengths was the trick of Olivier and Gielgud, but in order for you to do that you need to know what your weaknesses and strengths are.

No matter what the method, there is a physical pleasure the audience takes in watching someone display the mastery of a hard-won craft. If one way of working gets you consistently successful results, stick with it for as it long as it fits you into a play. Be careful, though, that the play is not reinterpreted to fit your way of working. The giveaway that this is happening is when the text undergoes massive cutting, bold-faced rewriting, shuffling of passages, or heavy-handed interpolation of new material.

Sometimes the text is realigned in order to gain a fresh understanding from a new point of view. Under the heading of *post-modernism* a number of classic texts have been shuffled to accommodate acting techniques and directorial concepts, often for the same reasons that, to accommodate romantic acting, *King Lear* was performed for two centuries with a happy ending and some of the more theatrical lines in the eighteenth-century staging of Shakespeare's *Macbeth* were added by another writer to include—among other up-to-date notions—sentimental repentance (125). Post-modern or sentimental, such "improvements," like the alterations to the ancient Greek drapery that transformed it into the "Gypsy" of the *Zingara*, can be very effective onstage. Sometimes they're not. The poet Coleridge said that to see the great romantic actor Kean perform Richard III was to read Shakespeare as if by flashes of lightning (126). The vividness of the metaphor is stirring—wouldn't most performers like to have the power of lightning? Yet, what Coleridge meant to suggest was that in between the bolts of illumination, most of the time the play was plunged into darkness.*

You can go on quite well keeping to the same way of working from play to play if you accept the limitations of the repertory that you can perform. Mae West built a rewarding career on her own terms. Once again, learn from Mae. Never much impressed by anyone else's writing, in her vaudeville days she used to sing a song called "Eugene O'Neill, You've Put a Curse on Broadway" (127).†

Look to See What the Text Suggests

Each of the plays discussed in the text will suggest certain ways to rehearse and perform. The chart lists some playwrights and which methods might prove successful and appropriate for their characteristic texts. Some choices are obvious. Brecht's plays come complete with headlined episodes; Chekhov's pauses imply a thoughtful subtext of actions and obstacles; the form of Shakespeare's verse demands a world of the play analysis.

Study the play's strengths in order to enhance them

When choosing an approach to a text it is often more effective to choose an acting technique that will complement, not duplicate, what the text already does well. There are many examples of how this might be done among the scenes we've considered for exercises.

- A text written by Brecht will state episodes so unambiguously it makes sense for a creative performer to work from images, so that the *gests* of the episodes gain dimension. This was Weigel's technique.
- The lush imagery of Shakespeare could use a structure of episodes provided by an actor; this will help avoid turning the performance into a poetry recitation. According to Tommaso Salvini, acting came down to *Voice! Voice! Voice!* Yet, his acting clearly defined episodes enough for him to perform in Italian throughout the world—and still be understood.
- The world of a play written by Ionesco or Beckett is its own, and not to be found in life. Paying attention to the rules of the world of the play will help an actor establish the meaning of behavior, but if actions that defer to or defy the rules are played in a through-line of tasks and obstacles, the *roles*, as well as the rules, will gain emotion and substance. This is De Niro's technique.

---

*It is possible that the critic was also referring to Kean's inspiration from a whiskey bottle.

†Mae was not the only one who felt this way. After seeing *Beyond the Horizon*, O'Neill's father said to him, "It's all right Gene, if that's what you want to do, but people come to the theater to forget their troubles, not be reminded of them. What are you trying to do—send the audience home to commit suicide?" (128).

- Ibsen's and Chekhov's subtle behavior can be made clear to an audience by episodic playing, and Duse, according to Eva Le Gallienne's report, seems to have done just that.
- The texts written by O'Neill, Genet, and Lorca present vibrant imagery and episodes so blatantly theatrical that in performance they can tip into melodrama. World of the play analysis or a structure of tasks and actions will make performances seem less overblown. It was Stanislavsky's pleasure to apply his system to melodramas and make their flat characters and lurid situations believable and moving.

These are just suggestions. For any and all texts, however, a performer should pay attention to the way a script provides a boost up for a performance or a series of pitfalls that a careful choice of method can help to skirt.

Distinguish between faithfulness and obedience to the text

A sense of responsibility and faithfulness to a text rewards a performer in the way that a sense of responsibility and faithfulness rewards the partners in a marriage. Still, as in a marriage, over time it does no good to ignore what's missing in a play or pretend that what's missing is unnecessary. Blind obedience is the role of a slave, not a partner. If you recognize that a text—say, a monologue—is long on images but short on events, by all means don't pretend it's not a bore: add some episodes by using a narrative analysis with a changing point of view. Many of the plays that call for storytelling can use some personalization for the story to gain emotional resonance. Sam Shepard's stories, or those by Aeschylus, work better onstage when they become *your* stories. When you can visualize what you are speaking about, you can erect images of your own to support the playwright's. While deciding which approach to use, don't just look at what words are on the page; imagine what the lines might *become*. Visualize them, like the artist who is studying an egg while he paints a picture of a bird in flight in *Clairvoyance*, the 1936 painting by René Magritte.

Assess the Time Available for Preparation

The length of time available for rehearsal often determines how you may prepare. A short rehearsal period will curtail certain approaches; a longer period will afford time for other approaches. A lengthy rehearsal period doesn't necessarily result in better performances; a down-and-dirty rehearsal period doesn't always end up with flashy bad *shtick*. The disastrous Moscow Art Theater *Julius Caesar* rehearsed for two years. Some of the better performances in Tennessee Williams's plays had to be done very quickly: the playwright had the disconcerting habit of showing up at the theater during previews with newly written pages of text that needed an immediate response in order to be inserted into the performance later that week—or even that night. Sometimes the speed and pressure of fast work bring out a bone-rattling intuitive response; sometimes a long time is just enough time to kill off good instincts and dull the spontaneity of execution.

Use all the time available (you will anyway)

Given a leisurely period—by commercial American standards, anything over six weeks—you can meander to enlightenment and have the pleasure of tumbling into unexpected successes. Even without meandering it takes time to specify tasks, try actions, adjust to obstacles, and rethink the process in order to refine choices and dependably repeat the path you've marked. Squeezed to a typically tight deadline of four weeks or less, you will need to chase after a solution with little chance to do more than obey the dictates of the text, establish episodes, learn your lines, and attempt to do tasks as improvisations.

The director's use of time is an essential to consider. Some directors permit experimentation, even in ways they don't initially understand. Shelley Winters reports that director George Stevens did just that at rehearsals for *A Place in the Sun*. Some directors will take time in rehearsal to set up improvisations that explore images and build the world of the play. When he's preparing a film, Robert De Niro has the respect—and star power—to be granted improvisation time. Other directors will work strictly with episodes and staging, and expect you to do any other work on your own. Laurence Olivier was proud to be such a director. "I'd rather run the scene eight times than have wasted time chattering away . . . arguing about motivations and so forth is a lot of rot"* (129).

You can maximize your handling of a director's use of time by translating the director's vagaries into the language of your approach. For example, for an actor patiently using Stanislavsky's system, the lazy catchall direction "Do it more" translates into a challenge to build up *obstacles*. When directing Marilyn Monroe, an exasperated Laurence Olivier reportedly demanded: "Be sexy!" Such a directive—or any demand to "be" something—means bite your tongue, go home, and find an *image*. "Do it like I just showed you"—which even Stanislavsky would say—means learn the *gest* and polish it. Don't explain your translations; traffic-cop directors resent even that much talk as time stolen from their opportunity to work. In such a situation you'll want to redouble your attention to what the other people are doing in order to compensate for the missed opportunity to include them in any experiments. There is no need, by the way, to translate a demand to "act better." Silence is best, but if you must reply, a pleasant response is: "I'll try. Do you think you can direct better?"

Some theater ensembles have the luxury of an open-ended period of preparation, and they rehearse hoping they will create something that the ensemble would like to share with an audience. Given such time to make ready, images can be thoroughly explored and the world of the play can be investigated with archeological precision.

That "work expands to the time allotted for it" is jokingly called Parkinson's Law, but it is no joke that whatever time you have will be filled. If you have three weeks to

---

*This conceptual distinction can be seen in various languages: the word for *rehearsal* in Italian and Russian is *repetizzi*, "repetition." In German, it's *probe*, "attempt." The English *rehearse*, with the *re-* prefix, implies *re-peat*.

rehearse, you will use all of them. If you have three months, likewise; if you have three days, the same. There is a theory that being ready too early runs the risk of a performance growing stale. It remains a theory because being ready too early doesn't happen often enough to confirm any side effects. One of the corniest (and maybe the oldest) of theater jokes is that Thespis's first comment after he stepped out of the Ancient Greek chorus to invent the role of actor was a self-deprecating "it needed another week."

Pack more into the rehearsal time by being prepared

The depth of some plays demands and inspires a lot more thinking than a four- or six-week rehearsal period allows. Like Brando as Marc Antony, if you cram preparation for highly complex work into a short time, you'll end up using someone else's images and trying out someone else's technique that will sit as an embarrassment on your shoulders like the ill-fitting clothes described in *Macbeth*.

You can make better use of available rehearsal time if you are already familiar with the play before you begin rehearsals, so that when you need to rehearse a demanding role you will have something to contribute with responses of your own. Read plays before you're cast in them; read plays in advance to learn what is to be expected of you. If you prefer, rather than read, go watch plays in performance. In theory, you want to become as familiar with the situations and characters as if they were gossip.

This is easier than you think for the classic repertory, which is the easiest and shortest set of literature to master. There are maybe two hundred great novelists, maybe two thousand great poets. There are fewer than twenty-five world-class playwrights. Who they are is not really debatable. Arguments rage about who else to include—Nigeria's Wole Soyinka? Japan's Chikamatsu? There is little argument whose company they would join. The "Borgia poison" of this book is that you've already been exposed to most of the playwrights. Drop Ionesco if you like, and replace him with Pirandello—although so far English translations don't do the Italian justice. Excuse the Americans on the list as patriotic prejudice.* Add Aristophanes and Strindberg and George Bernard Shaw and maybe Carlo Goldoni and you'll know practically all of the core authors, if not all their plays. A few others have contributed one or two more: Turgenev (*A Month in the Country*), Büchner (*Woyzeck, Danton's Death*), Wedekind (*Spring's Awakening, Earth Spirit*), Gogol (*The Government Inspector*), Alfred Jarry (*Ubu Roi*). Find more for yourself—how about the Restoration comedies? Texts by these playwrights have endured because they have something to say about human relationships: they remain destinations for an actor's ambition because they are satisfying places to visit and inhabit. Time has polished such plays with repetition, not just reputation.

As American actors you'll want to know about our own contemporary playwrights, if for no other reason than to avoid ending up like W.S. Gilbert's fool from *The Mikado* (130):

---

*And every country will have its own. Among others: Schiller in Germany, Corneille in France, Calderón in Spain, Ostrovsky in Russia; writers whose plays, though undeniably important in their natural culture, don't quite work in translation or in front of an audience that doesn't share the culture. There are also writers, Plautus among them, who are more important for their influence than for any single script or enduring performance history.

The idiot who praises in enthusiastic tones
All centuries but this one, and every country but his own.

The pragmatic reason for knowing contemporary plays, of course, is to get a job. The more lasting benefit will be our profession's gift to understanding the world. A play is a set of words that are a formula for human interactions. A contemporary play articulates contemporary relationships, which, in turn, influence interpretations and understanding of classic scripts. Knowing texts by August Wilson will open your eyes to racism and heroism among Americans; knowing the work of Caryl Churchill will open your eyes to the masks of sex, power, and class in England. David Mamet's dialogue reveals the musical rhythm of everyday speech; he once said that when he re-writes a line he tries to keep the same number of syllables and stresses (131).

If you live with an awareness of a text, over time it will reveal itself in your life. Births, deaths, failures, successes, and much more will be woven into the fabric of your understanding. If, for example, you are familiar with the text of *Hedda Gabler*, you will notice similar events in life. The hypocrites you meet will make you think of Judge Brack; the mediocre survivors, of Tesman; the suicides, of Hedda. It's not that you put your life on hold while you prepare—few of us can afford to do that, or would want to. The interlacing of other aspects of your life with the text fortify both.

Sometimes the best use of time is to wait and see

You don't need to pick any one approach at first. If you have no immediate inspiration to choose one approach, wait until something suggests itself. Before it does, trust that enough will happen in rehearsal to keep you occupied. In your notebook, if you're keeping one, you can jot down your experiences and impressions without knowing at first how to apply them: an image here (James Tyrone is like your father), a task there (he'd like to gain his son's respect), a rule of the world of the play that you can't help noticing (respect is beautiful, the truth is ugly), a change in a point of view that the playwright has stated as a stage direction (*sadly*) or indicated with a pause. If you're not keeping a notebook you will still be gathering sensations until they coalesce into an avalanche of a decision. The momentum of the other actors may persuade you to go along with what they are doing. The director may ask that you work in a certain way. Because certain approaches lead to certain results, going with the flow of rehearsal is one way to build a consistent world of the play for the production, although by no means the only way.

As your knowledge of the text and its situations and characters deepens, one method of working often leads to another, in the same way that you might take a plane across the ocean, a train from the airport, and a car from the train station to the boat landing—where you'll walk to your canoe and paddle to your island retreat. You may find that, with time, methods you do well can support and encourage other methods you would like to try. Meeting an immovable obstacle can set off the power of an emotional memory, prompting a decision to work with images. An image may suggest an episode. The clicking sound of the clasp on Mother Courage's moneybag set off Helene Weigel's imagination to a powerful opposition and evolved into a *gest* to be used while paying for her last living child's funeral: Weigel as Courage fished out a few coins and handed them over. Then she returned a single coin to the purse, closing the purse slowly and softly—in contrast to its usual business-like click (132).

Sitting back and watching what happens—waiting—may really be the best use of rehearsal time. When you are in performance, though, you should know what you are doing so that you can repeat it. No matter how long the rehearsal period, you want to face the audience with something you have to share. Bolstered by preparation, inspired by rehearsals, confident in technique, onstage you want to deliver dependable results.

As time goes on, the circle of your concentration grows wider; more of what happens in rehearsal and in your life will suggest itself for inclusion in playing your role—so many impressions and ideas that their range will often exceed what any one approach can organize. You don't need to choose one approach over the other; work can progress simultaneously on parallel routes. During the run of a performance, given a healthy instinct to consider more and more input, the impulse to combine techniques will be inevitable. The subjects of the next and last chapter are descriptions of how approaches might be combined, and a way to record such combinations.

CHAPTER 16

COMBINING APPROACHES

Braiding Your Work

When you combine approaches, you braid distinct trains of thought so that they wrap around each other and mutually support the progress of your work. Like a braid, the strand on top will be noticed, or seen, then it will be bent out of sight when another strand rises over it. As you continue to braid, each strand—even if out of sight—will once again rise back to the surface in its turn. Seen or not, each strand runs parallel to other strands as they, and it, extend in time. Turning your attention to images doesn't mean you will stop playing episodes; the episodes will keep going, laced with the inspiration of a line of images.

Technical skills and a vocabulary formed from different approaches will help you to identify and assign value to what happens in rehearsal and performance, and to place the results of your experiences where they might best support the ongoing process. Here are some suggestions for combining approaches to creating and performing a role. Circumstance, training, and personality will influence your choices.

Look for discrete units: episode, event, or image

Certain things will stand out as memorable when you first read a play: the death of your character, the role that reminds you of your Uncle Louie, the repetition of certain words in speeches. These kinds of responses will detach themselves from the rest of play and become, in your mind, discrete units.

This is analogous to the way a walk down a strange street gains landmarks once you recognize your hotel, or realize that the building with the flashing lights serves booze. Between those memorable highlights (or low-lifes), you will scratch out a route, and repetition will engrave it as habit—if you live in the same place long enough. When you prepare a role, a starting idea, separate by itself, will anchor the process of rehearsal, as a line would begin a drawing. You can naturally begin best with an episode, an event, or an image.

It's natural to begin with episodes

For Western thinkers, at least, the first impulse while reading a script is to figure out what happens. For a professional actor, *What do I do?* is usually the fourth inevitable question after *When is it scheduled?*, *How much do they pay?*, and *Where is it? What happens?* is the first thing an audience wants to know, and when the question isn't satisfied (although a complete answer can be delayed), "nothing is happening" and "the actors don't know what they're doing" are the most common criticisms.

The easiest way to rough-sketch an episode is to contrast the beginning and the end of a scene, and, if there are no noticeable differences, to imagine and investigate how there could be. A rough version of episodes, by clarifying the work of the ensemble, naturally becomes the armature on which the rest of the rehearsals hang. The episodes anchor the audience, too, so that they feel inclined to go with whatever else is part of the theatrical experience.

It is the essence of "braided thinking" that early rough sketches of an episode will be re-defined by later experience and knowledge. There is a dimension of time to rehearsal as to all aspects of theater; as rehearsals extend, your understanding of the episode will alter with the arrival of other approaches. Your first rough idea of an episode will be that RICHARD III TAKES A BRIDE; your later understanding of the world of the play might redefine the episode to RICHARD III TRAPS A VICTIM.

It's possible to begin with images

It's possible to begin an approach to a role with images, especially since they may be the first reaction you have to the text: that memory of Uncle Louie, or the fantasy of dressing up as Madame. When you first respond with images, they will sprout in a gloriously random and arbitrary order. Don't try to connect them with a logical cause-and-effect mechanism or to order them into a beginning, middle, and end. Wait, and they will unfold by themselves.

Yes, images too will unfold with time, unless they remain tableaux vivants, in which case you're not an actor, you're a mannequin. As images do unfold, a progression of beginning, middle, and end will establish an episode, some rules will lead to a world of the play analysis, and, if the image suggests a psychology, a substructure of desire will be established. Often an image is a trigger to a complex of ideas, and comes complete with the other aspects of a performance. Be warned: images will have a tendency to become "stray ends," and need to be twisted back into the braid by weaving them with the line of the episodes or the rules of the world of the play.

When an image occurs after the start of rehearsals, it can translate aspects of other analyses that have gone before it, reinterpreting and invigorating what you've found. Stanislavsky played the philandering writer Trigorin in the first production of Chekhov's *Seagull* with a white-suit elegance. Chekhov commented that the more proper image of the character was checked pants and shabby shoes. Stanislavsky reports the checked pants puzzled him, but when he thought more about the image it seized his imagination. The character of Trigorin was shabby, elegant only in the eyes of a hero-worshipping young girl, and it was just her looks of admiration that motivated Trigorin to notice and talk to her. Her attention glorified him, which played to his super-task: *I want to be admired*. The performance was completely reorganized.*

Beginning with actions and obstacles

When a text, like one of Chekhov's plays, has too many things happening at once to identify episodes, or too many people onstage to distinguish who is who, a very good way to begin is to notice what happens to other people when you say your lines. To make the process more active, you might try, at random, to play an action and see what the other person says or does in response. As Løvborg, you might try the action of *to probe* or *to test* Hedda; when she smiles back at you, you will notice something happened even if you don't label it as an episode: *she smiled at me, she lowered her guard*. If she frowns, you would notice that too.

When an action dependably repeats its collision with an obstacle, it detaches itself in your mind from other actions you took that had no reaction and no dependable outcome. Dependable actions have the potential to be used as a formula for a performance. Only when an action becomes such a formula will you label it, or even be aware of it. As with episodes and images, the rough tries at getting to the task will alter as the rehearsal time proceeds.

The use of tasks in performance is a good demonstration of how braiding works. On the surface of consciousness, the actor playing an action in performance is only paying attention to what he wants to do in order to accomplish his task. If you are the Professor in *The Lesson*, you will play *to probe, to test, to tease, to seduce* without a thought to the outcome of the play: the Professor kills the Pupil in order to teach her a lesson. Such thoughtlessness in performance is fruitful only if episodes have been structured in rehearsals beforehand to pace and build the play to that conclusion. Such previous work frees you to play the actions in what is called *moment to moment*. If the line of actions is not laced with an episode, the acting is in danger of wandering off track. Meyerhold, who played the student writer Treplev in the same production of *The Seagull* as Stanislavsky, criticized Stanislavsky's acting for what he called a "filigree of details" that obscured the meaning of the play (133).

Switching to storytelling

A temporary use of storytelling technique can be very helpful in rehearsals, even if the performance is ultimately staged without stories. Rehearsal storytelling is particularly useful for an actor when the emotional demands of the scene are such that repetition will be wearing, but necessary in order to perfect some technical business. For example, as Yerma, you need to be in high temper to strangle your husband. But you will want to rehearse that scene while you are at a distance emotionally from the action. Consistently rehearsing full out does not allow you the objectivity to apply craft to your inspiration.

Opera singers often "mark" certain rehearsals; they sing all the notes, but not full

---

*This is a famous theater story, not least because it is a recorded historic incidence of a playwright's suggestions helping a working actor.

out. Stage actors also experience their own rehearsals of just marking where they stand and what they do. It is not the same as performing full out; for one thing, you won't get enough from the other actors to really play with them. The events of the story will be clear, however, which is the purpose of such a rehearsal. A marked rehearsal often will be the last one before the premiere, as a way to finish and bind the work of the ensemble together so that everyone agrees to be telling the same story. Brecht considered these the most "epic" performances of all.

If the style of the text or the production (and the director) allows, storytelling may be incorporated into the performance itself. It is certainly necessary when telling a story that describes offstage action meant to be pictured by the audience.

World of the play analysis refines earlier choices

Since a world of the play analysis reorganizes the images, events, and episodes, it usually comes after there is something to reorganize in rehearsal or performance, not before. Yet, sometimes the strangeness of the world of the play will be the first thing that strikes you: Beckett's wasted landscape, Ionesco's word-rich wonderlands. Familiarity with a world can also be the first thing to provoke a response. Interestingly, the first time such information becomes useful for an actor is when it has jurisdiction over an action or obstacle. In Beckett's *Happy Days* a cheerful woman is buried in a mound, which defines her celebrating her life as a heroic overcoming of an insurmountable obstacle. On the first reading of any play by Ionesco, it becomes clear that words are important. When you prepare for the role of the Pupil or the Professor in Ionesco's *Lesson*, you will learn that saying the wrong words gets you punished and causes you pain. Gulliver among the tiny Lilliputians is an arresting image, but it becomes a dramatic image when Gulliver realizes he cannot move because he is tied down by a hundred little ropes and set on by a hundred little arrows. Among the giants of Brobdingnag, Gulliver turns picturesquely small; his situation turns theatrical when he thrashes against the helplessness of being picked up into the air like a mouse.

A well-known world is similarly made actable when it is wrapped around actions, episodes, and images; otherwise the impulse to build a realistic world remains static. This was one of Meyerhold's severest criticism of Stanislavsky-directed actors, that their efforts to make characters recognizable exhausted them from doing anything else.

While establishing a world of the play analysis in rehearsal, it is useful to notice the *values* of the production. Stage right is the house of safety; danger comes from stage left. Everyone is so slow; you are the fast one. These things take time to emerge from the process of rehearsing. Even if you're not conscious of them, they will measure your behavior for the audience; when you do understand them, you can take your own measure and some control over the significance of your actions in the audience's eyes.

Twisting the braid

Make an effort in rehearsal to have different approaches support each other, not compete for your attention and divert your concentration. Paying attention to another approach is a way to return to your own thoughts when you are confused by the director, lost in the technical aspects of a performance, or overwhelmed by the amount of work to be done.

Repetition will twist the braid tighter so that the individual strands of thought entwine each other. As you perform, however, you will not play all methods at once. One or two will predominate, depending on the challenges of the script, the time available, and your affinities. Attempts to fulfill tasks will twist the other strands tighter around the throughline of actions and obstacles. A performer's combination of approaches dominated by personal images will be different. Translated to the specifics of the text by the world of the play, a deeply felt image will fuse all things—including a technical need to communicate—by the heat of its passion and the force of its issuing.* In filming, certain directors will ask you to play the episode and subordinate all else to that. Certainly, everyone involved in recording the shot needs to agree what it is. As the performer being filmed, of course, you can work from an image or work on your task; but if you don't fulfil the episode—slam the door goodbye or scream at the unseen dragon on the blue screen—the director will need to retake the shot until the required episode is performed and recorded.

Onstage, an ongoing performance can be refreshed by turning your attention to strands of the braid that lie unnoticed. In this way, new ideas can be used to fortify existing lines of thought, or, in lucky cases, entirely new ideas can twist the whole coil one more time. This is what happened when Stanislavsky revised his ideas about the would-be dandy Trigorin and revamped his performance, even after having played the role with considerable success for over a year.

The formula used to repeat performance changes as a play extends into a run. From Mei Lanfang to John Gielgud, actors who have maintained a repertory of alternating roles have all described how their playing simplified once they learned to choose what was significant and discard the rest. To do that, they had to first have a range of choices to choose among. It is not a gift to be simple; it's an achievement.

Recording Your Work

For all the thinking required, acting is a physical activity and, like a dance, the physical pattern of acting must be established with the memory of your body. In order to discuss that physical and internal process, though, we've been using the model of a *notebook*, since notebook pages—rather than descriptions of what an actor might be thinking—give us something to share, to talk about, and examine. It does help to write something down while training yourself to recognize these new vocabularies and habits of work. Not everyone works by writing things down, however, and if you find something else that works for you, by all means use it.

Sometimes a notebook is a lifesaver, especially if the rehearsal is interrupted, or sparse, or if you are repeating something you haven't done in a while. Recording your work is a way of saving for later use what can easily be lost and forgotten. Here is a way to take notes for multiple and parallel approaches.

---

*Stanislavsky says the line of intuition will absorb all others.

Record three parallel columns on a page facing the text

Your notebook records the impressions that alter and the approaches that alternate during the processes of rehearsal and performance. Your notebook is not meant to be read by anyone else, so you can make up your own form if you like. You can write backwards to preserve your secrets from spies; you can use different inks. Keep whatever form you do use the same from role to role. Otherwise, you won't remember what you meant or be able to read your own handwriting. For now, use this form. Then invent your own, if you like. Once again, let's agree on a vocabulary and definitions in order to move on to a discussion.

On a page opposite the text, draw three parallel columns. Each column will contain a line of thought, organized by a method we've discussed. In theory, you should be able to read down a column and review that approach's organization of your performances:

What happens. / This is what I need to do. / This is what I'm thinking of.

A world of the play analysis will go in the same column as images. You could draw four columns, but that doesn't leave much room to write, and world of the play notes usually won't happen as often as the others. When acting switches to storytelling, the three columns are used in a different way, as you will see.

Episodes in the far left column

In the far left column, write down **headlines (captions)** parallel to where **episodes** occur in the text. Make these captions bold, or underlined, or any other way you can make them stand out. You want to be able to scan down the line, and read the list of *what happens*. Indented under the captions, or in lighter print, write down the **gests** and the **transactions**. You can draw little stick figures for the *gests*, if you like.

HEDDA *(opening the album)* You see this view of the mountains, Mr. Løvborg. That's the Ortler group. Tesman's labeled them underneath. Here it is: "The Ortler group, near Meran."	EPISODE: FRUSTRATED NEWLYWED BAITS OLD BEAU I set the trap *gest:* Spreading the book on his lap		
LØVBORG *(whose eyes have never left her, speaking in a low, soft voice)* Hedda—Gabler!	Transaction: *If you keep up appearances / we can still flirt*		

Actions and obstacles in the middle column

In the middle column facing the text, write down your notes for **actions** and **obstacles**. These will change, much more so than in the other columns, and you might want to make this column wider in order to have room. You will probably begin by writing down the actions you have tried and the obstacles they've encountered. Identify each, so you don't get confused between them. When you decide what the **tasks** are, they should be put in capital letters, or underlined, or somehow distinguished from the rest of the column.

SIMEON (*defiantly*) We hain't nobody's slaves from this out—nor no thin's slaves nuther. (*a pause—restlessly*) Speakin' o' milk, wonder how Eben's managin'? PETER I s'pose he's managin'. SIMEON Mebbe we'd ought t'help—this once. PETER Mebbe. The cows knows us. SIMEON An' likes us. They don't know him much. PETER An' the hosses, an' pigs, an' chickens. They don't know him much. SIMEON They knows us like brothers an likes us! (*proudly*) Hain't we raised 'em t' be fust-rate, number one prize stock? PETER We hain't—not no more. SIMEON (*dully*) I was fergittin.' (*then resignedly*) Waal, let's go help Eben a spell an' git waked up. PETER Suits me.	TASK: *TO FREE MYSELF (AND BROTHER)* Opportunity: My taskmaster father is away. Action: *Talking myself and my brother into bravery.* Obstacles: I run out of words, and spare time makes me feel ashamed that we're not doing chores. Opportunity: Talking about what we do well will make us feel better. Action: *to boost our confidence* Obstacles: Our sense of duty. We reinforce each other's slavery. Opportunity: If we obey one last time, we're free to go. Action: *to submit (in order to leave with a clear conscience).*

Images in the far right column

In the far right column, write down the list of your **images** parallel to where they occur in the text. Include the constellation of images. If you're Napoleon, who is Josephine? Or if you're Diana Ross, who are the Supremes? If there are photographs that inspire you or fuel your ideas (snapshots from your past? that tattered publicity photo of Diana Ross in concert?), you can clip them in the book. Later, you might want to have them next to you in your dressing room.

GLOS Vouchsafe to wear this ring.	Image: *Jackie and Ari Onassis*
ANNE To take is not to give. *(she puts on the ring)*	
GLOS Look, how this ring encompasseth finger.	Image: *The words are like a heady perfume*
Even so thy breast encloseth my poor heart;	
Wear both of them, for both of them are thine.	Image: *Like slipping on handcuffs*

World of the play notes go in the column with images

The **rules** discovered from a **world of the play analysis** go in the same column as the images. They will end up translating the images into the world of the play.

GLOS Vouchsafe to wear this ring.	Images: *Jackie and Ari Heady perfume Slipping on handcuffs*
ANNE To take is not to give. *(she puts on the ring)*	
GLOS Look, how this ring encompasseth finger.	Rule: *Love is a trick. Perfume is a drug.*
Even so thy breast encloseth my poor heart;	
Wear both of them, for both of them are thine.	*A ring is a link in a chain.*

Storytelling takes over all three columns

When the performance of the play switches from enactment to narrative, notes for storytelling take over all three columns. **Events** are described episodes, and go in the left column. The **shift in the point of view** should be written down next to them, in the second column. There will not be a conflict for space with a changing point of view, because tasks are always from the same point of view of the person doing them. If there is a **character quote**, notes for it go in the third column, as would any other image described in the story.

	Event:	Point of View:	Quote:
MADAME I've been trailing through corridors all night long. I've been seeing frozen men and stony faces, but I did manage to catch a glimpse of Monsieur. From a distance. I waved to him.	I went to visit jail. I met indifference. I saw my lover. He waved!	Third person, feeling sorry for herself ↓ First person: Reliving the glimpse	Mouthing *Bye-bye!* Fingers folded into the palm, like a child

Notebook: Combining Approaches

Here is what your notebook would look like combining approaches for *The Lesson*. We will use a very small part of the text, and show how notes analyzing it are laid down in layers. We'll begin with tasks.

PROFESSOR Tell me, if you're not exhausted, how many are four minus three? PUPIL Four minus three? . . . Four minus three? PROFESSOR Yes. I mean to say: subtract three from four. PUPIL That makes . . . seven? PROFESSOR I am sorry but I'm obliged to contradict you. Four minus three does not make seven. You are confused: four plus three makes seven, four minus three does not make seven . . . This is not addition anymore, we must subtract now. PUPIL *(trying to understand)* Yes . . . yes. PROFESSOR Four minus three makes . . . How many? . . . How many?	TASK: *TO TEACH HER A LESSON* Action: *to probe her for weaknesses (in order to correct them)* Obstacle: She stalls Opportunity: She doesn't know how to subtract Action: *to press* Obstacle: Her good spirits Action: *to humiliate* Opportunity: She's obedient, humble Action: *to corner*

The repetition of the action, obstacles, and opportunity will identify an episode here.

PROFESSOR Tell me, if you're not exhausted, how many are four minus three? PUPIL Four minus three? . . . Four minus three? PROFESSOR Yes. I mean to say: subtract three from four. PUPIL That makes . . . seven? PROFESSOR I am sorry but I'm obliged to contradict you. Four minus three does not make seven. You are confused: four plus three makes seven, four minus three does not make seven . . . This is not addition anymore, we must subtract now. PUPIL (trying to understand) Yes . . . yes. PROFESSOR Four minus three makes . . . How many? . . . How many?	HE FINDS HER WEAKNESS	TASK: *TO TEACH HER A LESSON* Action: *to probe her for weaknesses (in order to correct them)* Obstacle: She stalls Opportunity: She doesn't know how to subtract Action: *to press* Obstacle: Her good spirits Action: *to humiliate* Opportunity: She's obedient, humble Action: *to corner*	

Emotional recall might jog a sense memory of your sour-smelling piano teacher. World of the play analysis will reveal that as the Pupil gets weaker, the Professor gets stronger. A little research into Ionesco's life and times and you will identify the Professor—who wears an armband by the end of the play—with the Nazi (and later Communist) troops that overran Ionesco's homeland in Romania to erect a totalitarian system, where education was the murder of the soul.

PROFESSOR Tell me, if you're not exhausted, how many are four minus three? PUPIL Four minus three? . . . Four minus three? PROFESSOR Yes. I mean to say: subtract three from four. PUPIL That makes . . . seven? PROFESSOR I am sorry but I'm obliged to contradict you. Four minus three does not make seven. You are confused: four plus three makes seven, four minus three does not make seven. . . . This is not addition anymore, we must subtract now. PUPIL (*trying to understand*) Yes . . . yes. PROFESSOR Four minus three makes . . . How many? . . . How many?	HE FINDS HER WEAKNESS	TASK: *TO TEACH HER A LESSON* Action: *to probe her for weakness* Obstacle: She stalls Opportunity: She doesn't know how to subtract Action: *to press* Action: *to humiliate* Opportunity: She's obedient, humble Action: *to corner*	*Piano teacher insisting on the repetition of scales* *Gestapo border guard* Rules: *Her weakness is his strength.* *How to win:* *the right answer is all-important.*

315

This discovery of the rules of the world of the play will further identify the episode: HE GAINS STRENGTH. This might bring you to the image that the Professor is *a vampire*; this fantasy, complete with cornball Dracula accent, will inspire new rules and new actions.

PROFESSOR Tell me, if you're not exhausted, how many are four minus three? PUPIL Four minus three? . . . Four minus three? PROFESSOR Yes. I mean to say: subtract three from four. PUPIL That makes . . . seven? PROFESSOR I am sorry but I'm obliged to contradict you. Four minus three does not make seven. You are confused: four plus three makes seven, four minus three does not make seven. . . . This is not addition anymore, we must subtract now. PUPIL *(trying to understand)* Yes . . . yes. PROFESSOR Four minus three makes . . . How many? . . . How many?	~~HE FINDS HER WEAKNESS~~ HE GAINS STRENGTH HE DRAWS BLOOD	TASK: *TO FEED* Action: *to probe her for weakness* Obstacle: She stalls Opportunity: She doesn't know how to subtract ~~Action: to press~~ Action: *to pierce* ~~Action: to humiliate~~ Opportunity: She's obedient, humble *To sip, to savor*	~~Piano teacher insisting on the repetition of scales~~ *A VAMPIRE* *Gestapo border guard blinking in the light* Rules: *Her weakness is his strength.* *How to win:* *the right answer is all-important.* *To survive:* *He must drink her life*

Let's imagine such an exchange in performance. The cornball Dracula accent (not Romanian but Hungarian, by the way) has led the actor playing the Professor to the image of *a bat*. In this exchange of lines, he shyly leans forward ("If you're not too exhausted"), blinking at the light of the girl's good humor (her robustly repeated "Four minus three?")—the better to delicately sip at her ignorance ("That makes seven?") as if it were a fine wine. One of the memorable moments in Bela Lugosi's performance in the 1931 film *Dracula* is the pause the vampire takes when offered a drink: "I don't drink . . . wine." Lugosi had played the part on stage for years before it was filmed, and the pause was part of his shtick. A memory of this effect might inspire a sucked-in breathy pause for "I am sorry, but I'm obliged to . . . contradict you." Instead of humiliating the Pupil, this Professor glides like a bat to correct her (*correct* is the activity, *to pierce* is the action) with a look of intense concentration, which the Pupil—and the audience—may mistake for concern. Like a bat plumping its shoulders before spreading its wings, the Professor will swell a little when the Pupil gives the wrong answer, savoring her air of confusion. This fantasy image seems in keeping with the tone of the language. An actress playing the Pupil might work from more personal images—the memory of a torturous acting class, perhaps?

A Concluding Note on Notebooks

Throughout this book, and especially in this last chapter, we've agreed to use a notebook as a model in order to track a process that is internal and in motion. Notebook pages give a form to represent that process, like still photographs from a movie or prose descriptions in a book. A class can include demonstrations; a book must include descriptions.

Even so, don't confuse the map with the road. A notebook isn't necessary. The great American solo actress Ruth Draper not only didn't keep a notebook, she never had a written script. Miss Draper (never just "Ruth") wrote her own material and kept a repertory of over nine and a half hours of thirty-six monologues in her head—portraying fifty-three different characters and evoking a total of over three hundred others. Late in life, Miss Draper reluctantly agreed to her young managers' suggestion that a stenographer be hired to record the words in shorthand. You can picture her agreeing to the suggestion with a bemused, self-conscious smile and a patrician accent: "Oh, all right, boys."

By the way, the two preceding paragraphs braid the five approaches to acting. In justifying the use of notebooks, there is a:

task	to track a moving process
image	the still photographs from a movie
transaction	if you agree to definitions / we can move on to discussion
rules of the world	a book includes descriptions to make its points
story	the Ruth Draper anecdote, with the lady-like character quote

That you swallowed the example without knowing is the *gest*. Like Mei Lanfang, we could smile at this cleverness, but let's keep to the *Borgia poison* as an image for the episode, which can be captioned:

NOW YOU UNDERSTAND

Although episodes aren't linked by cause and effect, the next set of episodes might nevertheless be captioned:

YOU GO OUT AND USE WHAT YOU'VE LEARNED.

BIOGRAPHICAL DIRECTORY

Adler, Alfred psychologist (1870–1937)

Adler, Stella actress, teacher (1901–1992)

Aeschylus playwright (525–456 BCE)

Agee, James writer (1909–1955)

Akalitis, Jo Anne director (born 1937)

Albee Edward playwright (born 1928)

Aldridge, Ira Frederick actor (1807–1867)

Ann-Margret actress, singer (born 1941)

Aristophanes playwright (448–385 BCE)

Armstrong, Louis musician (1900–1971)

Arnheim, Rudolf psychologist (born 1904)

Arthur, Bea actress (born 1923)

Astaire, Fred dancer, singer (1899–1987)

Austen Jane novelist (1775–1817)

Baker, Josephine singer (1906–1975)

Balzac, Honoré de writer (1799–1850)

Barba, Eugenio director (born 1936)

Barrymore, John actor (1882–1942)

Barthes, Roland critic (1915–1980)

Beckett, Samuel playwright (1906–1989)

Belafonte, Harry actor (born 1927)

Belasco, David producer (1854–1931)

Benedict, Ruth anthropologist (1887–1948)

Bentley, Eric critic (born 1916)

Berg, Alban composer (1885–1935)

Bernhardt, Sarah actress (1844–1923)

Berlin, Isaiah critic (1909–1997)

Betty, Master (William Henry West) actor (1791–1874)

Blake, William poet (1757–1827)

Blanc, Mel actor (1908–1989)

Boas, Franz anthropologist (1858–1942)

Bogart, Anne director, teacher (born 1925)

Boleslavsky, Richard actor, teacher (1889–1937)

Bonaparte, Napoleon Emperor of France (1769–1821)

Bond, Edward playwright (born 1934)

Borghese, Camillo Fillipo Ludovico Italian prince (1775–1832)

Brando, Marlon actor (born 1924)

Braque, Georges artist (1882–1963)

Brecht, Bertolt playwright, director (1898–1956)

Brook, Peter director (born 1925)

Buchanan, Robert (Williams) critic (1841–1901)

Büchner, Georg playwright (1813–1837)

Bunny, Bugs cartoon character (born 1940)

Burton, Richard actor (1925–1984)

Calderón de la Barca, playwright (1600–1681)

Carnicke, Sharon Marie writer, teacher (born 1949)

Cézanne, Paul artist (1839–1906)

Chanel, Coco designer (1883–1971)

319

Chekhov, Anton playwright (1860–1904)

Chekhov, Michael actor, teacher (1891–1955)

Chikamatsu, Monzaemon playwright (1653–1725)

Churchill, Caryl playwright (born 1938)

Cleopatra VII Queen of Egypt (69–30 BCE)

Clift, Montgomery actor (1920–1966)

Clurman, Harold critic, teacher (1901–1980)

Cobb, Lee J. actor (1911–1976)

Cocteau, Jean writer (1889–1963)

Colbert, Claudette actress (1903–1996)

Coleridge, Samuel Taylor poet (1772–1834)

Coolidge, Calvin U.S. President (1872–1933)

Coppola, Francis Ford director (born 1939)

Corneille, Pierre playwright (1606–1684)

Cornell, Joseph sculptor (1903–1972)

Cortázar, Julio writer (1914–1984)

Cousteau, Jacques explorer (1910–1997)

Crosby, Bing singer (1903–1977)

Cukor, George director (1899–1983)

Curtis, Tony actor (born 1925)

Davis, Bette actress (1908–1989)

De Niro, Robert actor (born 1943)

Dean, James actor (1931–1955)

Delsarte, François scientist, writer (1811–1871)

DeMille, Cecil B. director (1881–1959)

Derrida, Jacques critic (born 1930)

Dickens, Charles writer (1812–1870)

Dietrich, Marlene actress, singer (1901–1992)

Dodin, Lev director (born 1944)

Dostoyevsky, Fyodor writer (1821–1881)

Draper, Ruth actress (1884–1956)

Dreiser, Theodore writer (1871–1945)

Dumas, Alexandre (père) writer (1802–1870)

Duncan, Isadora dancer (1877–1927)

Duse, Eleonora actress (1858–1924)

Easty, Edward Dwight writer, teacher (born 1930)

Einstein, Albert scientist (1879–1955)

Eisenstein, Sergei director (1898–1948)

Eliot, George writer (1819–1880)

Epstein, Raissa feminist (1873–1961)

Ernst, Max artist (1891–1976)

Euripides playwright (484–406 BCE)

Evans, Maurice actor (1901–1989

Felix, Eliza see *Rachel*

Fiorelli, Tiberio actor (1608?–1694)

Flaubert, Gustave writer (1821–1880)

Flint, F.S. poet (1885–1960)

Forrest, Edwin actor (1806–1872)

Forster, E.M. writer (1879–1970)

Freud, Anna psychologist (1895–1982)

Freud, Sigmund psychologist (1856–1939)

Gance, Abel director (1889–1981)

Gardner, Ava actress (1922–1990)

Garland, Judy actress, singer (1922–1969)

Genet, Jean playwright (1910–1986)

Gershwin, George composer (1898–1937)

Gibbon, Edmund historian (1737–1794)

Gielgud, John actor (1904–2000)

Gillespie, Dizzy musician (1917–1993)

Gish, Dorothy actress (1898–1968)

Gish, Lillian actress (1893–1993)

Gleason, Jackie actor (1916–1987)

Goethe, Johann Wolfgang von philosopher, critic (1749–1832)

Gogol, Nikolai playwright (1809–1852)

Goldberg, Whoopi actress (born 1949)

Goldoni, Carlo playwright (1707–1793)

Gran, Gerhard critic (1856–1925)

Griffith, D.W. director (1875–1948)

Gris, Juan artist (1887–1927)

Grosz, Georg artist (1893–1959)

Grotowski, Jerzy teacher, writer (1933–1999)

Grubb, Davis writer (born 1919)

Gurevich, Lyubov dramaturg (1866–1940)

Handke, Peter playwright (born 1942)

Hapgood, Elizabeth Reynolds translator (1894–1974)

Hapgood, Norman critic (1868–1937)

Hare, David playwright (born 1947)

Harlow, Jean actress (1911–1937)

Harris, Julie actress (born 1925)

Hazlitt, William critic (1778–1830)

Hepburn, Katharine actress (born 1907)

Heston, Charlton actor (born 1923)

Hill, Benny actor (1924–1992**)**

Hilliard, Bob songwriter (born 1918)

Hitchcock, Alfred director (1899–1980)

Hitler, Adolf German dictator (1889–1945)

Hochhuth, Rolf playwright (born 1931)

Hoffman, Dustin actor (born 1937)

Holiday, Billie singer (1915–1959)

Horney, Karen psychologist (1885–1952)

Hunt, Leigh (James Henry) critic (1784–1859)

Ibsen, Henrik playwright (1828–1906)

Ionesco, Eugene playwright (1909–1994)

Ivan IV (Ivan Grozny) Russian Tsar (1530–1584)

James, Henry writer (1843–1916)

Jarry, Alfred playwright (1873–1907)

Jensen, J.V. (Johannes Vilhelm) writer (1873–1950)

Johnson, Lyndon U.S. President (1908–1973)

Jones, Robert Edmund stage designer (1887–1954)

Joséphine Empress of France (1763–1814)

Jung, Carl psychologist (1875–1961)

Kaige, Chen director (born 1952)

Kean, Edmund actor (1787–1833)

Kemble, John Phillip actor (1757–1823)

Kennedy, Jacqueline U.S. First Lady (1929–1994)

Kennedy, John U.S. President (1917–1963)

Kline, Franz artist (1910–1962)

Knight, G. Wilson critic (1897–1985)

Knights, L.C. critic (born 1906)

Knipper, Olga actress (1869–1959)

Kommisarzhevskaya, Vera actress (1864–1910)

La Motta, Jake boxer (born 1921)

Laughton, Charles actor (1899–1962)

LaVerne, Lucille actress (1869–1943)

Le Gallienne, Eva actress (1899–1991)

Lee, Robert E. general (1807–1870)

Leigh, Janet actress (born 1927)

Lenin, Vladimir Ilyich First Premier of the U.S.S.R. (1870–1924)

Lichtenstein, Roy artist (1923–1997)

Lessitzky, El (for Eliezer, many variant spellings) sculptor (1890–1941)

Littlewood, Joan director (born 1914)

Logan, Joshua director (1908–1988)

Lorca, Federico García playwright (1898–1936)

Louis XIV King of France (1643–1715)

Lugosi, Bela actor (1882–1956)

Lumet, Sidney director (born 1924)

Macready, William actor (1793–1873)

Magritte, René artist (1898-1967)

Maintenon, Madame de (Françoise d'Aubigné, marquise) consort to Louis XIV (1652–1675)

Malina, Judith actress (born 1926)

Mamet, David playwright (born 1947)

BIOGRAPHICAL DIRECTORY

Mankiewicz, Joseph L. director, writer (1909–1992)
Mann, David songwriter (born 1916)
Marlowe Christopher playwright (1564–1593)
Marx, Karl economist (1818–1883)
Matthau, Walter actor (1920–2000)
McCambridge, Mercedes actress (born 1918)
McCullers, Carson writer (1917–1967)
Meadows, Audrey actress (1924–1996)
Mei Lanfang actor (1894–1961)
Melville, Herman writer (1819–1891)
Menken, Adah Isaacs actress (1835–1868)
Meyerhold, Vsevolod director (1874–1940)
Michelangelo, Buonarroti artist (1475–1564)
Miles, Sylvia actress (born 1932)
Miller, Arthur playwright (born 1915)
Mitchum, Robert actor (1917–1997)
Mnouckine, Ariane director (born 1938)
Moholy-Nagy, László artist (1895–1946)
Molière (Jean-Baptiste Poquelin) playwright, actor (1622–1673)
Monet, Claude artist (1840–1926)
Monk, Thelonious musician, composer (1917–1982)
Monroe, Marilyn actress (1926–1962)
Monsieur, Phillipe Duc d'Orleans (1640–1701)
Mrozek, Slawomir playwright (born 1930)
Müller, Heiner director, playwright (1929–1995)
Nemerovitch-Danchenko, Vladimir director, teacher (1858–1943)
Newman, Paul actor (born 1925)
Nietzsche, Friedrich philosopher (1844–1900)

O'Neill, Eugene playwright (1888–1953)
O'Neill, James actor (1849–1920)
Odets, Clifford playwright (1906–1963)
Oldenburg, Claes sculptor (born 1929)
Olivier, Laurence actor (1907–1989)
Onassis, Aristotle shipping tycoon (1906–1975)
Ostrovsky, Alexander playwright (1823–1886)
Ouspenskaya, Maria actress, teacher (1876–1949)
Pacino, Al actor (born 1940)
Page, Geraldine actress (1924–1987)
Parker, Charlie ("Bird") musician (1920–1955)
Parkinson, C. Northcote economist (1909–1993)
Perón, Evita First Lady of Argentina (1919–1952)
Picasso, Pablo artist (1881–1973)
Pig, Porky cartoon character (born 1935)
Pinter, Harold playwright, teacher (born 1930)
Pirandello, Luigi playwright, teacher (1867–1936)
Piscator, Erwin director, teacher (1893–1966)
Plautus, Titus Maccius playwright (254–184 BCE)
Poisson, Mademoiselle (Marie Angelique) actress (1657–1756)
Pollock, Jackson artist (1912–1956)
Polus actor (4th century BCE)
Poquelin, Jean-Baptiste see *Molière*
Post, Emily etiquette expert (1873–1960)
Presley, Elvis singer, actor (1935–1977)
Proust, Marcel writer (1871–1922)
Rachel (Felix, Eliza) actress (1820/21–1858)

Racine, Jean, playwright (1639–1699)

Radner, Gilda actress (1946–1989)

Reich, Wilhelm psychologist (1897–1957)

Repin, Ilya artist (1844–1930)

Reynolds, Joshua artist (1723–1792)

Ribot, Théodule-Armand psychologist (1839–1916)

Rimbaud, Arthur writer (1854–1891)

Robeson, Paul actor (1898–1976)

Rogers, Ginger actress (1911–1995)

Ross, Diana singer, actress (born 1944)

Rothko, Mark artist (1903–1970)

Salvini, Tommaso actor (1829–1916)

Schechner, Richard director (born 1934)

Schiller, Friedrich von playwright (1759–1805)

Schulberg, Budd writer (born 1914)

Schwitters, Kurt sculptor (1887–1948)

Scorsese, Martin director (born 1942)

Scott, Walter writer (1771–1832)

Seurat, Georges artist (1859–1891)

Shakespeare, William playwright (1564–1616)

Shaw, George Bernard playwright (1856–1950)

Shepkin, Michael actor (1788–1863)

Shchukin, Sergei art collector (1854–1936)

Shepard, Sam playwright (born 1943)

Shklovsky, Viktor critic (1893–1984)

Siddons, Mrs. Sarah actress (1755–1831)

Simon, Neil playwright (born 1927)

Sinatra, Frank singer, actor (1915–1998)

Skinner, Cornelia Otis actress, writer (1901–1979)

Smith, Anna Deveare playwright (born 1950)

Sophocles playwright (496–406 BCE)

Soyinka, Wole playwright (born 1934)

Stalin, Joseph Premier of the Soviet Union (1879–1953)

Stanislavsky, Konstantin (Alexeyev) actor, teacher (1863–1938)

Steiger, Rod actor (born 1925)

Stein, Gertrude writer (1874–1946)

Steinbeck, John writer (1902–1968)

Sterne, Laurence writer (1713–1768)

Stevens, George director (1904–1975)

Stoppard, Tom playwright (born 1937)

Strasberg, Lee teacher, actor (1901–1982)

Strauss, Richard composer (1864–1949)

Streep, Meryl actress (born 1949)

Strindberg, August playwright (1849–1912)

Stritch, Elaine actress (born 1925)

Suzuki, Tadeshi (sometimes spelled Tadashi) director (born 1939)

Swift, Jonathan writer (1667–1745)

Tabori, George actor (born 1914)

Tamiroff, Akim actor (1899–1972)

Taylor, Elizabeth actress (born 1932)

Terry, Ellen actress (1847–1928)

Thatcher, Margaret British Prime Minister (born 1925)

Tillyard, E.M.W. writer (1889–1962)

Tolstoy, Leo writer (1828–1910)

Trotsky, Leon revolutionary (1879–1940)

Turgenev, Ivan playwright (1818–1883)

Turner, Tina singer (born 1939)

Tynan, Kenneth critic (1937–1995)

Vakhtangov, Eugene director, teacher (1883–1922)

Victoria, Queen of England (1819–1901)

Wallach, Eli actor (born 1915)

Warhol, Andy artist (1928?–1987)

Warren, Lesley Anne actress (born 1946)

Washington, George First U.S. President (1732–1799)

Weaver, Dennis actor (born 1924)

Wedekind, Frank playwright (1864–1918)

Weigel, Helene actress (1900–1971)

Weill, Kurt composer (1900–1950)

Welles, Orson actor, director (1915–1985)

West, Mae actress (1892/3–1980)

White, Barry singer (born 1944)

Wilde, Oscar playwright (1854–1900)

Wilder, Thornton playwright (1897–1975)

Willett, John critic (born 1917)

Williams, Robin actor (born 1952)

Williams, Tennessee playwright (1911–1983)

Wilson, August playwright (born 1945)

Winters, Shelley actress (born 1922)

Wright, Orville inventor, aviator (1871–1948)

Yaroshenko, Nikolai artist (1846–1898)

Yesenin, Sergei poet (1895–1925)

Zeami (Kanze Motokiyo) actor, writer (1363–1443)

Zola, Emile writer (1840–1902)

GLOSSARY

Abstract Expressionists a school of American painters begun in the late 1940s that offered Method actors of the era a model for the process of making art. Abstract Expressionists like Jackson Pollock created their own forms rather than depicting or copying outer models. Certain Method actors relied exclusively on their own experiences and trusted that their impulses, if heartfelt enough, would result in communicating images onstage.

action in Stanislavsky's approach to acting, an action is what an actor does onstage in order to accomplish a task. If Hedda Gabler undertakes the task of freeing herself from a dull marriage, her action might be *to entice someone to rescue her*. The action answers the question *What do I do to get what I need?*

activity in Stanislavsky's approach to acting, an actor's behavior while performing an action. The specific activity—sweeping, bowling—is determined by the circumstances of the scene and its setting. Playing her action *to entice someone to rescue her*, Hedda Gabler's activity might be sitting and looking at an album of photographs with her old boyfriend. Activities can be assigned by the playwright or determined in rehearsal. An activity can change, but actions will still organize the performance.

Actors Studio founded in 1947 in New York City as a place to develop Stanislavsky's System among like-minded theater professionals experimenting with their craft. Lee Strasberg gained prominence there teaching his Stanislavsky-derived Method. Controversial for its emphasis on emotional memory and influential for the fame and accomplishment of its members, among them Shelley Winters and Dustin Hoffman.

affective memory a theory proposed by the French psychologist Théodule Ribot that events from the past settle into the mind and body and, when remembered, can affect the subject emotionally. Ribot claimed to find this phenomenon in a small percentage of sixty subjects. Stanislavsky claimed affective memory could be developed as a way for performers to access emotions. Lee Strasberg claimed affective memory could be developed as a way for performers to access emotional memories that could be put to use in rehearsal.

alexandrines a verse or line of poetry of twelve syllables. Used especially in classic French theater, the name itself derives from an Old French poem on the subject of Alexander the Great. According to the rules of classic French tragedy, alexandrines occur in pairs and each line ends a logical sequence with no carryover into the next line. A character's failure to complete the form indicates emotional disturbance.

alienation the term Bertolt Brecht used to identify the process of taking something familiar and *alienating* it from its surroundings so that it seems strange—and worthy of aesthetic consideration. Working with an episodic approach, actors alienate behavior so that the behavior becomes significant to the audience and illuminates the episode. In melodramas or horror films, a small, familiar gesture—such as the turn of a doorknob—can be alienated and thus understood to have life and death implications. The term was first used by the Russian critic Viktor Shklovsky to define a writer's technique of describing the commonplace as extraordinary.

archetypes the psychologist Carl Jung, who theorized that personality was a collection of masks called personae, further identified some personae as intrinsic to the human condition (Mother or Child, for example) rather than to a specific culture or family circumstance. An actor building a role out of images may include archetypes among other images, or trust that even the most personal images will connect to the archetypes of the audience.

"athletic acting" Usually called *heroic acting*, athletic acting displays physical feats such as horseback riding or stage fighting. In nineteenth-century America, this style of performing, robust and highly physical, was quite popular. Edwin Forrest was perhaps the greatest of the athletic actors. Athletic acting can be seen in Kung Fu movies and in America's version of "professional" wrestling.

beats within the system of acting organized by identifying tasks, a beat is the segment of a performance determined by a single task. The term is based on an American mishearing of the Russian-accented English "beads" (on a string), but the misinterpretation has been fruitful for its references to rhythm and musicality. There is confusion and controversy over this term, which is also referred to as "bits" and even "beets."

be-bop an avant-garde American jazz music movement of the mid-twentieth century. The word is a combination of nonsense syllables that refer to the bounce (*be bop!*) given to a melody, sometimes bent beyond recognition. Like Abstract Expressionism, *be-bop* offered contemporary Method actors a model for the process of making art. Relatively unconcerned with the composer's intentions, *bop* musicians brought a personal response to their musical interpretations. Method actors were more concerned with their own responses to the text than with the playwright's intentions. *Bop* musicians include Charlie Parker and Dizzy Gillespie.

biased point of view when storytelling, the narrator comments on the story being told. The audience is meant to synthesize the meaning of the text and the narrator's point of view to establish for themselves the character of the narrator and the nature of events. In order for the story to be effective, the audience should understand the narrator's bias, although they don't have to agree with it. Think of a wedding announcement read out loud by the bride's bitter ex-boyfriend. Bias can be revealed over time; it need not be apparent at once.

caption identifies an episode. The caption is analogous to a headline; it paraphrases or sums up the onstage event in unambiguous, simple language: MURDERER WOOS WIDOW. A caption answers the questions *What happens? Who makes it happen? To whom does it happen?* and is in the form of a complete sentence with a subject, verb, and object.

character quotes when storytelling, the narrator speaks or behaves in such a way as to identify characters who act or speak in the events of the story.

circle of concentration a Stanislavsky exercise, based on a Hatha Yoga practice, in which actors extend their awareness to consider new aspects of the production or their partner's ability to help or hinder accomplishment of their tasks.

classical acting a highly presentational style of rhetorical acting, prominent in Europe during the eighteenth and nineteenth centuries, that values balanced, stately movements and dignified, harmonious tones. Classical actors use as a model the classical ideal that the forms of art concentrate, refine, and express reality rather than imitate life. Even disorder is expressed in an orderly fashion. A leading exponent of the form in England was Mrs. Sarah Siddons.

collage artwork where the artist takes already-formed objects—or already-formed pictures—from other sources and places them together in order to produce an effect, or an image, greater than the sum of the parts. The word *collage* was coined to describe the work of a group of artists called the *Dadaists*, whose response to the First World War was to create art as an illogical combination of the wreckage of civilization. An actor combines images in a similar way. The word derives from the French word for "glue." Prominent collage artists include Max Ernst and Joseph Cornell.

collective unconscious according to the psychologist Carl Jung, all people share a realm where the archetypes of their unconscious minds coincide. As an actor, you can play from your own images knowing that you will connect to the archetypes of the audience in the realm of the collective unconscious.

comic pattern in world of the play analysis, a pattern is comic when rule-breaking is forgiven rather than punished.

Communism the theory of Karl Marx that property should be held in common, communally. Marx viewed human behavior as a series of economic transactions—at their best cooperative and reciprocal—that bind members of society together. In practice, European Communism has been an oligarchy, often run by a dictator, that continued the autocratic practices of the Tsars of Russia. The promulgators of episodic acting in the twentieth century—Brecht, Piscator, and Meyerhold—used the theories of Communism as their model for the mechanism of human behavior; their lives were shaped by the realities of the system.

composition in world of the play analysis, the characters in a play can acquire meaning through comparison with each other, as elements in a larger composition.

cooperation according to psychologist Alfred Adler, human behavior can be identified as a series of mutually beneficial transactions: *cooperation*. For example, an infant cooperates with its mother in order to be breast-fed. Adler's analysis provides an actor with a theory of transactions divorced from the historical reality of Communism, which used a similar analysis of economic transactions to explain behavior.

Cubism a movement among painters and sculptors at the beginning of the twentieth century that broke down the image of what was being depicted into planes and geometric shapes. Cubism allowed the point of view depicting an object to vary within an artwork, including views impossible to see simultaneously in life; for example, the silhouette of a nose alongside a frontal view of the full face. An actor telling a story also has the power to present similar shifts in point of view impossible to achieve in real life. Pablo Picasso, Juan Gris, and Georges Braque are examples of Cubist artists. The term was first used derisively by the artist Henri Matisse to describe a painting by Braque of houses reduced to cubes.

cultural anthropology the social science that examines behavior, relationships, emotion, and purpose in various populations and cultures. Like actors analyzing the world of a play, cultural anthropologists analyze the context of behavior, man-made and natural. Franz Boas and Ruth Benedict, among others, established the principles of twentieth-century cultural anthropology, especially the principle of relative value that no culture is superior to another. The psychologist Karen Horney was inspired by Benedict's writing to develop a theory of psychology that examines the meaning and value of an individual's behavior within social context.

deconstruction a process, identified by French critic Jacques Derrida, that separates a text into its parts in order to recognize that meaning is relative and dependent on the reader—no matter what the intentions of the writer. Deconstructed, no text has a meaning without an organizing interpretation. Derrida's first use of the term was in 1968, but the principles of the approach were set out by the Russian literary critic Viktor Shklovsky and by a school of Czech critics in Prague as early as the 1930s. Applied to a script, a performance text is broken down with an understanding that its meaning is subject to the way it is performed.

demonstration in episodic theater, performing the events of the play so that they are clearly understood by the audience. Demonstration may include enactment as well as asides, exaggeration, direct address, and playing to the house. As demonstration, these non-realistic elements call attention not to the actor, but to the events of the play.

description in storytelling, the words of a story that help the audience picture the events. Descriptions give meaning to action and behavior because they help to establish the world of the play—as it is presented in the story.

distanced point of view in storytelling, the narrator remains impartial while telling the story, and tries to keep personal bias out of the story. A newscaster reporting a disaster is a familiar example.

dramatic action has multiple definitions; it varies from approach to approach. For playwrights, the most famous definition, given by the Greek philosopher Aristotle (384–322 BCE), is that dramatic action is conflict. This is not always the case for an actor, not even in Greek tragedy. A performer telling a story, for example, may encounter no conflict and yet still establish dramatic action in performance. No matter what the approach, dramatic action always implies a significant change or a difference from what has gone before. In world of the play analysis, dramatic action is a significant breach in the rules of the world of the play. *See the Script Analysis Comparative Reference Chart for other specifics.*

Electra complex the psychologist Sigmund Freud's terminology for a daughter's unconscious desire for her father and competitive hatred for her mother, analogous to a son's Oedipus complex. Derived from the ancient Greek myth of Electra, who, avenging her father's death, arranges to have her own mother murdered. The story of Electra is the source material for Greek tragedies written by Aeschylus, Sophocles, and Euripides. The name means "shining" or "bright."

emotional memory emotions that renew their source in past and remembered events. For example, the joy felt when remembering a past triumph is an emotional memory. Method actors develop techniques of sense memory and emotional narrative in order to access emotional memories and harness them to the tasks of the script.

emotional narrative an event from an actor's past told as a story in order to retrieve a sense memory. A rehearsal technique, emotional narrative departs from the play's text entirely; not just the words, but the events and the characters the text describes. The actor is encouraged to relate, in his own words, an emotionally charged event from his past. Led by the director or acting teacher, emotional narrative reaches a point where the storyteller identifies emotionally with what he is describing.

epic theater a term coined by the director Erwin Piscator, and later appropriated by Bertolt Brecht, to describe a form of theater that includes demonstration along with enactment. Epic theatre openly acknowledges the presence of the audience and means to include the public in an emotionally charged judgmental response rather than an emotionally charged sympathetic response.

episode an event performed onstage as part of a play that is understood by its audience complete and by itself, separate from the whole of the play. Actors in an episode perform roles that fulfill the responsibility to demonstrate what is happening. The word is Greek in origin, and was used to refer to the segments of a play enacted between the songs of the chorus. In modern usage, the essence of an episode is that something changes in the course of its playing, and the audience notices that it has changed.

episodic acting the play is acted in segments, separated from each other, without continuity.

episodic structure an episodically structured performance acts out a *story*, or sequence of events, rather than presenting a *plot* linked together by cause and effect. In theory, each event in a story can be understood separately from the sequence.

event in storytelling, an episode that is described so that it can be understood in and of itself, separately from its sequence. The word is Latin in origin and stems from the word *evenire*, "to come out of"—the outcome. For an actor using narrative analysis, events are what a storyteller would like the audience to understand as happening so that they may enact an episode in their mind's eyes. Events are revealed by asking the questions *What happened?* and *Who did what to whom?*

Expressionism a style of art emphasizing an artist's response to the world rather than accurate depiction. Freed from the rules of resemblance, Expressionism may include distortion and exaggeration in what it depicts. In Germany, Expressionism was an alternative to the classical approach to art associated with Greece and Rome. Bertolt Brecht's earliest plays are Expressionist portraits of urban living, as are Georg Grosz's etchings depicting Berlin.

fantasy images A fantasy is anything an actor can imagine being and would like to act out. Children dressing up in their parents' clothing are playing fantasies; so are actors pretending to be someone other than themselves.

fourth wall the invisible wall that divides the actor from the audience, theoretically preserving the illusion of reality. Essential to naturalism, but not every approach to acting accepts the use of the fourth wall.

gest in episodic acting, a vivid physical moment onstage that happens when a trade is made or denied. The *gest* clarifies and reveals the episode and always involves a human gesture, an interaction between at least two people—or in some cases two aspects of one person's character. Think of the moment of the *gest* as the photograph in the tabloid that would accompany an episode's headline. The *gest* is not frozen in time like a tableau; a *gest* implies the *movement* of an offer, an exchange, or a rejection. Richard III slipping his ring onto Anne's finger is a *gest*. The word *gest* comes from the same root word as *gist* and *gesture*. Sometimes it is called, with a Latin flourish, *gestus*.

Hatha Yoga the school of Yoga that teaches the mind to observe the processes of the body in order to relax and ultimately eradicate stress. Stanislavsky had a life-long interest in Hatha Yoga and devised exercises for relaxation based on its practices.

identification in storytelling, the narrator emotionally identifies with the story being told. The words of the text are meant to be understood as a faithful description of the speaker's emotional state, and the actor is meant to use the power of images to persuade the audience that the description of the emotional state is true. In *A Streetcar Named Desire*, Blanche describes the death of her husband so that the audience understands that Blanche identifies emotionally with the events she recalls.

imagery analysis identifying ways an actor's idiosyncratic and personal set of images can be united with a script.

image a private idea evoked by the script, character, line, or moment in a play. For actors, an image is not always a picture; it can be a sound, a smell, a touch, a memory, a taste. Within imagery analysis, an image is labeled as a simile and answers the questions *What does this resemble? What is this like? What does this remind me of?* Images can be divided into two kinds: *fantasy* and *personal history*.

Impressionists a school of nineteenth-century painters who expanded the range of a painter's technique by evoking changes in light to capture shifting perceptions and the subjectivity of perception. While telling a story onstage, an actor uses similar shifts in the point of view. In its emphasis on the artist's impression of the subject—rather than the artist's responsibility to the subject's received meanings or appearance—Impressionism anticipates deconstruction and post-modernism. The name, used at first derisively, is taken from the title of Claude Monet's 1872 painting *Impression: Sunrise*. Among other later painters called *post-Impressionists*, Paul Cézanne and Georges Seurat were freed by the example and early practice of Impressionism to emphasize the formal technique of painting as subject matter, not unlike an episodic actor's calling attention to technique.

inner mask an actor's unseen image of the character or role being performed. Powerful inner masks often result in the illusion of transformation. Eleonora Duse and Ruth Draper are examples of actors who relied on inner masks.

Itinerants a group of nineteenth-century Russian painters, parallel in time to the French Impressionists, who insisted on expanding the subject matter of academic painting to include politically charged current events. Rebuffed by the official picture galleries, beginning in the 1870s joint exhibitions of these paintings toured from place to place—hence the name "Itinerants." Their emphasis on and detailed depiction of psychological relationships provided a contemporary model for Stanislavsky's depiction of psychological relationships on stage. Still little known in the West, the Itinerant movement's prominent members include world class artists such as Ilya Repin and skilled practitioners such as Nikolai Yaronshenko.

justification within the vocabulary of Method actors, the reason something happens onstage. To avoid the danger that an actor's fascination with private imagery might overwhelm an investigation of the text, images in the Method are never allowed to articulate their own forms and language the way a fantasy image might. Yoking an image to a task "justifies" the onstage behavior.

making a transition in Stanislavsky's approach to acting, moving from task to task. An actor makes a transition after a task is completed or when the task is abandoned in the face of an immovable obstacle. Switching tasks doesn't happen as often as switching actions, but when it does happen, it is more significant.

making an adjustment in Stanislavsky's approach to acting, moving from action to action. An actor pursuing a task makes an adjustment after encountering an obstacle. The actor tries a *different* action in order to meet the demands of the *same* task. Making adjustments to onstage obstacles is a constant process in rehearsal and in performance.

melodrama a form of theatrical entertainment, especially popular during the nineteenth century, often featuring everyday characters caught up in sensational situations. Usually associated nowadays with simplistic characterization, to the lower-class audiences of its day, melodrama seemed lifelike, realistic, and truthful, not least because its characters included working people.

the Method a systematic use of personal images popularized by acting teacher Lee Strasberg at the Actors Studio.

narrative analysis identifying the structure of the story that is told in a play before deciding on its meaning or interpretation. It helps to concentrate on answering the question *How does the story mean?* before proceeding to the equally important question *What does the story mean?*

"naturalism" Among actors, French writer François Delsarte's quasi-scientific approach to the recorded observation, translation, and categorization of people's physical postures and behavior. Delsarte made charts, drawings, and schemes for the physical representation of human emotions found "in nature." *Naturalistic acting* was derived from these formulae for the "accurate" representation of emotion on stage. The name is taken from a literary movement championed by Emile Zola that also proposed a scientific approach to the observation and depiction of life. The so-called naturalistic "slice of life" was meant to present reality without idealization or avoidance of ugliness.

object lesson in episodic acting, the use of a physical object to demonstrate the *gest*. The object, onstage, represents an essential part of the episode and is understood by the audience in this way. When Richard III offers himself to Anne, the ring he slips on her finger is essential to the audience's understanding that Anne has given herself to Richard.

obstacle in Stanislavsky's approach to acting, whatever interrupts the progress of an actor's actions in pursuit of an onstage task. Obstacles thwart the fulfillment of desire. Obstacles are often the other actor(s), but they can also be encountered in the physical environment, costume, or any other aspect of the production or the role.

Oedipus complex the psychologist Sigmund Freud's terminology for a son's unconscious desire for his mother, in competition with his father. Derived from the ancient Greek myth of Oedipus, who killed his father and married his own mother. The story of Oedipus is the source material for two Greek tragedies written by Sophocles. The name means "swollen foot"; in order to avoid the prophecy that the child would kill his father, the infant Oedipus was deliberately abandoned on a mountain, with a spike driven through his ankles.

opportunity anything that helps an actor get a task done onstage.

pattern with a world of the play analysis, a more or less consistent configuration of words and action in the play. The pattern is the context, the system of meaning within which roles are characterized and actions evaluated. World of the play analysis identifies and collects details of behavior and dialogue in order to relate them to deeper patterns embedded in the text.

persona Latin for an "actor's mask." The psychologist Carl Jung used this term to identify personality as a collection of masks—which he called personae—carved for us and by us as a result of our life experiences. These are roles played out during a lifetime; for example, Son, Husband, Father.

personal history images remembered from an individual actor's past.

personal myth The psychologist Carl Jung's insight that sometimes people behave in certain ways because, consciously or not, they are acting out an image. These images fill a pattern in a story so deeply believed that the story can be called a personal myth. Jung's theories apply to the work of an actor because for Jung images are not isolated or self-sufficient, they are entire systems of relationships, to other people and to the world.

personalization within the vocabulary of Method acting, an actor's use of personal experience in performing a role. The actor forms an image that parallels his personal history. The question to be answered is not only *What is this like?* but also *How is this like me?* Using personalization, an actor playing a horse might imagine what aspects of himself resemble a horse. Using a slightly different technique—substitution—an actor unfamiliar with horses might substitute motorcycles for stallions.

playing oppositions in episodic acting, when a character performs a role in an episode reluctantly—his reactions at odds with his actions even as he performs them. When a role played in one episode contradicts another of the same character's roles in other episodes, that is also playing an opposition. The guilt-ridden murderer Macbeth can be played as an example of the first; the inconsistent Hamlet can be played as an example of the second. The use of opposition is meant to provoke the audience to stand apart from any one side of the opposition—including the feelings of any one character—in order to respond to the dynamic of the opposed forces.

point of view the storyteller's reaction to the story being told. Broadly speaking, the point of view in performance can be characterized as identified, distanced, or biased.

post-modernism the late twentieth century's label for itself as an inheritor and caretaker of systems and texts it no longer had faith in. In architecture, music, dance, literature, and other arts, post-modernists quote, replicate, and combine forms separated from their cultural associations. Post-modern acting relies on deconstruction, as well as quotation and unexpected combinations of images, to perform traditional texts with new, deliberately inconclusive, interpretations. More often associated with directorial style than specific actors.

projection the storyteller characterizes a listening audience. When the storyteller projects onto the audience a response that influences the telling of the story, the audience is cast as a partner, in a role. There are many examples in plays written by William Shakespeare.

psychoanalysis the systematic investigation of the subconscious in order to identify the sources of behavior. Developed by Sigmund Freud, who insisted on the primacy of the sexual drive, and expanded by his younger colleagues Carl Jung, Alfred Adler, and Wilhelm Reich—who identified other drives as primary. The development of psychoanalysis parallels the rise in interest in the psychology of acting; changes in psychoanalytic theory parallel changes in an actor's approach to characterization.

psychological blocks a theory that holds that a person's traumatic experiences are stored as tension that blocks feeling and free expression in the body and the brain. Applying the theory, the goal of the psychologist, artist, or actor is to uncover these psychological blocks—under the assumption that once blocks are removed, the true character of a person reveals itself. Abandoned by Freud, promulgated by Wilhelm Reich, and adapted by popular culture in America—and especially by Method actors.

Raja Yoga the school of Yoga that teaches the mind to observe its inner desires in order to choose which desires to pursue, with the ultimate goal of refining and eradicating those desires. Stanislavsky's identification of tasks, actions, and obstacles as the structures of behavior was influenced by his lifelong interest in Raja Yoga.

role in episodic acting, the actor enacts a role in order to participate in the performance of an episode. The defining question of a role is not so much *Who am I?* as it is *What do I do?* or *How does it fit in with what other people do?* In order for the episode to work, its roles must interconnect—all the actors play roles that fit together like the parts of a machine in order to produce the effect of the episode.

romantic acting a school of performing popular in the nineteenth century that was, in a way, the antithesis of the more decorous classical style. Romantic actors believed in the romantic ideal that the forms of art arise spontaneously from a performer's genius. A romantic actor's poses and vocal expression could be unbalanced and wild, although often just as deliberate as a classical actor's. Edmund Kean was the British exemplar of this dynamic style.

Rosetta Stone In 1799, French archeologists exploring the Rosetta arm of the River Nile discovered a slab of granite inscribed with writing in two languages, ancient

Greek and Egyptian hieroglyphics. This stone with the same information in two languages became a key to reading hieroglyphics once the decipherers compared the hieroglyphics to the Greek. The process is the same for actors using their own images—the language they know—to decipher initially perplexing images of a script.

rules of the world what measures the behavior in the world of a play. The rules of the world of the play organize the behavior and the environment in that world. Rules are often said out loud by a character, given by the playwright in a stage direction, or derived from the action of the play.

script analysis an in-depth exploration of the play's text, reorganizing its meanings in order to rehearse and perform.

sense memory a cluster of sensations that, when remembered, induce emotion for an actor. For example, the sound of a passing train, or the sway of the train in motion, might be connected in a performer's mind and body to the childhood pleasure of going on vacation.

shift in the point of view a change in the storyteller's attitude as a story is told, felt by the audience as dramatic action. To identify a change or changes in the point of view onstage, it helps to look at what is different about the narrator at the beginning of the story compared to the end. The question is *What happens to the teller while telling the story?*

social novel a fictional account that investigates the role of its characters in society. Pioneered by the nineteenth-century French writer Emile Zola, the social novel anticipates the episodic analysis definition of personality as a role in an episode.

Socialist Realism a Soviet government-sanctioned approach to art dedicated to the display of positive role models. It took as its mission the inclusion of groups that had not previously been represented or active in art—especially the lower classes—and meant to invite those previously excluded groups to participate in art as creators and enthusiasts. The emphasis was on realism, under the assumption that realistic art is most accessible to all groups.

soliloquy a speech said by an actor onstage and alone. Soliloquies are used in different ways by different playwrights. In *The Glass Menagerie*, for example, Tom performs soliloquies as memories or stories. In *Richard III*, Richard delivers his soliloquies as if the audience were a confidante, or a projected aspect of Richard's own mind.

spatial analysis in world of the play analysis, looking at all the episodes of the play as if they happened at once, in order to define a repeated pattern. The word "spatial" is used because the actions are imagined to form a pattern in space, rather than lining up chronologically as a sequence in time. This technique was identified by the Shakespeare critic G. Wilson Knight and can be used by a performer not only to examine a text, but to review and reorganize what has taken place in rehearsals.

Stanislavsky System an approach to the craft of an actor's preparation and performance developed by the Russian Konstantin Stanislavsky. Although consistently combining the physical aspects of performance with the subconscious, Stanislavsky's System changed its emphasis over time. The earlier versions (1909–1934) stressed internal preparation; the later version (begun in 1934) stressed physical action. The earlier versions have been taught primarily in America, the later in Russia.

story apparatus words used as technical aspects of telling a story onstage, necessary for grammar, narrative devices, or the conventions of storytelling—conventions that call attention to the story as story. The most frequent words of story apparatus are probably *she said, he said.*

stringing masks assembling a character from a collection of personae.

subconscious the realm of the mind of which the thinker is unaware. Interest in the subconscious developed in the nineteenth-century novel, in the turn of that century's psychology, and ultimately in Stanislavsky's approach to acting, which aimed to rouse the subconscious through conscious means. Not every psychological theory admits the existence of the subconscious, nor does every approach to acting. For example, episodic analysis does not necessarily involve the subconscious; neither does a world of the play analysis.

substitution In some approaches to acting, rather than imagining a sensation or an emotion called for by the script, actors substitute their own. Childhood memories are particularly useful for substitution because the experiences of a child are often dramatic.

super-task in Stanislavsky's approach to acting, the overriding task a character needs to do throughout the entire play; sometimes called the *spine* of the character.

task in Stanislavsky's approach to acting, what the character needs to do onstage at any given moment. The text sets a task, which in turn challenges an actor to answer the question *What do I need to do?* The task provides the need that drives an actor's activities, speeches, relationships, and behavior on stage. Hedda Gabler's task is *to free herself.* The Russian word—*z'dacha*—can also be translated as "problem," for which an actor provides a solution.

theater of the absurd a term coined by the critic Martin Esslin to describe a group of playwrights who create parallel worlds onstage that echo reality in a distorted way, and with a logic of their own. Samuel Beckett and Eugene Ionesco are examples of absurdist playwrights. Actors performing an absurdist play use a world of the play analysis to identify the logic of the parallel world.

through-line in Stanislavsky's approach to acting, a repeatable progression of actions in pursuit of a task encountering obstacles and opportunities. The word in Russian is based on the word for channel.

tragic pattern in world of the play analysis, a play's pattern can be thought of as tragic when rule-breaking is punished.

transaction according to some models of psychology, economics, history, and politics, the underlying structure of behavior. Trade: something is bought or sold or rejected as an offer. The founders of twentieth-century episodic acting—Brecht, Piscator, and Meyerhold—would all have agreed that an actor's performance of an episode should bring the political aspects of transactions into focus for an audience. An episode suggests a set of questions for the actor to ask: *What is being bought or sold? Who is the buyer? Who is the seller? What is the price? Is the deal concluded?*

GLOSSARY

transactional analysis a psychological practice of uncovering the unspoken contracts and exchanges that determine behavior.

transforming actors performers with no readily identifiable "types" who change appearance, voice, and sometimes even body shape to conform to the role they are playing. Meryl Streep and Robert De Niro are examples.

transitive verb requires an *object* to complete its action. Useful for defining tasks in acting a scene because a transitive verb describes an active relationship with somebody else.

translating images an actor translates the images of the text or dramatic situation into personal metaphors and then applies those images in performance by reassigning a value to the rest of the specific words and situations in the play. It is especially important to translate the other characters and the environment into the language of image.

type actors performers who trade on personality, often playing the same type of characters over and over again. Mae West and John Wayne are examples.

vocal mask a characteristic way of speaking, a way of masking a performer's voice. Vocal masks are created when an actor changes pitch or tone, or when the voice is placed differently in the throat or mouth. A vocal mask may be exaggerated, unrealistic, even inconsistent. A vocal mask is different from an *accent*, which refers to a specific place, time, and social status.

world of the play the place where the action of the play takes place. This includes the specific environments within which the play is set and performed, the form in which the play is written, and the rules that measure the behavior of characters set within the world.

world of the play analysis an investigation of the play's environment and how that environment can organize and motivate rehearsals and performance. The world of the play—created or implied by the script—frames, explains, restricts, amplifies, motivates, and organizes the action of the play and the identity of its characters.

Yoga the Indian practice of self-observation and physical refinement, often begun in order to eradicate desire. The discipline of Yoga can take many paths. The path best known in the West, Hatha Yoga, concentrates on the removal of stress through physical exercises, especially controlled breathing. Raja Yoga emphasizes the processes of the mind. Stanislavsky was influenced by Yogic practices in developing physical and mental exercises that became part of the Stanislavsky System. The word *yoga* means "union," but as a discipline it also refers to the same root as *yoke*.

Zingara literally Italian for "gypsy," the name of an ancient Greek sculpture of a torso to which a head, arms, and bronze feet were added in order to give it its gypsy identity. Over time, the knowledge that these were additions was lost. As a metaphor, artwork whose meaning or function is obscured by later additions unrecognized as additions; for example, the performance of Shakespeare's soliloquies while ignoring the audience.

READING AND VIEWING LISTS

Part I: Getting to the Task

Reading List

The Lesson, by Eugene Ionesco (Donald Allen, trans.). In: *Four Plays by Ionesco*. New York: Grove Press, 1958.

Hedda Gabler, by Henrik Ibsen (Rolf Fjelde, trans.). In: *Ibsen: The Complete Major Prose Plays*, Rolf Fjelde (ed.). New York: New American Library, 1965.

An Actor Prepares, by Konstantin Stanislavsky (Elizabeth Reynolds Hapgood, trans.). Chapter 3: "Action," Chapter 5: "Concentration of Attention," Chapter 7: "Units and Objectives," Chapter 15: "The Super Objective." New York: Theater Arts Books, 1936.

Stanislavsky in Focus, by Sharon Marie Carnicke. Chapter 3: "The Classroom Circuit," Chapter 4: "The Publication Maze." Amsterdam: Harwood Academic Publishers, Gordon and Breach International, 1998.

Viewing List

Orphans of the Storm, directed by D.W. Griffith, 1921. Video: Kino Video/DVD: Image Entertainment.

A Place in the Sun, directed by George Stevens, 1951. Video/DVD: MGM/UA.

Part II: Playing Episodes

Reading List

In the Jungle of Cities, by Bertolt Brecht (Gerhard Nellhaus, trans.). New York: Vintage (Random House), 1971.

King Richard III, by William Shakespeare.

Brecht on Theater, by Bertolt Brecht (John Willett, trans.). Section 24: "Epic Theater and Chinese Alienation Techniques." New York: Hill and Wang, Farrar Strauss Giroux, 1964.

Viewing List

The Night of the Hunter, directed by Charles Laughton, 1955. Video/DVD: MGM Vintage Classics.

Raging Bull, directed by Martin Scorsese, 1980. Video/DVD: MGM/UA.

Part III: Building Images

Reading List

The Maids, by Jean Genet (Bernard Frechtman, trans.). New York: Grove Press, 1954.
Yerma, by Federico García Lorca (James Graham-Luján and Richard L. O'Connell, trans.). New York: New Directions, 1947.
Stanislavsky in Focus, by Sharon Marie Carnicke. Chapter 2: "New York Adopts Stanislavsky," Chapter 6: "Emotion and Human Spirit of the Role." Amsterdam: Harwood Academic Publishers, Gordon and Breach International, 1998.

Viewing List

Dinner at Eight, directed by George Cukor, 1933. Video: MGM Vintage Classics.
Touch of Evil, directed by Orson Welles, 1958. Video/DVD: Universal Special Edition.

Part IV: Inhabiting the World of the Play

Reading List

Desire Under the Elms, by Eugene O'Neill. In: *Nine Plays of Eugene O'Neill*. New York: Modern Library, Random House, 1932.
The Odd Couple, by Neil Simon. New York: Random House, 1966.
Patterns of Culture, by Ruth Benedict. Chapter 8: "The Individual and the Pattern of Culture." Boston: Houghton Mifflin, 1934.

Part V: Telling a Story

Reading List

Iphigenia in Aulis, by Euripides (Nicholas Rudall, trans.). Chicago: Ivan R. Dee, 1997.
Buried Child, by Sam Shepard. In: *Seven Plays*. New York: Bantam Books, 1984.

Viewing List

Long Day's Journey into Night, directed by Sidney Lumet, 1962. Video: Republic Pictures Home Video.

BIBLIOGRAPHIC NOTES AND REFERENCES

Chapter 1: What Should I Do?

1. Benedetti, Jean. *Stanislavsky: A Biography*. New York: Routledge, 1990.
2. Stanislavsky, Konstantin (Robbins, J. J., trans.). *My Life in Art*. New York: Little Brown, 1924.
3. Carnicke, Sharon Marie. *Stanislavsky in Focus*. Amsterdam: Harwood Academic Publishers, Gordon and Breach International, 1998.
4. Eliot, George. *Adam Bede*. London, 1859.
5. Eliot, George. *Adam Bede*. London, 1859.
6. Ionesco, Eugene (Allen, Donald, trans.). *The Lesson*. In: *Four Plays by Ionesco*. New York: Grove Press, 1958.
7. Stanislavsky, Konstantin (Hapgood, Elizabeth Reynolds, trans.). *An Actor Prepares*. New York: Theater Arts Books, 1936.

Chapter 2: The Importance of Obstacles

8. Caesar, Irving and Youmans, Vincent. "Sometimes I'm Happy" (music and lyrics). Miami: WB Music Corp., 1925.
9. Cole, Toby, and Chinoy, Helen Krich (eds.). *Actors on Acting, new revised edition*. New York: Crown, 1970.
10. Manvell, Roger. *Sarah Siddons, Portrait of an Actress*. New York: Putnam, 1971.
11. Odell, George C.D. *Shakespeare from Betterton to Irving*. New York: Charles Scribner & Sons, 1920.
12. Cole, Toby, and Chinoy, Helen Krich (eds.). *Actors on Acting, new revised edition*. New York: Crown, 1970.
13. Irving, Henry. Lecture at Harvard University (March 30, 1885). In: Cole, Toby, and Chinoy, Helen Krich (eds.). *Actors on Acting, new revised edition*. New York: Crown, 1970.
14. Manvell, Roger. *Sarah Siddons, Portrait of an Actress*. New York: Putnam, 1971.
15. Hill, Aaron. "An Essay on the Art of Acting" (London, 1746): Hill, John. "The Actor: A Treatise on the Art of Playing" (London, 1750). Cited in: Cole, Toby, and Chinoy, Helen Krich (eds.). *Actors on Acting, new revised edition*. New York: Crown, 1970.
16. Oderman, Stuart. *Lillian Gish: A Life on Stage and Screen*. London: MacFarland, 2000.
17. Archer, William. "The Mausoleum of Ibsen." In: *Fortnightly Review* (London, July 1893). Quoted in: Meyer, Michael (ed.). *Ibsen, A Biography*. New York: Doubleday, 1971.
18. Gran, Gerhard. Review of *Hedda Gabler*. In: *Samtiden* (1891). Quoted in: Meyer, Michael (ed.). *Ibsen, A Biography*. New York: Doubleday, 1971.
19. Ibsen, Henrik (Fjelde, Rolf, trans.). *Hedda Gabler*. In: Fjelde, Rolf (ed.). *Ibsen: The Complete Major Prose Plays*. New York: New American Library, 1965.
20. Ibsen, Henrik. Letter to Constance Bruun (March 25, 1887). Quoted in: Meyer, Michael (ed.). *Ibsen, A Biography*. New York: Doubleday, 1971.
21. Tolstoy, Lev Nikolaevich (Maude, Louise, trans.). *Resurrection*. Russia: 1899.

Chapter 3: Stanislavsky's Legacy

22. Stanislavsky, Konstantin (Hapgood, Elizabeth Reynolds, trans.). *An Actor Prepares*. New York: Theater Arts Books, 1936.
23. Carnicke, Sharon Marie. *Stanislavsky in Focus*. Amsterdam: Harwood Academic Publishers, Gordon and Breach International, 1998.
24. Sivananda, Sri Swami. "Raja Yoga." In: *Bliss Divine, A Book of Spiritual Essays on the Lofty Purpose of Human Life and the Means to Its Achievement, third edition* (originally published in 1938). Himalayas: The Divine Life Society, 1974.
25. Logan, Joshua. *Josh: My Up and Down, In and Out Life*. New York: Delacorte Press, 1976.
26. Winters, Shelley. *Shelley, Also Known as Shirley*. New York: William Morrow, 1980.

Chapter 4: Episodes

27. Stanislavsky, Konstantin (Robbins, J. J., trans.). *My Life in Art*. New York: Little Brown, 1924.
28. Berlin, Isaiah. Introductory Note to *A Month in the Country* by Ivan Turgenev. New York: Viking Press, 1981.
29. Forster, E.M. *Aspects of the Novel*. New York: Harcourt Brace & World, 1927.
30. Nabokov, Nicholas. "Time in Reverse: 1959 Talk in BBC Third Programme, broadcast 6.11.1958." Quoted in: Esslin, Martin. *Brecht, The Man and His Work*. New York: Doubleday, 1959.
31. Thomson, Peter. "Brecht and Actor Training." In: Hodge, Alison (ed.). *Twentieth Century Acting Training*. New York: Routledge, 2000.
32. Keegan, John. *The Face of Battle*. New York: Viking Press, 1976.
33. Flint, F.S. "Lament." In: Silkin, John (ed.). *The Penguin Book of First World War Poetry, second edition*. New York: Penguin Books, 1979.
34. Von Eckardt, Wolf, and Gilman, Sander L. *Bertolt Brecht's Berlin, A Scrapbook of the Twenties*. Garden City: Anchor Press/Doubleday, 1975.
35. Meyers, Bernard (ed.). *The German Expressionists: A Generation in Revolt*. New York: Praeger, 1966. Citing a manifesto excerpt quoted in: Von Eckardt, Wolf and Gilman, Sander L. *Bertolt Brecht's Berlin, A Scrapbook of the Twenties*. Garden City: Anchor Press/Doubleday, 1975.
36. Willett, John. "Piscator & Brecht: Closeness Through Distance." *IcarbS*, I(2), Spring-Summer 1974.
37. Brecht, Bertolt (Nellhaus, Gerhard, trans.). *In the Jungle of Cities*. New York: Vintage (Random House), 1971.
38. Thomson, Peter. "Brecht and Actor Training." In: Hodge, Alison, (ed.). *Twentieth Century Acting Training*. New York: Routledge, 2000.

Chapter 5: Combining Episodes

39. Carnicke, Sharon Marie. *Stanislavsky in Focus*. Amsterdam: Harwood Academic Publishers, Gordon and Breach International, 1998.
40. Carnicke, Sharon Marie. *Stanislavsky in Focus*. Amsterdam: Harwood Academic Publishers, Gordon and Breach International, 1998.

Chapter 6: Three Lives in the Episodic Theater

41. Meyerhold, Vsevolod (Braun, Edward, trans.). "The Naturalistic Theater and the Theater of Mood," 1906. In: Braun, Edward (ed.). *Meyerhold on Theater*. New York: Hill and Wang, 1969.
42. Conversation with Lou Criss, New York, June 19, 2000.
43. Willett, John. "Piscator and Brecht: Closeness Through Distance." *IcarbS*, I(2), Spring-Summer 1974.
44. Flanagan, Hallie. *Arena*. New York: Arno Press, 1980.
45. Esslin, Martin. *Brecht, The Man and His Work*. New York: W.W. Norton, 1971.

46. Torres, M.L.F. "Anticipating Freedom in Theatre: Brecht in Asia and Africa." *The Brecht Yearbook* XIV, University of Hong Kong, 1989.

47. Kerr, David. *African Popular Theatre*. London: James Currey, 1995.

48. Winters, Shelley. *Shelley, Also Known as Shirley*. New York: William Morrow, 1980.

Chapter 7: Masks

49. Cottrell, John. *Laurence Olivier*. Englewood Cliffs: Prentice Hall, 1975.

50. Tynan, Kenneth. Interview with Laurence Olivier. (First published in the U.S. in *Tulane Drama Review*, XI(3), Winter, 1966 [© authors and BBC 1966–1967].) In: Burton, Hal (ed.). *Great Acting*. Quoted in: Cole, Toby, and Chinoy, Helen Krich (eds.). *Actors on Acting, new revised edition*. New York: Crown, 1970.

51. Skinner, Cornelia Otis. *Madame Sarah*. Boston: Houghton Mifflin, 1967.

52. Strindberg, August. "Author's Note to *A Dream Play*." In: Meyer, Michael (trans.). *The Plays of Strindberg, Vol. II*. New York: Vintage, 1976.

53. Balzac, Honoré de (Sedgwick, Jane Minot, trans.). *Father Goriot*. Philadelphia: George Barrie & Son, 1897.

54. Hirsch, Foster. *A Method to Their Madness: The History of the Actors Studio*. New York: W.W. Norton, 1984.

55. Hull, Lorraine S. *Strasberg's Method As Taught by Lorrie Hull*. Woodbridge: Ox Bow Publishing, 1985. Quoted in: Carnicke, Sharon Marie. *Stanislavsky in Focus*. Amsterdam: Harwood Academic Publishers, Gordon and Breach International, 1998.

56. Genet, Jean (Frechtman, Bernard, trans.). *The Maids*. New York: Grove Press, 1954.

57. Hammerstein II, Oscar. "Life Upon the Wicked Stage" (lyric). From: Hammerstein II, Oscar, and Kern, Jerome. *Showboat*. Los Angeles: Universal-PolyGram International Publishing, Inc., 1927.

58. Staggs, Sam. *All About "All About Eve": The Complete Behind-the-Scenes Story of the Bitchiest Film Ever Made*. New York: St. Martin's Press, 2000.

59. Cottrell, John. *Laurence Olivier*. Englewood Cliffs: Prentice-Hall, 1975.

Chapter 8: The Language of Images

60. Moore, Irene. *The Stanislavsky System*. New York: Viking Press, 1965.

61. Solomon, Deborah. *Jackson Pollock, A Biography*. New York: Simon and Schuster, 1987.

62. Stanislavsky, Konstantin (Hapgood, Elizabeth Reynolds, trans.). *Building a Character*. New York: Theater Arts Books, 1949.

63. Easty, Edward D. *On Method Acting*. New York: Ivy Books, 1981.

64. Winters, Shelley. *Shelley, Also Known as Shirley*. New York: William Morrow, 1980.

65. Cocteau, Jean (Fitts, Dudley, trans.). Preface to *The Eiffel Tower Wedding*. In: *The Infernal Machine and Other Plays*. New York: New Direction, 1963.

Chapter 9: Comparison

66. Benedict, Ruth. *Patterns of Culture*. Boston: Houghton Mifflin, 1934.

67. Caffrey, Margaret M. *Ruth Benedict, Stranger in This Land*. Austin: University of Texas Press, 1989.

68. Benedict, Ruth. *Patterns of Culture*. Boston: Houghton Mifflin, 1934.

69. Benedict, Ruth. "Anthropology and the Abnormal," *Journal of General Psychology* 10, 1934. Reprinted in: Mead, Margaret (ed.). *An Anthropologist at Work: Writings of Ruth Benedict*. Quoted in: Caffrey, Margaret M. *Ruth Benedict, Stranger in This Land*. Austin: University of Texas Press, 1989.

70. Benedict, Ruth. "Anthropology and the Humanities." In: *American Anthropologist* 50: 585, 593, 1948. Reprinted in: Mead, Margaret (ed.). *An Anthropologist at Work: Writings of Ruth Benedict*. Boston: Houghton Mifflin, 1959.

71. Knight, G. Wilson. "On Principles of Shakespeare Interpretation." In: *The Wheel of Fire*, New York: Oxford University Press, 1930.

72. Knights, L.C. "How Many Children Had Lady Macbeth?" In: *Explorations*. New York: George W. Stewart, 1933.

73. O'Neill, Eugene. *Desire Under the Elms*. In: *Nine Plays of Eugene O'Neill*. New York: Modern Library, Random House, 1932.

74. O'Neill, Eugene. *Long Day's Journey into Night* (1941). New Haven: Yale University Press, 1956.

75. Benedict, Ruth. *Patterns of Culture*. Boston: Houghton Mifflin, 1934.

76. Annenkov, Pavel. Quoted in: Senelick, Laurence, "Rachel in Russia." *Theatre Research International*, III(2), February 1978, 99. In: Brownstein, Rachel M. *Tragic Muse*. New York: Knopf, 1993.

Chapter 10: Playing by the Rules—or Not

77. Bray, Rene. "The Actor." From: Hollander, Anne. *Molière, homme de théâtre*, (1954). In: Guicharnaud, Jacques (ed.). *Molière, A Collection of Critical Essays*. Englewood Cliffs: Prentice-Hall, 1964.

78. Molière. "Lettre sur la comédie de l'Imposteur," 1667. Cited in: "Molière," *Encyclopædia Britannica Online*, 2000.

79. Simon, Neil. *The Odd Couple*. New York: Random House, 1966.

80. Beckett, Samuel. *Happy Days*. New York: Grove Press, 1961.

81. Ionesco, Eugene (Allen, Donald M., trans.). *The Bald Soprano*. In: *Four Plays by Ionesco*. New York: Grove Press, 1950.

82. Beckett, Samuel. *Endgame*. New York: Grove Press, 1958.

83. De Niro, Robert. "Dialogue on Film." Interview in: *American Film*, March 1981.

84. Skinner, Cornelia Otis. *Madame Sarah*. Boston: Houghton Mifflin, 1967.

Chapter 11: Storytelling

85. Skinner, Cornelia Otis. *Madame Sarah*. Boston: Houghton Mifflin, 1967.

86. Aeschylus (Vellacot, Phillip, trans.). *The Persians*. In: Vellacot, Phillip (trans.). *Prometheus and Other Plays by Aeschylus*. New York: Penguin Classics, 1961.

87. Sophocles (Storr, F., trans.). *Oedipus the King*. Loeb Library Edition. London: William Heinemann, 1912.

88. Sophocles (Storr, F., trans.). *Oedipus at Colonus*. Loeb Library Edition. London: William Heinemann, 1912.

89. Plautus. *The Braggart Warrior* (*Miles Gloriosus*). 205 BCE.

90. Sterne, Laurence. *Tristram Shandy*. London, 1776.

91. Molière (Wilbur, Richard, trans.). *The School for Wives*. New York: Harcourt Brace Jovanovich, Inc., 1971.

92. Williams, Tennessee. *The Glass Menagerie*. In: *The Theatre of Tennessee Williams*, Vol. 1. New York: New Directions, 1971.

93. Willett, John. *The Theatre of Erwin Piscator*. New York: Holmes and Meier, 1979.

94. Williams, Tennessee. *A Streetcar Named Desire*. In: *The Theatre of Tennessee Williams, Vol. 1*. New York: New Directions, 1971.

95. Shepard, Sam. *Buried Child*. In: *Sam Shepard, Seven Plays*. New York: Bantam Books, 1984.

96. Beckett, Samuel. *Endgame*. New York: Grove Press, 1958.

Chapter 12: Dramatic Action and Illusion of Character

97. West, Mae. *Goodness Had Nothing to Do With It*. New York: Prentice-Hall, 1959.

98. Weintraub, Joseph (ed.). *The Wit and Wisdom of Mae West*. New York: Avon, 1967.

99. Brecht, Bertolt (Smith, William E. and Manheim, Ralph, trans.). *Drums in the Night*. In: Manheim, Ralph, and Willett, John (eds.). *Bertolt Brecht: Collected Plays, Vol. 1*. New York: Vintage, 1971.
100. Stanislavsky, Konstantin (Robbins, J. J., trans.). *My Life in Art*. New York: Little Brown, 1924.
101. Stanislavsky, Konstantin (Robbins, J. J., trans.). *My Life in Art*. New York: Little Brown, 1924.
102. O'Neill, Eugene. *Strange Interlude*. In: *Nine Plays of Eugene O'Neill*. New York: Modern Library, Random House, 1932.
103. Euripides (Rudall, Nicholas, trans.). *Iphigenia in Aulis*. Chicago: Ivan R. Dee, 1997.
104. Euripides. *Iphigenia in Tauris*. 414 BCE.
105. Thucydides, circa 413 BCE.
106. Chekhov, Anton (Dunnigan, Ann, trans.). *The Three Sisters*. New York: New American Library, 1964.

Chapter 13: Shakespeare's Soliloquies

107. Haskell, Francis, and Penny, Nicholas. *Taste and the Antique*. New Haven: Yale University Press, 1981.
108. Haskell, Francis, and Penny, Nicholas. *Taste and the Antique*. New Haven: Yale University Press, 1981.

Chapter 14: Comparing Approaches

109. Macready, William Charles. Extract from diary (Cincinnati, April 1849) "whilst playing Hamlet on tour in America." In: Rigg, Diana (ed.). *No Turn Unstoned*. Los Angeles: Silman-James Press, 1982.
110. Le Gallienne, Eva. *The Mystic in the Theater: Eleonora Duse*. Carbondale: Southern Illinois University Press, 1965.
111. Le Gallienne, Eva. *The Mystic in the Theater: Eleonora Duse*. Carbondale: Southern Illinois University Press, 1965.
112. Rigg, Diana (ed.). *No Turn Unstoned*. Los Angeles: Silman-James Press, 1982
113. Bernhardt, Sarah. *Memoirs*. In: Le Gallienne, Eva. *The Mystic in the Theater: Eleonora Duse*. Carbondale: Southern Illinois University Press, 1965.
114. Gielgud, John. *An Actor and His Time: A Memoir*. New York: Clarkson N. Potter, 1980.
115. Shaw, George Bernard. *Saturday Review*, June 1895. In: Rigg, Diana (ed.). *No Turn Unstoned*. Los Angeles: Silman-James Press, 1982.
116. Brien, Allen. Quoted in: Cottrell, John. *Laurence Olivier*. Englewood Cliffs: Prentice-Hall, 1975.
117. Skinner, Cornelia Otis. *Madame Sarah*. Boston: Houghton Mifflin, 1967.
118. O'Neill, Eugene. *Long Day's Journey into Night*. New Haven: Yale University Press, 1956.
119. Cottrell, John. *Laurence Olivier*. Englewood Cliffs: Prentice-Hall, 1975.
120. Cottrell, John. *Laurence Olivier*. Englewood Cliffs: Prentice-Hall, 1975.
121. Winters, Shelley. *Shelley, Also Known as Shirley*. New York: William Morrow, 1980.
122. Brecht, Bertolt (Willett, John, trans.). "Dialog über Schauspielkunst." From: *Berliner Börsen-Courier*, February 17, 1929. In: *Brecht on Theatre*. New York: Hill and Wang, Farrar Strauss Giroux, 1964.
123. Weigel, Helene (Bernstein, Joseph M., trans.). *Theaterarbeit*. Dresden: VVV Dresdner Verlag, 1952. In: Cole, Toby, and Chinoy, Helen Krich (eds.). *Actors on Acting, new revised edition*. New York: Crown, 1970.
124. Le Gallienne, Eva. *The Mystic in the Theater: Eleonora Duse*. Carbondale: Southern Illinois University Press, 1965.

Chapter 15: Choosing an Approach

125. Odell, George C.D. *Shakespeare from Betterton to Irving*. New York: Charles Scribner & Sons, 1920.
126. Cole, Toby, and Chinoy, Helen Krich (eds.). *Actors on Acting, new revised edition*. New York: Crown, 1970.
127. Wortis Leider, Emily. *Becoming Mae West*. New York: Farrar Strauss Giroux, 1997.
128. Rigg, Diana (ed.). *No Turn Unstoned*. Los Angeles: Silman-James Press, 1982.

129. Olivier, Laurence. "The Olivier Method." Interview in: the *New York Times*, February 7, 1960, X:1–3. In: Cole, Toby, and Chinoy, Helen Krich (eds.). *Directors on Directing, revised edition.* Indianapolis: Bobbs-Merrill, 1963.
130. Gilbert, W.S. "I Have a Little List" (lyric). From: Gilbert, W.S., and Sullivan, Arthur. *The Mikado,* 1885.
131. Mamet, David. Conversation during rehearsals for *Reunion/Dark Pony* at the Yale Repertory Theater, 1978.
132. Weigel, Helene (Bernstein, Joseph M., trans.). *Theaterarbeit.* Dresden: VVV Dresdner Verlag, 1952. In: Cole, Toby, and Chinoy, Helen Krich (eds.). *Actors on Acting, new revised edition.* New York: Crown, 1970.

Chapter 16: Combining Approaches

133. Braun, Edward (ed.). *Meyerhold on Theater.* New York: Hill and Wang, 1969.

INDEX

INDEX

CPSIA information can be obtained
at www.ICGtesting.com
Printed in the USA
LVOW09s0004050118

561919LV00006B/52/P